THE LOWER YOU RIDE, THE COOLER YOU ARE

Andrews McMeel
Publishing

Kansas City

ISBN: 0-7407-1840-1

01 02 03 04 05 BAH 10 9 8 7 6 5 4 3 2 1

Library of Congress Catalog Card Number: 2001087913

———— **ATTENTION: SCHOOLS AND BUSINESSES** ————

Andrews McMeel books are available at quantity discounts with bulk purchase for educational, business, or sales promotional use. For information, please write to: Special Sales Department, Andrews McMeel Publishing, 4520 Main Street, Kansas City, Missouri 64111.

READ BALDO IN YOUR LOCAL NEWSPAPER. IF IT'S NOT IN THERE, CALL AND ASK FOR IT. IF IT IS THERE, CALL AND THANK THEM.

Acknowledgments

We throw collective props to John McMeel, Kathy Andrews, Lee Salem, John Vivona, Erin Friedrich, Alberto Bernal, and all the good people at Universal Press Syndicate and Andrews McMeel for their dedication and faith ... and especially our editor Greg Melvin, who's forced to deal with us on a weekly basis, explaining things like why Tia Carmen's chickens probably shouldn't hold extensive conversations with each other. Hey, they're *smart* chickens!

Hector thanks ... Linda (this would not have happened without you, mi amor), Maya, Sofia, Max (mis hijos chulos), and Teresa, Amancio, Gloria, David, Leonel, Kim, Mike, Mercy, Gilda, Ralph, Marinela, Greg, Alma, Ruben y las familias Longoria, Closner y Garcia (for their inspiration and support). Andale pues ...

Carlos thanks ... my beautiful wife and best friend, Maria—
your love and support make it *all* possible.
Chase and Alec, my beautiful sons, for the endless wonder over rocks, ants, and flowers. You show me magic and miracles every day.
My parents, Lourdes and Juan I. Castellanos, for your love and courage.
Mis abuelitas, Lucrecia Martinez y Caridad Gonzalez.
My brother, Alex. Herena Escar, Spencer, Fian, Brian, Maggie y las familias Alfonso, Fuentes, Biskup y Couvertiers ... for their friendship, encouragement, and support.

Send Hector and Carlos e-mail at:
baldomail@baldocomics.com

Send snail mail, furry dice, and velas to:
BALDO
c/o Universal Press Syndicate
4520 Main St.
Kansas City, MO 64111

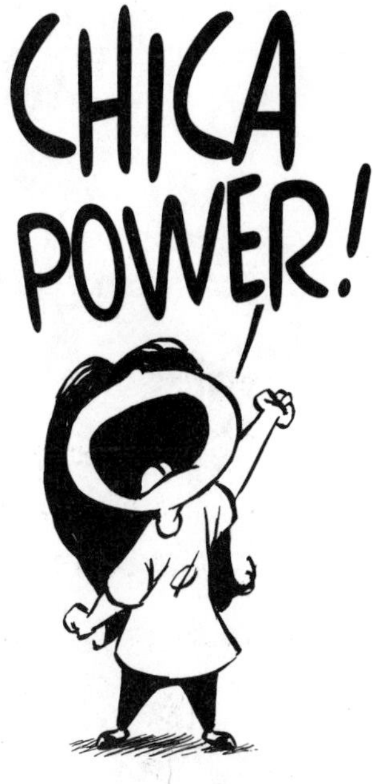

CHICA POWER!

Introduction

The newspaper comic strip is a true American art form. Starting in the late nineteenth century as political commentary, it evolved later into a mainstream form of entertainment. The simplicity of the presentation made comics easy to follow on a daily basis.

Characters such as Blondie, Mutt & Jeff, Pogo, Charlie Brown, Felix the Cat and many others became as famous and recognizable as any movie star or political leader, maybe more so. Through the years, Hispanic cartoonists also have contributed to the comic pages. Gus Arriola's Gordo and Bill De La Torre's Lil Pedro were popular, if not controversial, in the 1950s and '60s.

And now, following in that tradition, comes Baldo, a wonderful new comic created by the very gifted team of Hector Cant' and Carlos Castellanos.

I was among the first outsiders to lay eyes on Baldo and his family - sister Gracie, Dad and Tìa Carmen. It was 1998 when Hector came to my office, told me he had partnered with Carlos and wanted to start a comic. I imagine everyone dreams of having a comic strip. It looks so simple! Just four drawings and a gag. Yet, that simplicity is what makes cartooning so formidable and challenging.

Hector showed me a few strips and asked for my advice. I immediately liked what I saw. Good characters, a warm and humorous story line, all drawn in a bold and graceful style. Hector and Carlos had captured the true essence of a comic strip. I quickly realized that any advice would be meaningless since they already were on the right track. The only challenge I saw was delivering and maintaining this quality on a daily basis. And that they have done. The strip continues to grow in confidence and style.

Looking over this collection from Baldo's first year, I see it has everything needed to be a successful comic strip. It's witty, well-drawn and has a family of likable characters. Baldo, I believe, has the potential to be the next great American comic strip.

Phil Roman, Phil Roman Entertainment
Executive Producer, 1992-1999
The Simpsons and *King of the Hill*

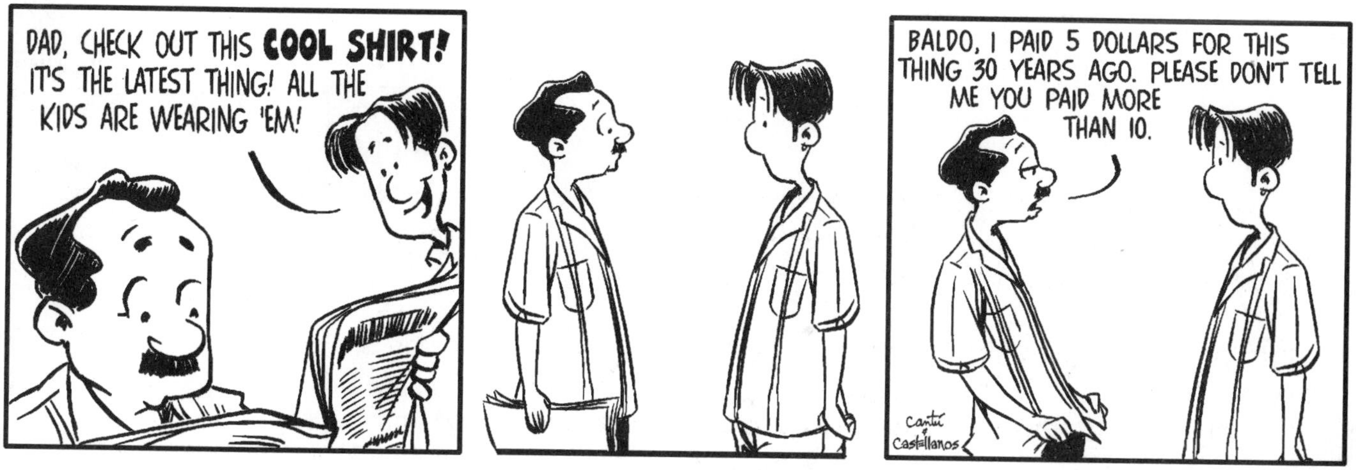
DAD, CHECK OUT THIS COOL SHIRT! IT'S THE LATEST THING! ALL THE KIDS ARE WEARING 'EM!
BALDO, I PAID 5 DOLLARS FOR THIS THING 30 YEARS AGO. PLEASE DON'T TELL ME YOU PAID MORE THAN 10.
Cantú & Castellanos

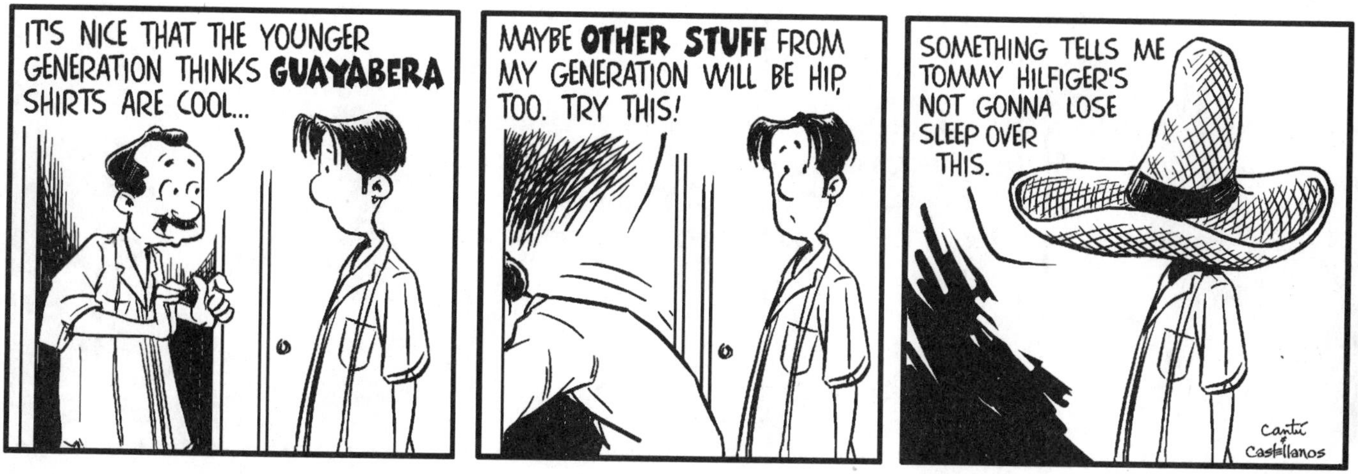
IT'S NICE THAT THE YOUNGER GENERATION THINKS GUAYABERA SHIRTS ARE COOL...
MAYBE OTHER STUFF FROM MY GENERATION WILL BE HIP, TOO. TRY THIS!
SOMETHING TELLS ME TOMMY HILFIGER'S NOT GONNA LOSE SLEEP OVER THIS.
Cantú & Castellanos

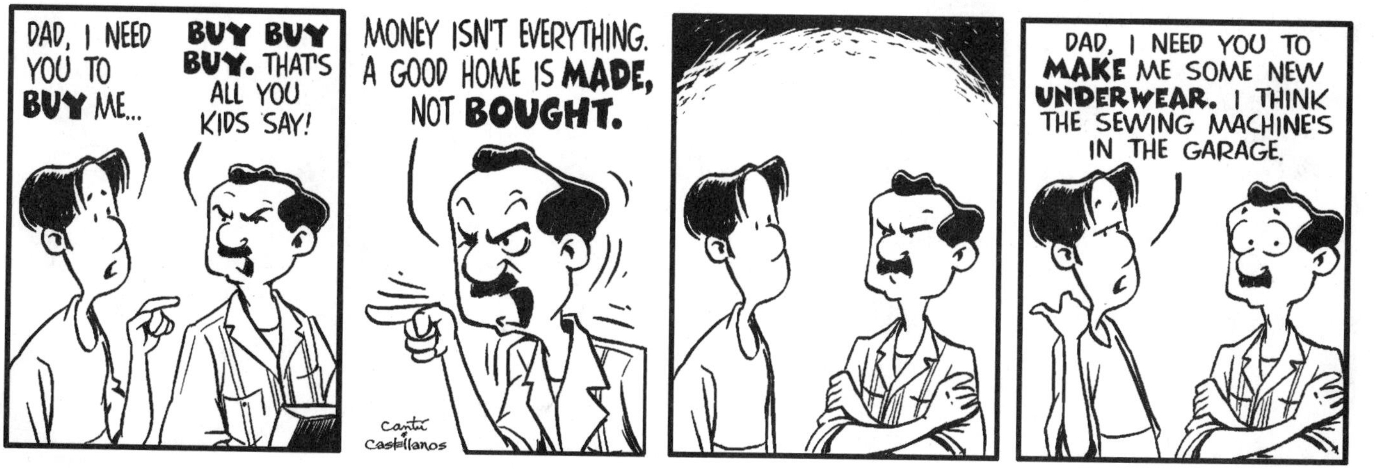
DAD, I NEED YOU TO BUY ME...
BUY BUY BUY. THAT'S ALL YOU KIDS SAY!
MONEY ISN'T EVERYTHING. A GOOD HOME IS MADE, NOT BOUGHT.
Cantú & Castellanos
DAD, I NEED YOU TO MAKE ME SOME NEW UNDERWEAR. I THINK THE SEWING MACHINE'S IN THE GARAGE.

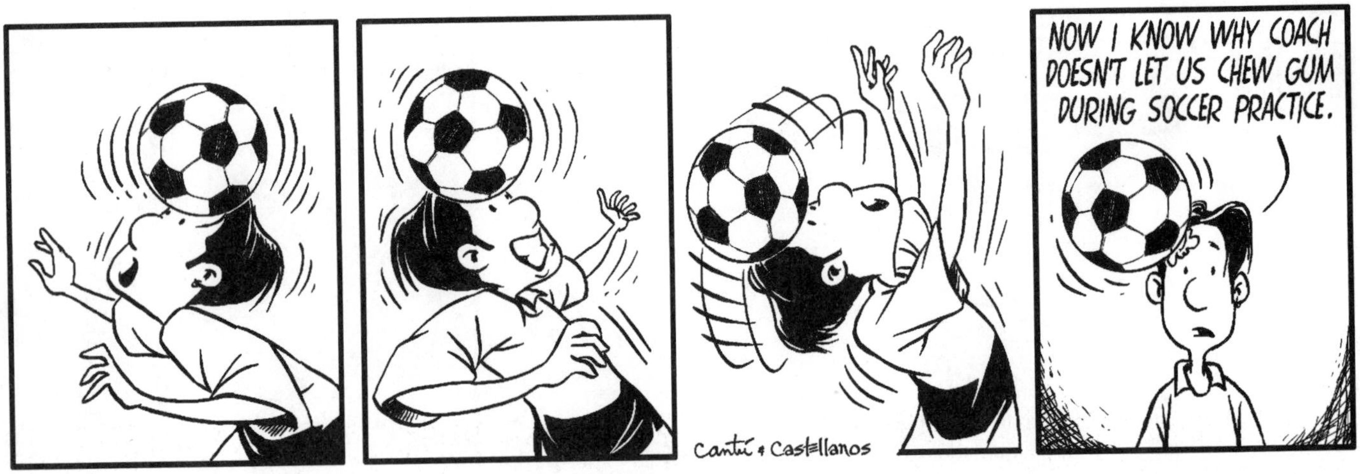
Cantú & Castellanos
NOW I KNOW WHY COACH DOESN'T LET US CHEW GUM DURING SOCCER PRACTICE.

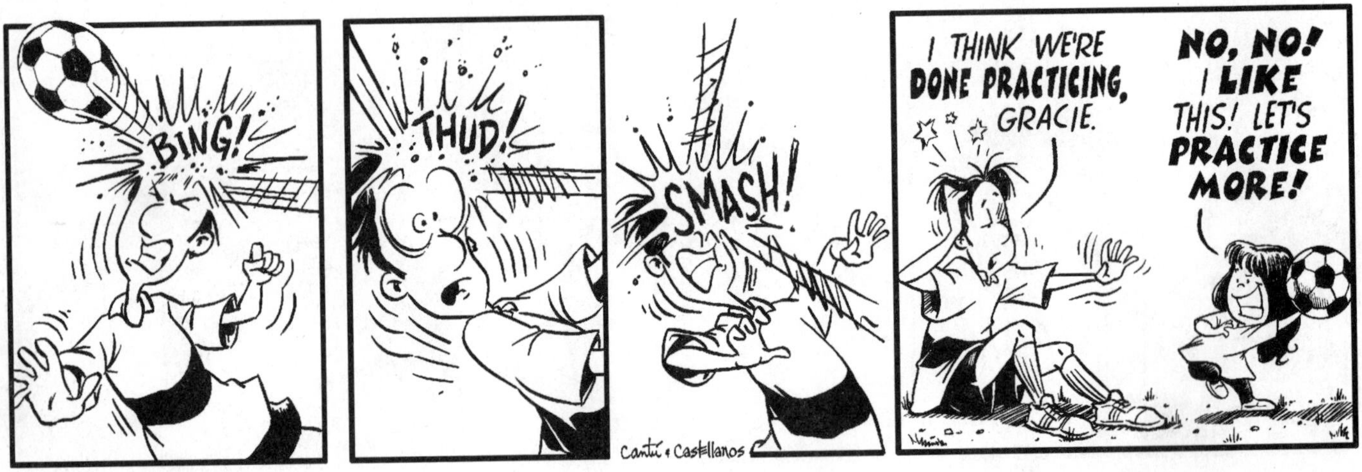
BING!
THUD!
SMASH!
Cantú & Castellanos
I THINK WE'RE **DONE PRACTICING,** GRACIE.
NO, NO! I **LIKE** THIS! LET'S **PRACTICE MORE!**

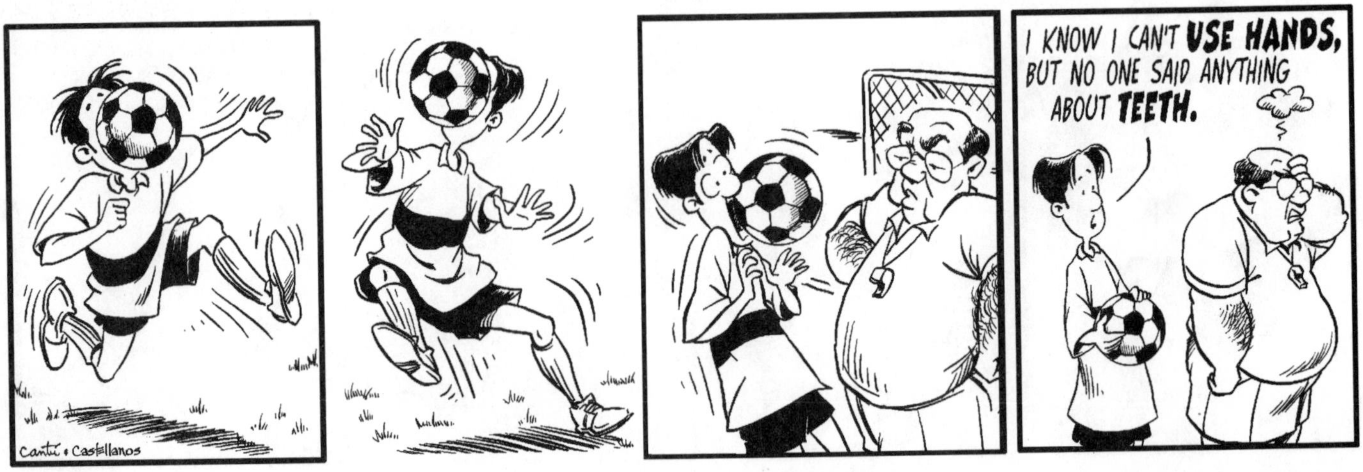
Cantú & Castellanos
I KNOW I CAN'T **USE HANDS,** BUT NO ONE SAID ANYTHING ABOUT **TEETH.**

MOON?
COCONUT?
BALLOON?
SOCCER BALL!
Cantú • Castellanos
OOOOF!
SOCCER AND DAYDREAMING JUST DON'T MIX.

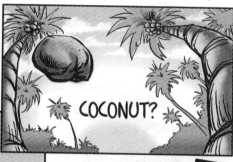

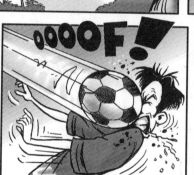

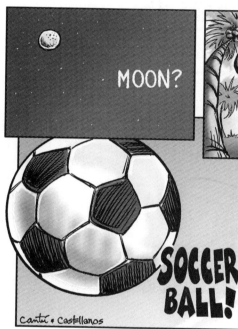

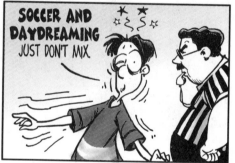

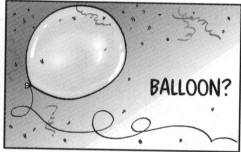

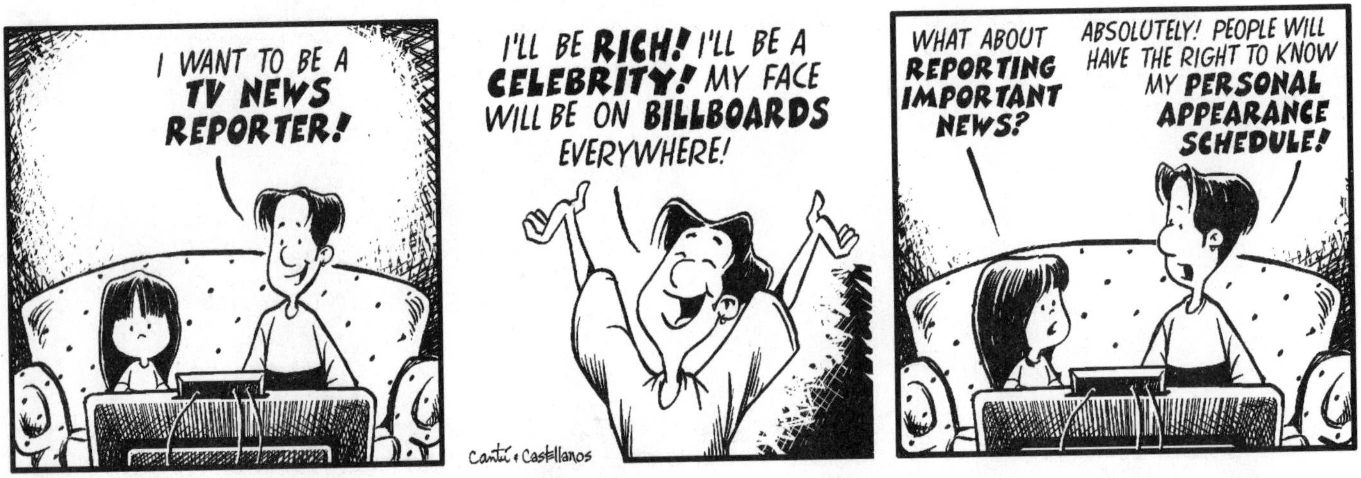
I WANT TO BE A **TV NEWS REPORTER!**
I'LL BE **RICH!** I'LL BE A **CELEBRITY!** MY FACE WILL BE ON **BILLBOARDS** EVERYWHERE!
Cantú & Castellanos
WHAT ABOUT **REPORTING IMPORTANT NEWS?**
ABSOLUTELY! PEOPLE WILL HAVE THE RIGHT TO KNOW MY **PERSONAL APPEARANCE SCHEDULE!**

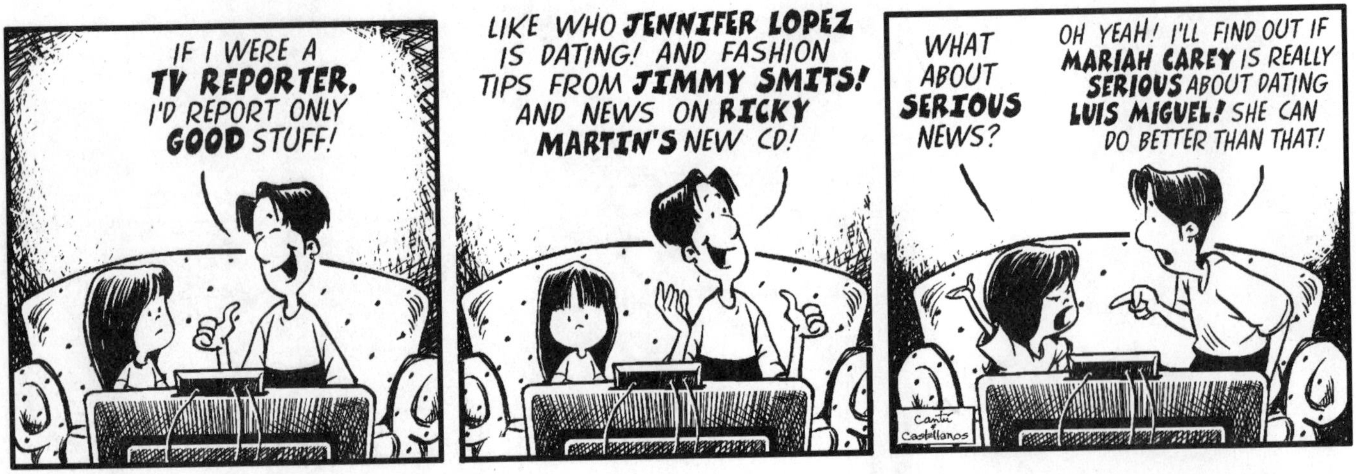
IF I WERE A **TV REPORTER,** I'D REPORT ONLY **GOOD** STUFF!
LIKE WHO **JENNIFER LOPEZ** IS DATING! AND FASHION TIPS FROM **JIMMY SMITS!** AND NEWS ON **RICKY MARTIN'S** NEW CD!
WHAT ABOUT **SERIOUS** NEWS?
OH YEAH! I'LL FIND OUT IF **MARIAH CAREY** IS REALLY **SERIOUS** ABOUT DATING **LUIS MIGUEL!** SHE CAN DO BETTER THAN THAT!
Cantú Castellanos

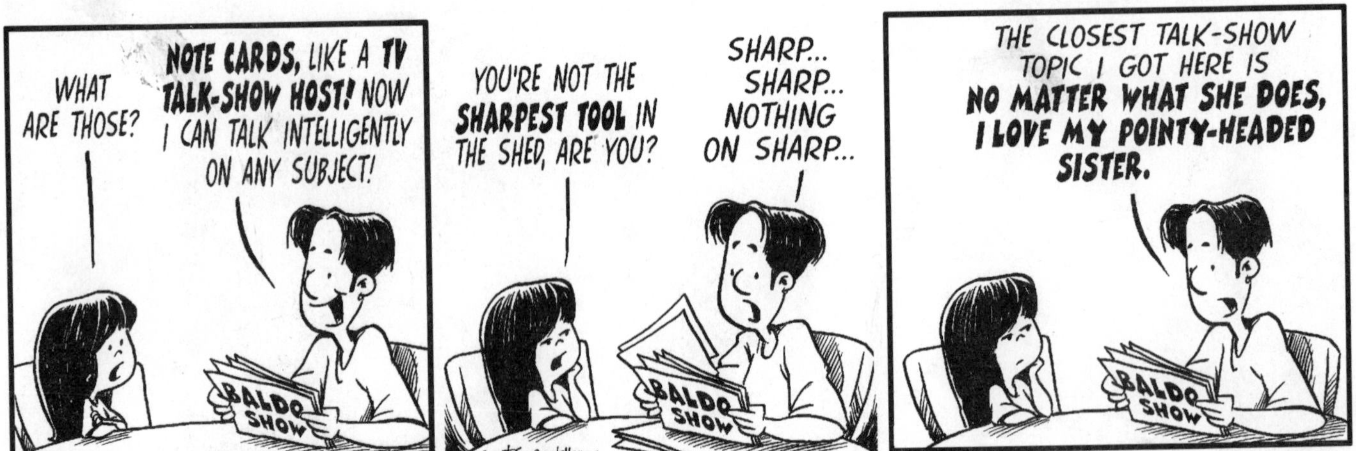
WHAT ARE THOSE?
NOTE CARDS, LIKE A **TV TALK-SHOW HOST!** NOW I CAN TALK INTELLIGENTLY ON ANY SUBJECT!
BALDO SHOW
YOU'RE NOT THE **SHARPEST TOOL** IN THE SHED, ARE YOU?
SHARP... SHARP... NOTHING ON SHARP...
BALDO SHOW
Cantú & Castellanos
THE CLOSEST TALK-SHOW TOPIC I GOT HERE IS **NO MATTER WHAT SHE DOES, I LOVE MY POINTY-HEADED SISTER.**
BALDO SHOW

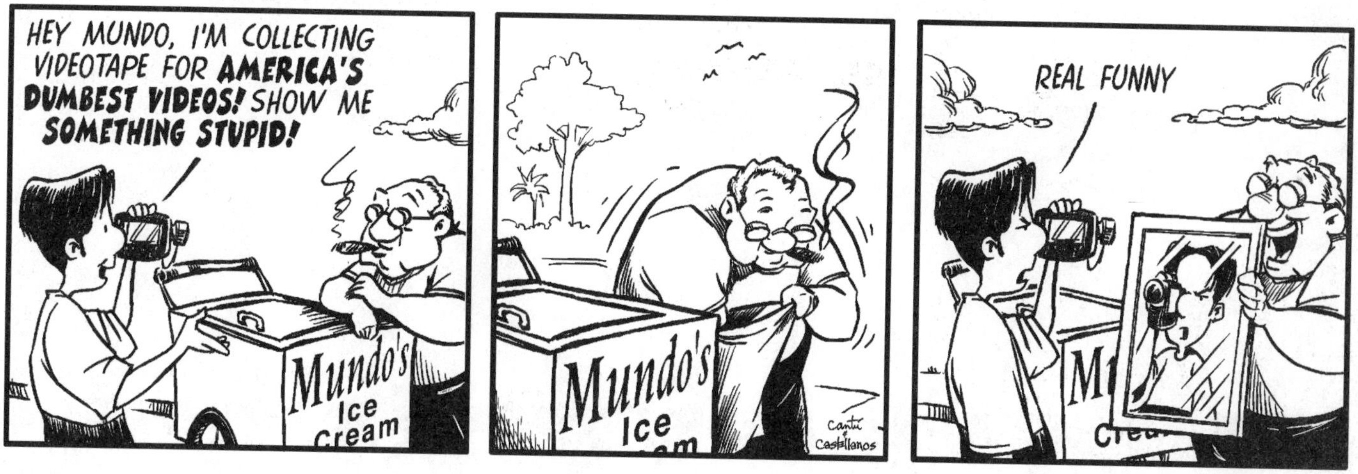
HEY MUNDO, I'M COLLECTING VIDEOTAPE FOR AMERICA'S DUMBEST VIDEOS! SHOW ME SOMETHING STUPID!
Mundo's Ice Cream
REAL FUNNY
Cantú Castellanos

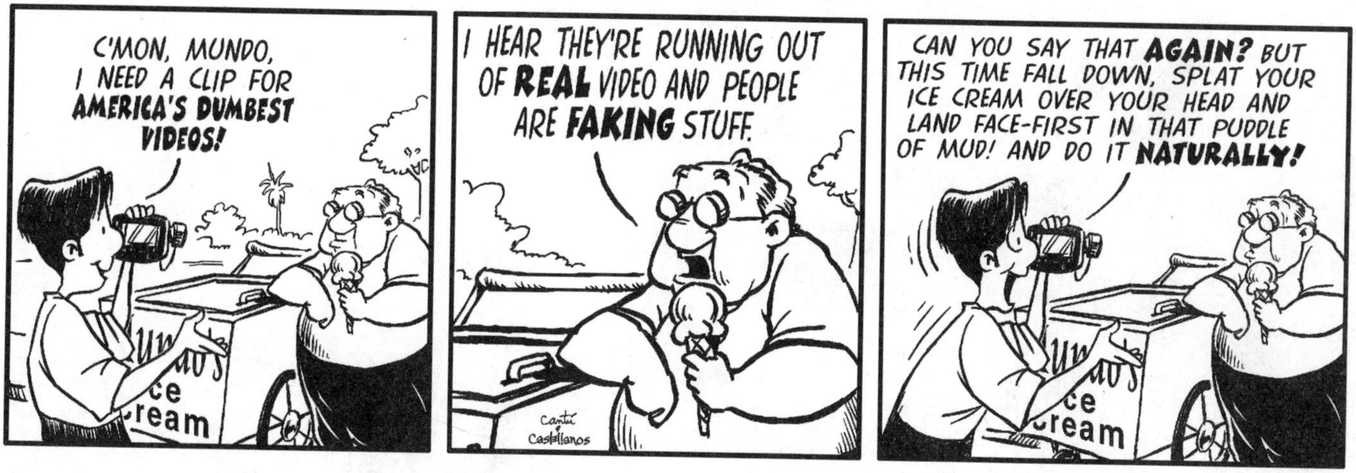
C'MON, MUNDO, I NEED A CLIP FOR AMERICA'S DUMBEST VIDEOS!
I HEAR THEY'RE RUNNING OUT OF REAL VIDEO AND PEOPLE ARE FAKING STUFF.
CAN YOU SAY THAT AGAIN? BUT THIS TIME FALL DOWN, SPLAT YOUR ICE CREAM OVER YOUR HEAD AND LAND FACE-FIRST IN THAT PUDDLE OF MUD! AND DO IT NATURALLY!
Cantú Castellanos

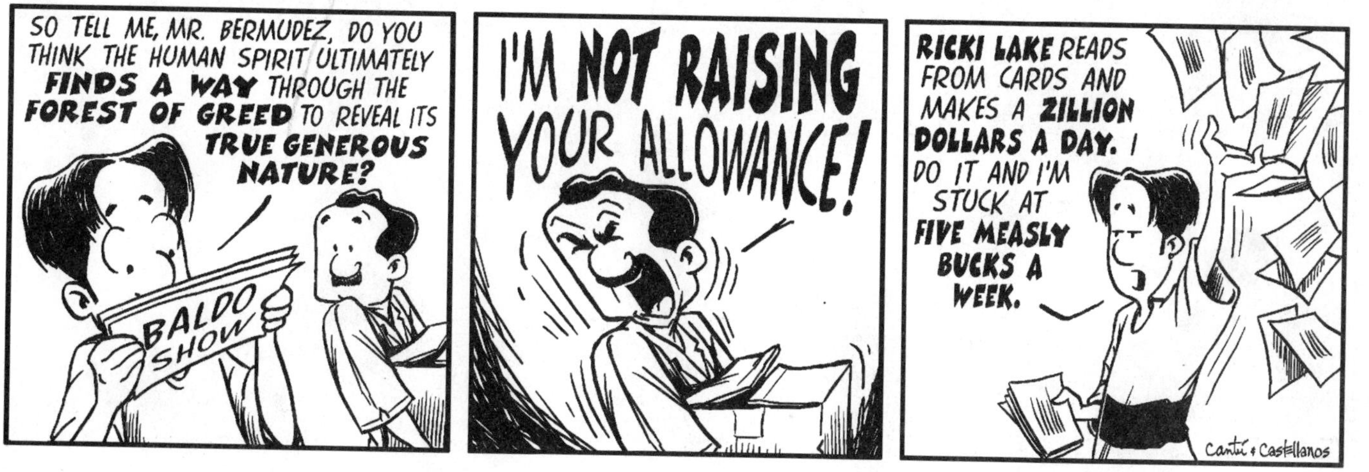
SO TELL ME, MR. BERMUDEZ, DO YOU THINK THE HUMAN SPIRIT ULTIMATELY FINDS A WAY THROUGH THE FOREST OF GREED TO REVEAL ITS TRUE GENEROUS NATURE?
BALDO SHOW
I'M NOT RAISING YOUR ALLOWANCE!
RICKI LAKE READS FROM CARDS AND MAKES A ZILLION DOLLARS A DAY. I DO IT AND I'M STUCK AT FIVE MEASLY BUCKS A WEEK.
Cantú & Castellanos

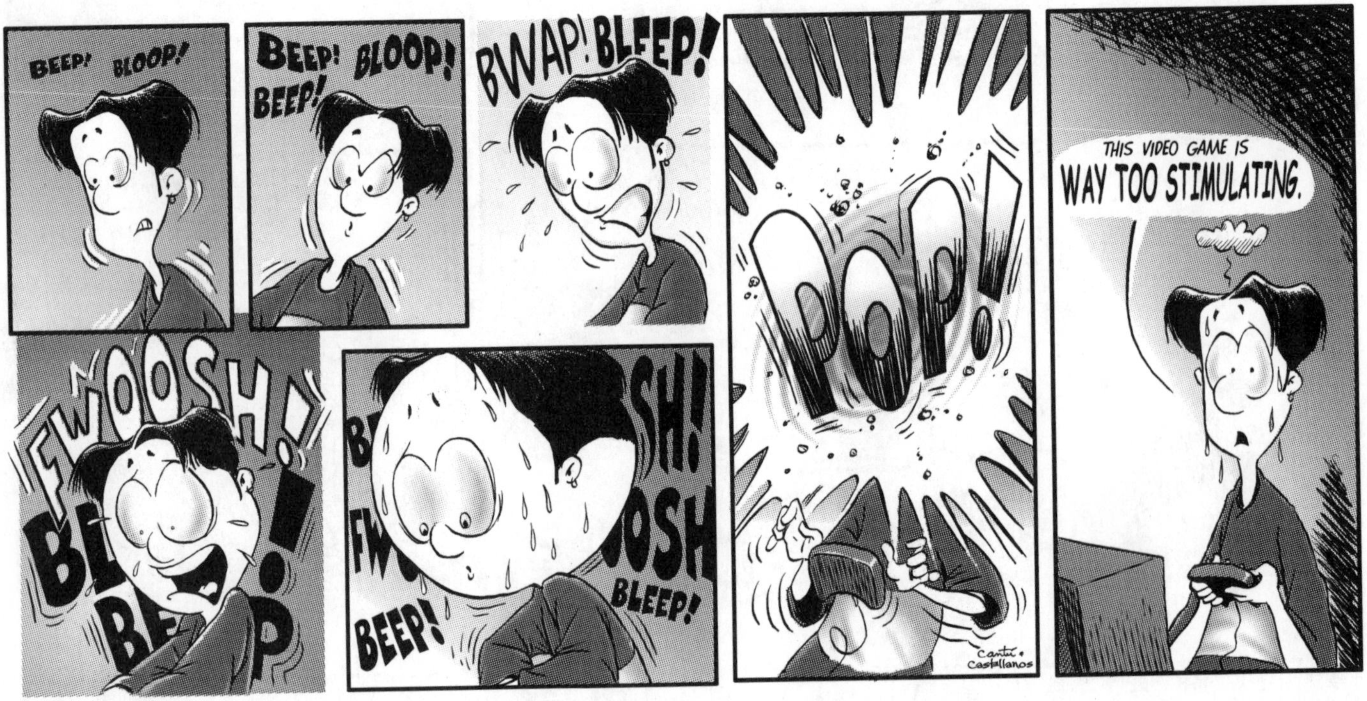
BEEP! BLOOP!
BEEP! BLOOP! BEEP!
BWAP! BLEEP!
FWOOSH!
BEEP!
BLEEP!
POP!!
Cantú • Castellanos
THIS VIDEO GAME IS WAY TOO STIMULATING.

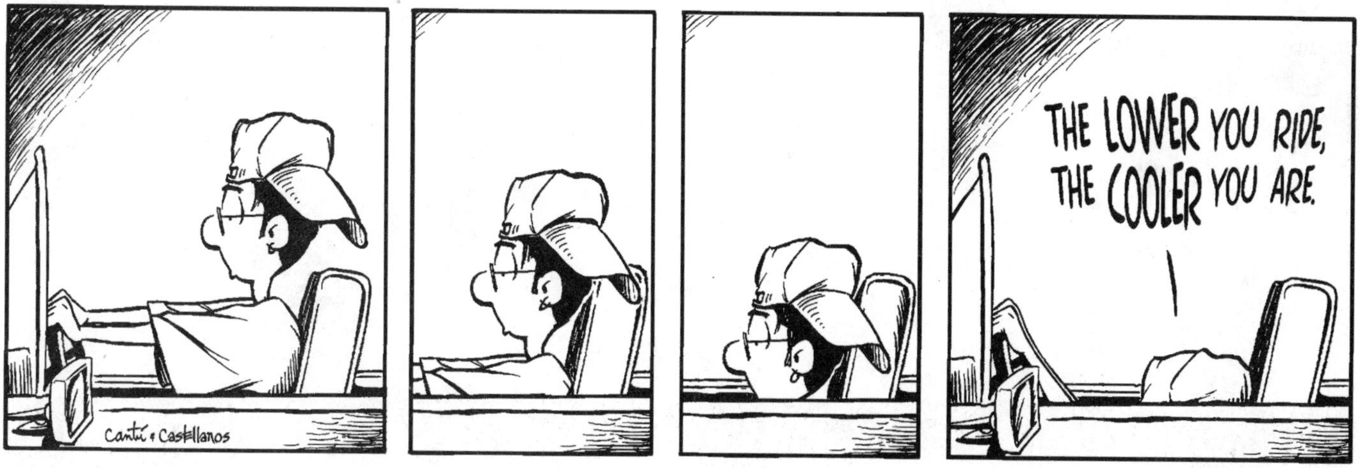
Cantú & Castellanos
THE LOWER YOU RIDE, THE COOLER YOU ARE.

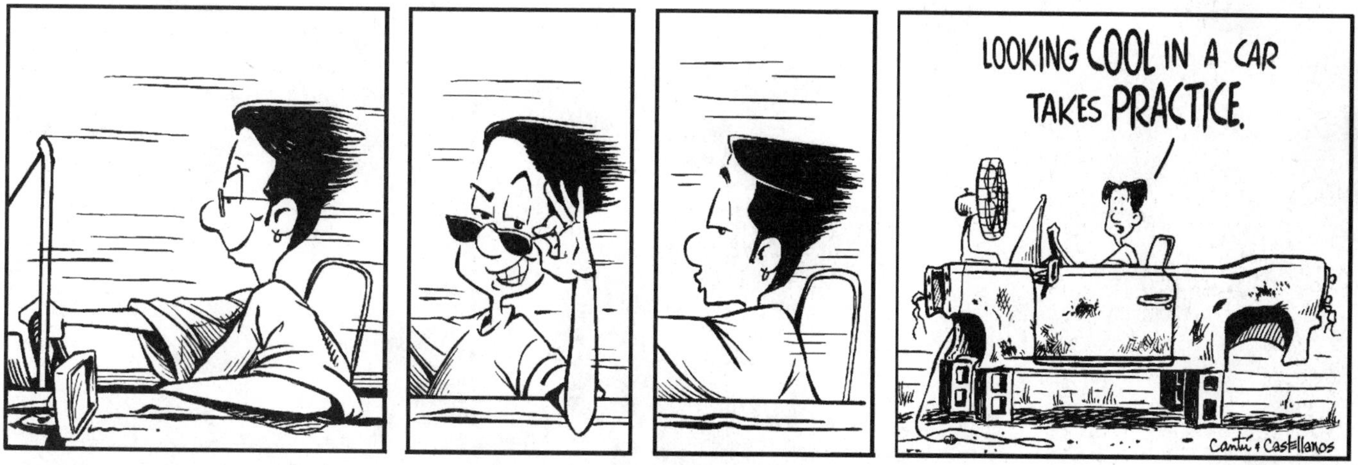
LOOKING COOL IN A CAR TAKES PRACTICE.
Cantú & Castellanos

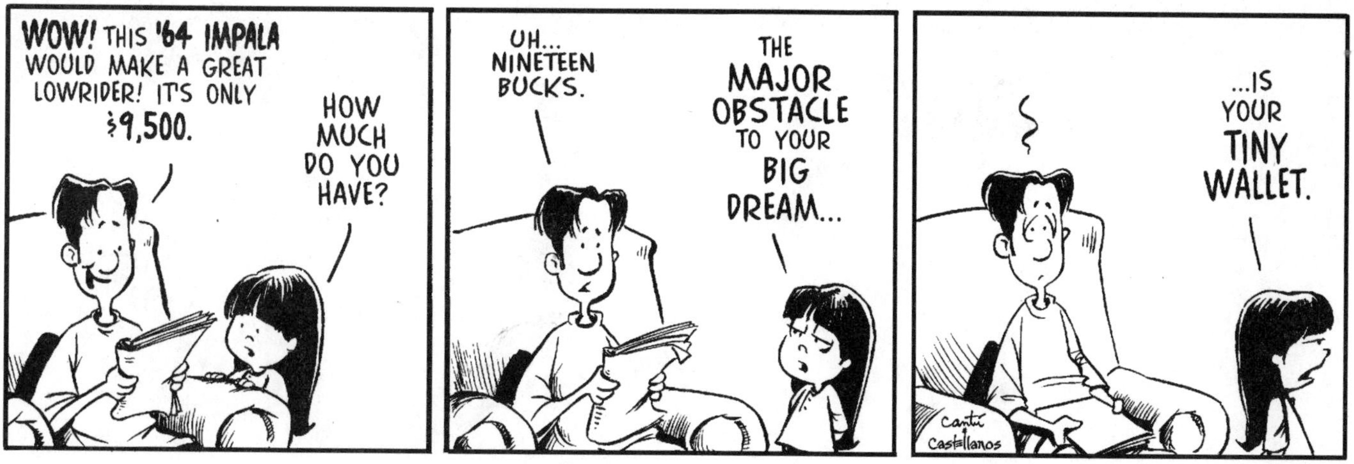
WOW! THIS '64 IMPALA WOULD MAKE A GREAT LOWRIDER! IT'S ONLY $9,500.
HOW MUCH DO YOU HAVE?
UH... NINETEEN BUCKS.
THE MAJOR OBSTACLE TO YOUR BIG DREAM...
...IS YOUR TINY WALLET.
Cantú Castellanos

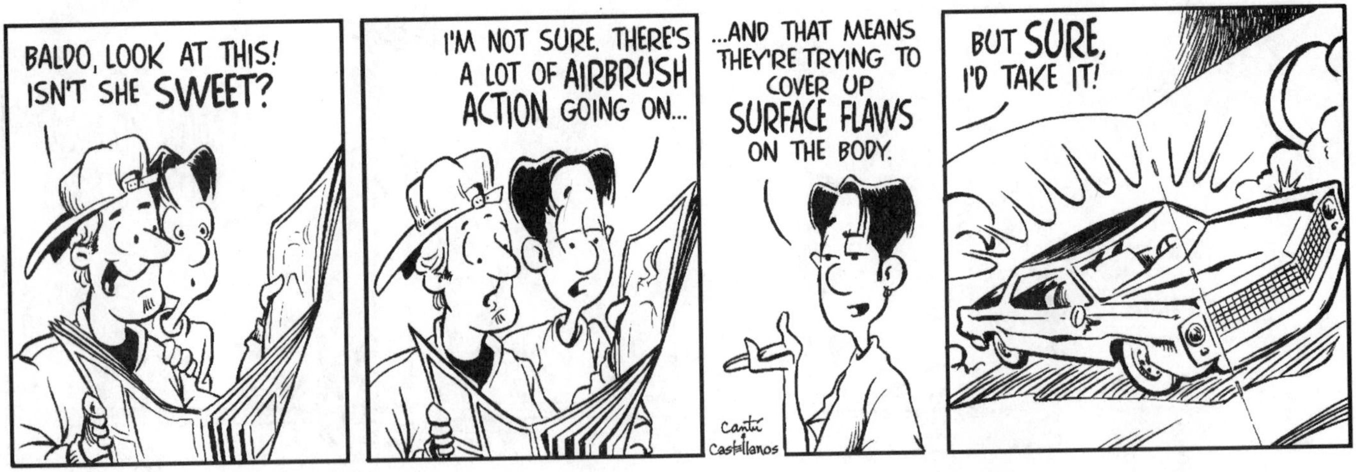
BALDO, LOOK AT THIS! ISN'T SHE SWEET?
I'M NOT SURE. THERE'S A LOT OF AIRBRUSH ACTION GOING ON...
...AND THAT MEANS THEY'RE TRYING TO COVER UP SURFACE FLAWS ON THE BODY.
Cantú Castellanos
BUT SURE, I'D TAKE IT!

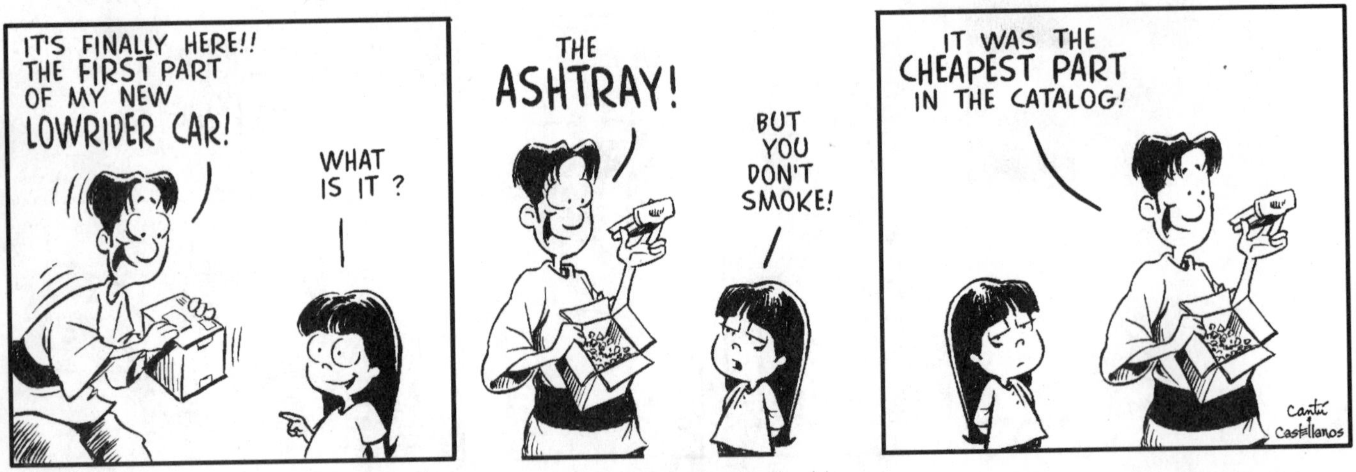
IT'S FINALLY HERE!! THE FIRST PART OF MY NEW LOWRIDER CAR!
WHAT IS IT ?
THE ASHTRAY!
BUT YOU DON'T SMOKE!
IT WAS THE CHEAPEST PART IN THE CATALOG!
Cantú Castellanos

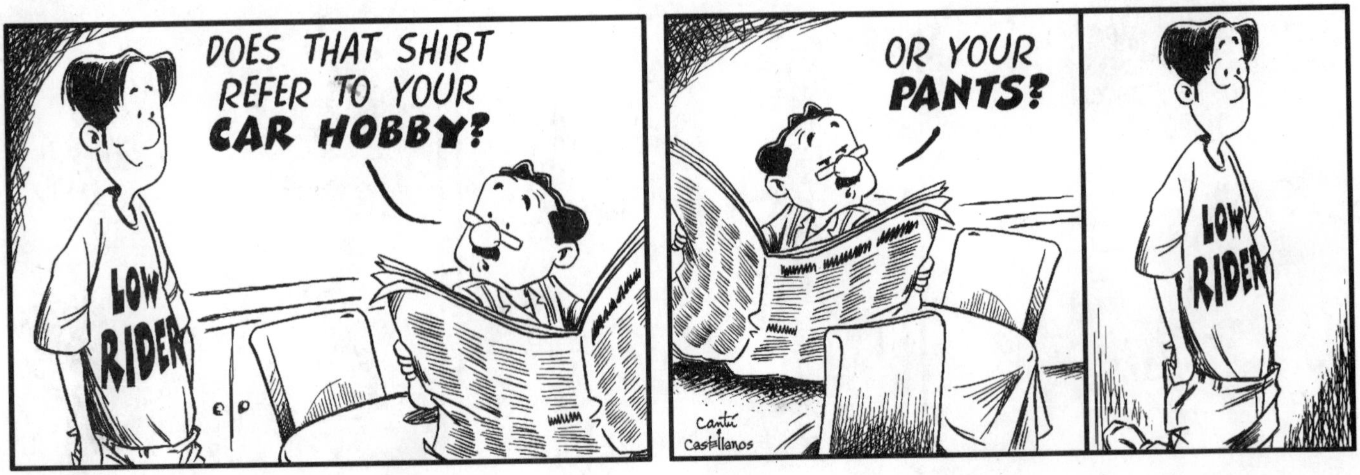
DOES THAT SHIRT REFER TO YOUR CAR HOBBY?
LOW RIDER
OR YOUR PANTS?
Cantú Castellanos
LOW RIDER

HEY DAD! THESE CHICHARONE CHIPS ARE GREAT! WHAT EXACTLY IS THIS STUFF? CORN? POTATOES?
CHICHARONES
ACTUALLY, YOU TAKE A DEAD PIG AND CHOP ITS SKIN INTO BITE-SIZED MORSELS...
THEN YOU BOIL IT IN A BIG VAT OF GREASY LARD...
...AND FRY IT TO A NICE SALTY CRISP! DELICIOSO!
JUST TALKING ABOUT IT IS MAKING ME HUNGRY! CAN YOU PASS SOME OVER HERE?
Cantú & Castellanos
GO AHEAD AND TAKE'EM ALL...
CHICHARONES

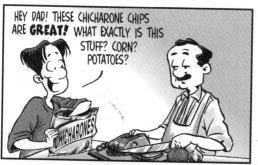

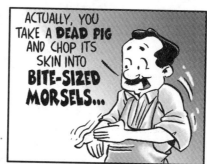

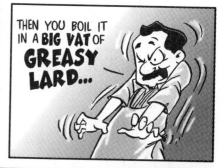

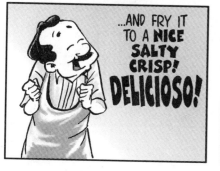

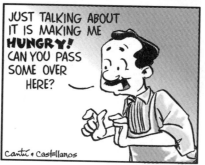

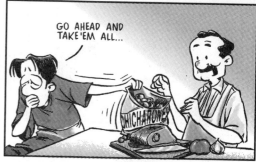

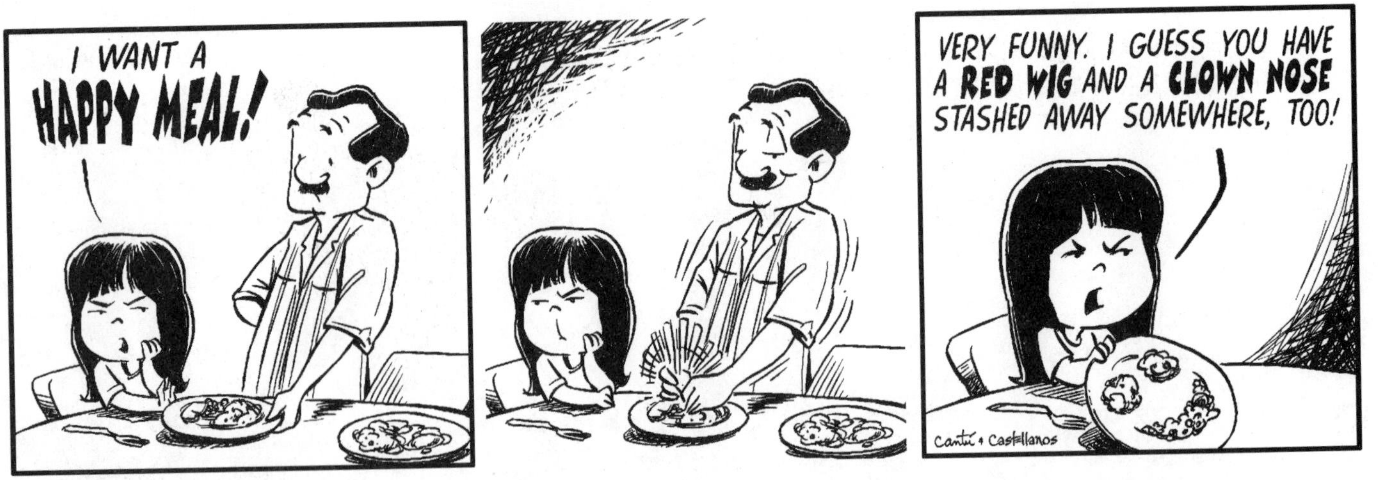
I WANT A HAPPY MEAL!
VERY FUNNY. I GUESS YOU HAVE A RED WIG AND A CLOWN NOSE STASHED AWAY SOMEWHERE, TOO!
Cantú + Castellanos

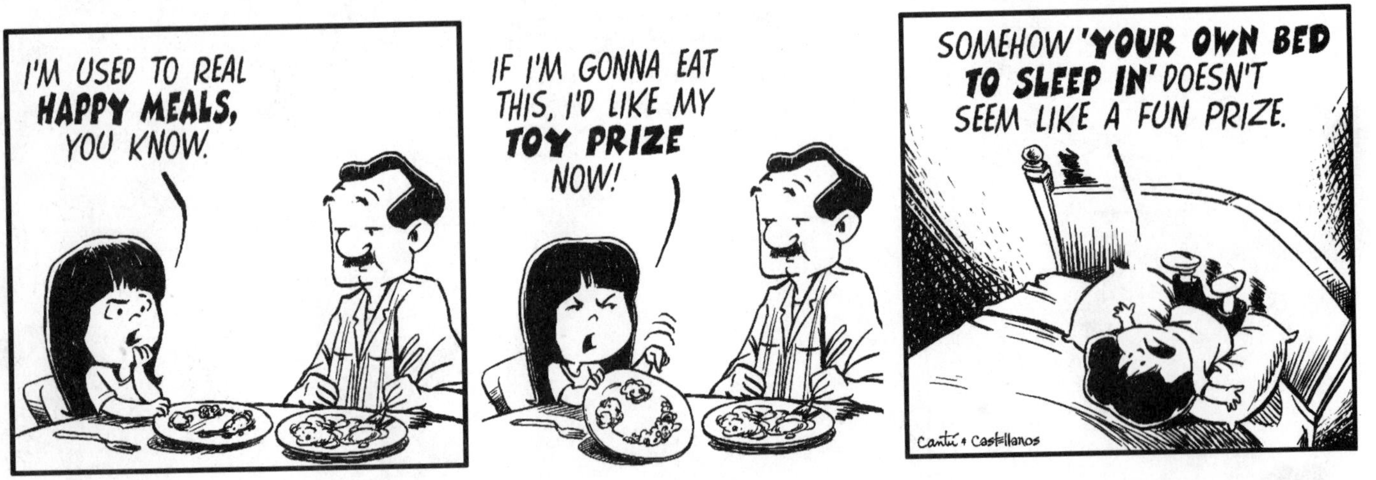
I'M USED TO REAL HAPPY MEALS, YOU KNOW.
IF I'M GONNA EAT THIS, I'D LIKE MY TOY PRIZE NOW!
SOMEHOW 'YOUR OWN BED TO SLEEP IN' DOESN'T SEEM LIKE A FUN PRIZE.
Cantú + Castellanos

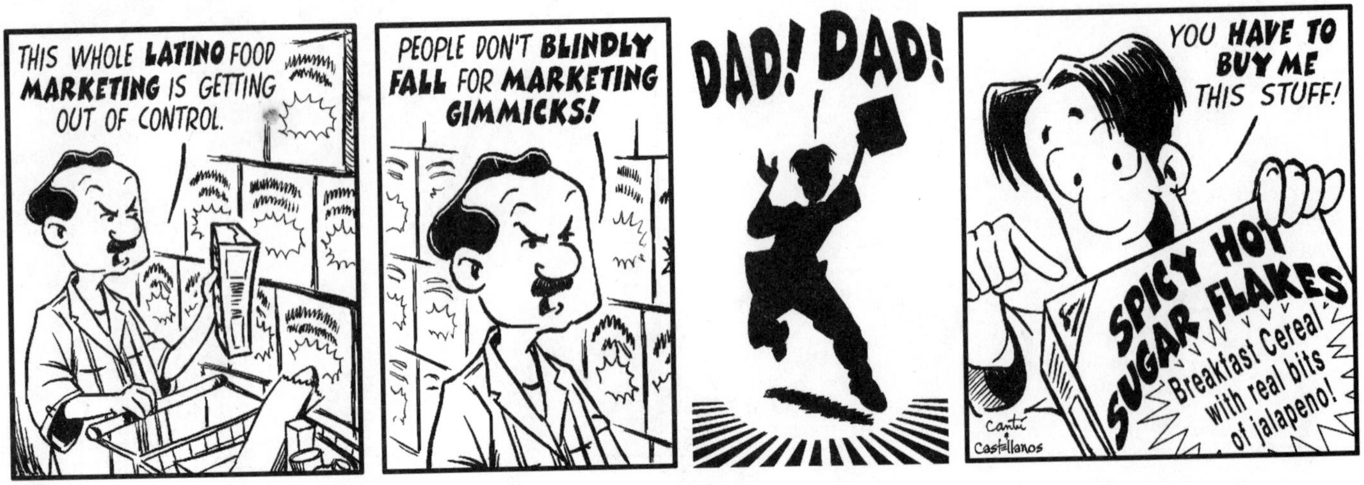
THIS WHOLE LATINO FOOD MARKETING IS GETTING OUT OF CONTROL.
PEOPLE DON'T BLINDLY FALL FOR MARKETING GIMMICKS!
DAD! DAD!
YOU HAVE TO BUY ME THIS STUFF!
SPICY HOT SUGAR FLAKES
Breakfast Cereal with real bits of jalapeno!
Cantú + Castellanos

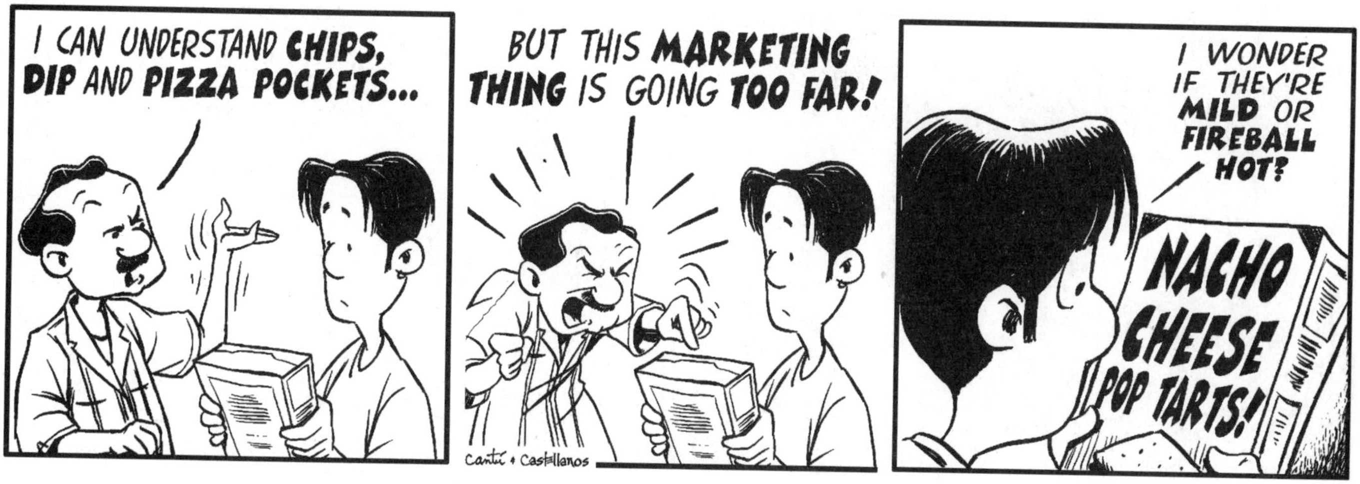
I CAN UNDERSTAND CHIPS, DIP AND PIZZA POCKETS...
BUT THIS MARKETING THING IS GOING TOO FAR!
Cantú & Castellanos
I WONDER IF THEY'RE MILD OR FIREBALL HOT?
NACHO CHEESE POP TARTS!

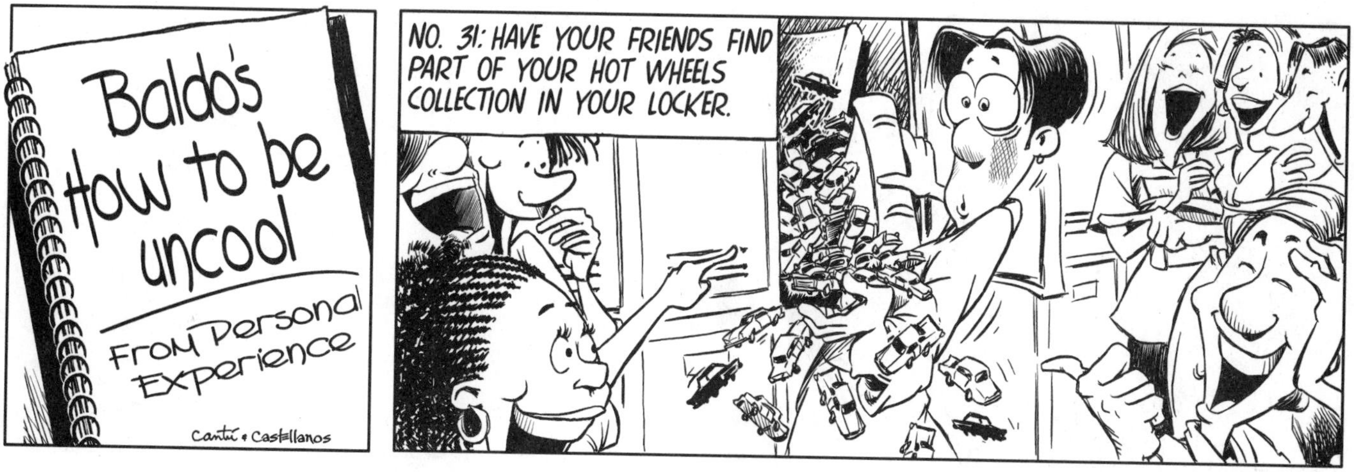
Baldo's How to be uncool
From Personal Experience
Cantú & Castellanos
NO. 31: HAVE YOUR FRIENDS FIND PART OF YOUR HOT WHEELS COLLECTION IN YOUR LOCKER.

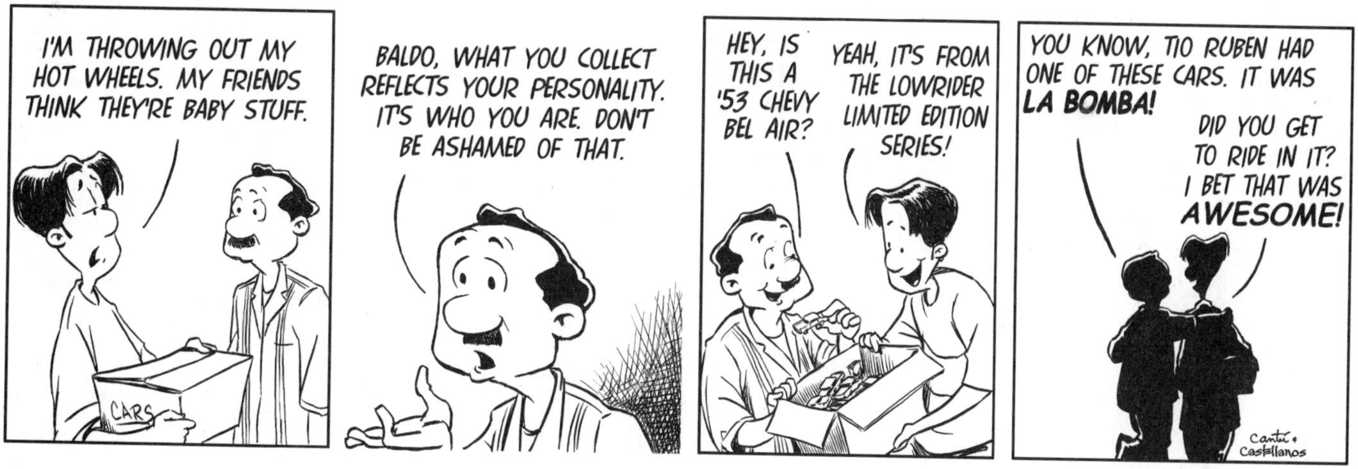
I'M THROWING OUT MY HOT WHEELS. MY FRIENDS THINK THEY'RE BABY STUFF.
CARS
BALDO, WHAT YOU COLLECT REFLECTS YOUR PERSONALITY. IT'S WHO YOU ARE. DON'T BE ASHAMED OF THAT.
HEY, IS THIS A '53 CHEVY BEL AIR?
YEAH, IT'S FROM THE LOWRIDER LIMITED EDITION SERIES!
YOU KNOW, TIO RUBEN HAD ONE OF THESE CARS. IT WAS LA BOMBA!
DID YOU GET TO RIDE IN IT? I BET THAT WAS AWESOME!
Cantú & Castellanos

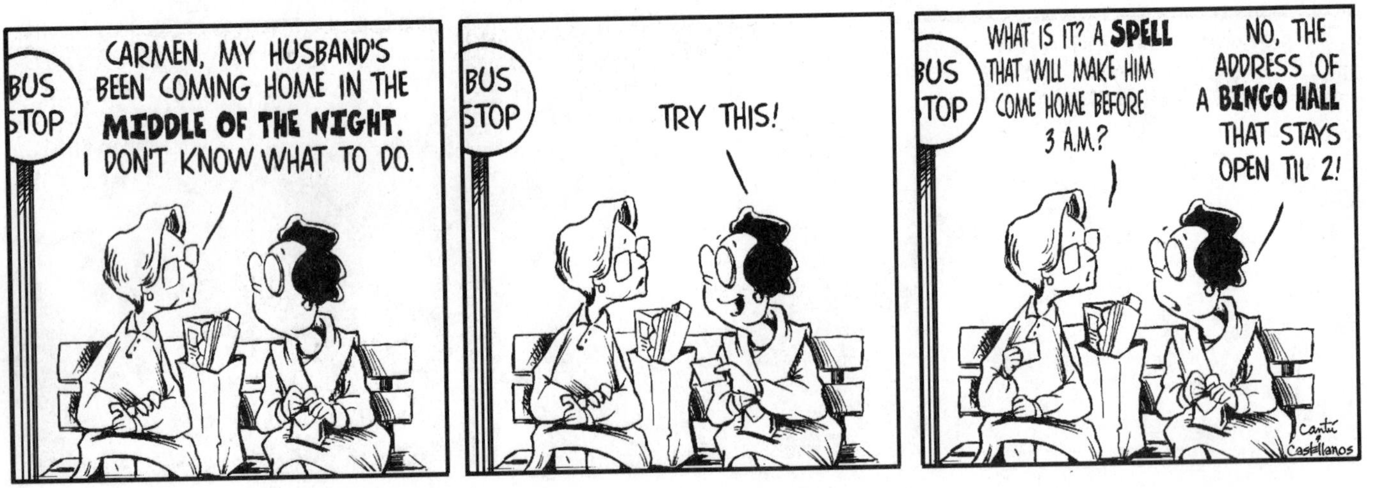
BUS STOP
CARMEN, MY HUSBAND'S BEEN COMING HOME IN THE **MIDDLE OF THE NIGHT.** I DON'T KNOW WHAT TO DO.
TRY THIS!
WHAT IS IT? A **SPELL** THAT WILL MAKE HIM COME HOME BEFORE 3 A.M.?
NO, THE ADDRESS OF A **BINGO HALL** THAT STAYS OPEN TIL 2!

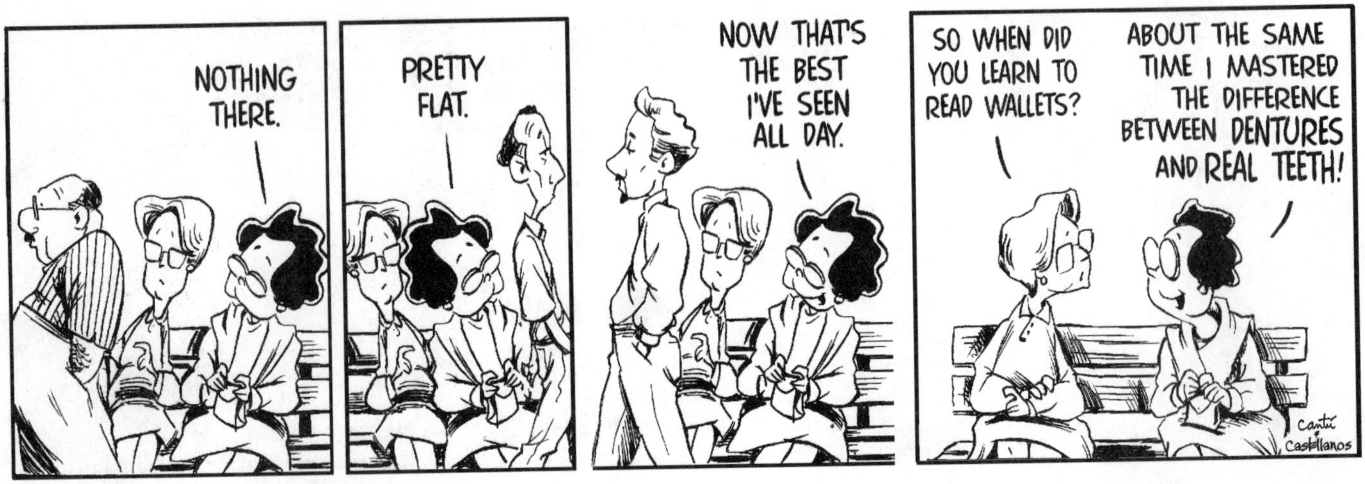
NOTHING THERE.
PRETTY FLAT.
NOW THAT'S THE BEST I'VE SEEN ALL DAY.
SO WHEN DID YOU LEARN TO READ WALLETS?
ABOUT THE SAME TIME I MASTERED THE DIFFERENCE BETWEEN DENTURES AND REAL TEETH!

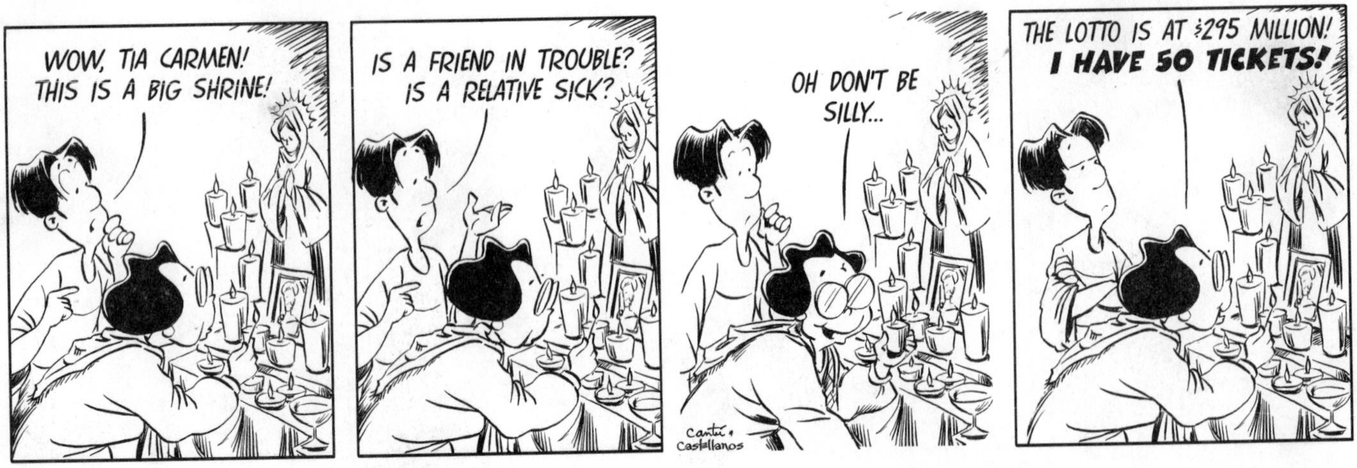
WOW, TIA CARMEN! THIS IS A BIG SHRINE!
IS A FRIEND IN TROUBLE? IS A RELATIVE SICK?
OH DON'T BE SILLY...
THE LOTTO IS AT $295 MILLION! **I HAVE 50 TICKETS!**

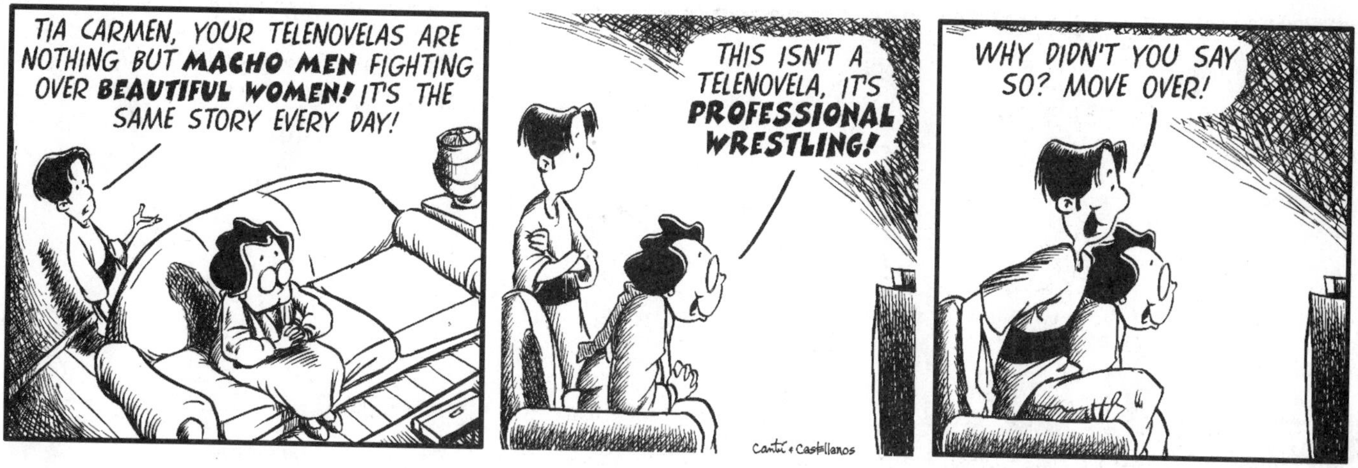
TIA CARMEN, YOUR TELENOVELAS ARE NOTHING BUT MACHO MEN FIGHTING OVER BEAUTIFUL WOMEN! IT'S THE SAME STORY EVERY DAY!
THIS ISN'T A TELENOVELA, IT'S PROFESSIONAL WRESTLING!
WHY DIDN'T YOU SAY SO? MOVE OVER!
Cantú & Castellanos

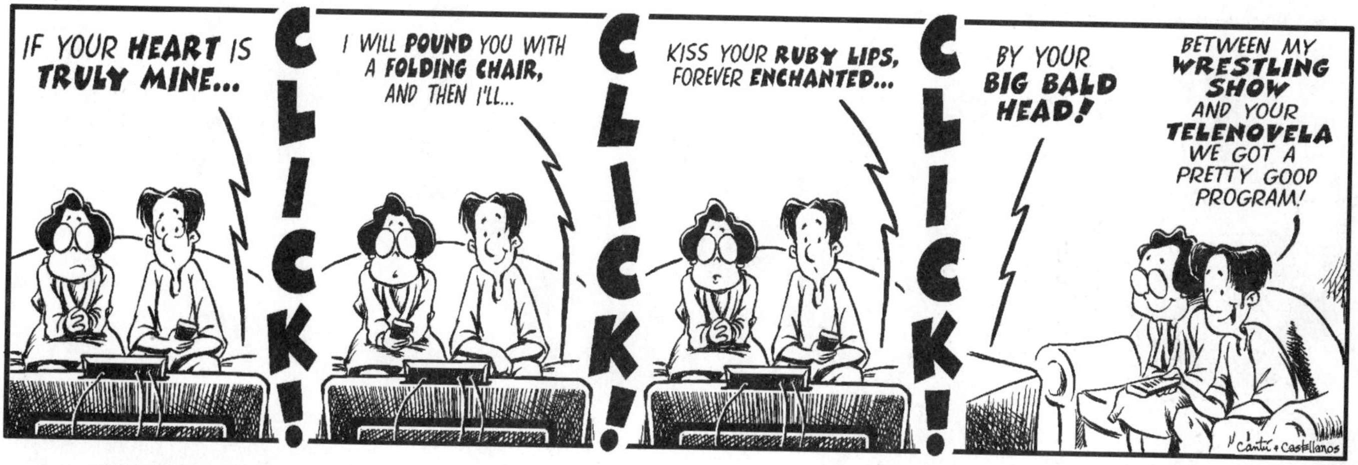
IF YOUR HEART IS TRULY MINE...
CLICK!
I WILL POUND YOU WITH A FOLDING CHAIR, AND THEN I'LL...
CLICK!
KISS YOUR RUBY LIPS, FOREVER ENCHANTED...
CLICK!
BY YOUR BIG BALD HEAD!
BETWEEN MY WRESTLING SHOW AND YOUR TELENOVELA WE GOT A PRETTY GOOD PROGRAM!
Cantú & Castellanos

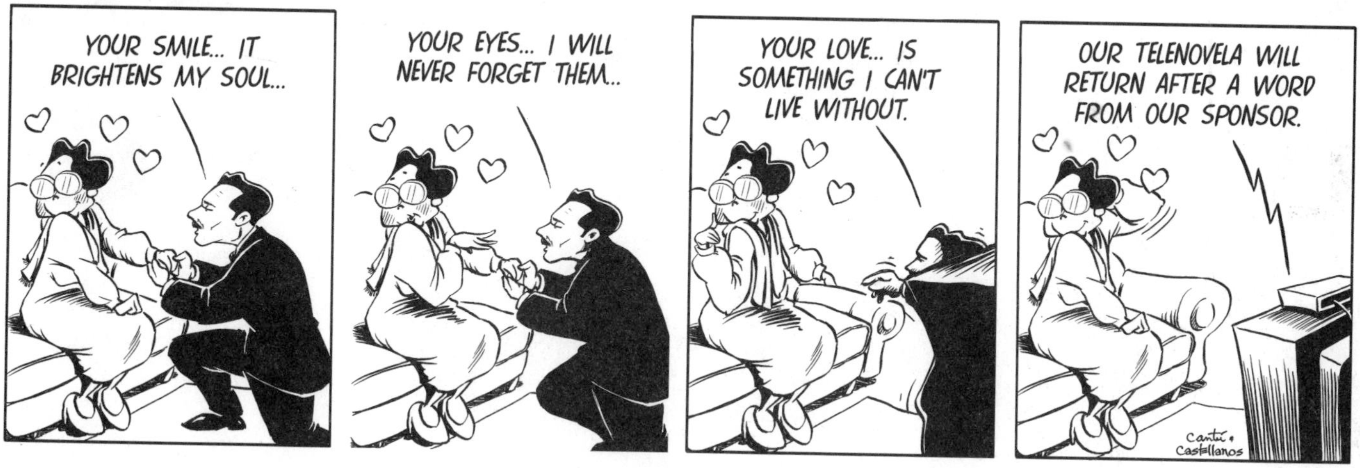
YOUR SMILE... IT BRIGHTENS MY SOUL...
YOUR EYES... I WILL NEVER FORGET THEM...
YOUR LOVE... IS SOMETHING I CAN'T LIVE WITHOUT.
OUR TELENOVELA WILL RETURN AFTER A WORD FROM OUR SPONSOR.
Cantú & Castellanos

AIEE! IT'S BAACK!
AIEE! IT'S BAACK!
AIEE! IT'S BAACK!
IS IT ME, OR ARE THEY CRAMMING A LOT MORE COMMERCIAL BREAKS IN TIA CARMEN'S TELE-NOVELA?

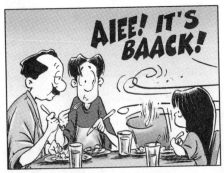

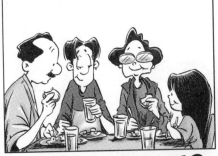

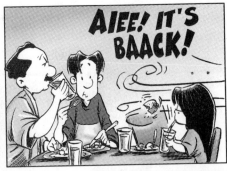

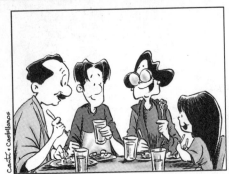

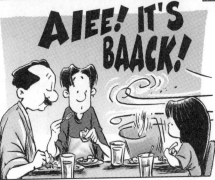

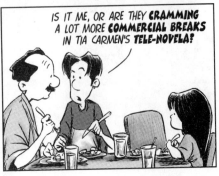

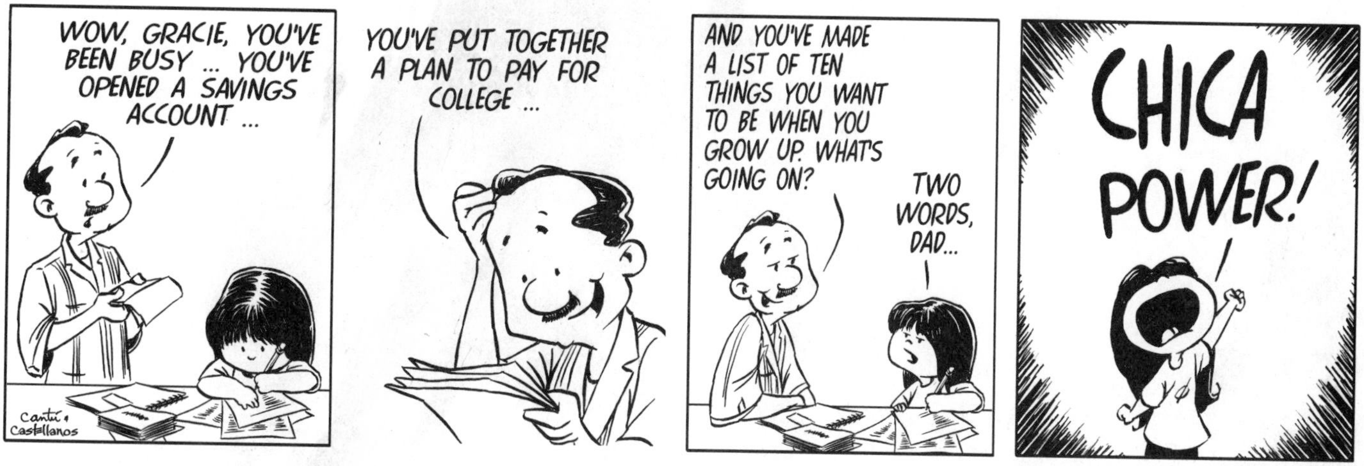
WOW, GRACIE, YOU'VE BEEN BUSY ... YOU'VE OPENED A SAVINGS ACCOUNT ...
YOU'VE PUT TOGETHER A PLAN TO PAY FOR COLLEGE ...
AND YOU'VE MADE A LIST OF TEN THINGS YOU WANT TO BE WHEN YOU GROW UP. WHAT'S GOING ON?
TWO WORDS, DAD...
CHICA POWER!

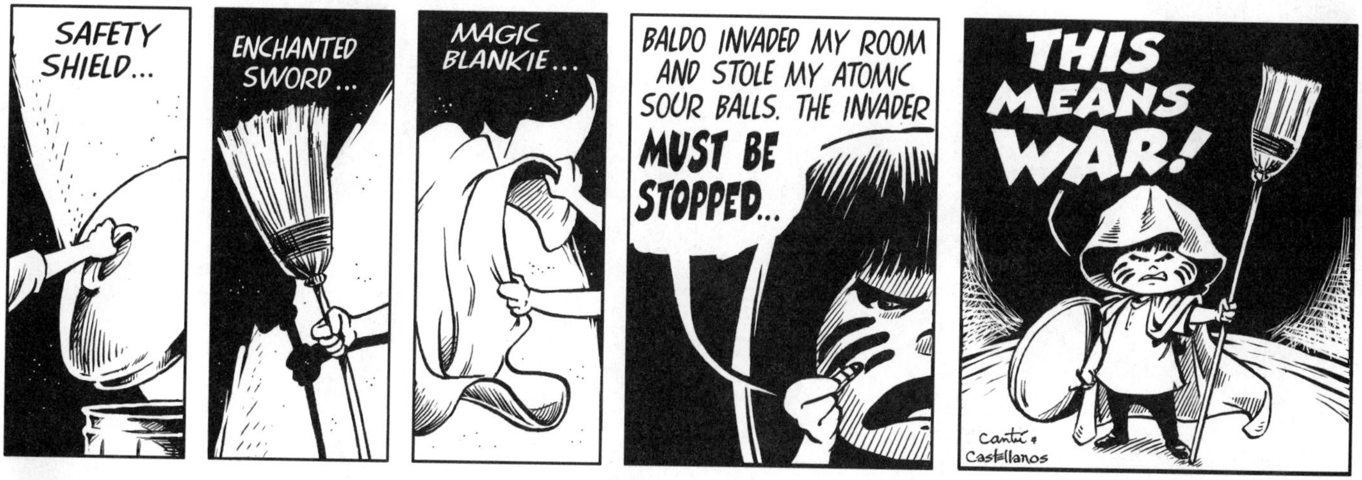
SAFETY SHIELD...
ENCHANTED SWORD...
MAGIC BLANKIE...
BALDO INVADED MY ROOM AND STOLE MY ATOMIC SOUR BALLS. THE INVADER MUST BE STOPPED...
THIS MEANS WAR!

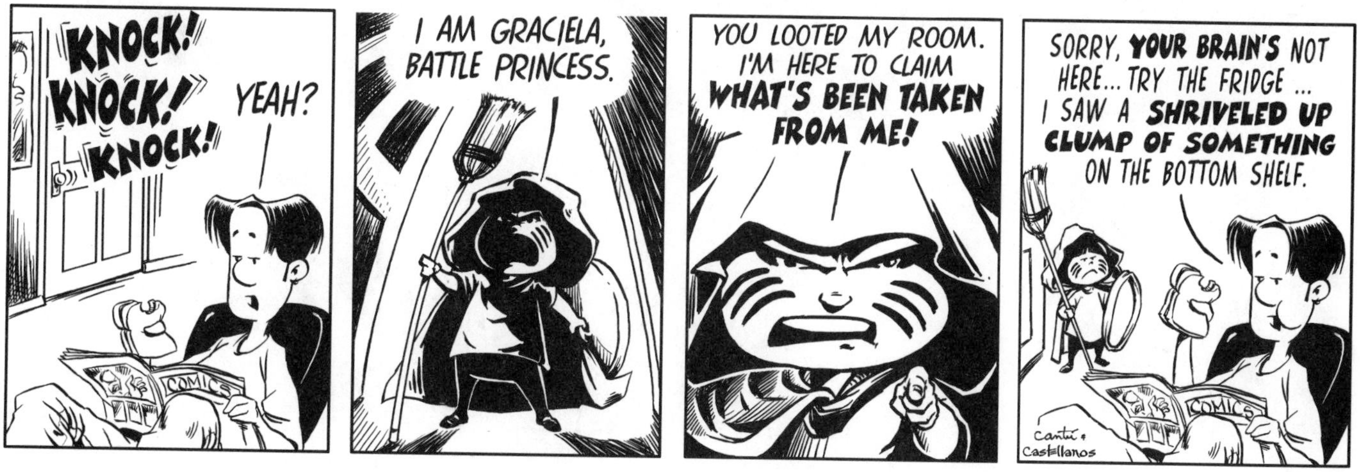
KNOCK! KNOCK! KNOCK!
YEAH?
COMICS
I AM GRACIELA, BATTLE PRINCESS.
YOU LOOTED MY ROOM. I'M HERE TO CLAIM WHAT'S BEEN TAKEN FROM ME!
SORRY, YOUR BRAIN'S NOT HERE... TRY THE FRIDGE ... I SAW A SHRIVELED UP CLUMP OF SOMETHING ON THE BOTTOM SHELF.
COMICS

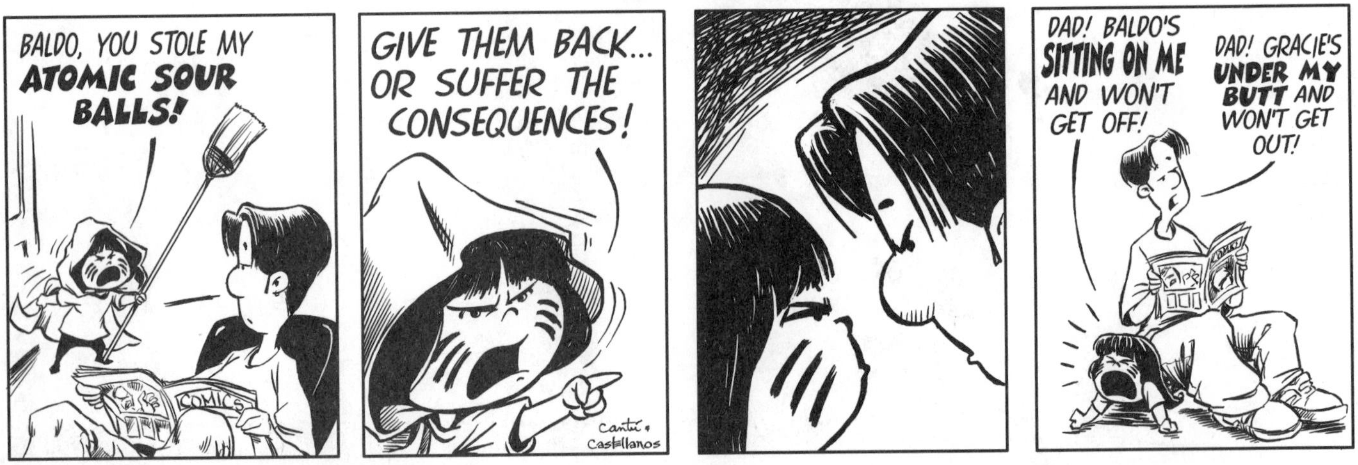
BALDO, YOU STOLE MY ATOMIC SOUR BALLS!
COMICS
GIVE THEM BACK... OR SUFFER THE CONSEQUENCES!
Cantú & Castellanos
DAD! BALDO'S SITTING ON ME AND WON'T GET OFF!
DAD! GRACIE'S UNDER MY BUTT AND WON'T GET OUT!

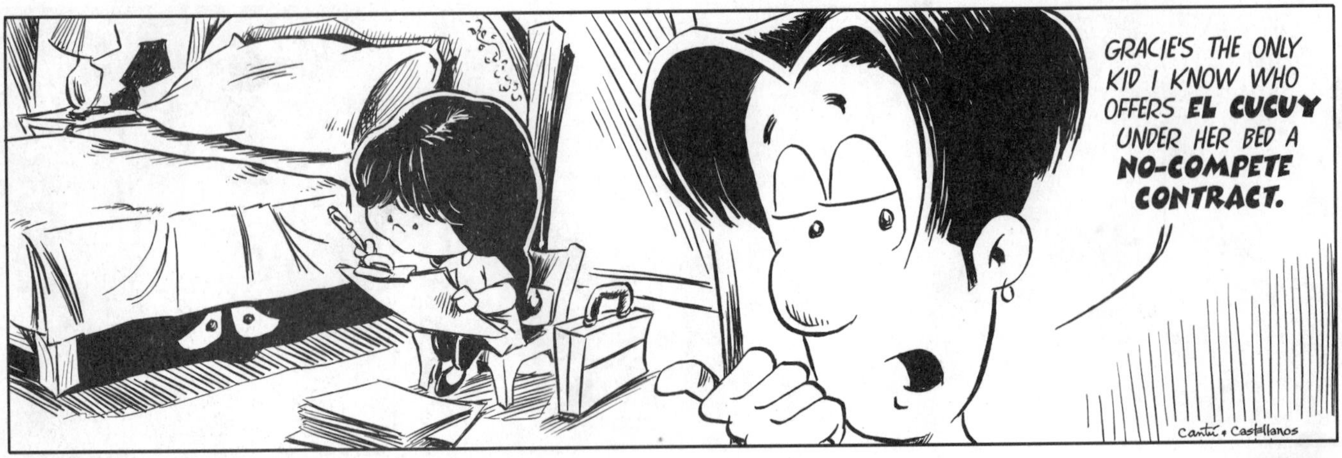
GRACIE'S THE ONLY KID I KNOW WHO OFFERS EL CUCUY UNDER HER BED A NO-COMPETE CONTRACT.
Cantú & Castellanos

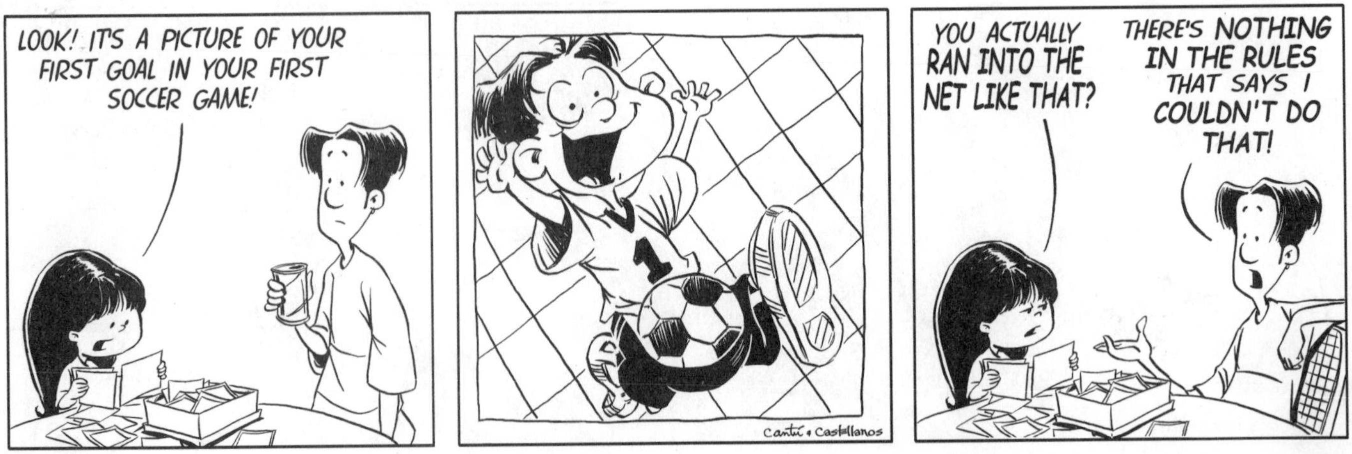
LOOK! IT'S A PICTURE OF YOUR FIRST GOAL IN YOUR FIRST SOCCER GAME!
Cantú & Castellanos
YOU ACTUALLY RAN INTO THE NET LIKE THAT?
THERE'S NOTHING IN THE RULES THAT SAYS I COULDN'T DO THAT!

Cantú • Castellanos
THERE!
Conserve our Resources

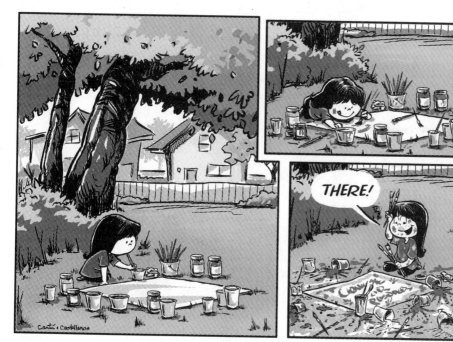

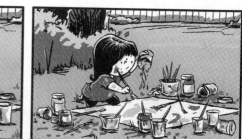

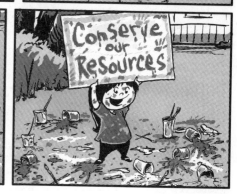

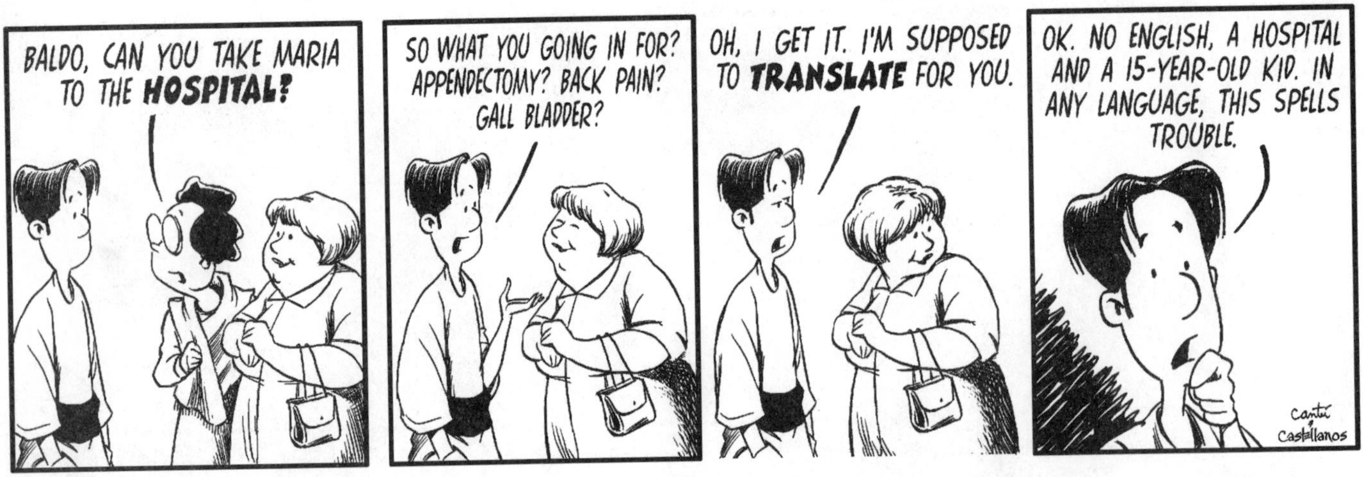
BALDO, CAN YOU TAKE MARIA TO THE **HOSPITAL?**
SO WHAT YOU GOING IN FOR? APPENDECTOMY? BACK PAIN? GALL BLADDER?
OH, I GET IT. I'M SUPPOSED TO **TRANSLATE** FOR YOU.
OK. NO ENGLISH, A HOSPITAL AND A 15-YEAR-OLD KID. IN ANY LANGUAGE, THIS SPELLS TROUBLE.
Cantú Castellanos

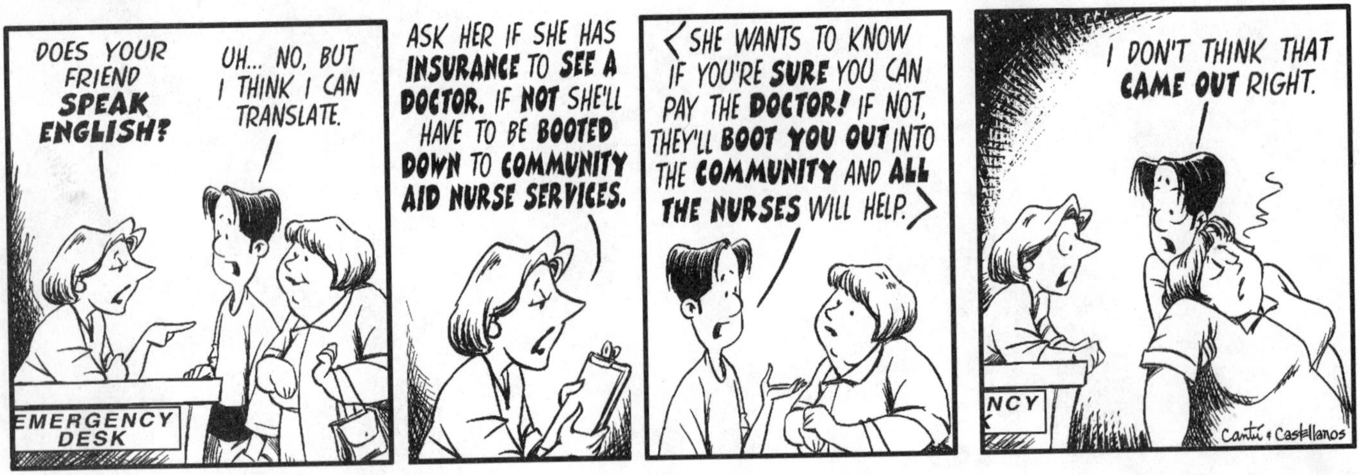
DOES YOUR FRIEND **SPEAK ENGLISH?**
UH... NO, BUT I THINK I CAN TRANSLATE.
EMERGENCY DESK
ASK HER IF SHE HAS **INSURANCE** TO **SEE A DOCTOR.** IF **NOT** SHE'LL HAVE TO BE **BOOTED DOWN** TO **COMMUNITY AID NURSE SERVICES.**
<SHE WANTS TO KNOW IF YOU'RE **SURE** YOU CAN PAY THE **DOCTOR!** IF NOT, THEY'LL **BOOT YOU OUT** INTO THE **COMMUNITY** AND **ALL THE NURSES** WILL HELP.>
I DON'T THINK THAT **CAME OUT** RIGHT.
NCY
Cantú & Castellanos

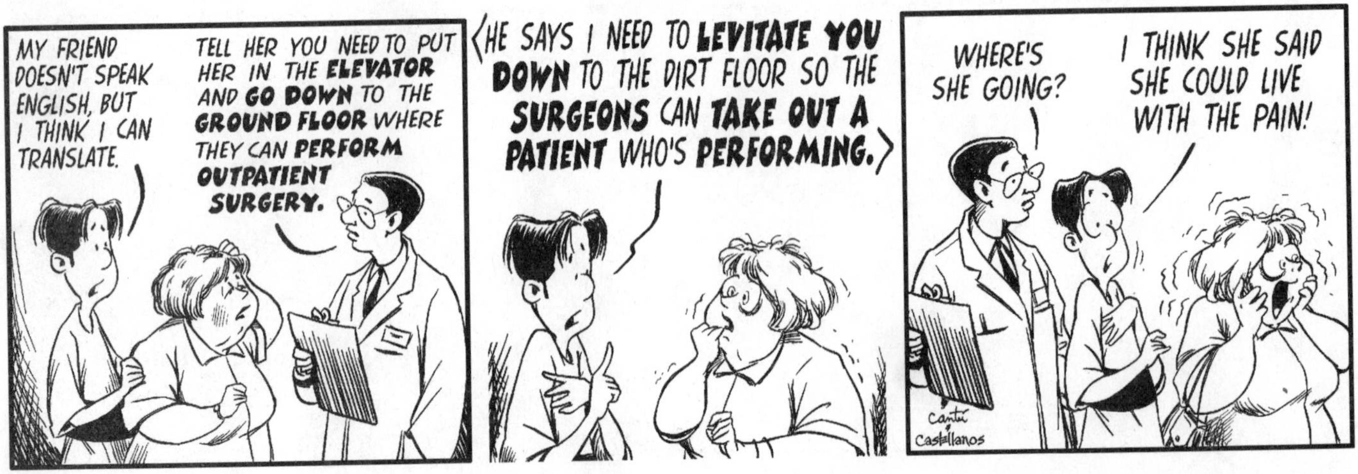
MY FRIEND DOESN'T SPEAK ENGLISH, BUT I THINK I CAN TRANSLATE.
TELL HER YOU NEED TO PUT HER IN THE **ELEVATOR** AND **GO DOWN** TO THE **GROUND FLOOR** WHERE THEY CAN **PERFORM OUTPATIENT SURGERY.**
<HE SAYS I NEED TO **LEVITATE YOU DOWN** TO THE DIRT FLOOR SO THE **SURGEONS** CAN **TAKE OUT A PATIENT** WHO'S **PERFORMING.**>
WHERE'S SHE GOING?
I THINK SHE SAID SHE COULD LIVE WITH THE PAIN!
Cantú Castellanos

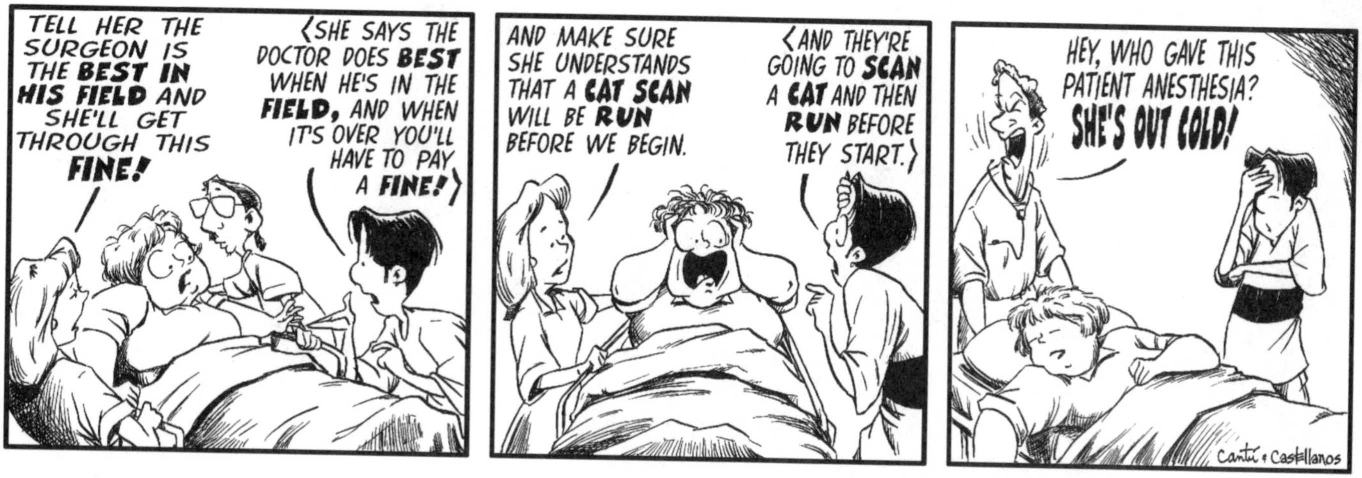
TELL HER THE SURGEON IS THE BEST IN HIS FIELD AND SHE'LL GET THROUGH THIS FINE!
{SHE SAYS THE DOCTOR DOES BEST WHEN HE'S IN THE FIELD, AND WHEN IT'S OVER YOU'LL HAVE TO PAY A FINE!}
AND MAKE SURE SHE UNDERSTANDS THAT A CAT SCAN WILL BE RUN BEFORE WE BEGIN.
{AND THEY'RE GOING TO SCAN A CAT AND THEN RUN BEFORE THEY START.}
HEY, WHO GAVE THIS PATIENT ANESTHESIA? SHE'S OUT COLD!
Cantú & Castellanos

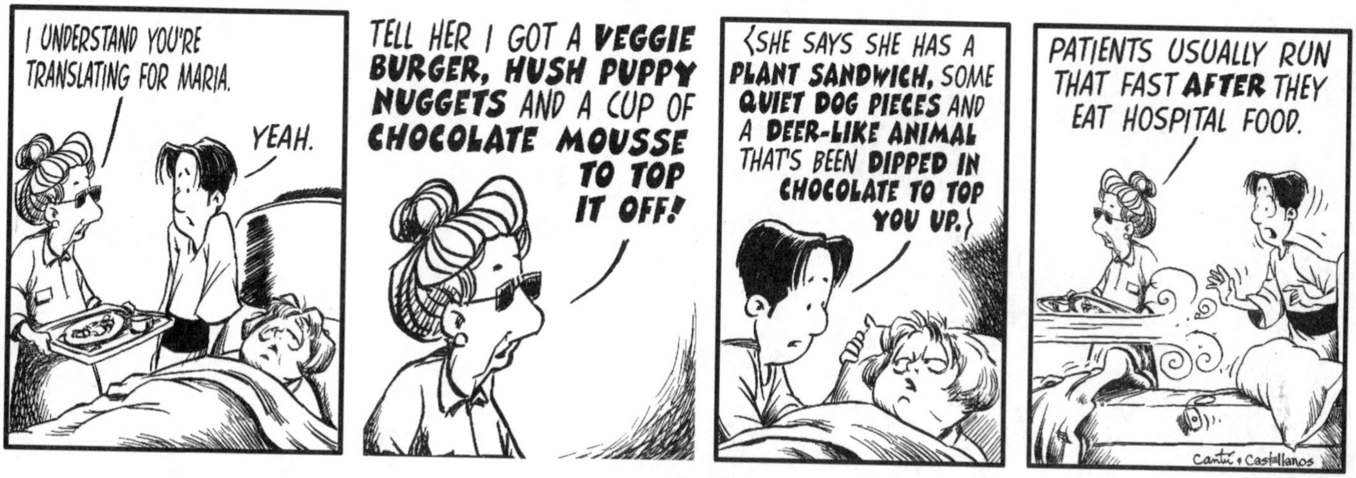
I UNDERSTAND YOU'RE TRANSLATING FOR MARIA.
YEAH.
TELL HER I GOT A VEGGIE BURGER, HUSH PUPPY NUGGETS AND A CUP OF CHOCOLATE MOUSSE TO TOP IT OFF!
{SHE SAYS SHE HAS A PLANT SANDWICH, SOME QUIET DOG PIECES AND A DEER-LIKE ANIMAL THAT'S BEEN DIPPED IN CHOCOLATE TO TOP YOU UP.}
PATIENTS USUALLY RUN THAT FAST AFTER THEY EAT HOSPITAL FOOD.
Cantú & Castellanos

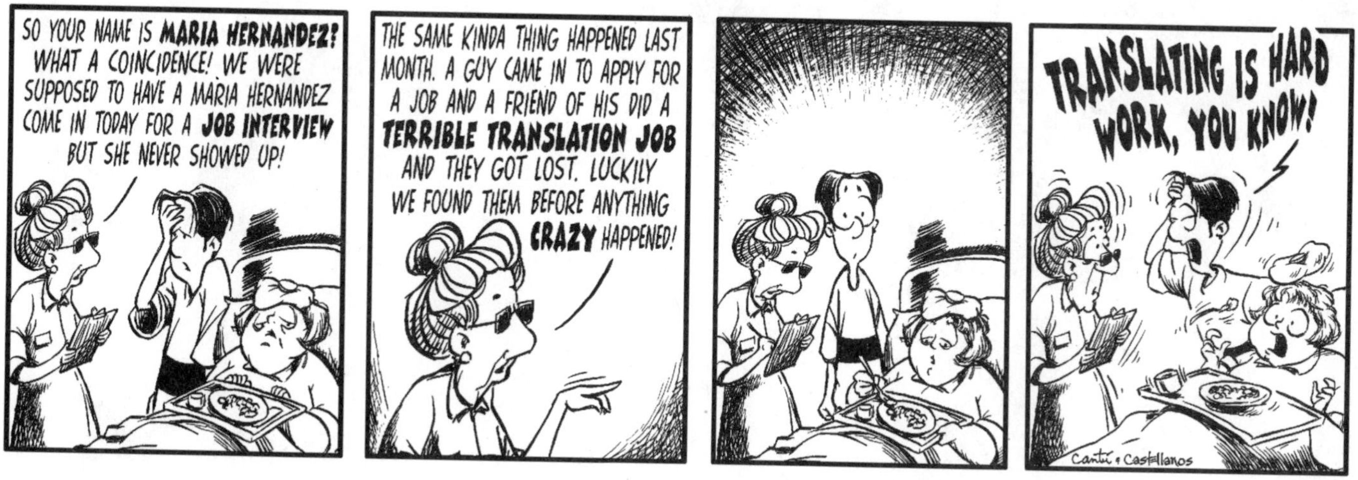
SO YOUR NAME IS MARIA HERNANDEZ? WHAT A COINCIDENCE! WE WERE SUPPOSED TO HAVE A MARIA HERNANDEZ COME IN TODAY FOR A JOB INTERVIEW BUT SHE NEVER SHOWED UP!
THE SAME KINDA THING HAPPENED LAST MONTH. A GUY CAME IN TO APPLY FOR A JOB AND A FRIEND OF HIS DID A TERRIBLE TRANSLATION JOB AND THEY GOT LOST. LUCKILY WE FOUND THEM BEFORE ANYTHING CRAZY HAPPENED!
TRANSLATING IS HARD WORK, YOU KNOW!
Cantú & Castellanos

IT'S SYLVIA SANCHEZ, THE PRETTIEST GIRL IN SCHOOL! WHAT DO I SAY?
HEY BALDO, HOW ARE YOU?
GREAT! HOW 'BOUT YOU?
Cantú + Castellanos

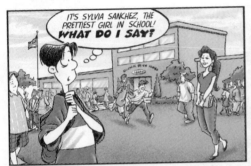

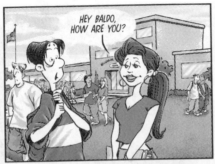

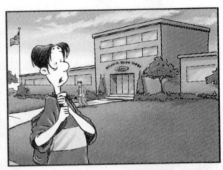

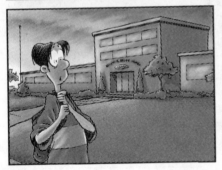

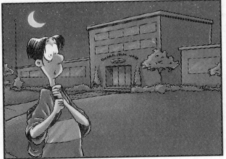

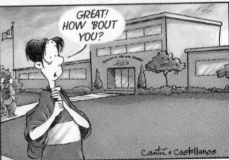

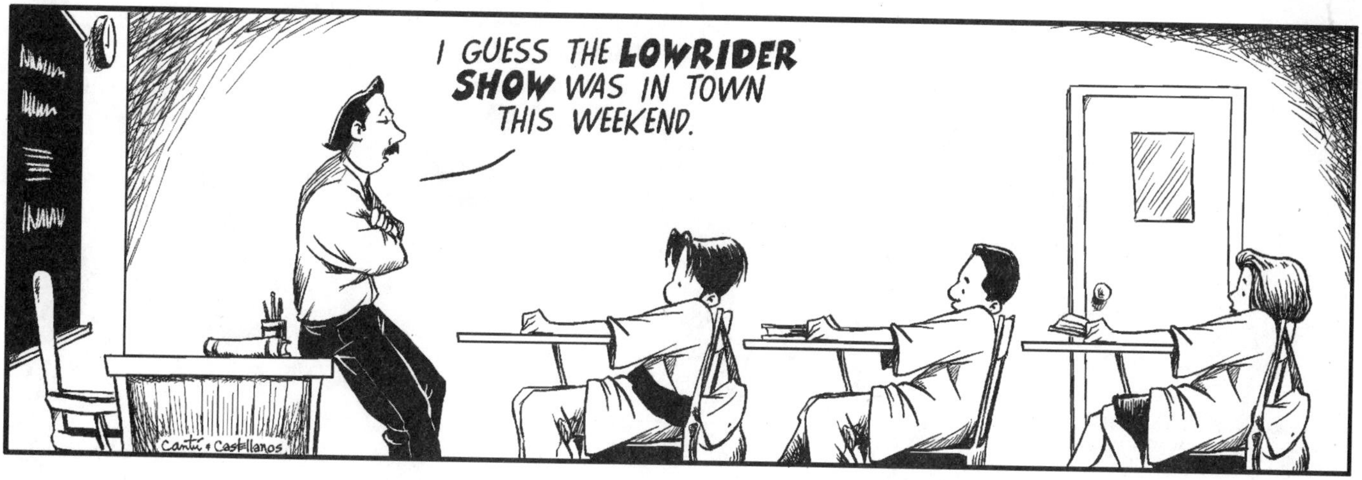
I GUESS THE **LOWRIDER SHOW** WAS IN TOWN THIS WEEKEND.
Cantú & Castellanos

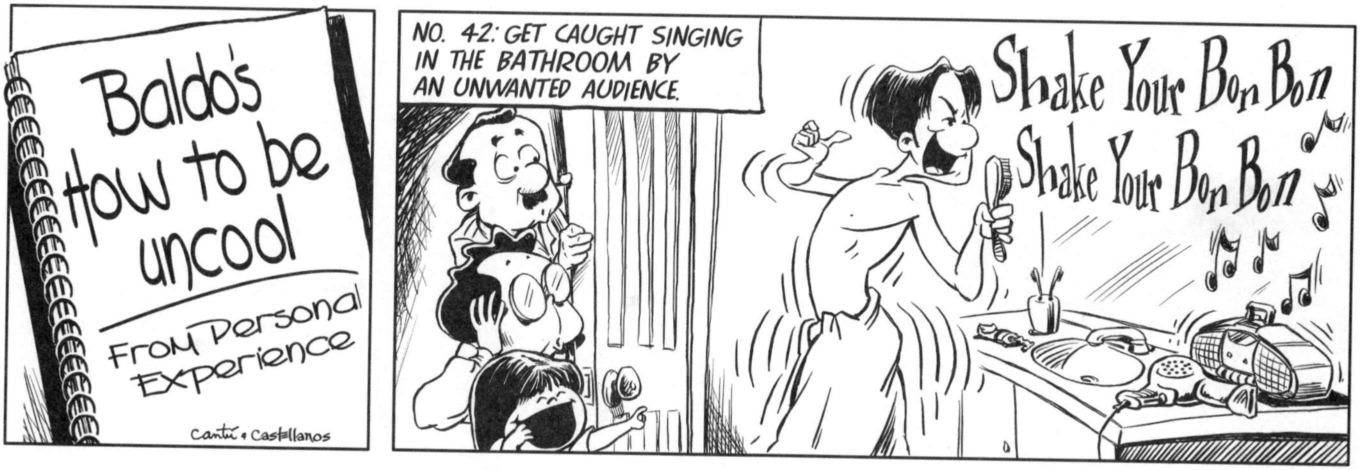
Baldo's How to be uncool
From Personal Experience
Cantú & Castellanos
NO. 42: GET CAUGHT SINGING IN THE BATHROOM BY AN UNWANTED AUDIENCE.
Shake Your Bon Bon
Shake Your Bon Bon

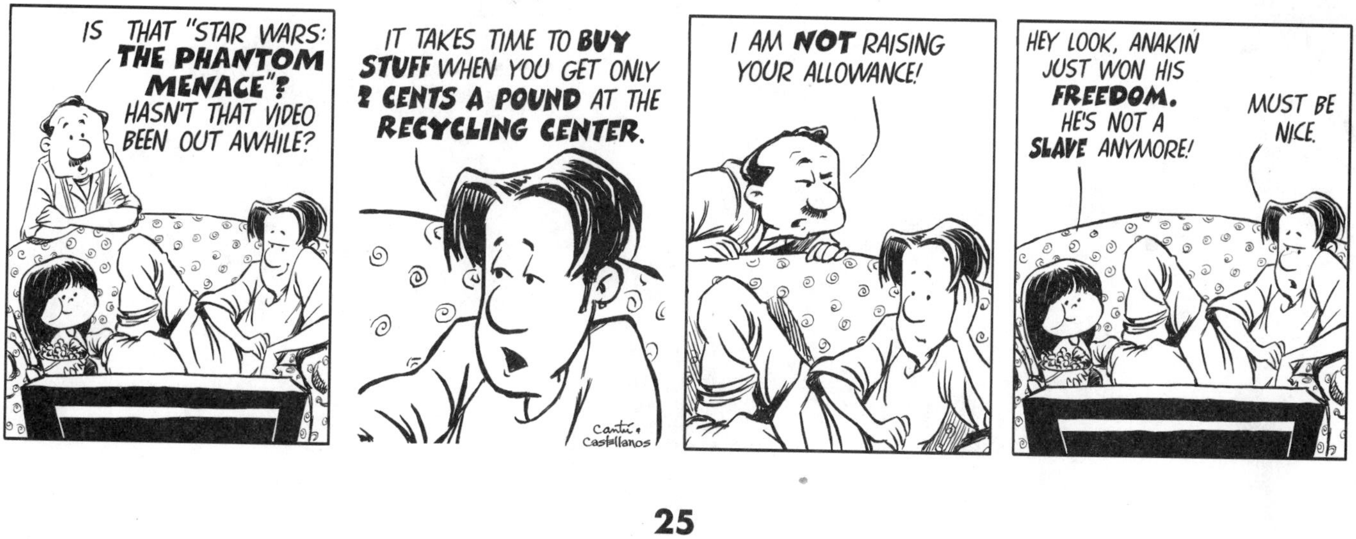
IS THAT "STAR WARS: **THE PHANTOM MENACE"?** HASN'T THAT VIDEO BEEN OUT AWHILE?
IT TAKES TIME TO **BUY STUFF** WHEN YOU GET ONLY **2 CENTS A POUND** AT THE **RECYCLING CENTER.**
Cantú & Castellanos
I AM **NOT** RAISING YOUR ALLOWANCE!
HEY LOOK, ANAKIN JUST WON HIS **FREEDOM.** HE'S NOT A **SLAVE** ANYMORE!
MUST BE NICE.

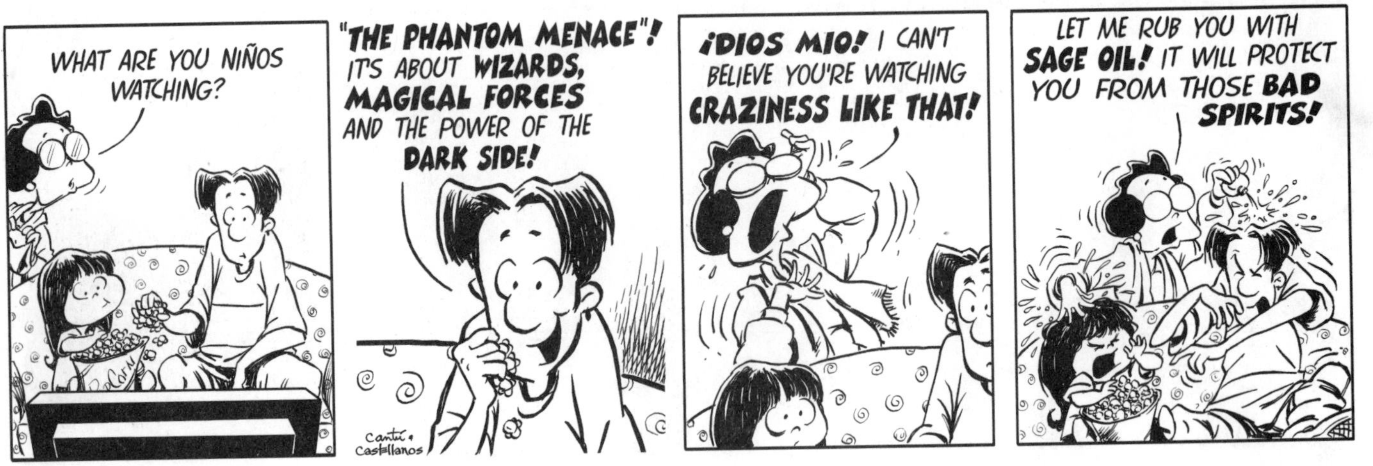
WHAT ARE YOU NIÑOS WATCHING?
"THE PHANTOM MENACE"! IT'S ABOUT WIZARDS, MAGICAL FORCES AND THE POWER OF THE DARK SIDE!
¡DIOS MIO! I CAN'T BELIEVE YOU'RE WATCHING CRAZINESS LIKE THAT!
LET ME RUB YOU WITH SAGE OIL! IT WILL PROTECT YOU FROM THOSE BAD SPIRITS!

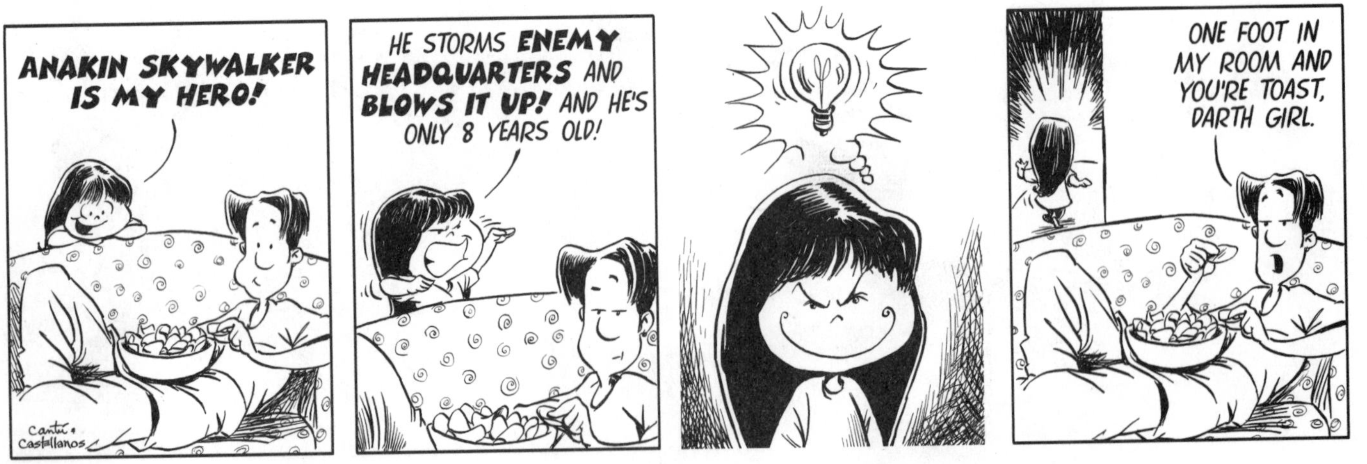
ANAKIN SKYWALKER IS MY HERO!
HE STORMS ENEMY HEADQUARTERS AND BLOWS IT UP! AND HE'S ONLY 8 YEARS OLD!
ONE FOOT IN MY ROOM AND YOU'RE TOAST, DARTH GIRL.

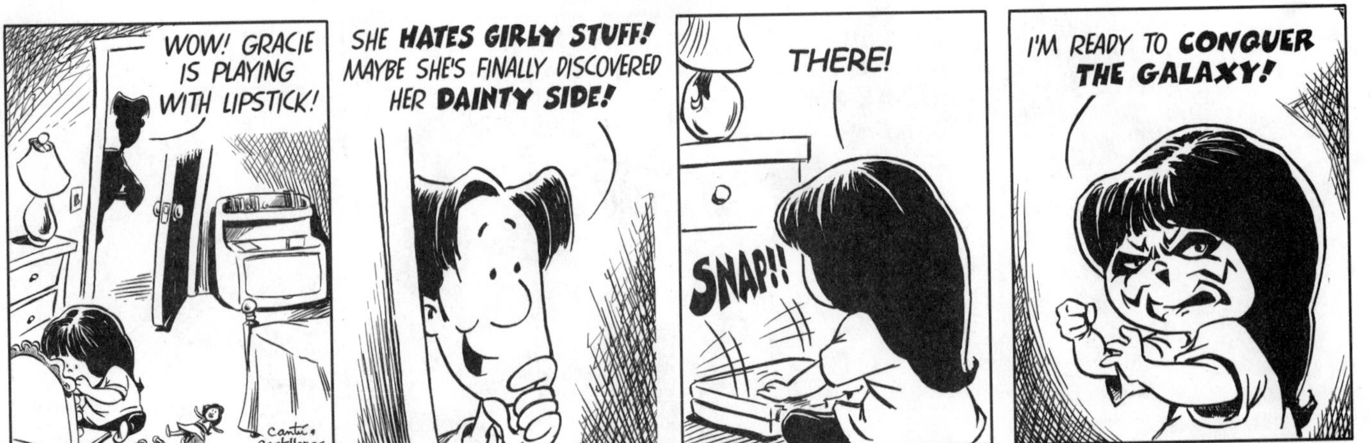
WOW! GRACIE IS PLAYING WITH LIPSTICK!
SHE HATES GIRLY STUFF! MAYBE SHE'S FINALLY DISCOVERED HER DAINTY SIDE!
THERE!
SNAP!!
I'M READY TO CONQUER THE GALAXY!

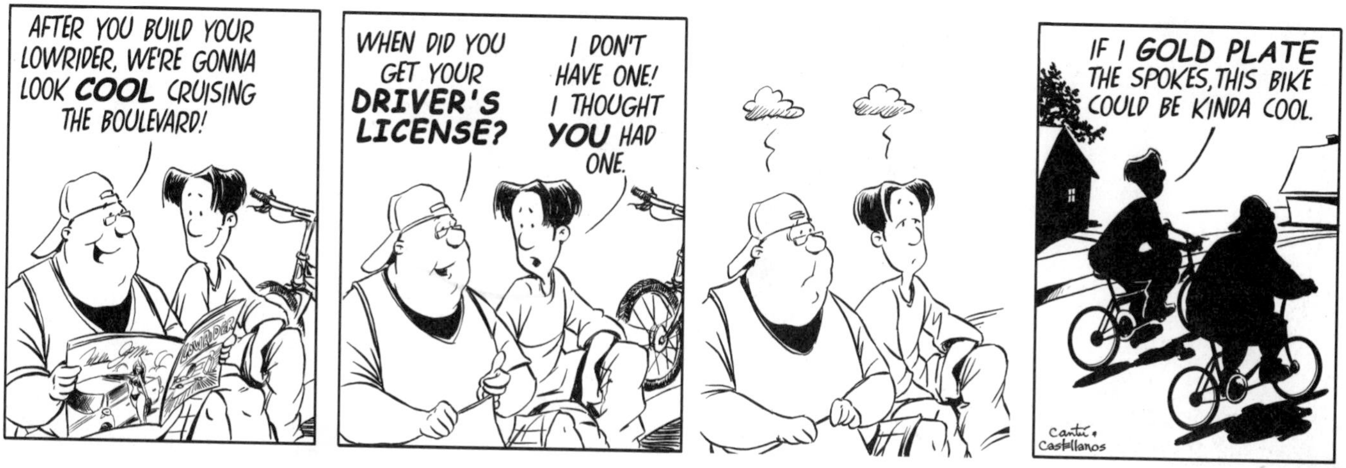
AFTER YOU BUILD YOUR LOWRIDER, WE'RE GONNA LOOK **COOL** CRUISING THE BOULEVARD!
LOWRIDER
WHEN DID YOU GET YOUR **DRIVER'S LICENSE?**
I DON'T HAVE ONE! I THOUGHT **YOU** HAD ONE.
IF I **GOLD PLATE** THE SPOKES, THIS BIKE COULD BE KINDA COOL.
Cantú & Castellanos

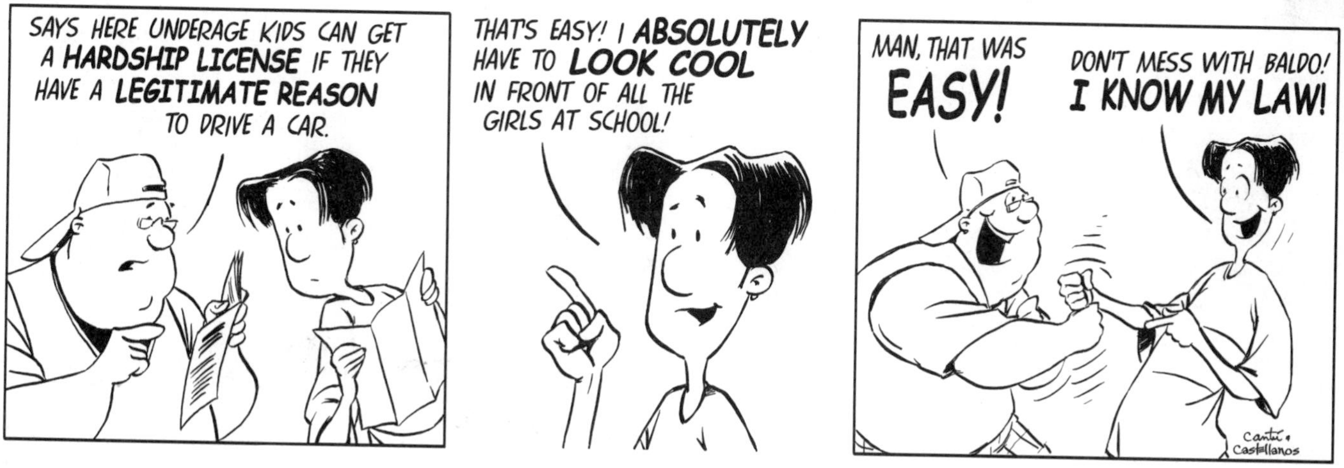
SAYS HERE UNDERAGE KIDS CAN GET A **HARDSHIP LICENSE** IF THEY HAVE A **LEGITIMATE REASON** TO DRIVE A CAR.
THAT'S EASY! I **ABSOLUTELY** HAVE TO **LOOK COOL** IN FRONT OF ALL THE GIRLS AT SCHOOL!
MAN, THAT WAS **EASY!**
DON'T MESS WITH BALDO! **I KNOW MY LAW!**
Cantú & Castellanos

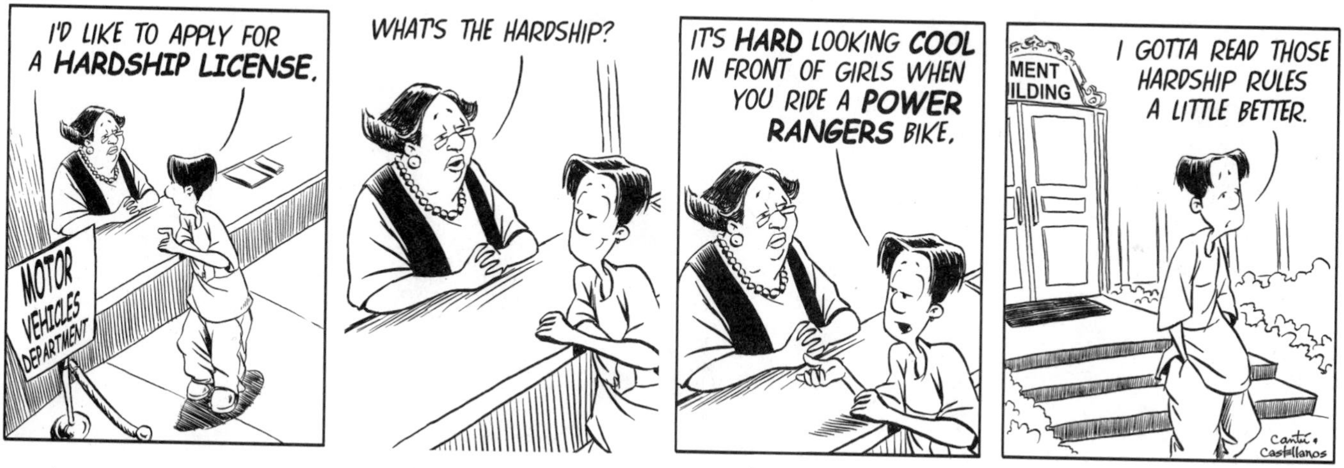
I'D LIKE TO APPLY FOR A **HARDSHIP LICENSE.**
MOTOR VEHICLES DEPARTMENT
WHAT'S THE HARDSHIP?
IT'S **HARD** LOOKING **COOL** IN FRONT OF GIRLS WHEN YOU RIDE A **POWER RANGERS** BIKE.
MENT
ILDING
I GOTTA READ THOSE HARDSHIP RULES A LITTLE BETTER.
Cantú & Castellanos

HEY, LOOK! I'M FROM THE PLANET NAREEZ AND THESE ARE MY NOSE ANTENNAE!
I'M FROM THE PLANET VOSNO AND THIS IS MY VOICE AMPLIFICATION CHAMBER!
I CAN FLY ACROSS THE NAREEZ TERRAIN WITH MY NAP-KAPE!
WITH THESE HIGH-TECH EYELIDS, I CAN SEE FOR MILES!
OOOOOOHHH!
HEY, ISN'T THAT SYLVIA, THE PRETTIEST GIRL IN SCHOOL?
YOU THINK SHE SAW US?
ONLY UNTIL SODA SPRAYED OUT OF HER NOSE FROM LAUGHING SO HARD, THEN SHE LOOKED MORE PREOCCUPIED WITH THAT.
Cantú & Castellanos

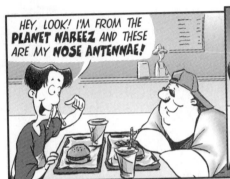

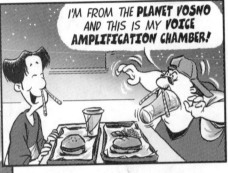

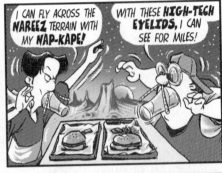

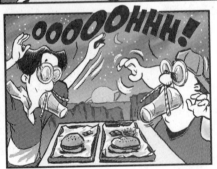

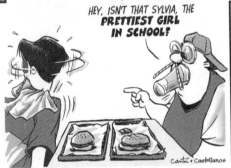

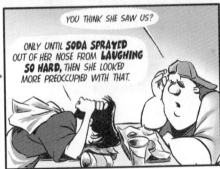

NO HANDS.
NO HANDS.
NO HANDS.
NO HANDS.
NO HANDS.
POOF!
I'M TAKING SOCCER PRACTICE WAY TOO SERIOUSLY.

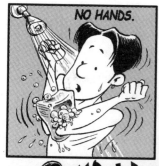

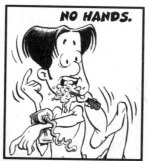

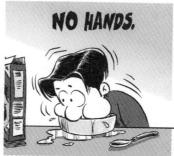

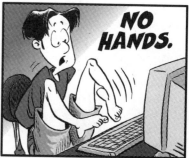

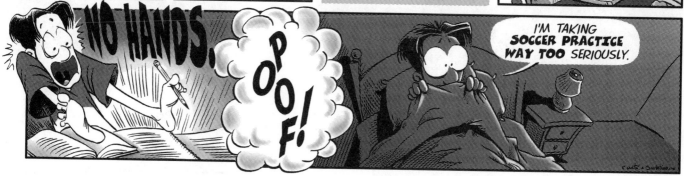

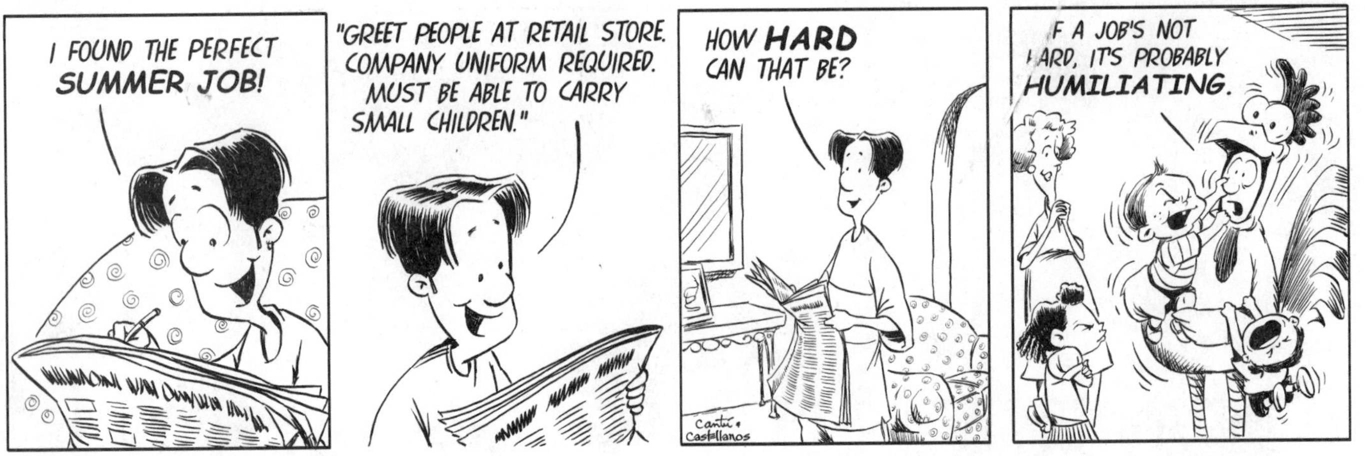
I FOUND THE PERFECT **SUMMER JOB!**
"GREET PEOPLE AT RETAIL STORE. COMPANY UNIFORM REQUIRED. MUST BE ABLE TO CARRY SMALL CHILDREN."
HOW **HARD** CAN THAT BE?
Cantú & Castellanos
F A JOB'S NOT ARD, IT'S PROBABLY **HUMILIATING.**

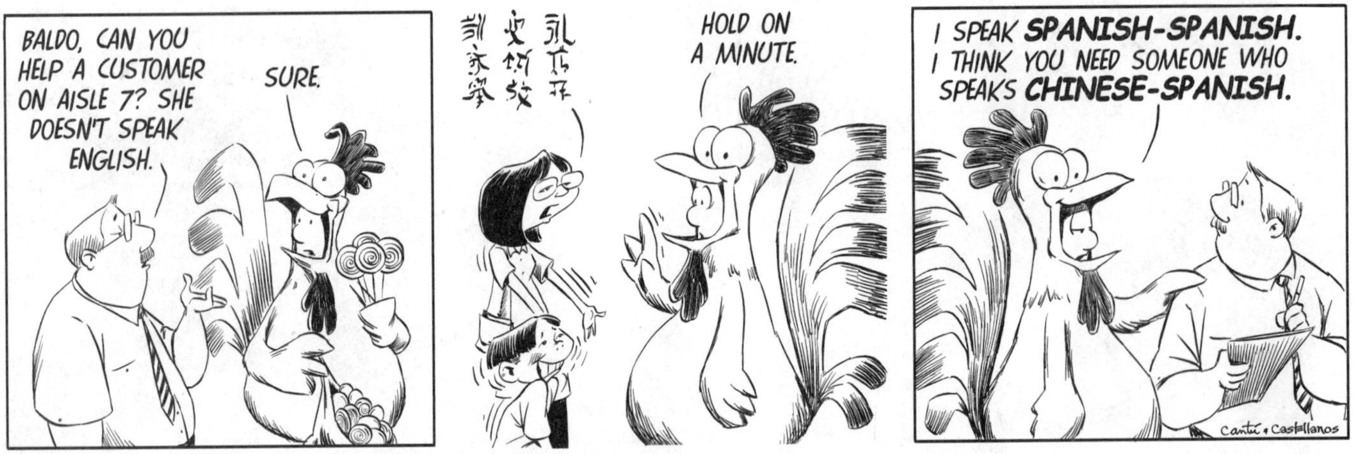
BALDO, CAN YOU HELP A CUSTOMER ON AISLE 7? SHE DOESN'T SPEAK ENGLISH.
SURE.
HOLD ON A MINUTE.
I SPEAK **SPANISH-SPANISH.** I THINK YOU NEED SOMEONE WHO SPEAKS **CHINESE-SPANISH.**
Cantú & Castellanos

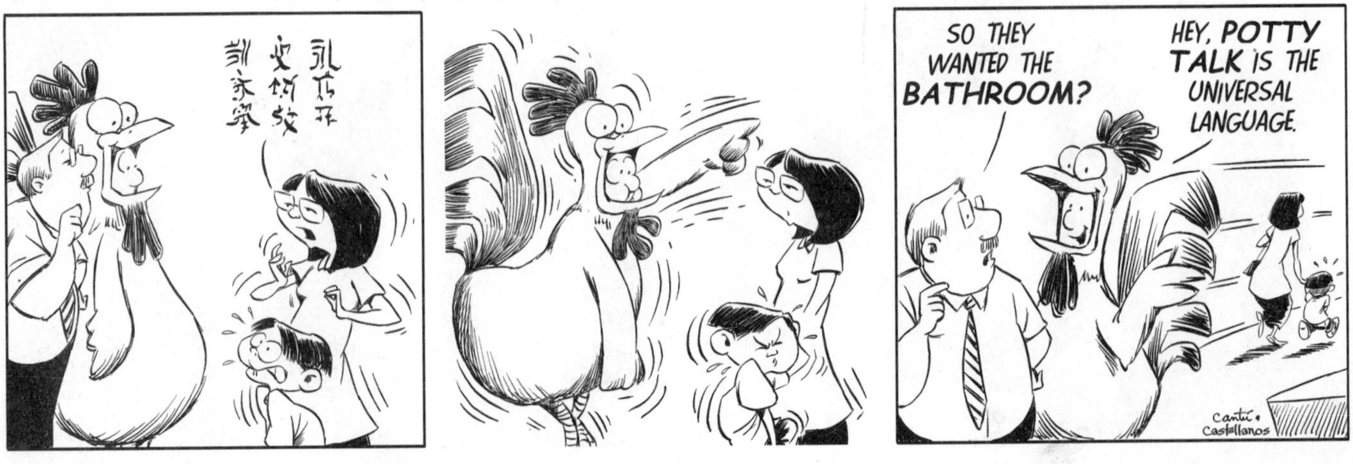
SO THEY WANTED THE **BATHROOM?**
HEY, **POTTY TALK** IS THE UNIVERSAL LANGUAGE.
Cantú & Castellanos

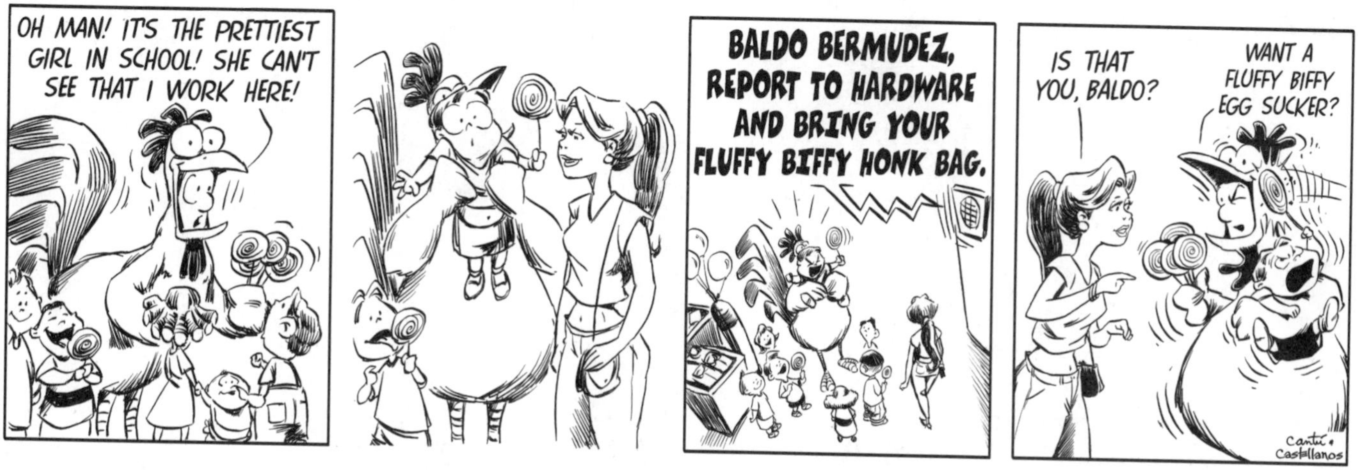
OH MAN! IT'S THE PRETTIEST GIRL IN SCHOOL! SHE CAN'T SEE THAT I WORK HERE!
BALDO BERMUDEZ, REPORT TO HARDWARE AND BRING YOUR FLUFFY BIFFY HONK BAG.
IS THAT YOU, BALDO?
WANT A FLUFFY BIFFY EGG SUCKER?
Cantú • Castellanos

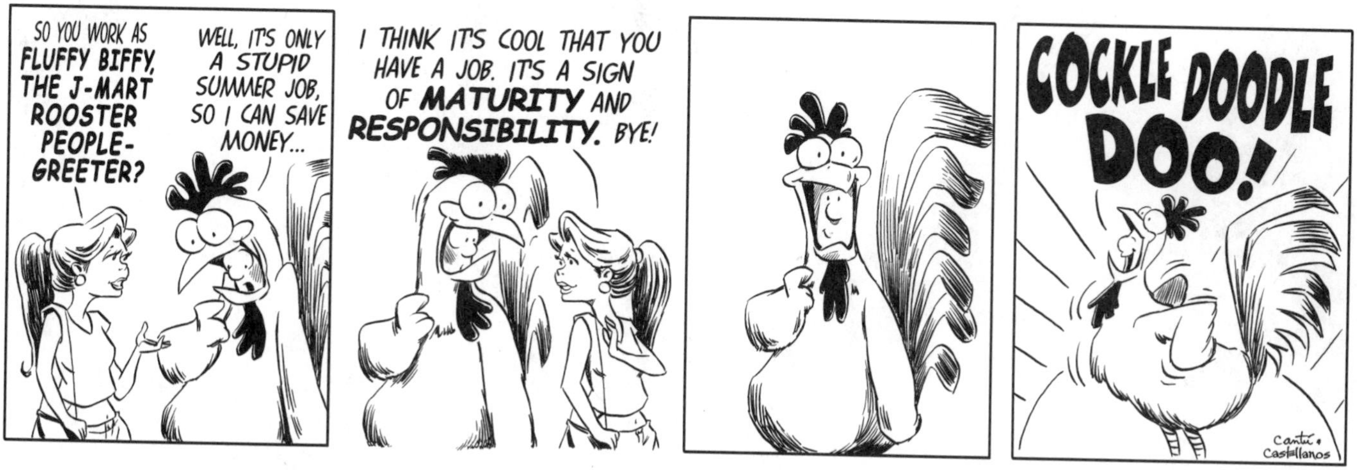
SO YOU WORK AS FLUFFY BIFFY, THE J-MART ROOSTER PEOPLE-GREETER?
WELL, IT'S ONLY A STUPID SUMMER JOB, SO I CAN SAVE MONEY...
I THINK IT'S COOL THAT YOU HAVE A JOB. IT'S A SIGN OF MATURITY AND RESPONSIBILITY. BYE!
COCKLE DOODLE DOO!
Cantú • Castellanos

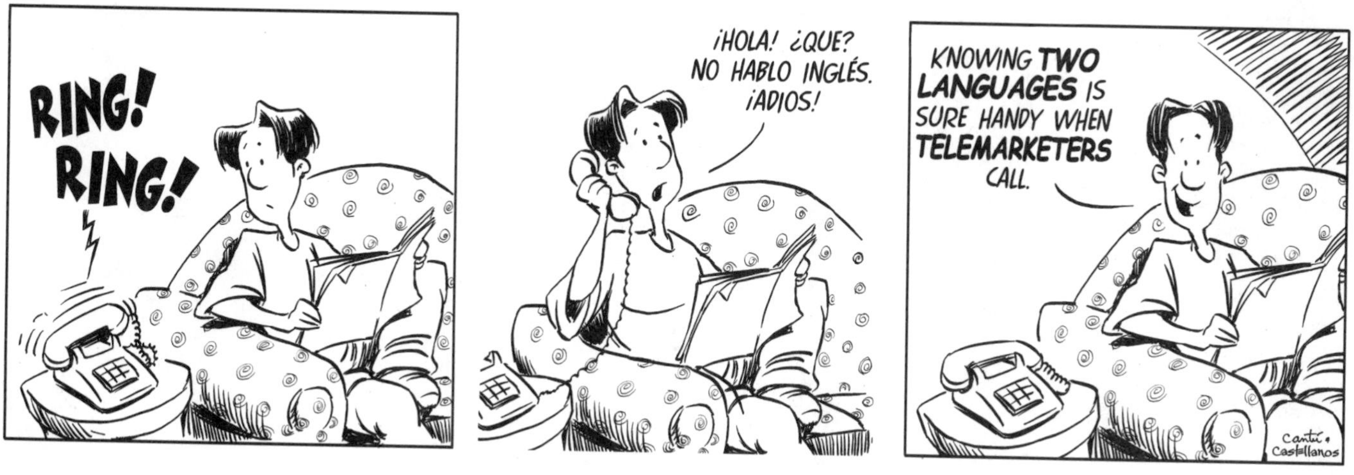
RING! RING!
¡HOLA! ¿QUE? NO HABLO INGLÉS. ¡ADIOS!
KNOWING TWO LANGUAGES IS SURE HANDY WHEN TELEMARKETERS CALL.
Cantú • Castellanos

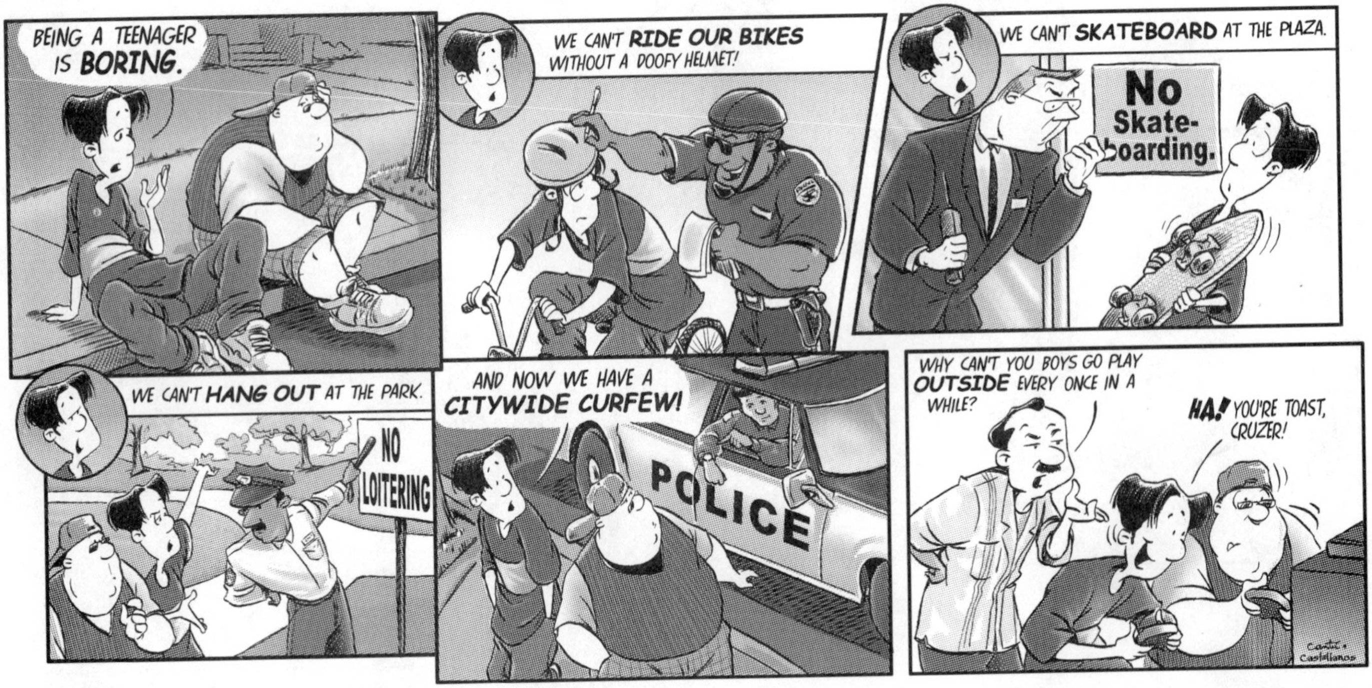
BEING A TEENAGER IS BORING.
WE CAN'T RIDE OUR BIKES WITHOUT A DOOFY HELMET!
WE CAN'T SKATEBOARD AT THE PLAZA.
No Skate-boarding.
WE CAN'T HANG OUT AT THE PARK.
NO LOITERING
AND NOW WE HAVE A CITYWIDE CURFEW!
POLICE
WHY CAN'T YOU BOYS GO PLAY OUTSIDE EVERY ONCE IN A WHILE?
HA! YOU'RE TOAST, CRUZER!

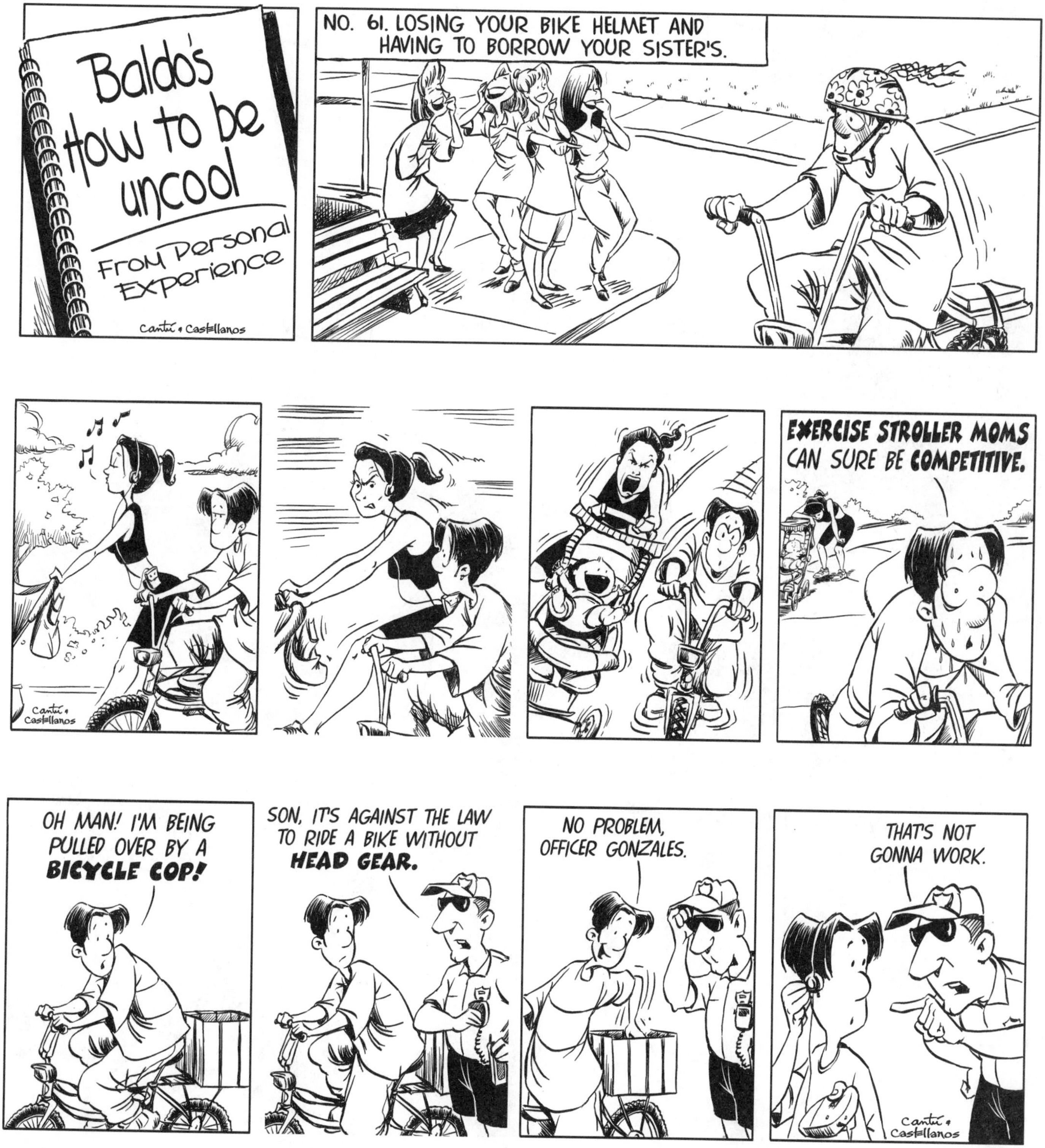
Baldo's How to be uncool
From Personal Experience
Cantú & Castellanos
NO. 61. LOSING YOUR BIKE HELMET AND HAVING TO BORROW YOUR SISTER'S.
Cantú & Castellanos
EXERCISE STROLLER MOMS CAN SURE BE COMPETITIVE.
OH MAN! I'M BEING PULLED OVER BY A BICYCLE COP!
SON, IT'S AGAINST THE LAW TO RIDE A BIKE WITHOUT HEAD GEAR.
NO PROBLEM, OFFICER GONZALES.
THAT'S NOT GONNA WORK.
Cantú & Castellanos

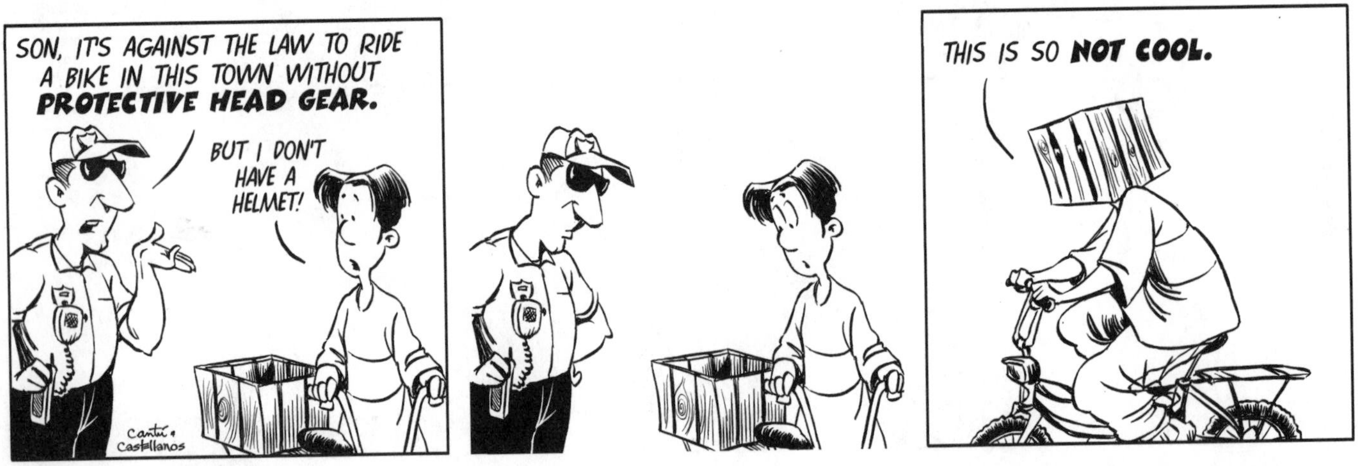
SON, IT'S AGAINST THE LAW TO RIDE A BIKE IN THIS TOWN WITHOUT **PROTECTIVE HEAD GEAR.**
BUT I DON'T HAVE A HELMET!
Cantú & Castellanos
THIS IS SO **NOT COOL.**

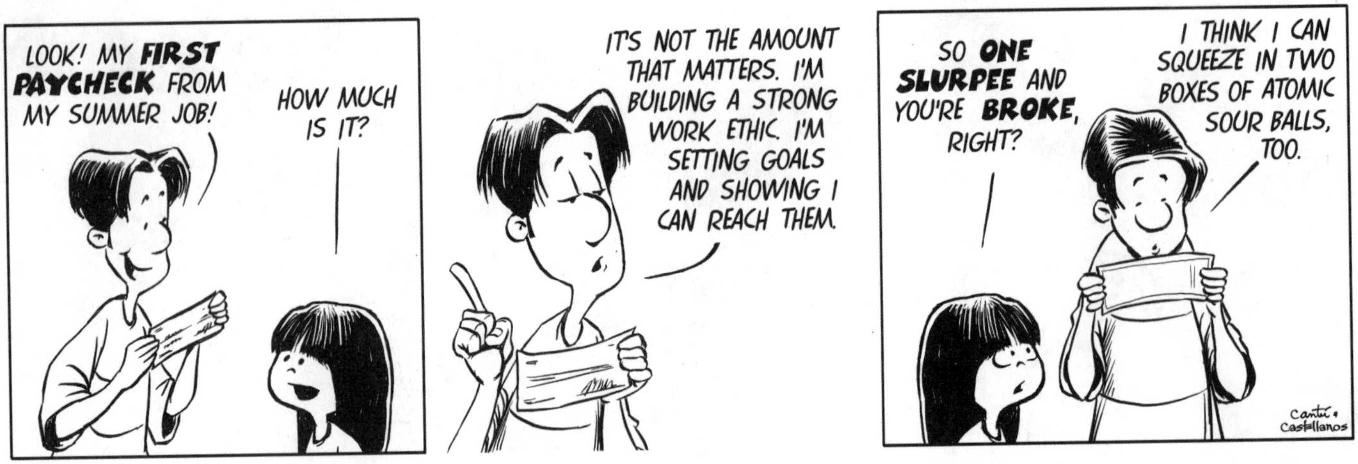
LOOK! MY **FIRST PAYCHECK** FROM MY SUMMER JOB!
HOW MUCH IS IT?
IT'S NOT THE AMOUNT THAT MATTERS. I'M BUILDING A STRONG WORK ETHIC. I'M SETTING GOALS AND SHOWING I CAN REACH THEM.
SO **ONE SLURPEE** AND YOU'RE **BROKE**, RIGHT?
I THINK I CAN SQUEEZE IN TWO BOXES OF ATOMIC SOUR BALLS, TOO.
Cantú & Castellanos

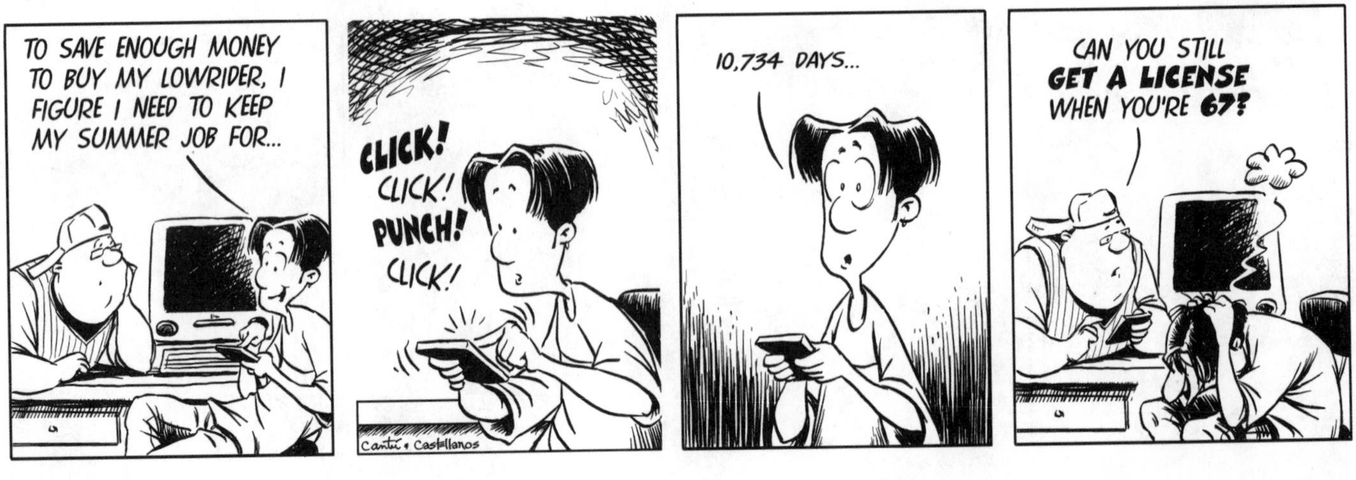
TO SAVE ENOUGH MONEY TO BUY MY LOWRIDER, I FIGURE I NEED TO KEEP MY SUMMER JOB FOR...
CLICK!
CLICK!
PUNCH!
CLICK!
Cantú & Castellanos
10,734 DAYS...
CAN YOU STILL **GET A LICENSE** WHEN YOU'RE **67?**

Find Edit Character Tools Parag
Dear Tio Celestino, how is Tia Abundia?
Tell Cousin Flaco I said hola.
And Cousin Reyes dropped by and said
Luz was marrying some muchacho from
Nueve Puntos. Bye.
Find Edit Cha Tools Parag
CLICK!
Spell Check...
Thesaurus...
Display...
Hyphenate...
Dear Tio Celestino, how is Tia Abundia?
Tell Cousin Flaco I said hola.
And Cousin Reyes dropped by and said
Luz was marrying some muchacho from
Nueve Puntos. Bye.
Find Edit Character Tools Parag
Dear It Selection, how is It Abound?
Tell Cousin Flak I said holler.
And Cousin Recess dropped by and said
Lug was marrying some mutate from
Never Punts. Bye.
THIS SPELL CHECK OBVIOUSLY ISN'T BALDO FAMILY COMPLIANT.

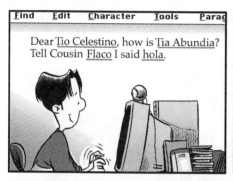

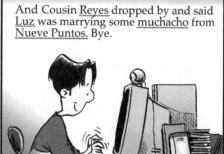

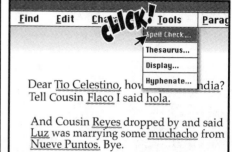

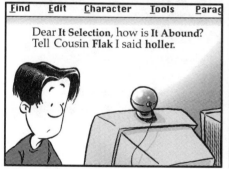

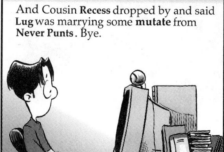

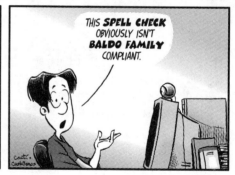

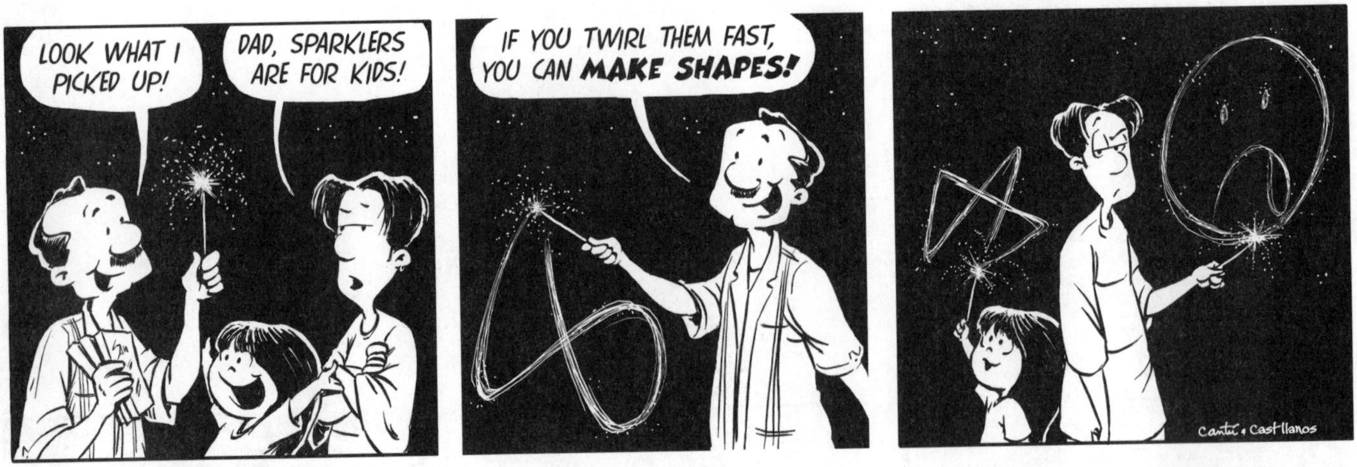
LOOK WHAT I PICKED UP!
DAD, SPARKLERS ARE FOR KIDS!
IF YOU TWIRL THEM FAST, YOU CAN **MAKE SHAPES!**
Cantú & Castellanos

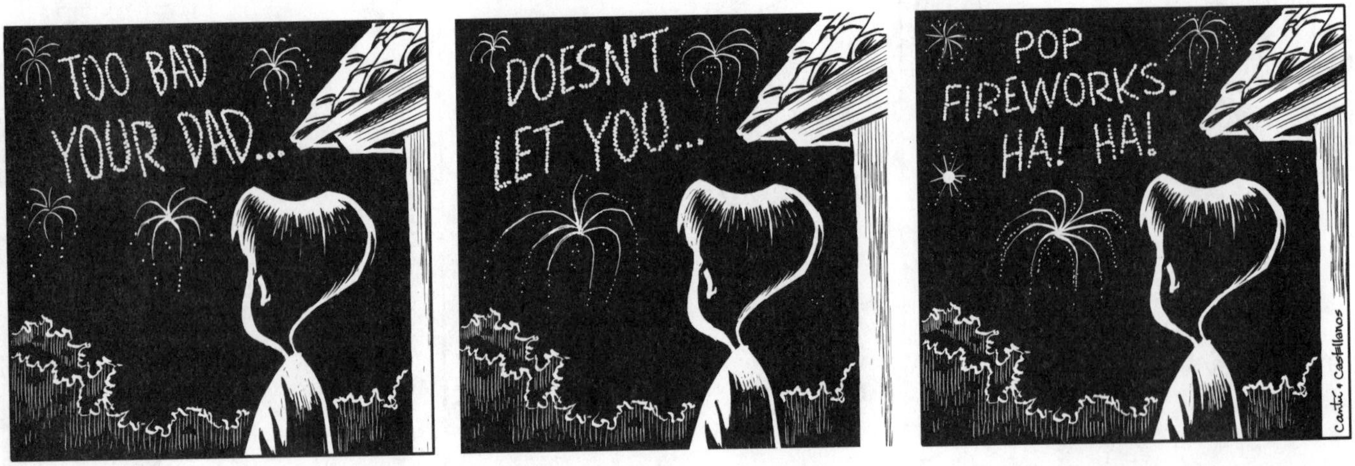
TOO BAD YOUR DAD...
DOESN'T LET YOU...
POP FIREWORKS. HA! HA!
Cantú & Castellanos

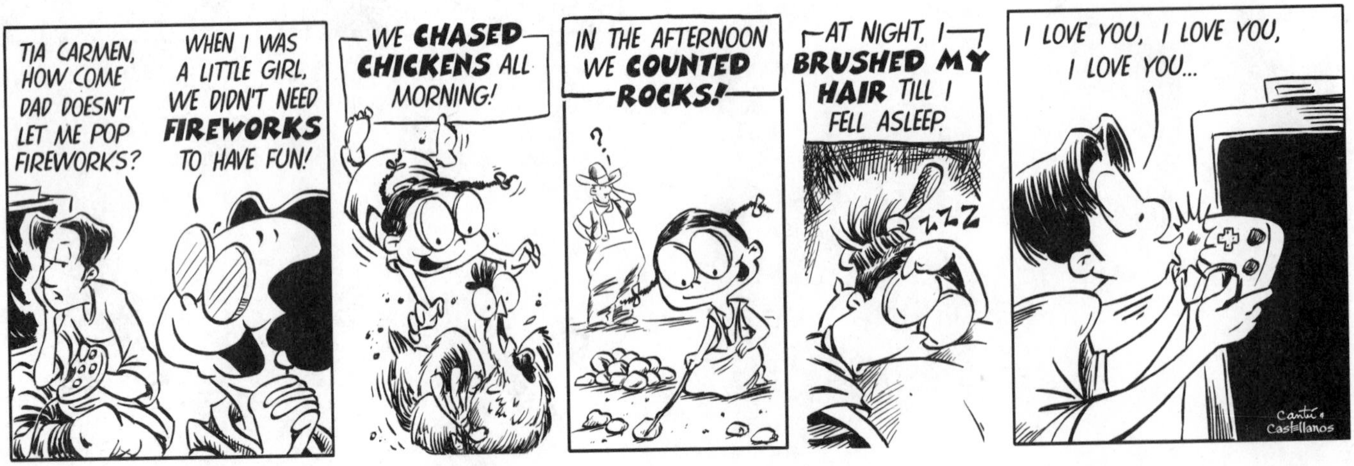
TIA CARMEN, HOW COME DAD DOESN'T LET ME POP FIREWORKS?
WHEN I WAS A LITTLE GIRL, WE DIDN'T NEED **FIREWORKS** TO HAVE FUN!
WE **CHASED CHICKENS** ALL MORNING!
IN THE AFTERNOON WE **COUNTED ROCKS!**
?
AT NIGHT, I **BRUSHED MY HAIR** TILL I FELL ASLEEP.
ZZZ
I LOVE YOU, I LOVE YOU, I LOVE YOU...
Cantú & Castellanos

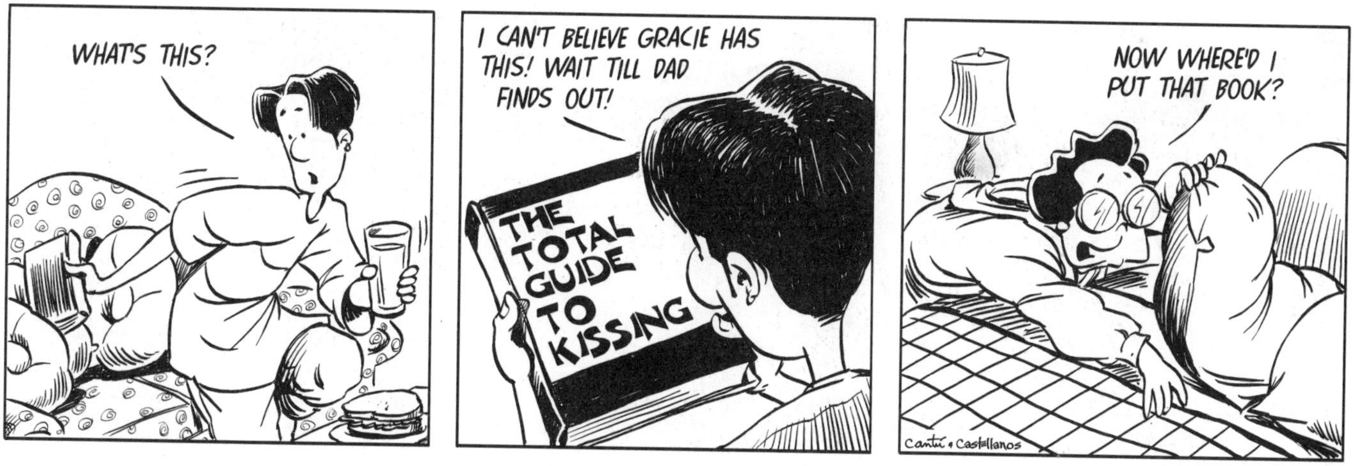
WHAT'S THIS?
I CAN'T BELIEVE GRACIE HAS THIS! WAIT TILL DAD FINDS OUT!
THE TOTAL GUIDE TO KISSING
NOW WHERE'D I PUT THAT BOOK?
Cantú & Castellanos

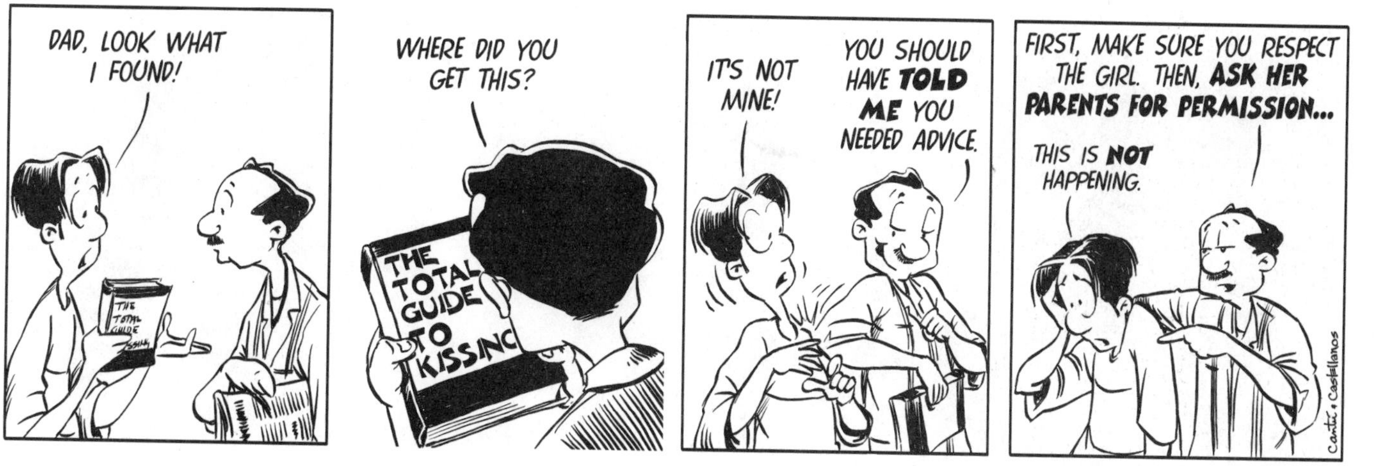
DAD, LOOK WHAT I FOUND!
WHERE DID YOU GET THIS?
THE TOTAL GUIDE TO KISSING
IT'S NOT MINE!
YOU SHOULD HAVE **TOLD ME** YOU NEEDED ADVICE.
FIRST, MAKE SURE YOU RESPECT THE GIRL. THEN, **ASK HER PARENTS FOR PERMISSION...**
THIS IS **NOT** HAPPENING.
Cantú & Castellanos

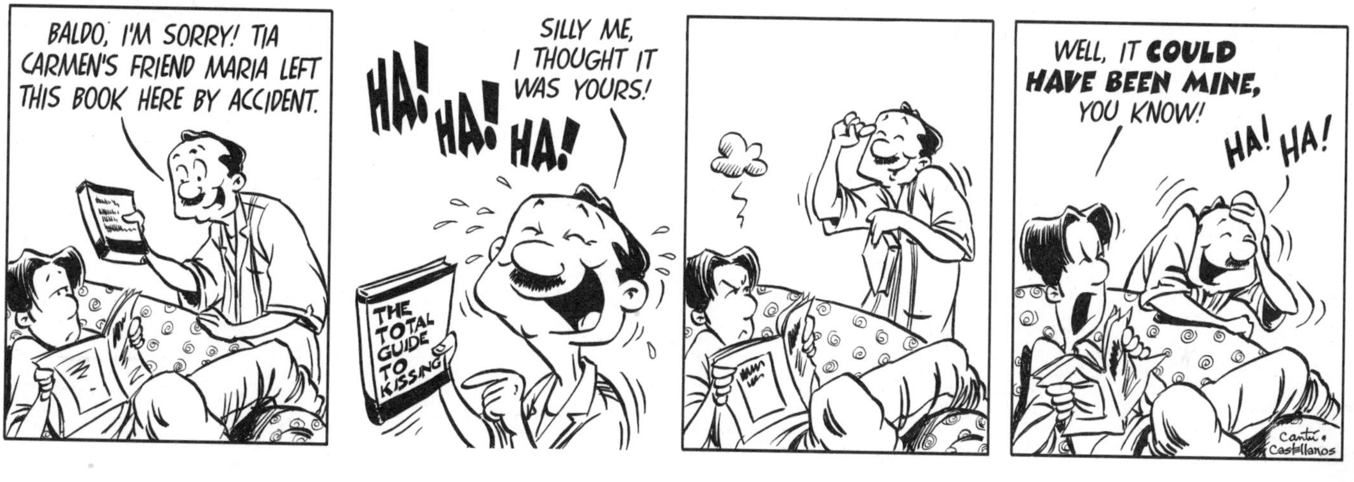
BALDO, I'M SORRY! TIA CARMEN'S FRIEND MARIA LEFT THIS BOOK HERE BY ACCIDENT.
HA! HA! HA!
SILLY ME, I THOUGHT IT WAS YOURS!
THE TOTAL GUIDE TO KISSING
WELL, IT **COULD HAVE BEEN MINE,** YOU KNOW!
HA! HA!
Cantú & Castellanos

I CAN'T BELIEVE IT! AFTER ALL THIS TIME... MY CAR'S FINISHED!

AN '84 BUICK REGAL WITH ALL THE SWEETEST AMENITIES!

A FINE CANDY BRANDYWINE PAINT JOB WITH A FULL SET OF BLUE, BROWN AND RED PINSTRIPES...

A SAND-COLORED PHANTOM TOP ROOF WITH THREE RIBS...

CHROME FENDER MOLDINGS AND MIRROR ROCKER PANELS ON THE DOOR.

Cantú + Castellanos

HEY, **PAINT THIS LIKE A LOWRIDER, TOO!**

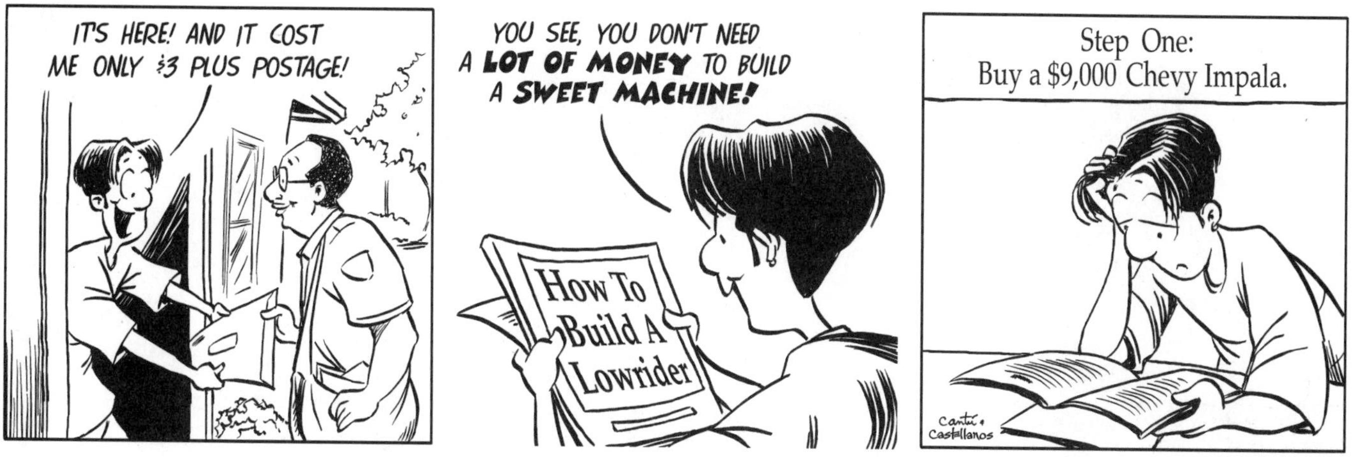
IT'S HERE! AND IT COST ME ONLY $3 PLUS POSTAGE!
YOU SEE, YOU DON'T NEED A LOT OF MONEY TO BUILD A SWEET MACHINE!
How To Build A Lowrider
Step One:
Buy a $9,000 Chevy Impala.

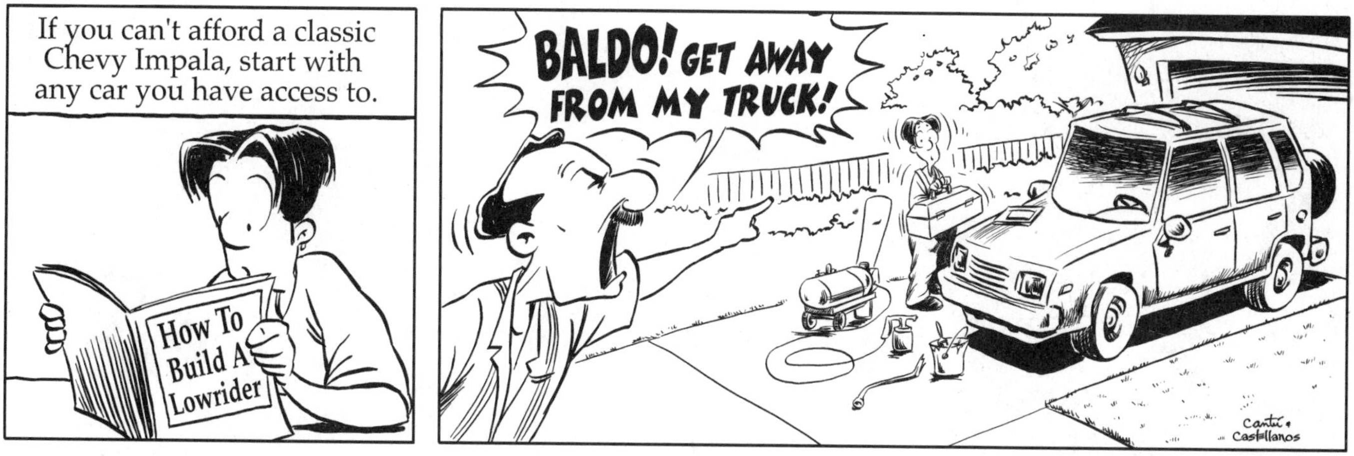
If you can't afford a classic Chevy Impala, start with any car you have access to.
How To Build A Lowrider
BALDO! GET AWAY FROM MY TRUCK!

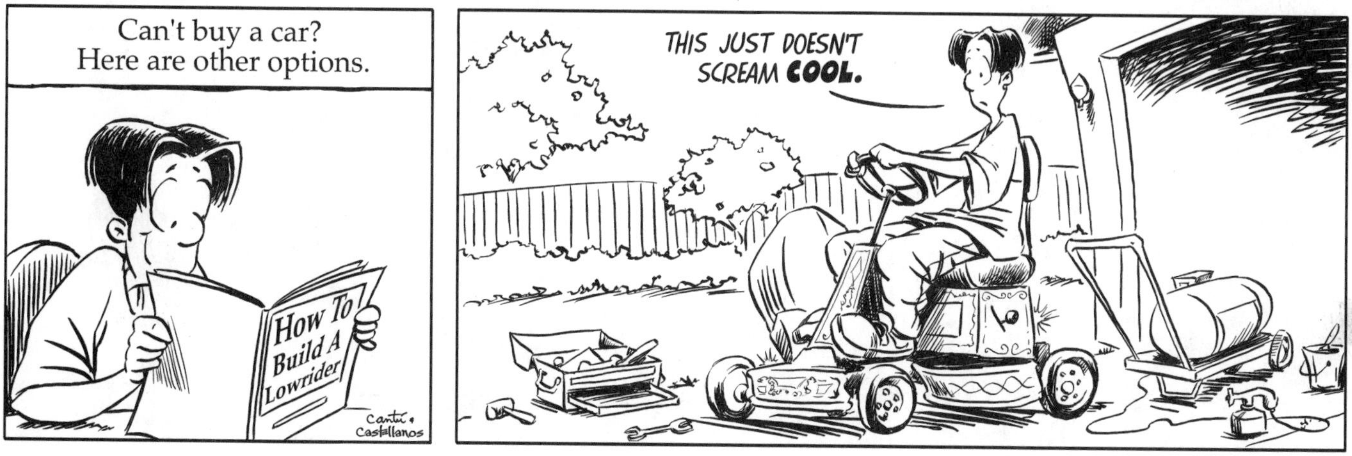
Can't buy a car?
Here are other options.
How To Build A Lowrider
THIS JUST DOESN'T SCREAM COOL.

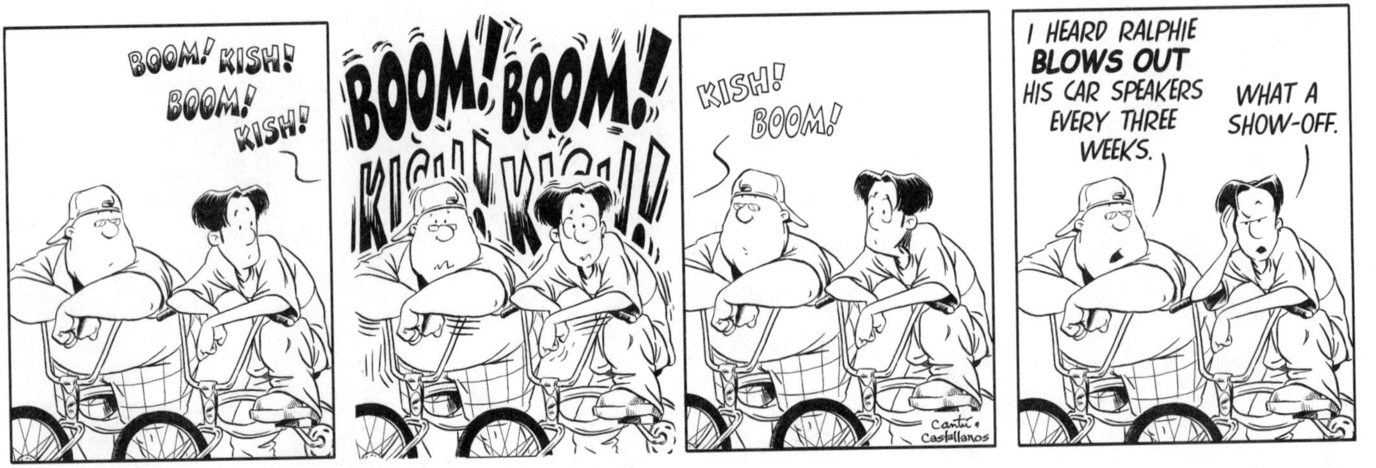
BOOM! KISH!
BOOM!
KISH!
BOOM! BOOM!
KISH!
BOOM!
I HEARD RALPHIE **BLOWS OUT** HIS CAR SPEAKERS EVERY THREE WEEKS.
WHAT A SHOW-OFF.
Cantú & Castellanos

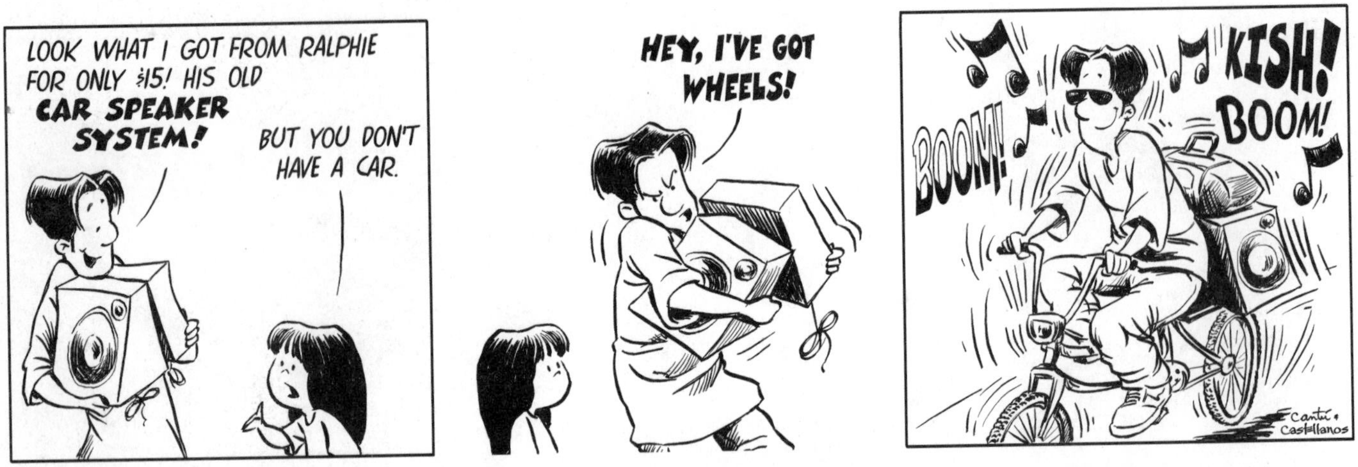
LOOK WHAT I GOT FROM RALPHIE FOR ONLY $15! HIS OLD **CAR SPEAKER SYSTEM!**
BUT YOU DON'T HAVE A CAR.
HEY, I'VE GOT WHEELS!
BOOM!
KISH!
BOOM!
Cantú & Castellanos

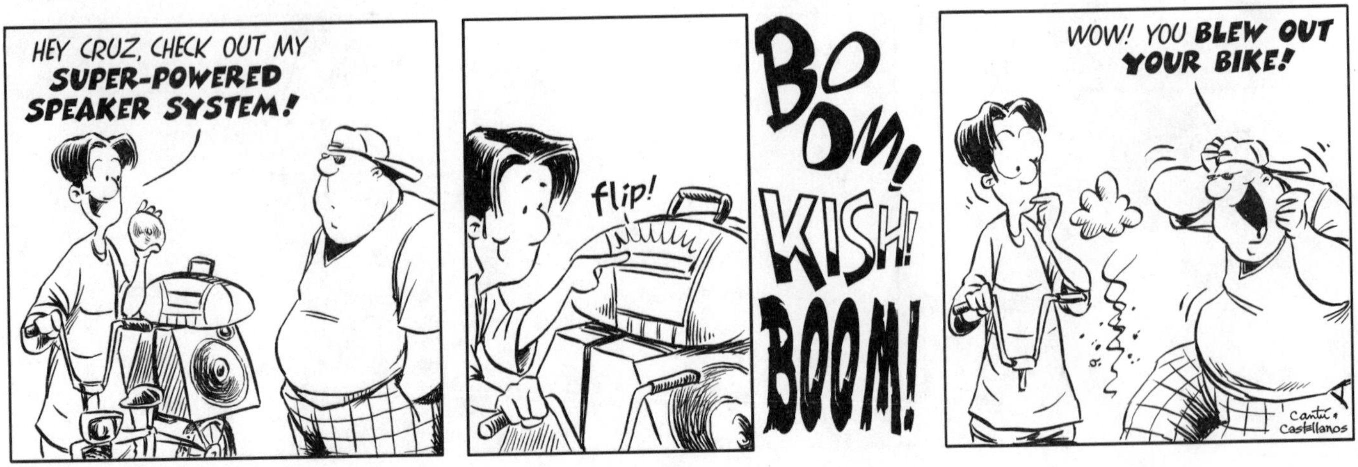
HEY CRUZ, CHECK OUT MY **SUPER-POWERED SPEAKER SYSTEM!**
flip!
BOOM!
KISH!
BOOM!
WOW! YOU **BLEW OUT YOUR BIKE!**
Cantú & Castellanos

Jennifer Lopez
Christina Aguilera
OH NO!
INVADERS FROM ANOTHER PLANET HAVE DEVISED AN INGENIOUS PLAN...
TO RID THE EARTH OF HUMANS!
STRAWS THAT SUCK BACK!
MY IMAGINATION BEATS BAD TV ANY DAY.
Christina Aguilera
Cantú • Castellanos

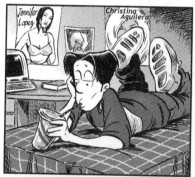

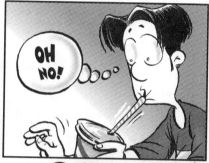

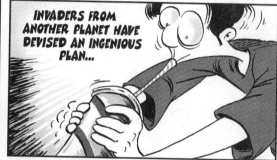

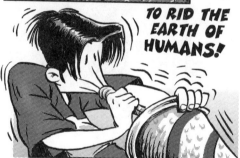

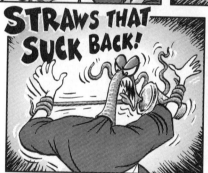

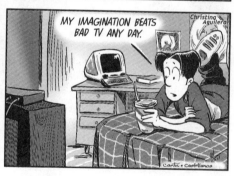

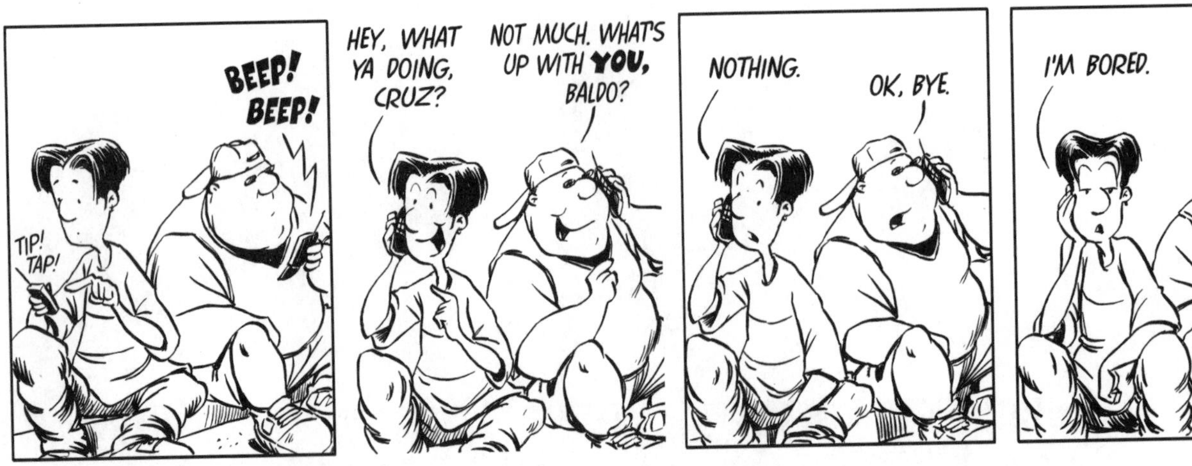
BEEP! BEEP!
TIP! TAP!
HEY, WHAT YA DOING, CRUZ?
NOT MUCH. WHAT'S UP WITH **YOU**, BALDO?
NOTHING.
OK, BYE.
I'M BORED.
YEAH, I HEARD.
Cantú & Castellanos

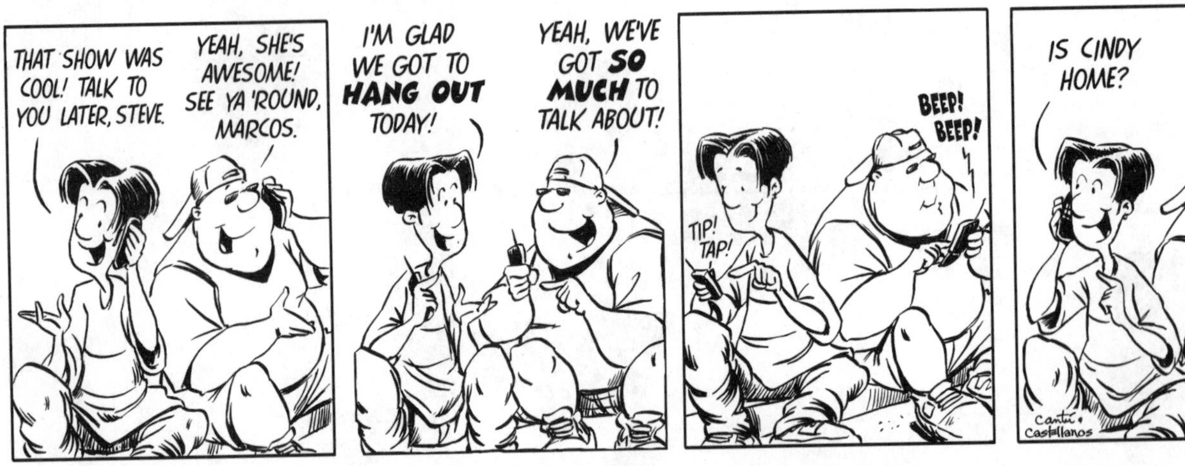
THAT SHOW WAS COOL! TALK TO YOU LATER, STEVE.
YEAH, SHE'S AWESOME! SEE YA 'ROUND, MARCOS.
I'M GLAD WE GOT TO **HANG OUT** TODAY!
YEAH, WE'VE GOT **SO MUCH** TO TALK ABOUT!
BEEP! BEEP!
TIP! TAP!
IS CINDY HOME?
WHAT UP, JUAN?
Cantú & Castellanos

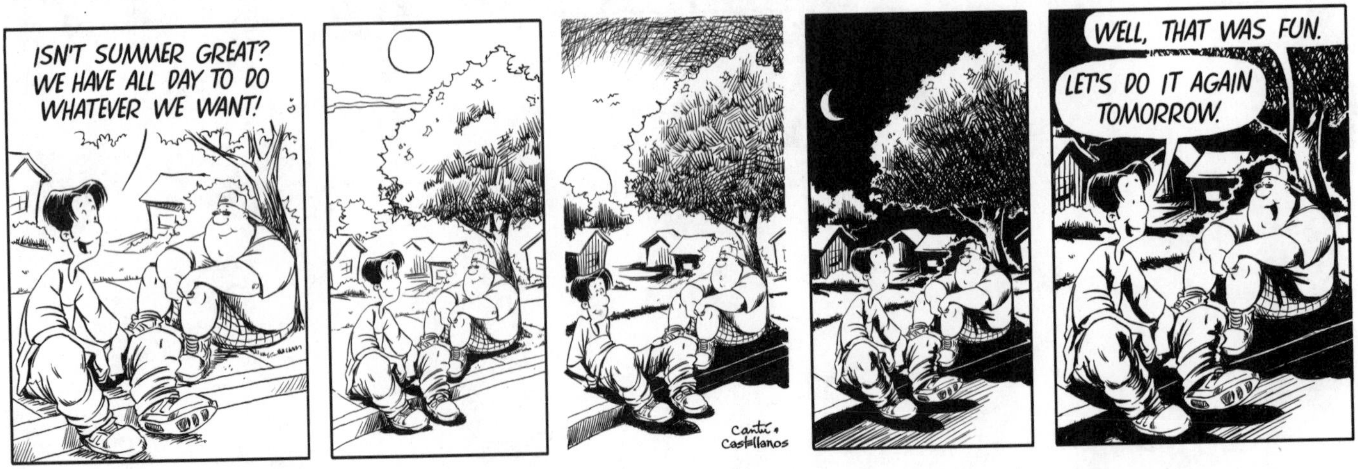
ISN'T SUMMER GREAT? WE HAVE ALL DAY TO DO WHATEVER WE WANT!
Cantú & Castellanos
WELL, THAT WAS FUN.
LET'S DO IT AGAIN TOMORROW.

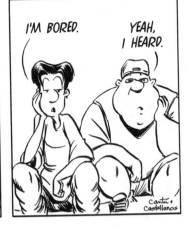

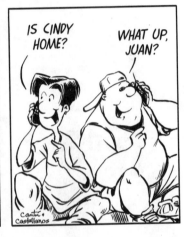

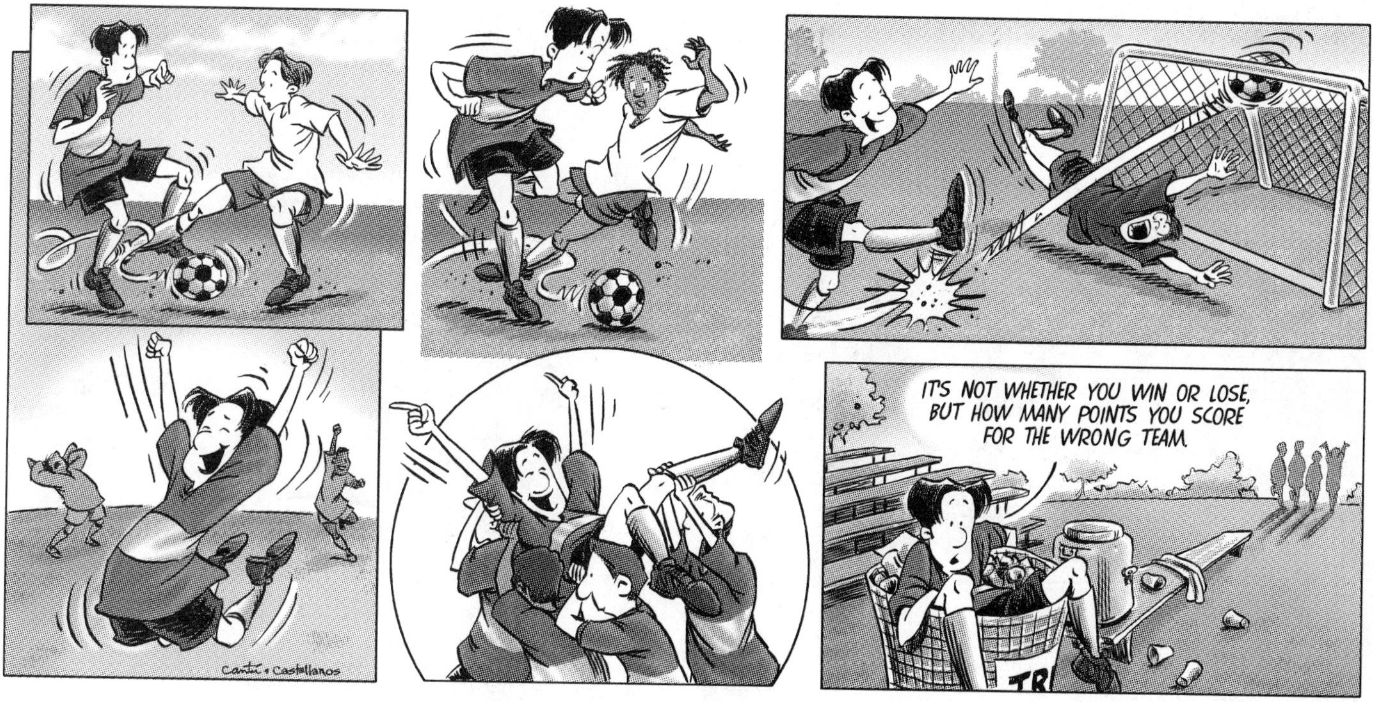
IT'S NOT WHETHER YOU WIN OR LOSE, BUT HOW MANY POINTS YOU SCORE FOR THE WRONG TEAM.
Cantú • Castellanos

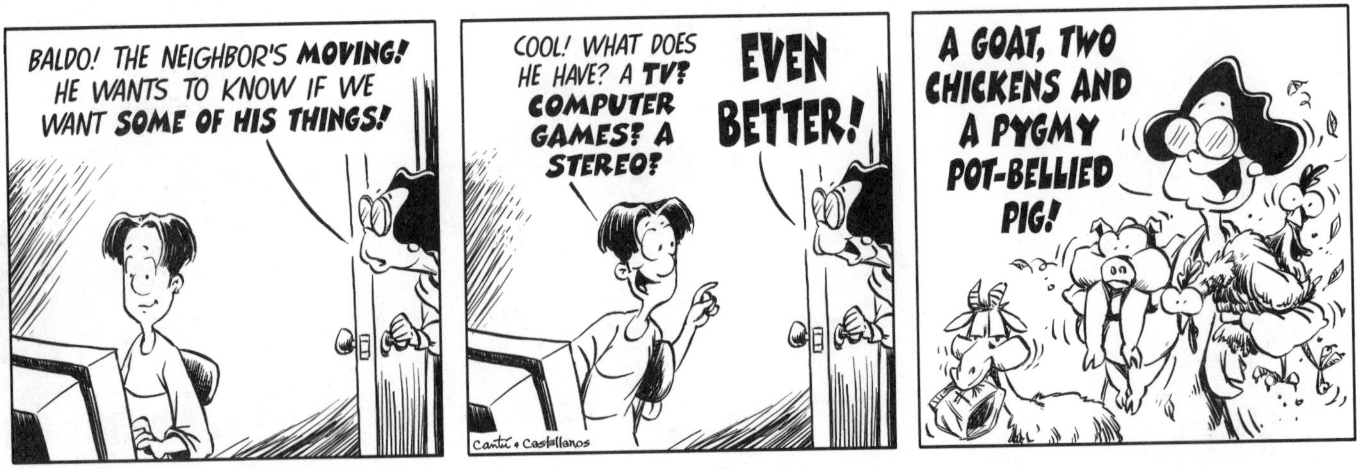
BALDO! THE NEIGHBOR'S MOVING! HE WANTS TO KNOW IF WE WANT SOME OF HIS THINGS!
COOL! WHAT DOES HE HAVE? A TV? COMPUTER GAMES? A STEREO?
EVEN BETTER!
A GOAT, TWO CHICKENS AND A PYGMY POT-BELLIED PIG!
Cantú & Castellanos

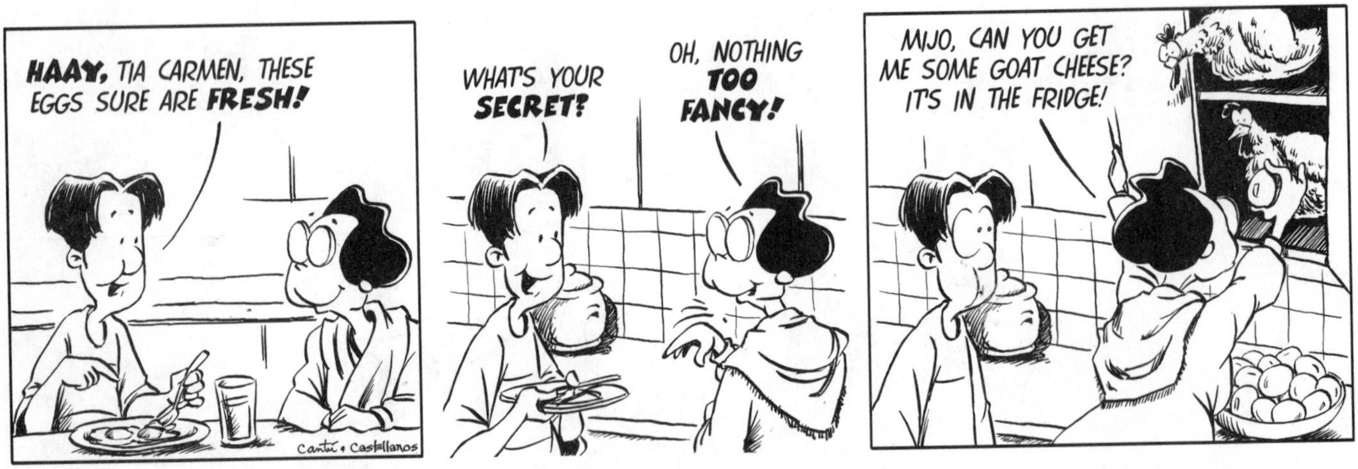
HAAY, TIA CARMEN, THESE EGGS SURE ARE FRESH!
WHAT'S YOUR SECRET?
OH, NOTHING TOO FANCY!
MIJO, CAN YOU GET ME SOME GOAT CHEESE? IT'S IN THE FRIDGE!
Cantú & Castellanos

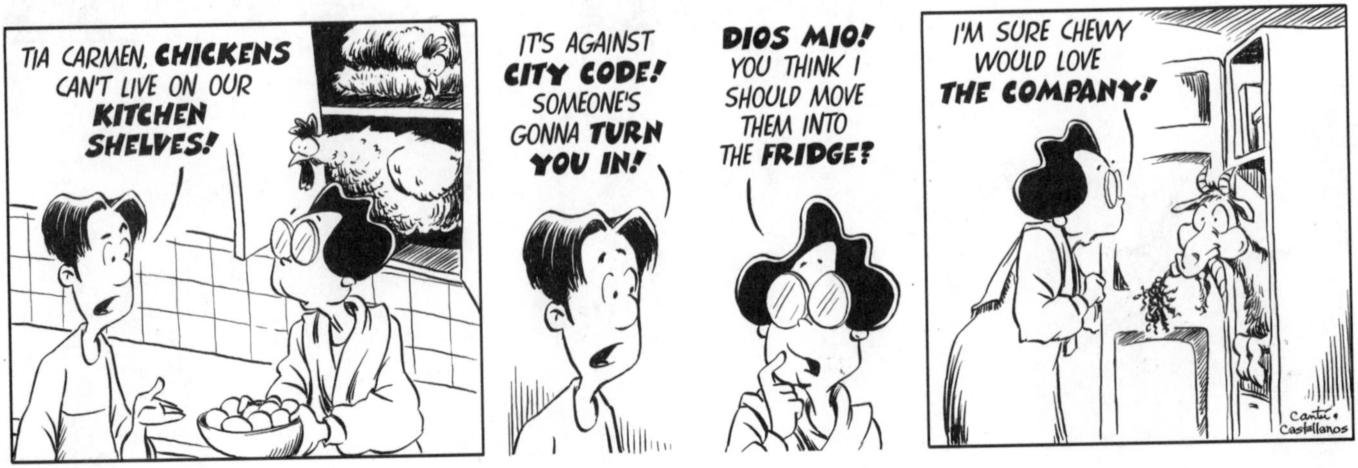
TIA CARMEN, CHICKENS CAN'T LIVE ON OUR KITCHEN SHELVES!
IT'S AGAINST CITY CODE! SOMEONE'S GONNA TURN YOU IN!
DIOS MIO! YOU THINK I SHOULD MOVE THEM INTO THE FRIDGE?
I'M SURE CHEWY WOULD LOVE THE COMPANY!
Cantú & Castellanos

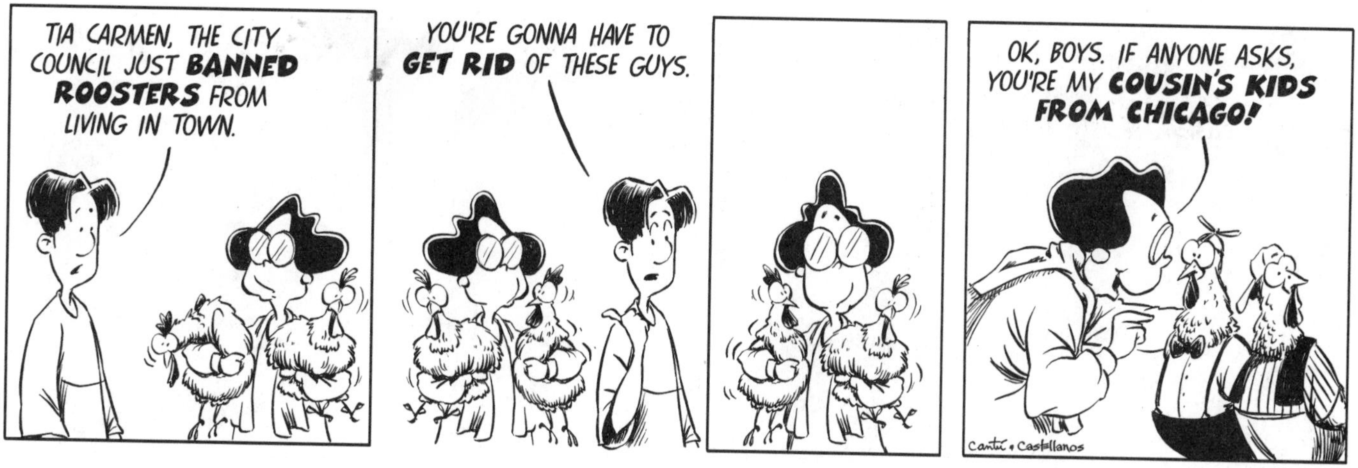
TIA CARMEN, THE CITY COUNCIL JUST BANNED ROOSTERS FROM LIVING IN TOWN.
YOU'RE GONNA HAVE TO GET RID OF THESE GUYS.
OK, BOYS. IF ANYONE ASKS, YOU'RE MY COUSIN'S KIDS FROM CHICAGO!
Cantú & Castellanos

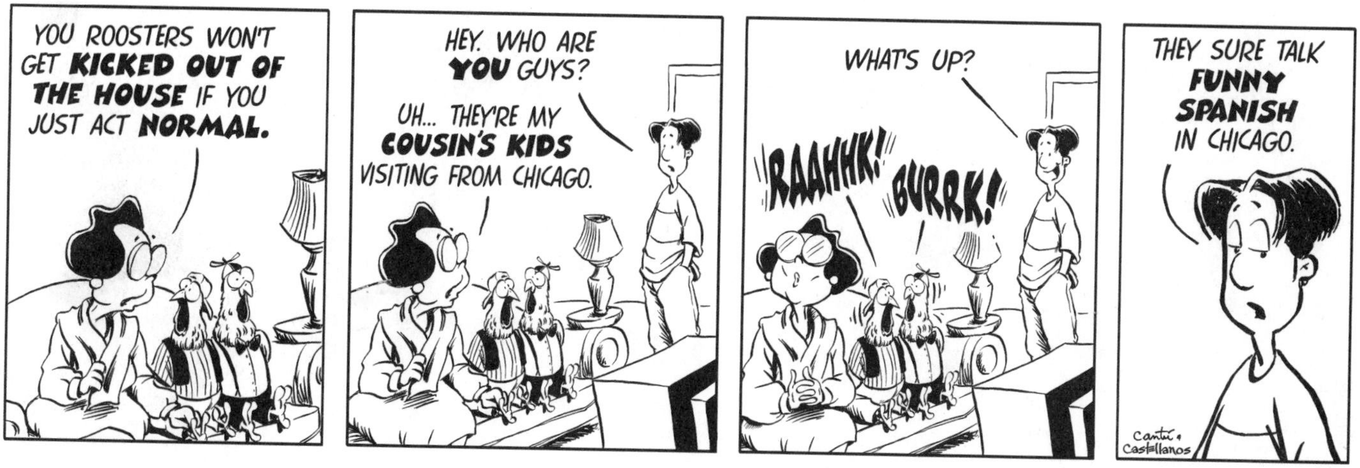
YOU ROOSTERS WON'T GET KICKED OUT OF THE HOUSE IF YOU JUST ACT NORMAL.
HEY. WHO ARE YOU GUYS?
UH... THEY'RE MY COUSIN'S KIDS VISITING FROM CHICAGO.
WHAT'S UP?
RAAHHK!
BURRK!
THEY SURE TALK FUNNY SPANISH IN CHICAGO.
Cantú & Castellanos

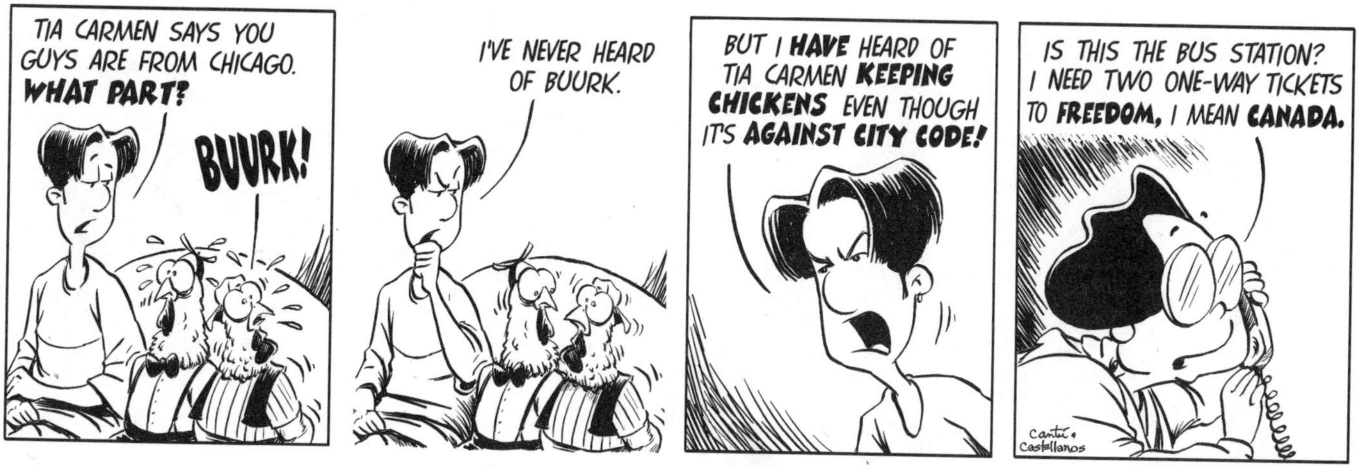
TIA CARMEN SAYS YOU GUYS ARE FROM CHICAGO. WHAT PART?
BUURK!
I'VE NEVER HEARD OF BUURK.
BUT I HAVE HEARD OF TIA CARMEN KEEPING CHICKENS EVEN THOUGH IT'S AGAINST CITY CODE!
IS THIS THE BUS STATION? I NEED TWO ONE-WAY TICKETS TO FREEDOM, I MEAN CANADA.
Cantú & Castellanos

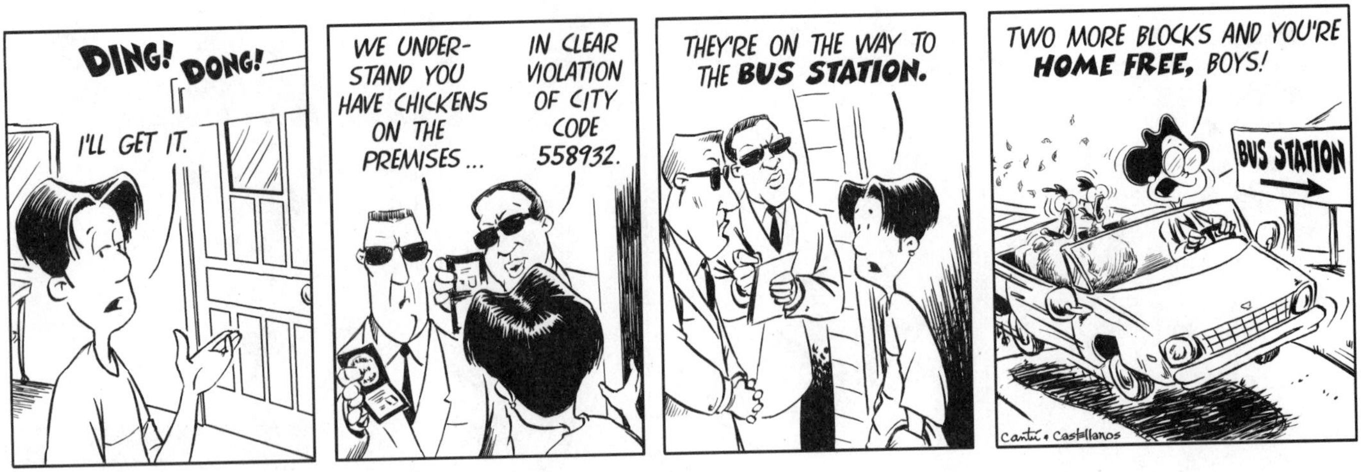
DING! DONG!
I'LL GET IT.
WE UNDERSTAND YOU HAVE CHICKENS ON THE PREMISES ...
IN CLEAR VIOLATION OF CITY CODE 558932.
THEY'RE ON THE WAY TO THE BUS STATION.
TWO MORE BLOCKS AND YOU'RE HOME FREE, BOYS!
BUS STATION
Cantú • Castellanos

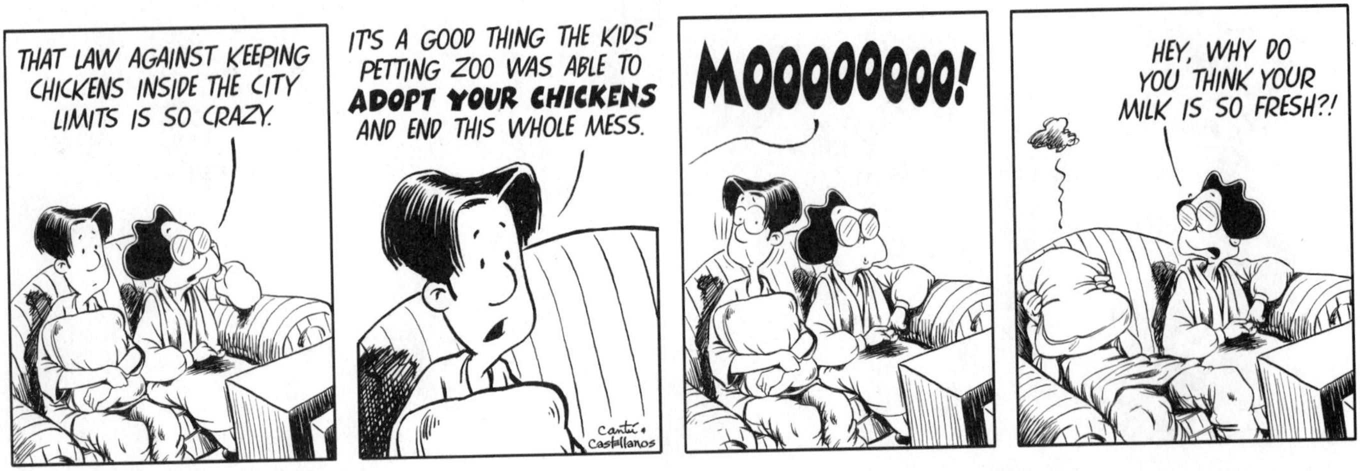
THAT LAW AGAINST KEEPING CHICKENS INSIDE THE CITY LIMITS IS SO CRAZY.
IT'S A GOOD THING THE KIDS' PETTING ZOO WAS ABLE TO ADOPT YOUR CHICKENS AND END THIS WHOLE MESS.
Cantú • Castellanos
MOOOOOOOO!
HEY, WHY DO YOU THINK YOUR MILK IS SO FRESH?!

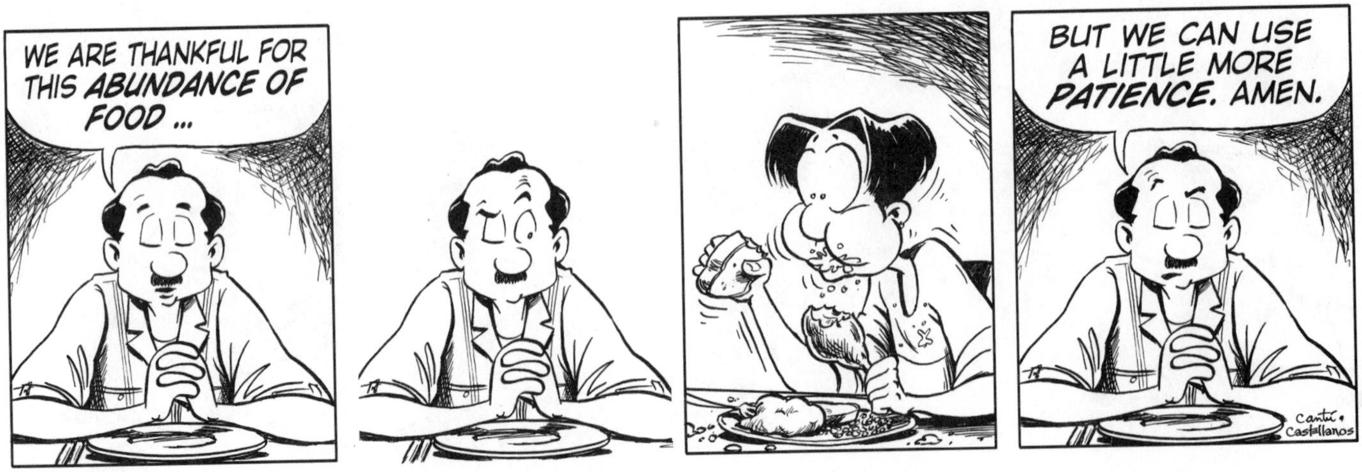
WE ARE THANKFUL FOR THIS ABUNDANCE OF FOOD ...
BUT WE CAN USE A LITTLE MORE PATIENCE. AMEN.
Cantú • Castellanos

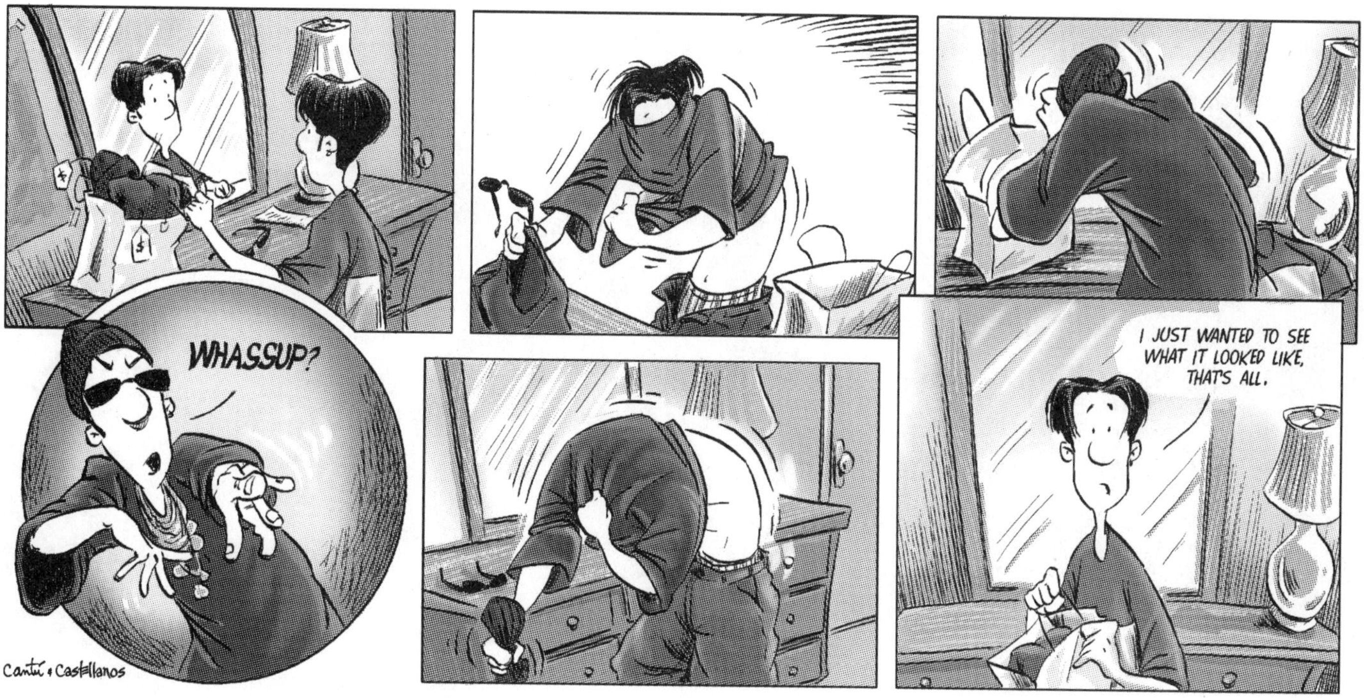
WHASSUP?
I JUST WANTED TO SEE WHAT IT LOOKED LIKE, THAT'S ALL.
Cantú & Castellanos

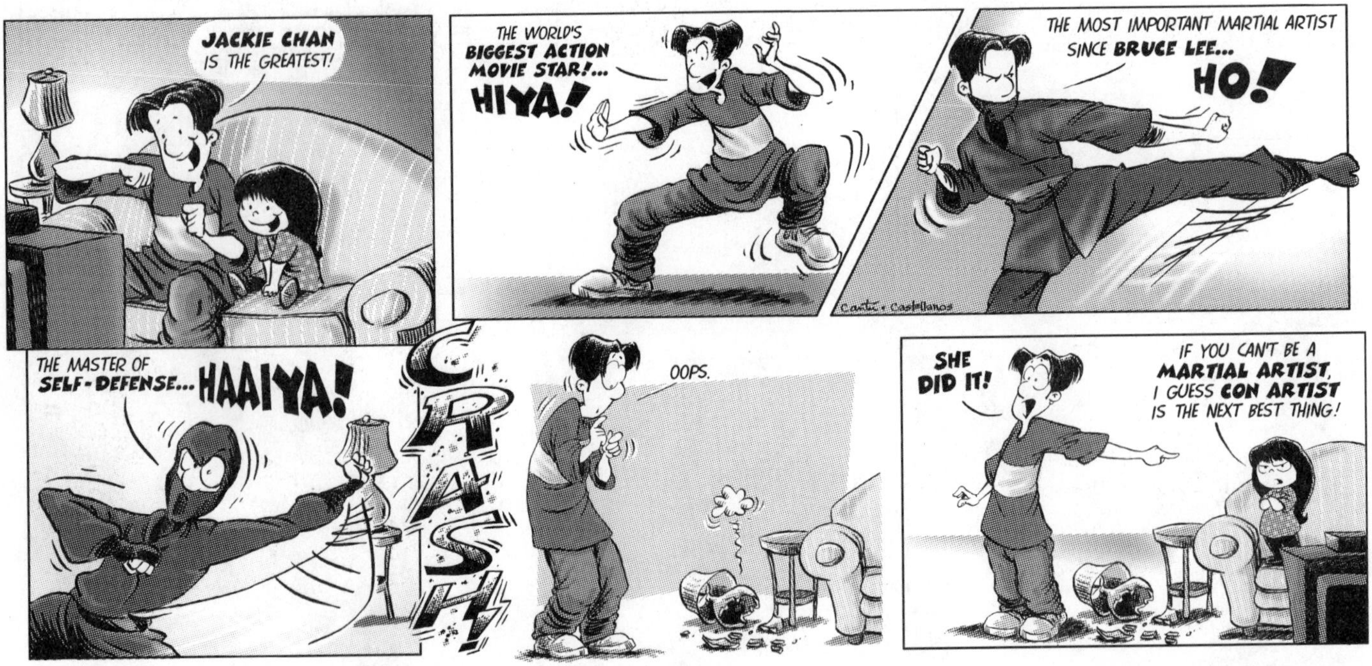
JACKIE CHAN IS THE GREATEST!
THE WORLD'S BIGGEST ACTION MOVIE STAR!... HIYA!
THE MOST IMPORTANT MARTIAL ARTIST SINCE BRUCE LEE... HO!
THE MASTER OF SELF-DEFENSE... HAAIYA!
CRASH!
OOPS.
SHE DID IT!
IF YOU CAN'T BE A MARTIAL ARTIST, I GUESS CON ARTIST IS THE NEXT BEST THING!

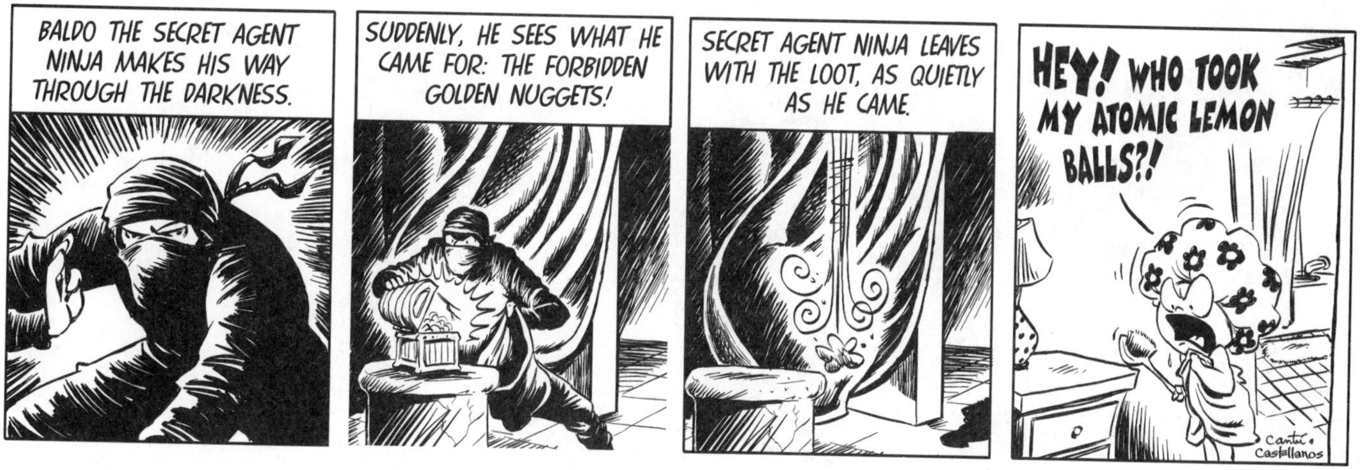
BALDO THE SECRET AGENT NINJA MAKES HIS WAY THROUGH THE DARKNESS.
SUDDENLY, HE SEES WHAT HE CAME FOR: THE FORBIDDEN GOLDEN NUGGETS!
SECRET AGENT NINJA LEAVES WITH THE LOOT, AS QUIETLY AS HE CAME.
HEY! WHO TOOK MY ATOMIC LEMON BALLS?!

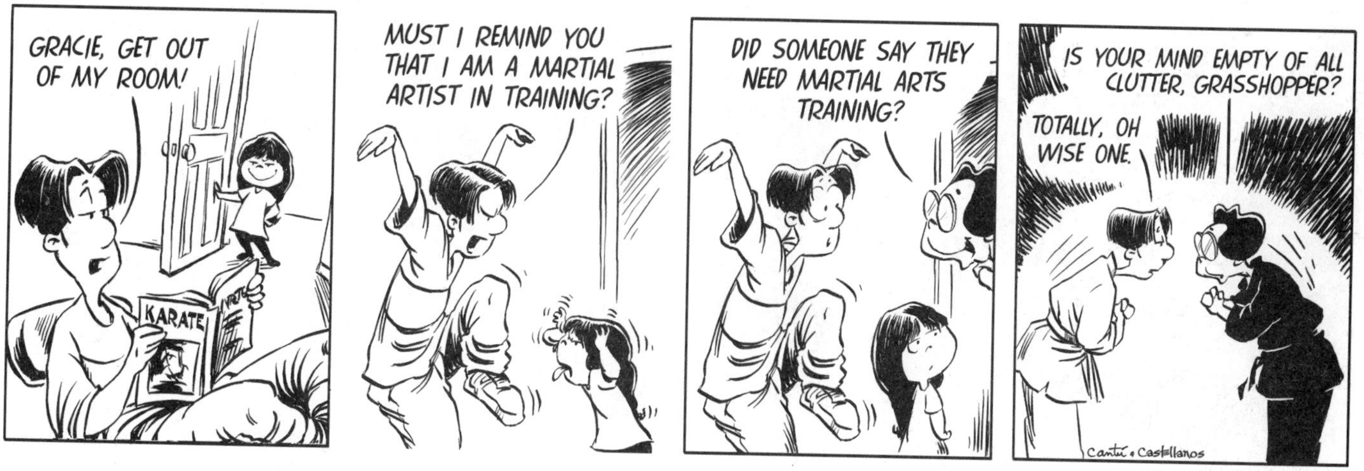
GRACIE, GET OUT OF MY ROOM!
KARATE
MUST I REMIND YOU THAT I AM A MARTIAL ARTIST IN TRAINING?
DID SOMEONE SAY THEY NEED MARTIAL ARTS TRAINING?
IS YOUR MIND EMPTY OF ALL CLUTTER, GRASSHOPPER?
TOTALLY, OH WISE ONE.

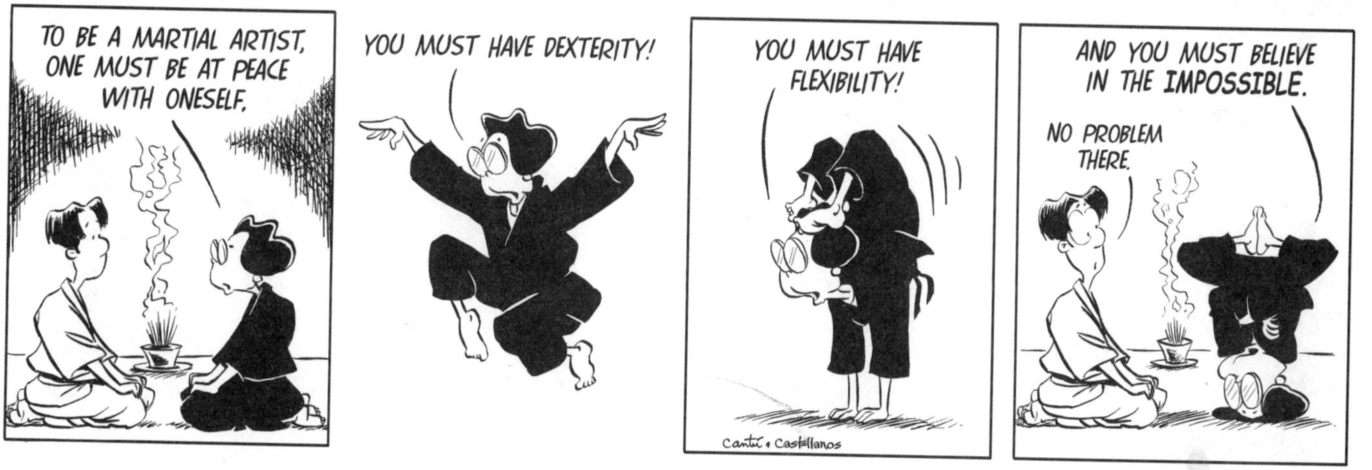
TO BE A MARTIAL ARTIST, ONE MUST BE AT PEACE WITH ONESELF.
YOU MUST HAVE DEXTERITY!
YOU MUST HAVE FLEXIBILITY!
AND YOU MUST BELIEVE IN THE IMPOSSIBLE.
NO PROBLEM THERE.

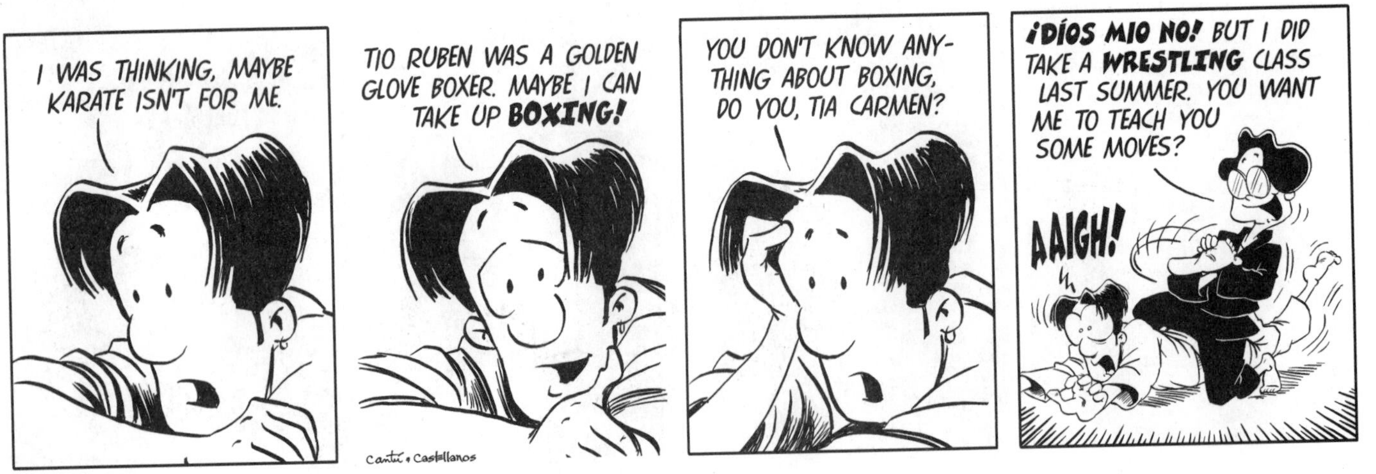
I WAS THINKING, MAYBE KARATE ISN'T FOR ME.
TIO RUBEN WAS A GOLDEN GLOVE BOXER. MAYBE I CAN TAKE UP BOXING!
YOU DON'T KNOW ANYTHING ABOUT BOXING, DO YOU, TIA CARMEN?
¡DÍOS MIO NO! BUT I DID TAKE A WRESTLING CLASS LAST SUMMER. YOU WANT ME TO TEACH YOU SOME MOVES?
AAIGH!
Cantú & Castellanos

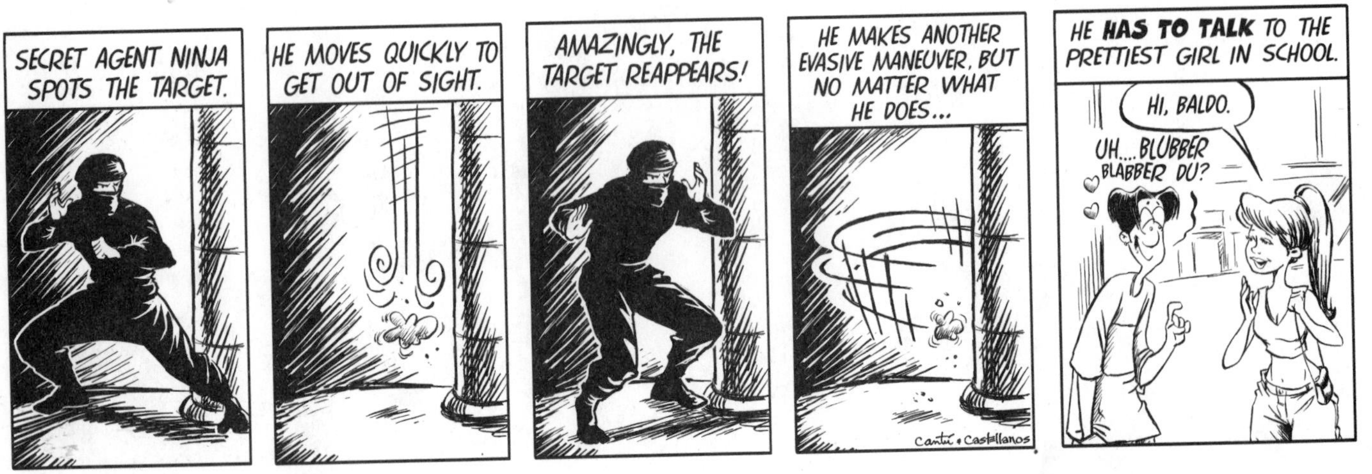
SECRET AGENT NINJA SPOTS THE TARGET.
HE MOVES QUICKLY TO GET OUT OF SIGHT.
AMAZINGLY, THE TARGET REAPPEARS!
HE MAKES ANOTHER EVASIVE MANEUVER, BUT NO MATTER WHAT HE DOES...
HE HAS TO TALK TO THE PRETTIEST GIRL IN SCHOOL.
HI, BALDO.
UH... BLUBBER BLABBER DU?
Cantú & Castellanos

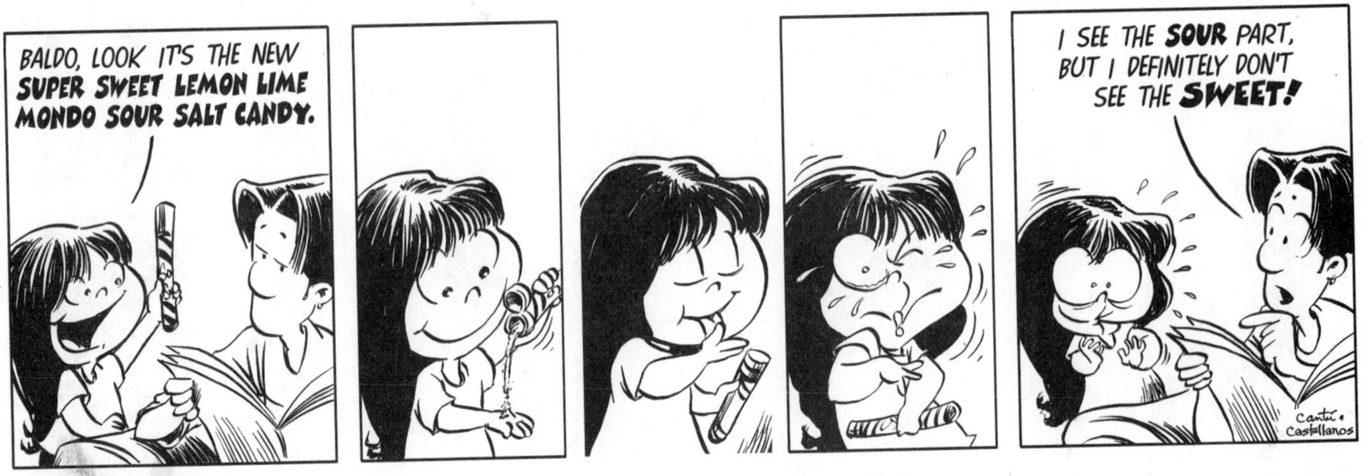
BALDO, LOOK IT'S THE NEW SUPER SWEET LEMON LIME MONDO SOUR SALT CANDY.
I SEE THE SOUR PART, BUT I DEFINITELY DON'T SEE THE SWEET!
Cantú & Castellanos

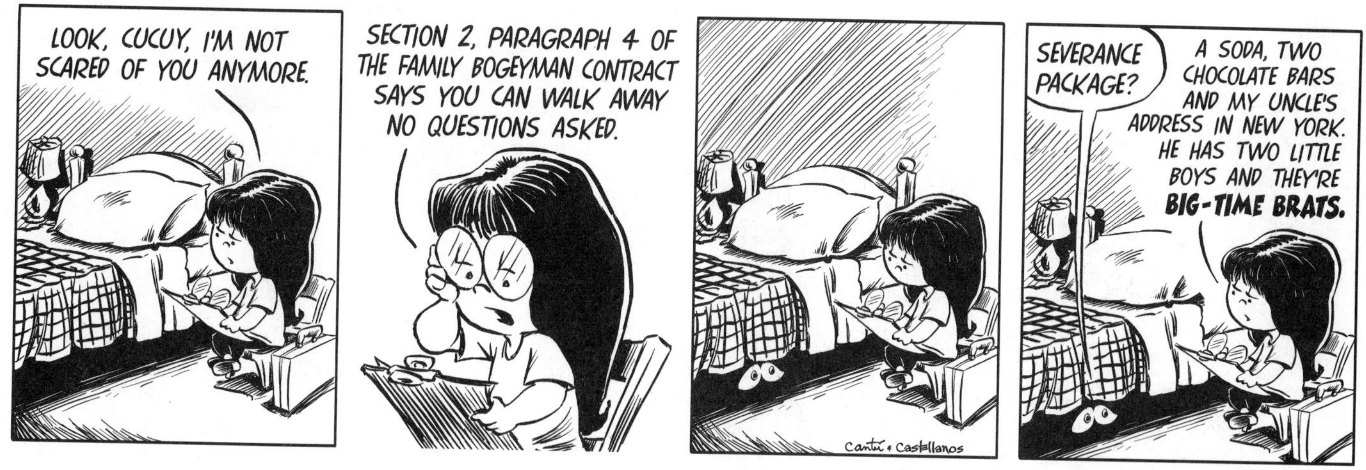
LOOK, CUCUY, I'M NOT SCARED OF YOU ANYMORE.
SECTION 2, PARAGRAPH 4 OF THE FAMILY BOGEYMAN CONTRACT SAYS YOU CAN WALK AWAY NO QUESTIONS ASKED.
SEVERANCE PACKAGE?
A SODA, TWO CHOCOLATE BARS AND MY UNCLE'S ADDRESS IN NEW YORK. HE HAS TWO LITTLE BOYS AND THEY'RE **BIG-TIME BRATS.**

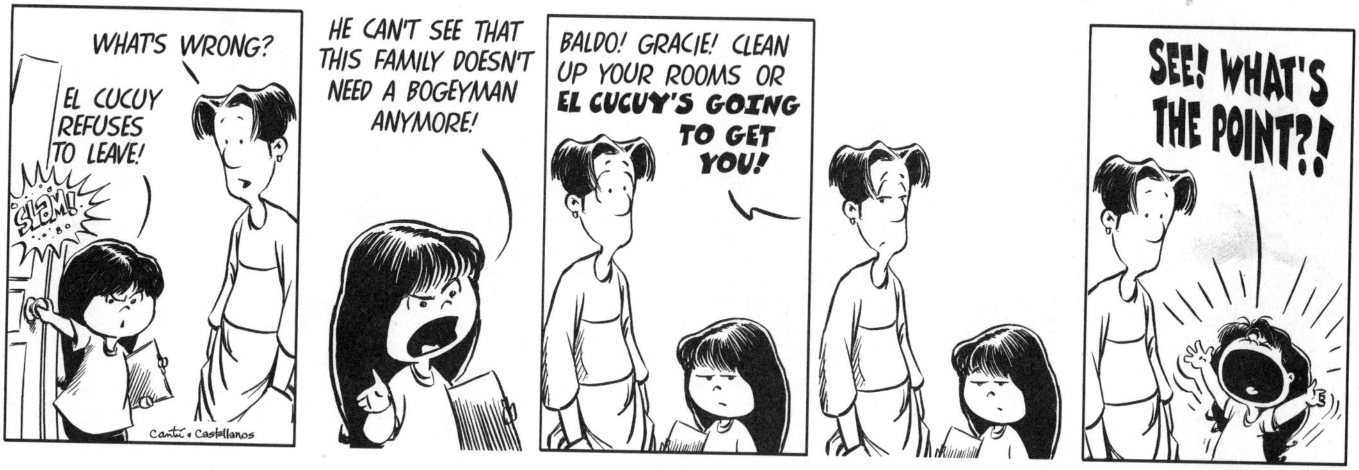
WHAT'S WRONG?
SLAM!
EL CUCUY REFUSES TO LEAVE!
HE CAN'T SEE THAT THIS FAMILY DOESN'T NEED A BOGEYMAN ANYMORE!
BALDO! GRACIE! CLEAN UP YOUR ROOMS OR **EL CUCUY'S GOING TO GET YOU!**
SEE! WHAT'S THE POINT?!

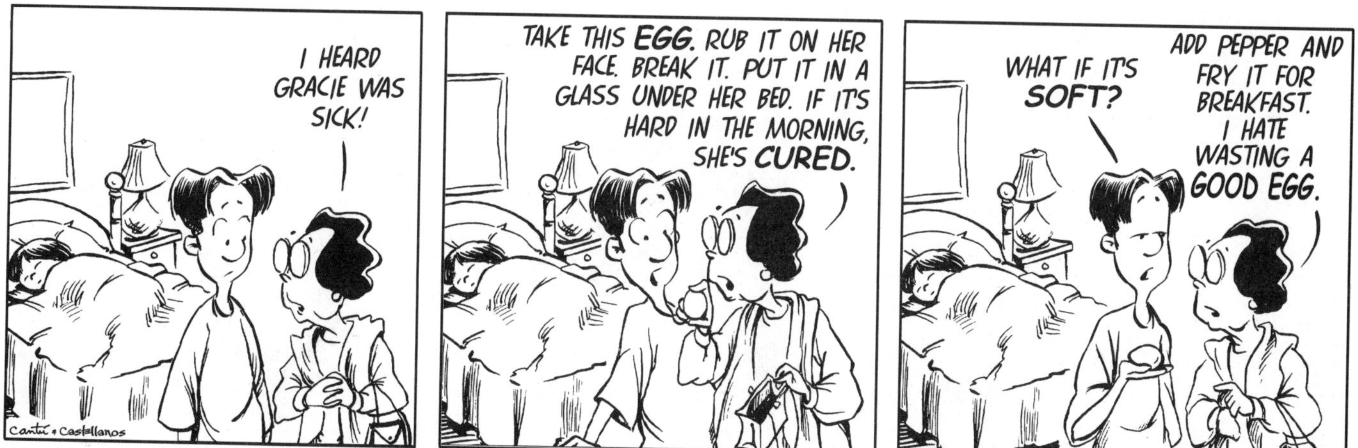
I HEARD GRACIE WAS SICK!
TAKE THIS **EGG**. RUB IT ON HER FACE. BREAK IT. PUT IT IN A GLASS UNDER HER BED. IF IT'S HARD IN THE MORNING, SHE'S **CURED**.
WHAT IF IT'S **SOFT?**
ADD PEPPER AND FRY IT FOR BREAKFAST. I HATE WASTING A **GOOD EGG**.

HA! YOU BROKE THE CD PLAYER. YOU'RE IN **BIG TROUBLE** NOW!
OOOO... DOESN'T LOOK LIKE LITTLE SIS IS GETTING OUT OF THIS ONE.
BOINK!
UH-OH, SOMETHING'S HAPPENING...
IT'S KINDA HARD TO MAKE OUT. IS IT ...?
YES IT IS! IT'S A BRUISE!
LITTLE SIS HAS A **NASTY BRUISE** ON HER ARM!
OOW! YOU BRUISED ME! YOU'RE IN **BIG TROUBLE!** **DAD!**
WHAT A COMEBACK! BALDO'S ON THE ROPES! TURN OUT THE LIGHTS!
Cantú • Castellanos

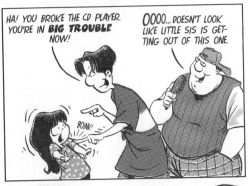

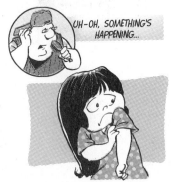

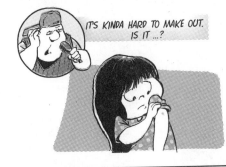

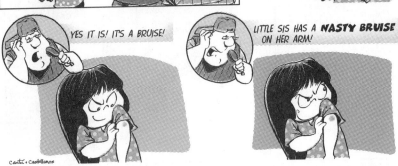

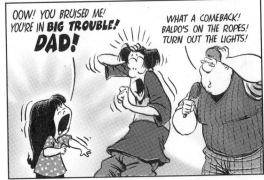

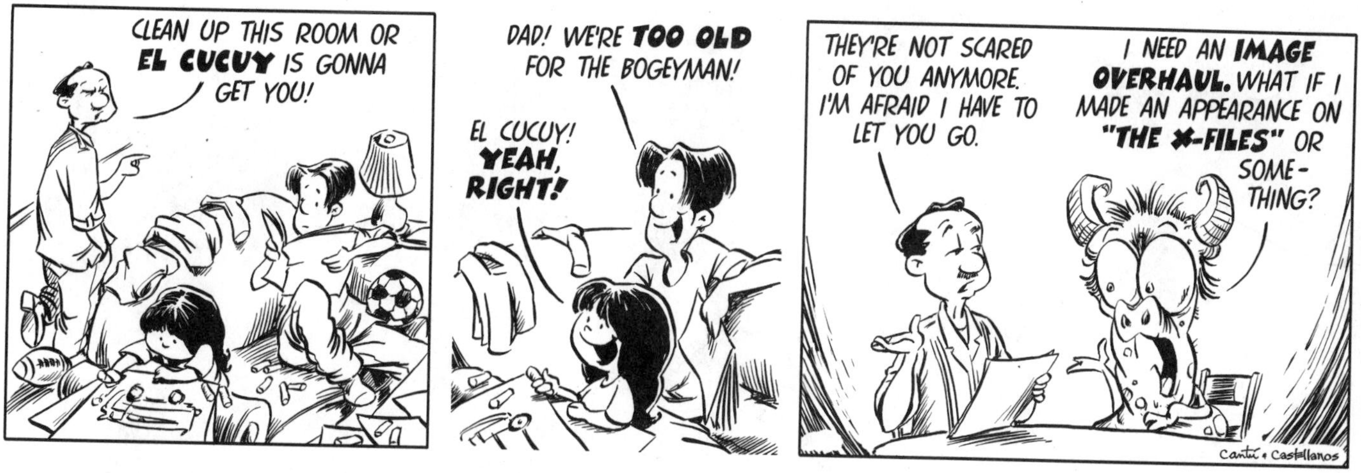
CLEAN UP THIS ROOM OR EL CUCUY IS GONNA GET YOU!
DAD! WE'RE TOO OLD FOR THE BOGEYMAN!
EL CUCUY! YEAH, RIGHT!
THEY'RE NOT SCARED OF YOU ANYMORE. I'M AFRAID I HAVE TO LET YOU GO.
I NEED AN IMAGE OVERHAUL. WHAT IF I MADE AN APPEARANCE ON "THE X-FILES" OR SOME-THING?
Cantú & Castellanos

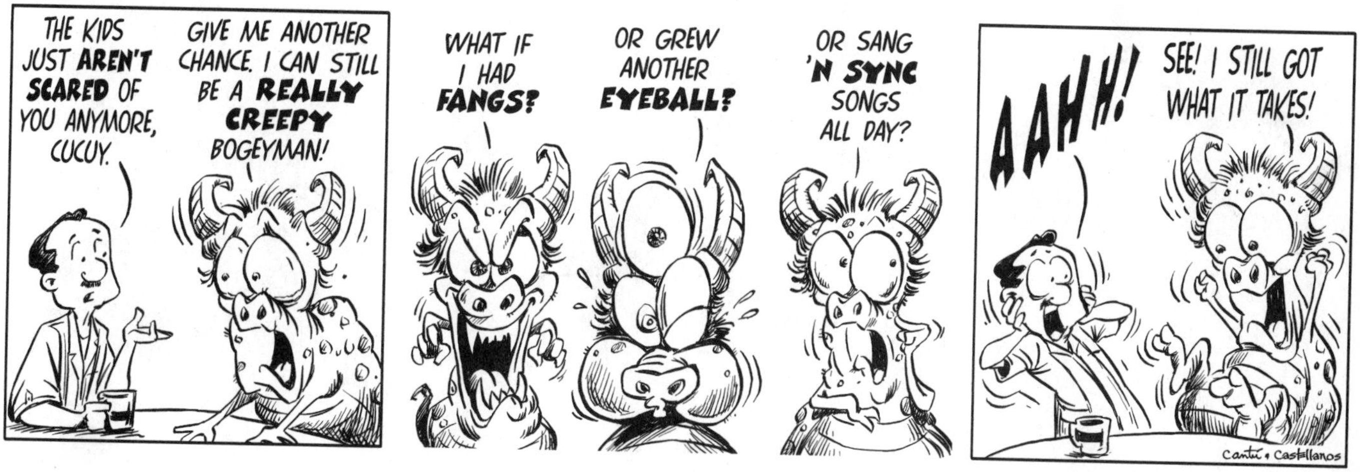
THE KIDS JUST AREN'T SCARED OF YOU ANYMORE, CUCUY.
GIVE ME ANOTHER CHANCE. I CAN STILL BE A REALLY CREEPY BOGEYMAN!
WHAT IF I HAD FANGS?
OR GREW ANOTHER EYEBALL?
OR SANG 'N SYNC SONGS ALL DAY?
AAHH!
SEE! I STILL GOT WHAT IT TAKES!
Cantú & Castellanos

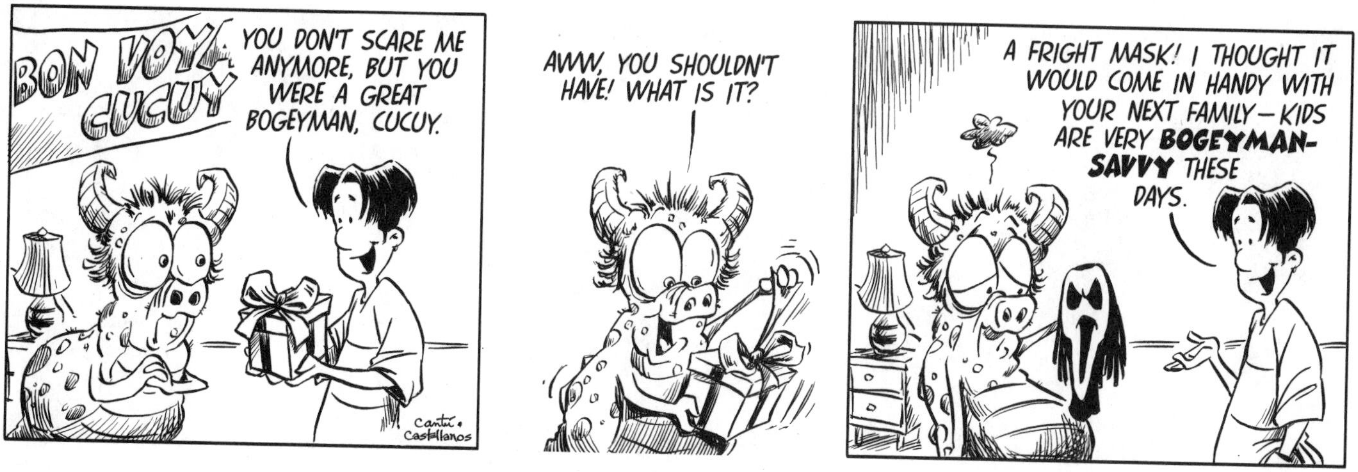
BON VOYAGE CUCUY
YOU DON'T SCARE ME ANYMORE, BUT YOU WERE A GREAT BOGEYMAN, CUCUY.
AWW, YOU SHOULDN'T HAVE! WHAT IS IT?
A FRIGHT MASK! I THOUGHT IT WOULD COME IN HANDY WITH YOUR NEXT FAMILY—KIDS ARE VERY BOGEYMAN-SAVVY THESE DAYS.
Cantú & Castellanos

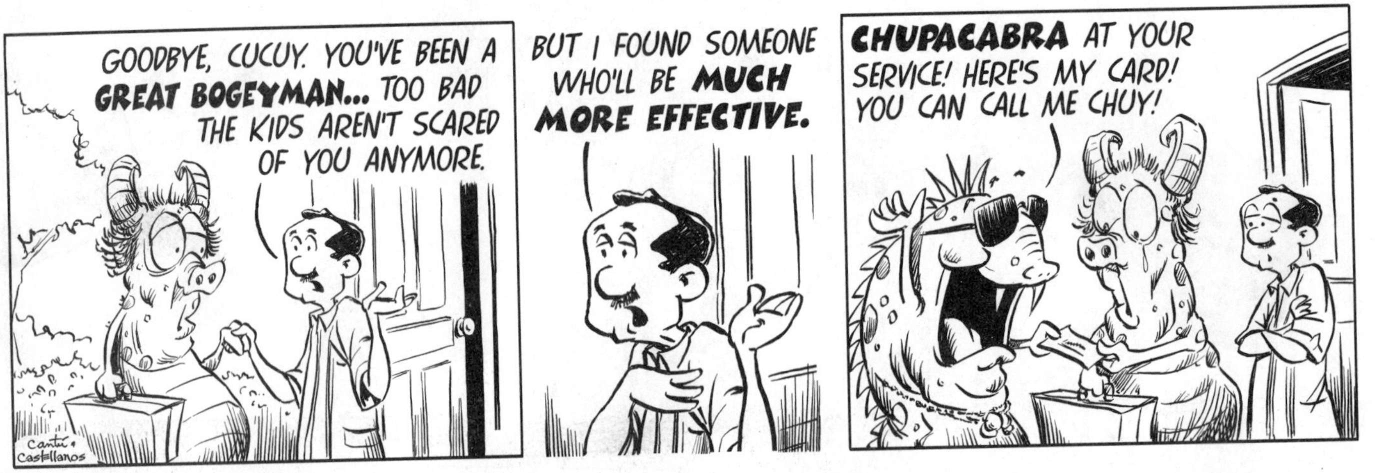
GOODBYE, CUCUY. YOU'VE BEEN A **GREAT BOGEYMAN...** TOO BAD THE KIDS AREN'T SCARED OF YOU ANYMORE.
Cantú & Castellanos
BUT I FOUND SOMEONE WHO'LL BE **MUCH MORE EFFECTIVE.**
CHUPACABRA AT YOUR SERVICE! HERE'S MY CARD! YOU CAN CALL ME CHUY!

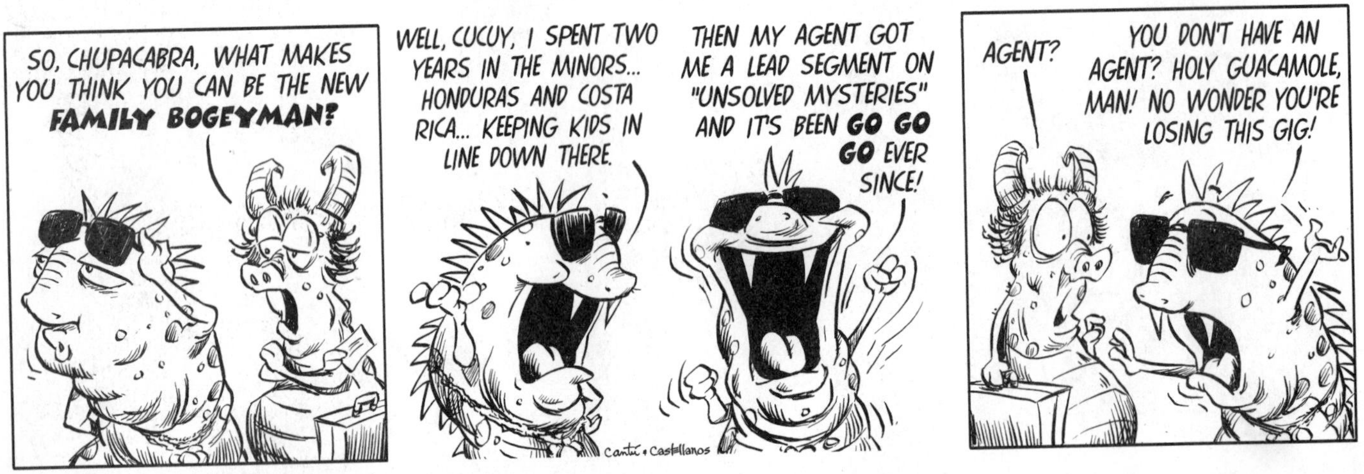
SO, CHUPACABRA, WHAT MAKES YOU THINK YOU CAN BE THE NEW **FAMILY BOGEYMAN?**
WELL, CUCUY, I SPENT TWO YEARS IN THE MINORS... HONDURAS AND COSTA RICA... KEEPING KIDS IN LINE DOWN THERE.
THEN MY AGENT GOT ME A LEAD SEGMENT ON "UNSOLVED MYSTERIES" AND IT'S BEEN **GO GO GO** EVER SINCE!
Cantú & Castellanos
AGENT?
YOU DON'T HAVE AN AGENT? HOLY GUACAMOLE, MAN! NO WONDER YOU'RE LOSING THIS GIG!

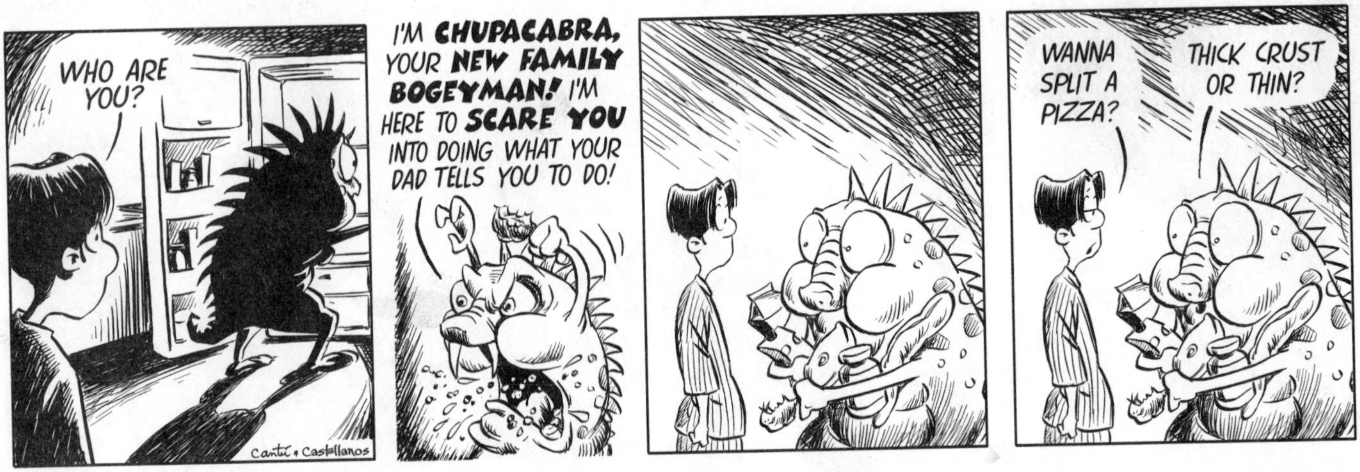
WHO ARE YOU?
Cantú & Castellanos
I'M **CHUPACABRA,** YOUR **NEW FAMILY BOGEYMAN!** I'M HERE TO **SCARE YOU** INTO DOING WHAT YOUR DAD TELLS YOU TO DO!
WANNA SPLIT A PIZZA?
THICK CRUST OR THIN?

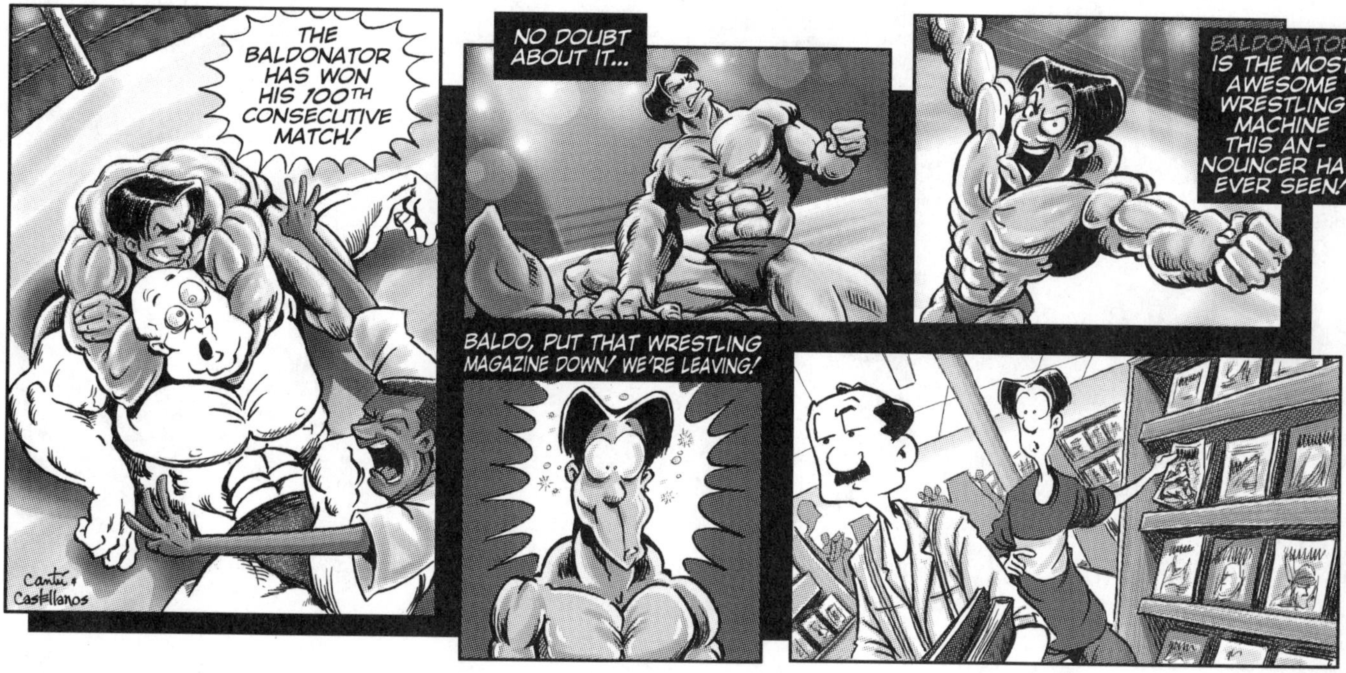
THE BALDONATOR HAS WON HIS 100TH CONSECUTIVE MATCH!
Cantú & Castellanos
NO DOUBT ABOUT IT...
BALDONATOR IS THE MOST AWESOME WRESTLING MACHINE THIS AN-NOUNCER HAS EVER SEEN!
BALDO, PUT THAT WRESTLING MAGAZINE DOWN! WE'RE LEAVING!

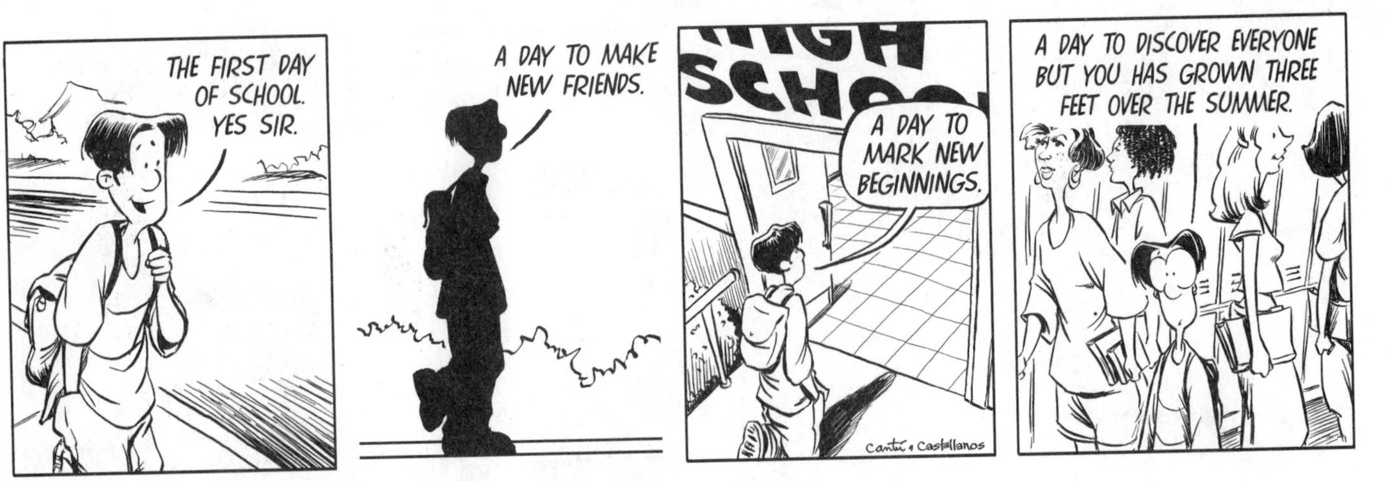
THE FIRST DAY OF SCHOOL. YES SIR.
A DAY TO MAKE NEW FRIENDS.
HIGH SCHOOL
A DAY TO MARK NEW BEGINNINGS.
A DAY TO DISCOVER EVERYONE BUT YOU HAS GROWN THREE FEET OVER THE SUMMER.
Cantú & Castellanos

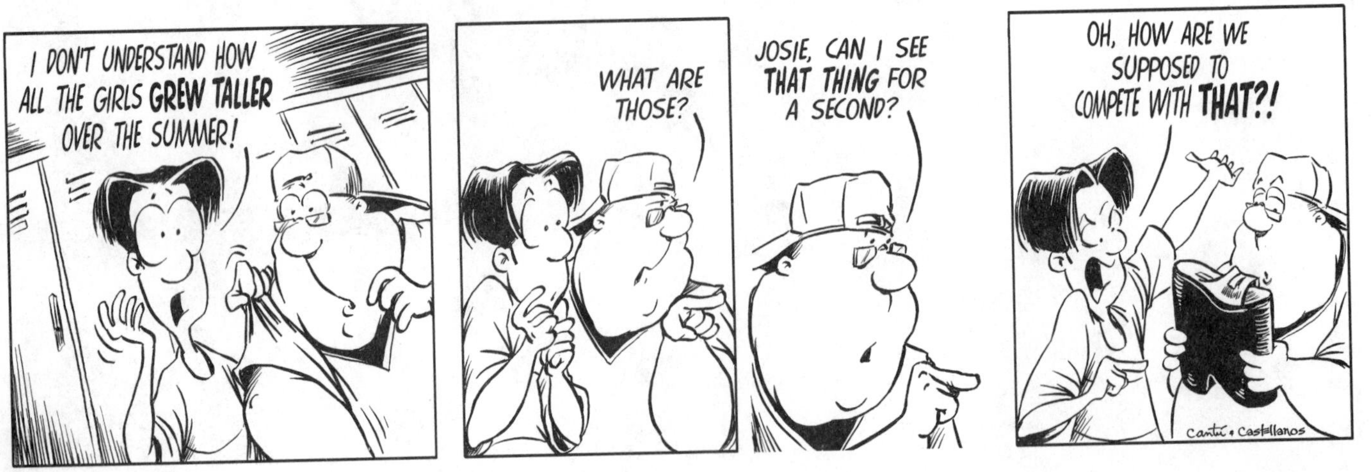
I DON'T UNDERSTAND HOW ALL THE GIRLS GREW TALLER OVER THE SUMMER!
WHAT ARE THOSE?
JOSIE, CAN I SEE THAT THING FOR A SECOND?
OH, HOW ARE WE SUPPOSED TO COMPETE WITH THAT?!
Cantú & Castellanos

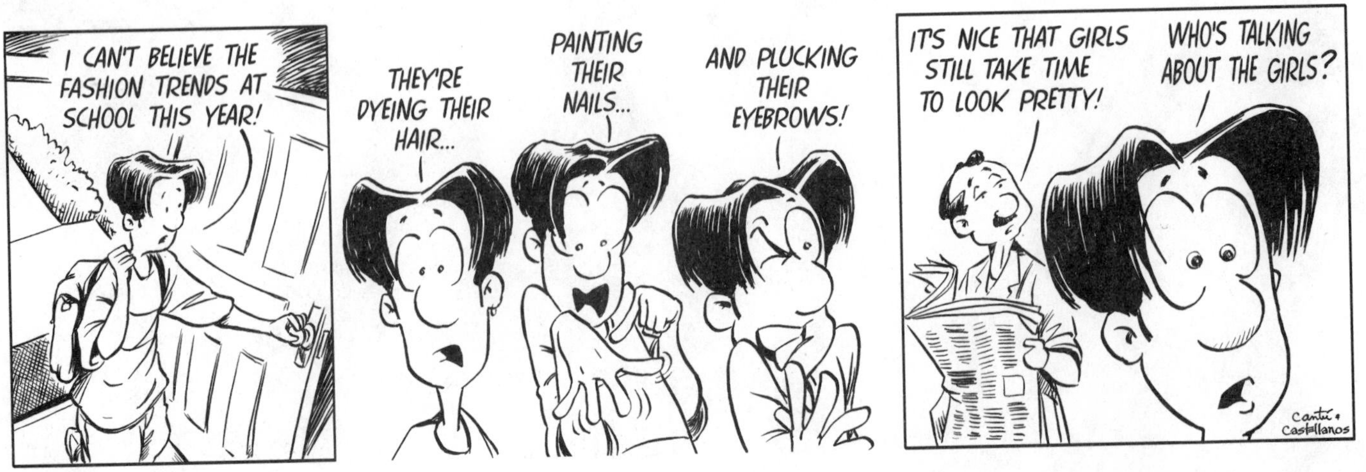
I CAN'T BELIEVE THE FASHION TRENDS AT SCHOOL THIS YEAR!
THEY'RE DYEING THEIR HAIR...
PAINTING THEIR NAILS...
AND PLUCKING THEIR EYEBROWS!
IT'S NICE THAT GIRLS STILL TAKE TIME TO LOOK PRETTY!
WHO'S TALKING ABOUT THE GIRLS?
Cantú & Castellanos

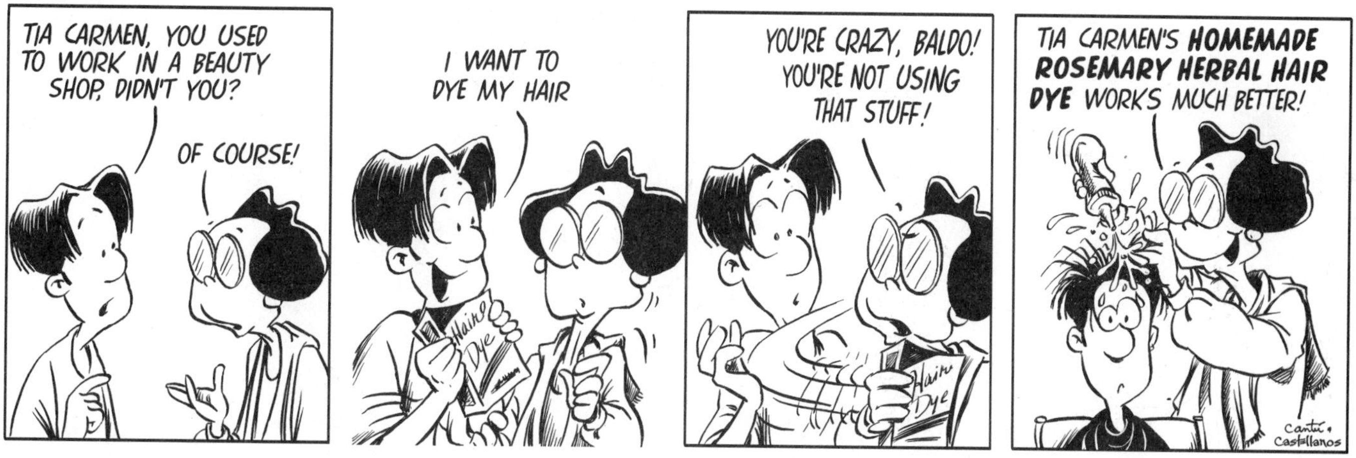
TIA CARMEN, YOU USED TO WORK IN A BEAUTY SHOP, DIDN'T YOU?
OF COURSE!
I WANT TO DYE MY HAIR
Hair Dye
YOU'RE CRAZY, BALDO! YOU'RE NOT USING THAT STUFF!
Hair Dye
TIA CARMEN'S **HOMEMADE ROSEMARY HERBAL HAIR DYE** WORKS MUCH BETTER!
Cantú & Castellanos

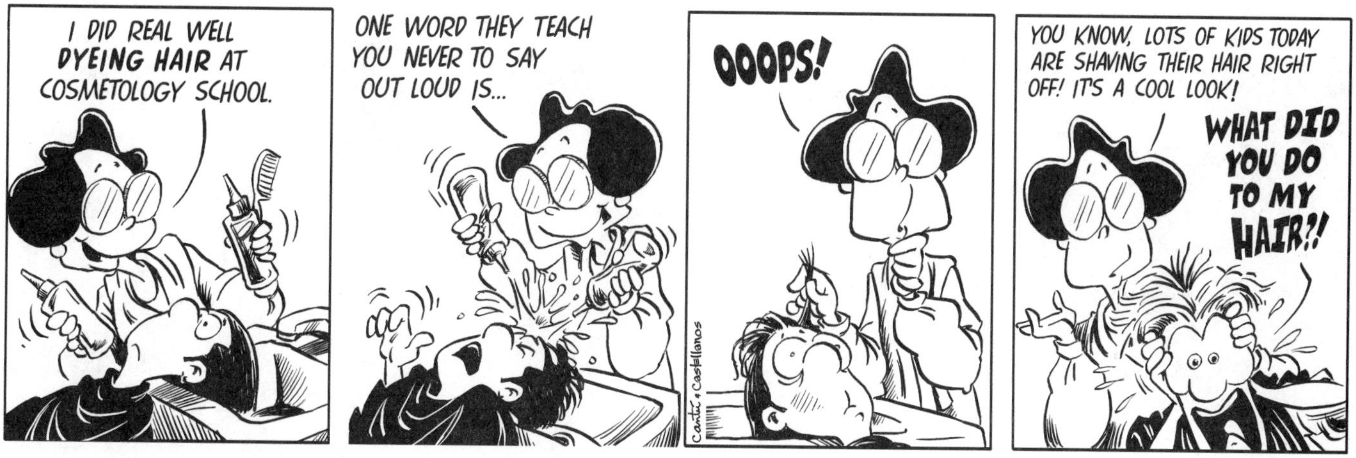
I DID REAL WELL **DYEING HAIR** AT COSMETOLOGY SCHOOL.
ONE WORD THEY TEACH YOU NEVER TO SAY OUT LOUD IS...
OOOPS!
Cantú & Castellanos
YOU KNOW, LOTS OF KIDS TODAY ARE SHAVING THEIR HAIR RIGHT OFF! IT'S A COOL LOOK!
WHAT DID YOU DO TO MY HAIR?!

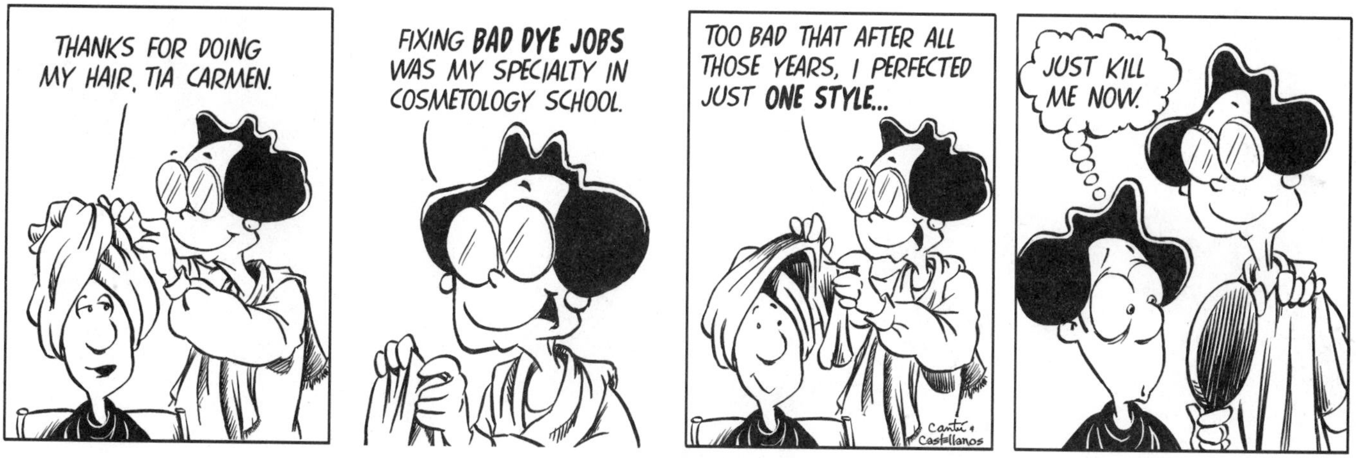
THANKS FOR DOING MY HAIR, TIA CARMEN.
FIXING **BAD DYE JOBS** WAS MY SPECIALTY IN COSMETOLOGY SCHOOL.
TOO BAD THAT AFTER ALL THOSE YEARS, I PERFECTED JUST **ONE STYLE...**
Cantú & Castellanos
JUST KILL ME NOW.

Dear Abuelita,
Just a note on this Grandparents Day to say how much I miss you.
I miss the wild smells when I stuck my nose in your spice cabinet.
I miss the underwear you always gave me for my birthday.
I miss finding old coffee cans filled with pennies that you hid around the house.
I miss your elegant handwritten letters, always with a 5-dollar bill inside, wishing me a happy future and telling me to always do my best at whatever I do.
Te quiero,
your grandson,
Baldo
Cantú & Castellanos

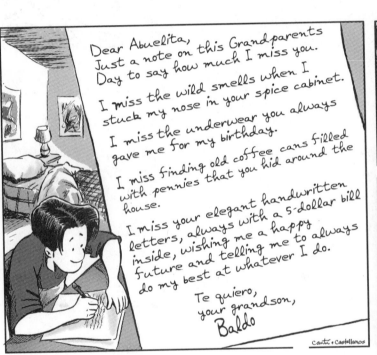

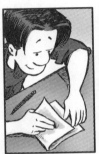

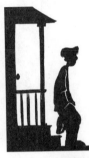

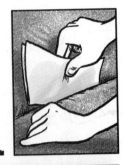

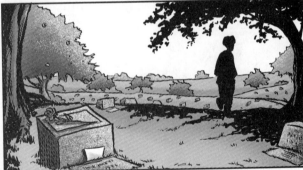

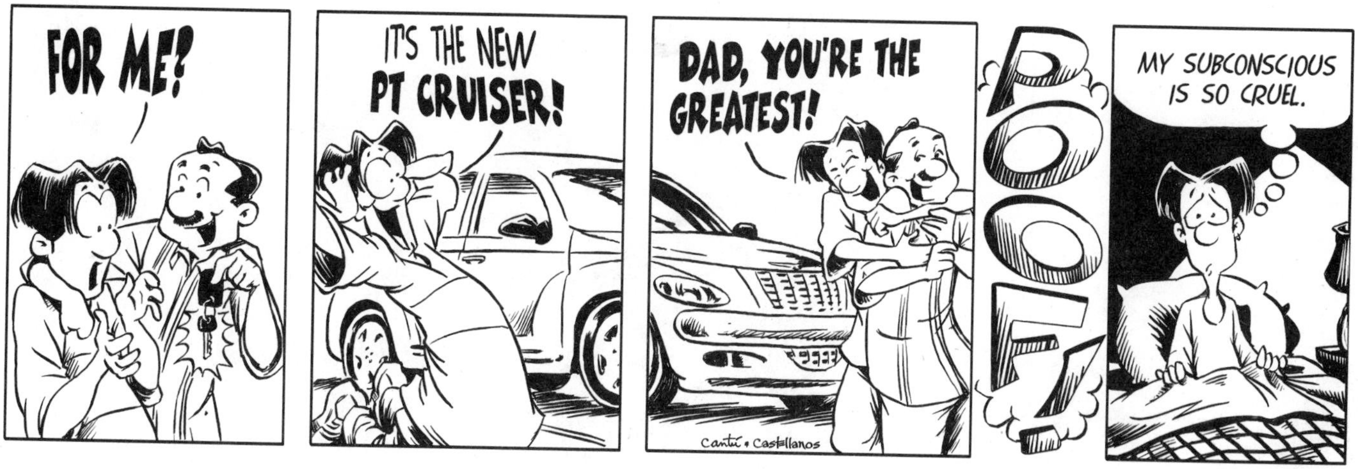
FOR ME?
IT'S THE NEW PT CRUISER!
DAD, YOU'RE THE GREATEST!
POOF
MY SUBCONSCIOUS IS SO CRUEL.

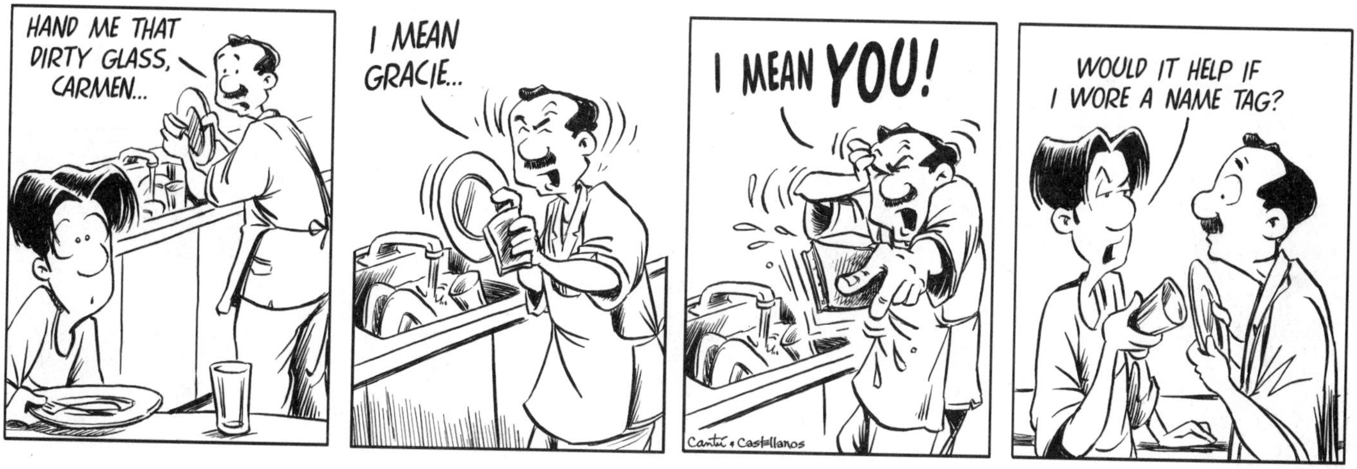
HAND ME THAT DIRTY GLASS, CARMEN...
I MEAN GRACIE...
I MEAN YOU!
WOULD IT HELP IF I WORE A NAME TAG?

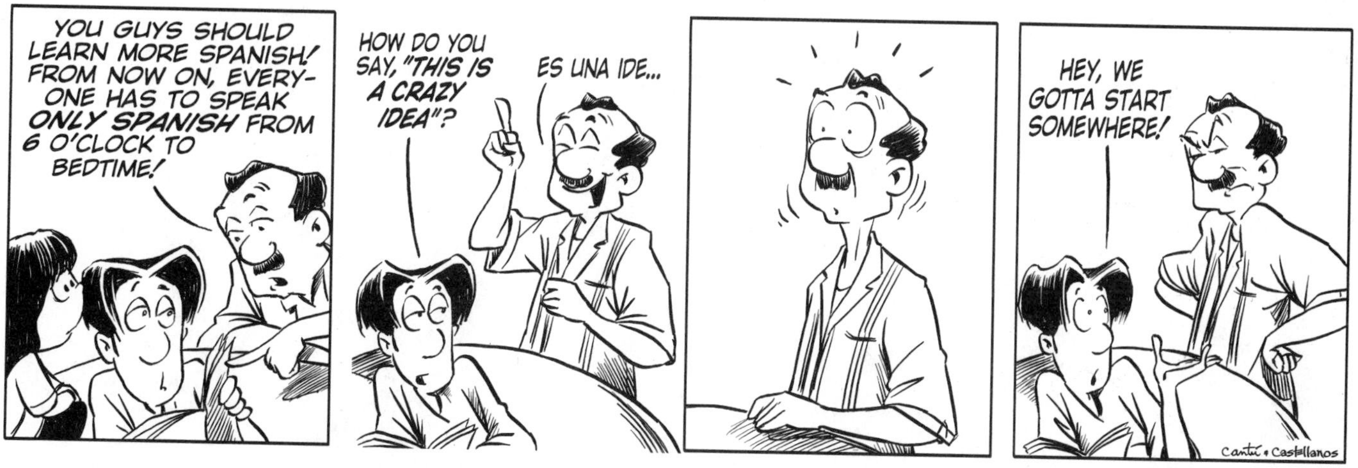
YOU GUYS SHOULD LEARN MORE SPANISH! FROM NOW ON, EVERY-ONE HAS TO SPEAK ONLY SPANISH FROM 6 O'CLOCK TO BEDTIME!
HOW DO YOU SAY, "THIS IS A CRAZY IDEA"?
ES UNA IDE...
HEY, WE GOTTA START SOMEWHERE!

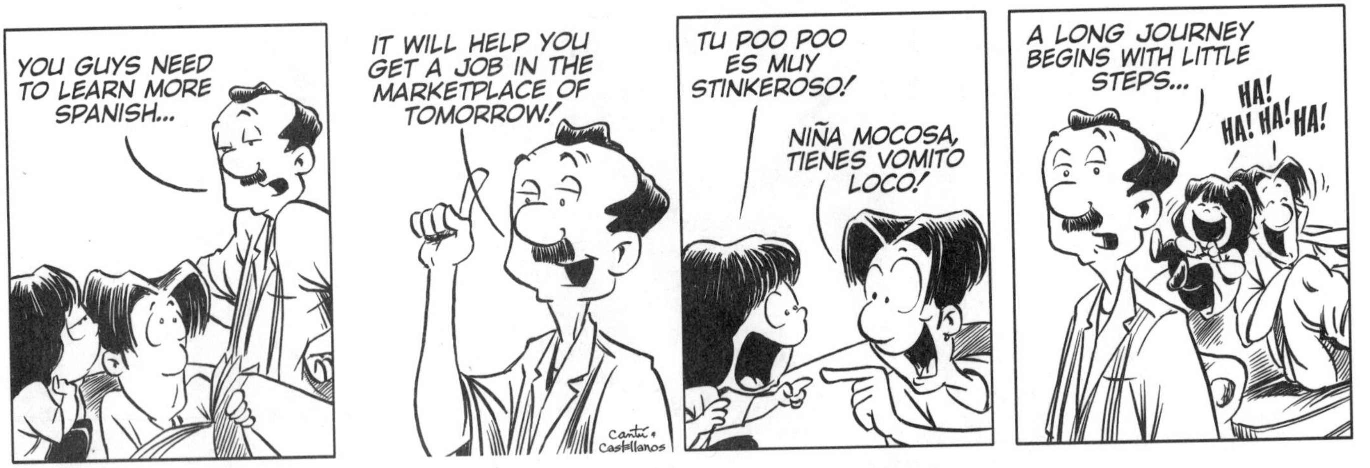
YOU GUYS NEED TO LEARN MORE SPANISH...
IT WILL HELP YOU GET A JOB IN THE MARKETPLACE OF TOMORROW!
TU POO POO ES MUY STINKEROSO!
NIÑA MOCOSA, TIENES VOMITO LOCO!
A LONG JOURNEY BEGINS WITH LITTLE STEPS...
HA! HA! HA! HA!

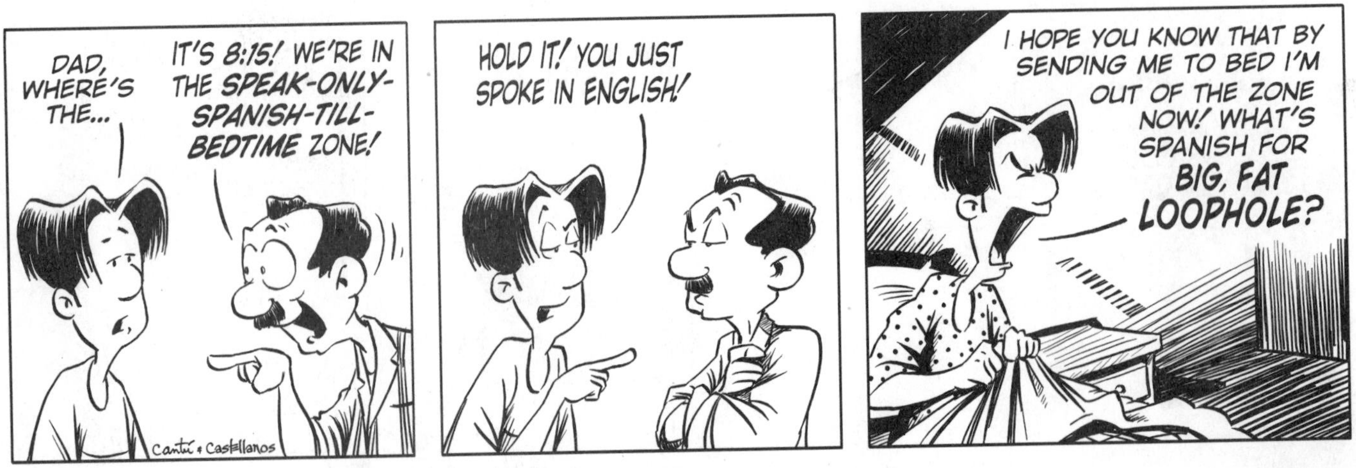
DAD, WHERE'S THE...
IT'S 8:15! WE'RE IN THE SPEAK-ONLY-SPANISH-TILL-BEDTIME ZONE!
HOLD IT! YOU JUST SPOKE IN ENGLISH!
I HOPE YOU KNOW THAT BY SENDING ME TO BED I'M OUT OF THE ZONE NOW! WHAT'S SPANISH FOR BIG, FAT LOOPHOLE?

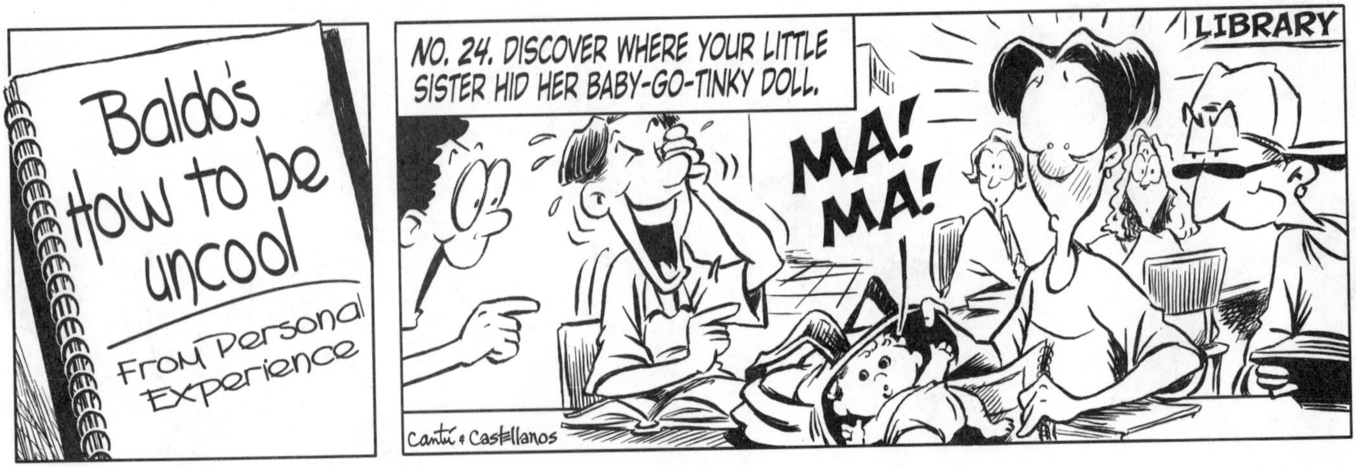
Baldo's How to be uncool
From Personal Experience
NO. 24. DISCOVER WHERE YOUR LITTLE SISTER HID HER BABY-GO-TINKY DOLL.
LIBRARY
MA! MA!

LOOK, BALDO! SCIENTIFIC RESEARCH SAYS **BOREDOM IS GOOD FOR YOU!**
Legend of el Chupacabra
IT STIMULATES YOUR IMAGINATION...
STUDIES SAY A STATE OF INACTIVITY MAKES YOUR BRAIN WORK HARDER TO **ENTERTAIN ITSELF.**
SO THOSE "IMAGINATION NEURONS" IN THAT LITTLE HEAD OF YOURS GET A **WELL-NEEDED WORKOUT!**
WHAT DO YOU THINK OF THAT?
I'M NOT SURE ... GO BACK TO THAT BORING PART ABOUT **SCIENTIFIC RESEARCH ...**
Cantú • Castellanos

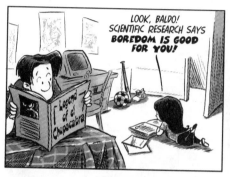

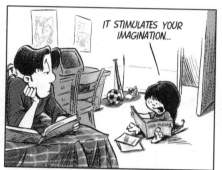

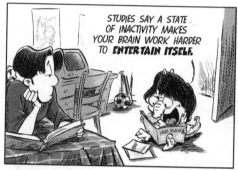

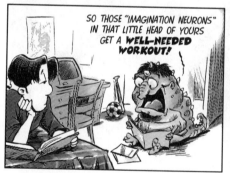

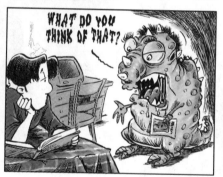

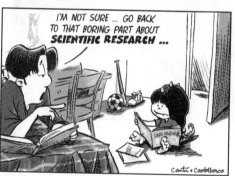

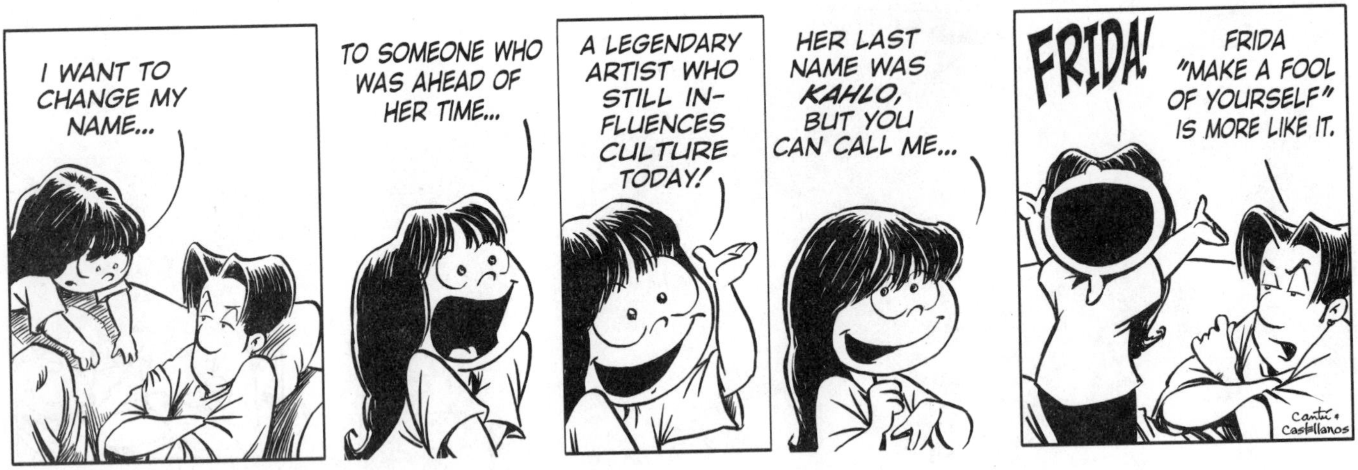
I WANT TO CHANGE MY NAME...
TO SOMEONE WHO WAS AHEAD OF HER TIME...
A LEGENDARY ARTIST WHO STILL IN-FLUENCES CULTURE TODAY!
HER LAST NAME WAS KAHLO, BUT YOU CAN CALL ME...
FRIDA!
FRIDA "MAKE A FOOL OF YOURSELF" IS MORE LIKE IT.
Cantú & Castellanos

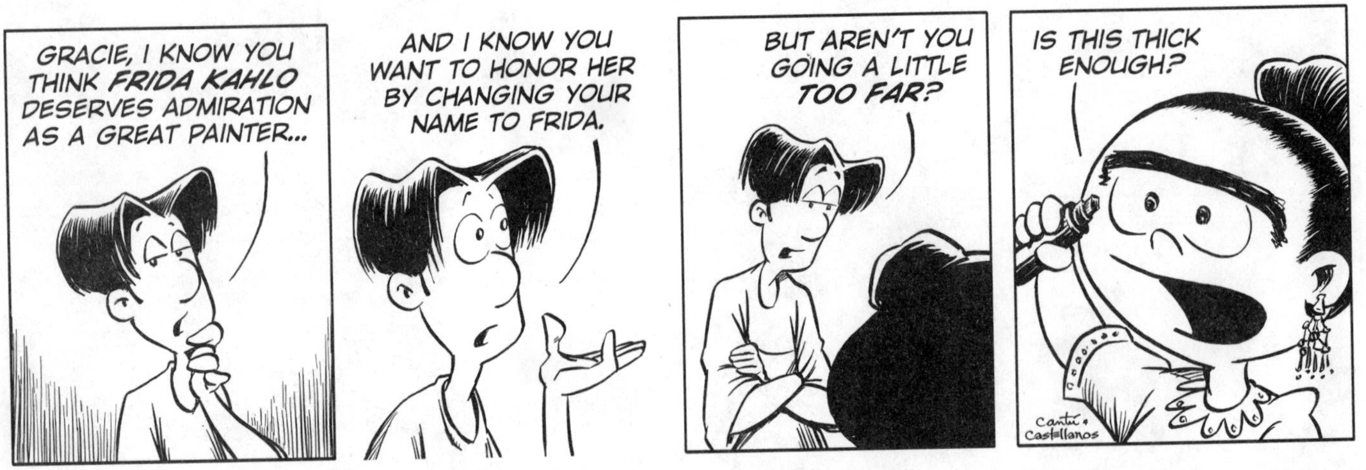
GRACIE, I KNOW YOU THINK FRIDA KAHLO DESERVES ADMIRATION AS A GREAT PAINTER...
AND I KNOW YOU WANT TO HONOR HER BY CHANGING YOUR NAME TO FRIDA.
BUT AREN'T YOU GOING A LITTLE TOO FAR?
IS THIS THICK ENOUGH?
Cantú & Castellanos

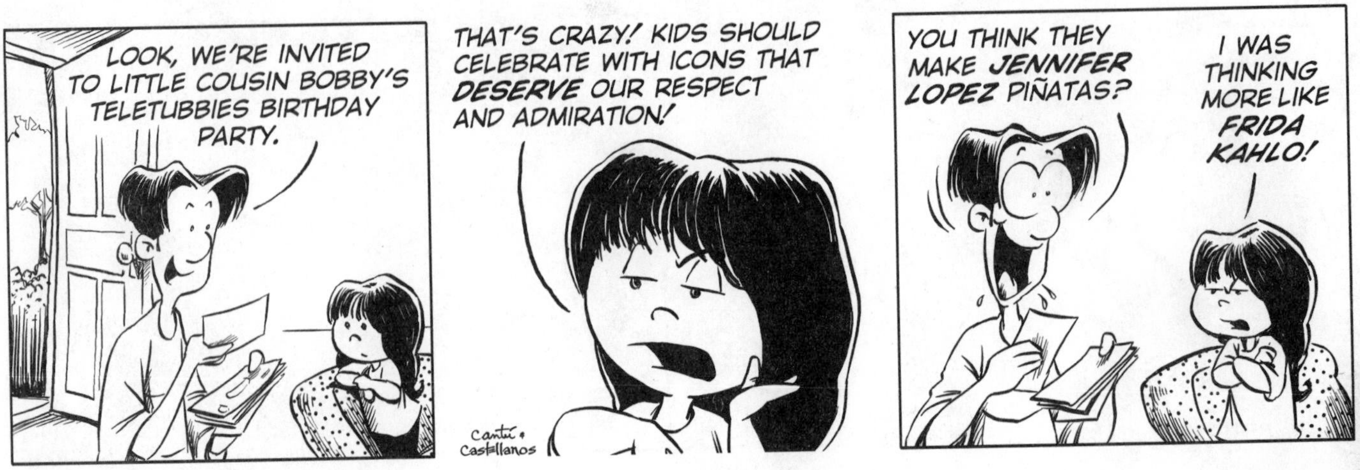
LOOK, WE'RE INVITED TO LITTLE COUSIN BOBBY'S TELETUBBIES BIRTHDAY PARTY.
THAT'S CRAZY! KIDS SHOULD CELEBRATE WITH ICONS THAT DESERVE OUR RESPECT AND ADMIRATION!
YOU THINK THEY MAKE JENNIFER LOPEZ PIÑATAS?
I WAS THINKING MORE LIKE FRIDA KAHLO!
Cantú & Castellanos

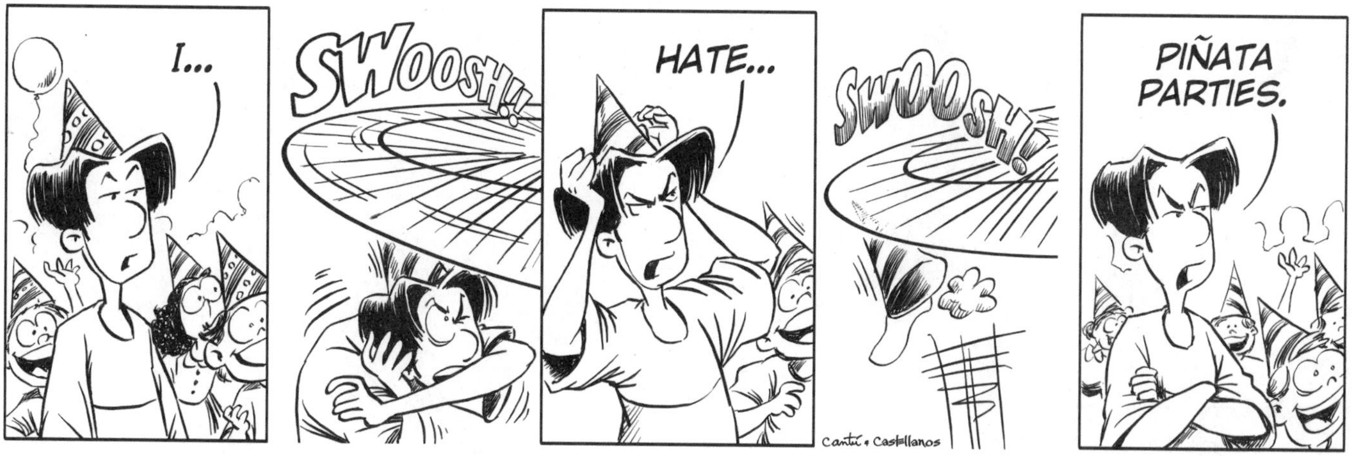
I...
SWOOSH!!
HATE...
SWOOSH!
PIÑATA PARTIES.
Cantú & Castellanos

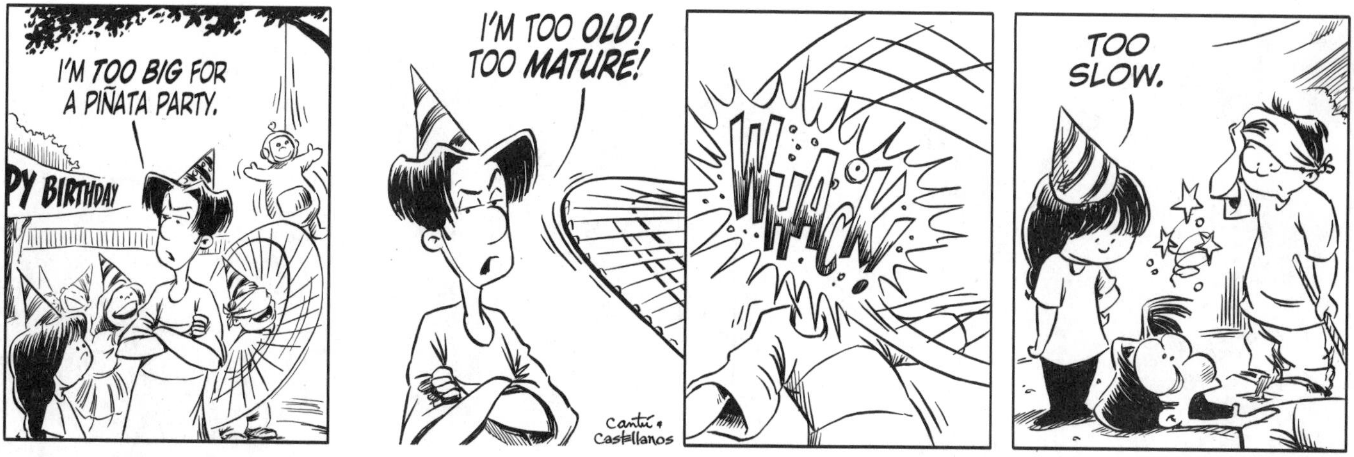
I'M TOO BIG FOR A PIÑATA PARTY.
PY BIRTHDAY
I'M TOO OLD! TOO MATURE!
Cantú & Castellanos
WHACK!
TOO SLOW.

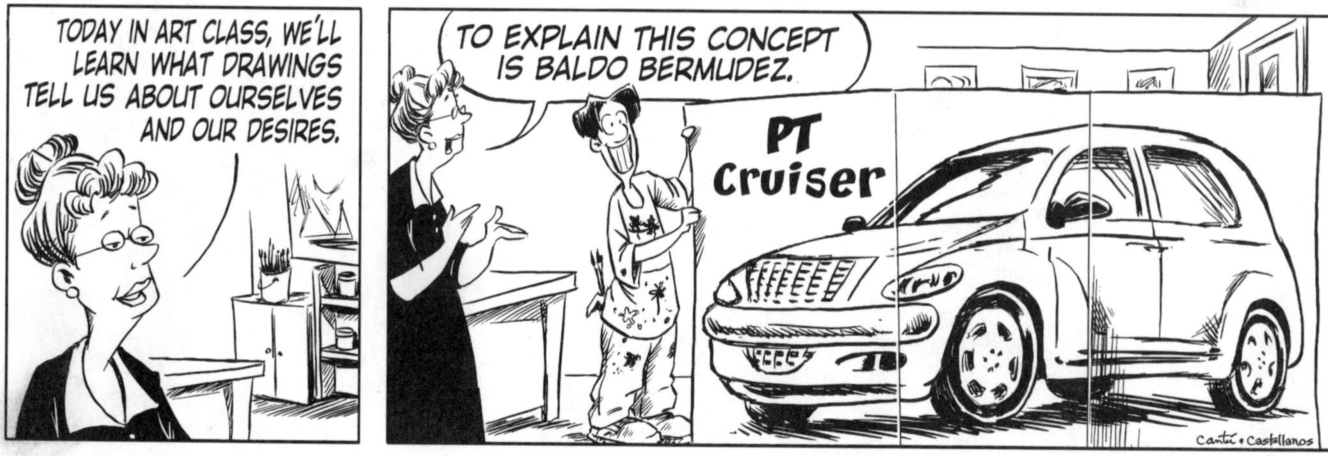
TODAY IN ART CLASS, WE'LL LEARN WHAT DRAWINGS TELL US ABOUT OURSELVES AND OUR DESIRES.
TO EXPLAIN THIS CONCEPT IS BALDO BERMUDEZ.
PT Cruiser
Cantú & Castellanos

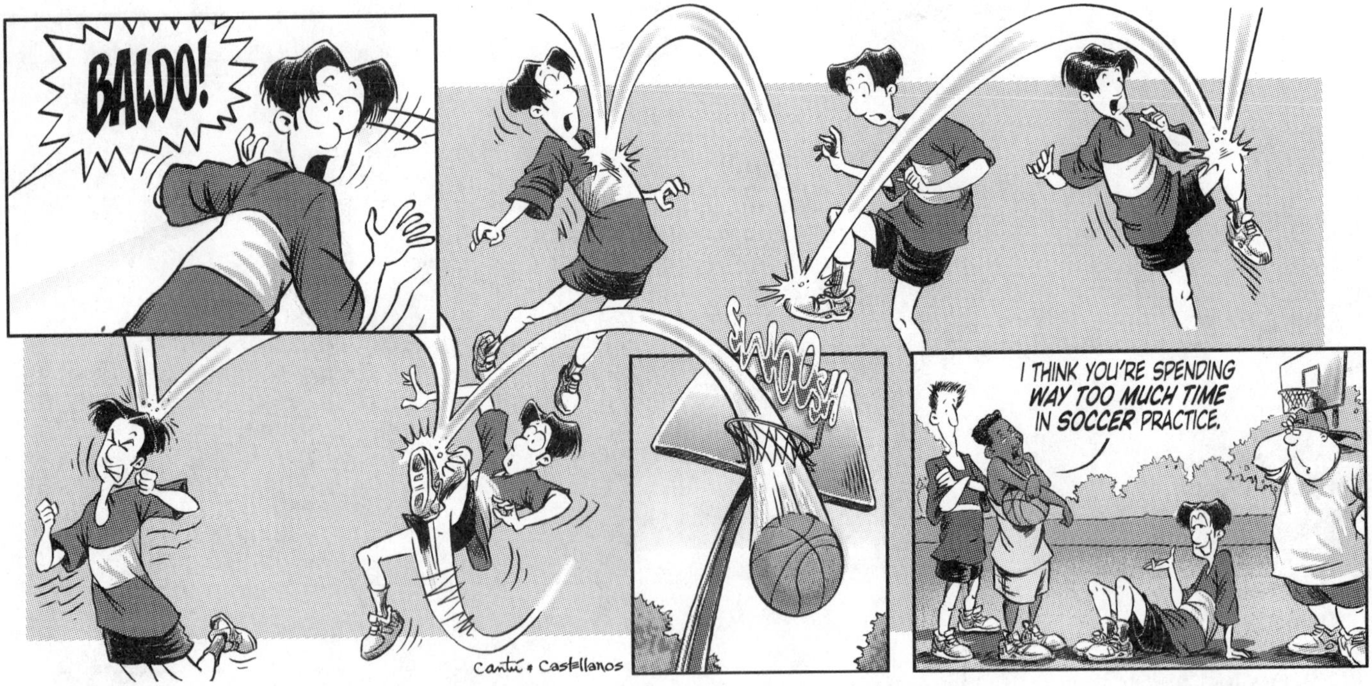
BALDO!
SWOOSH
I THINK YOU'RE SPENDING WAY TOO MUCH TIME IN SOCCER PRACTICE.
Cantú & Castellanos

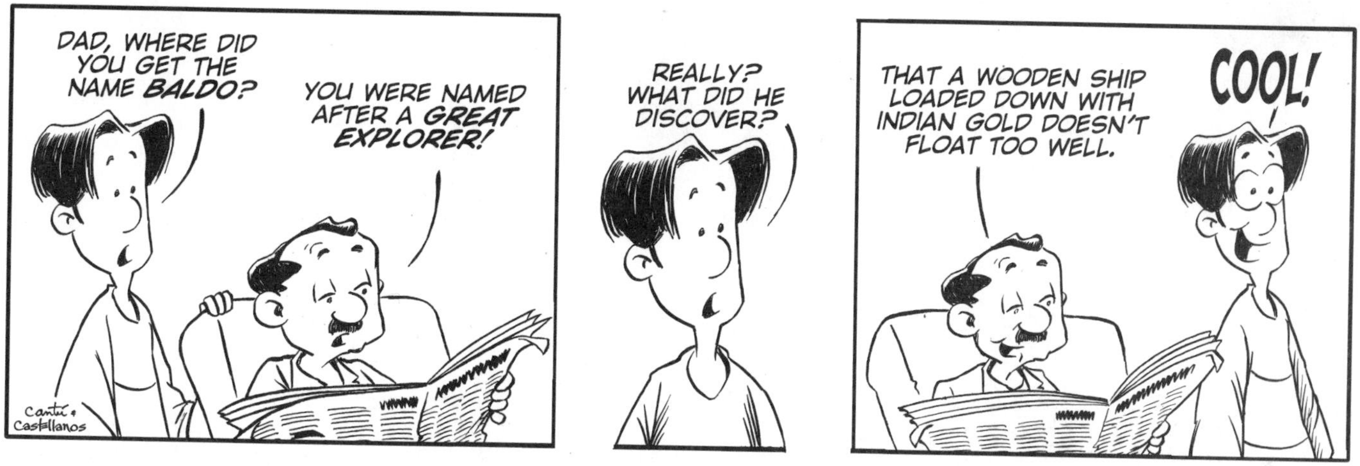
DAD, WHERE DID YOU GET THE NAME BALDO?
YOU WERE NAMED AFTER A GREAT EXPLORER!
REALLY? WHAT DID HE DISCOVER?
THAT A WOODEN SHIP LOADED DOWN WITH INDIAN GOLD DOESN'T FLOAT TOO WELL.
COOL!
Cantú & Castellanos

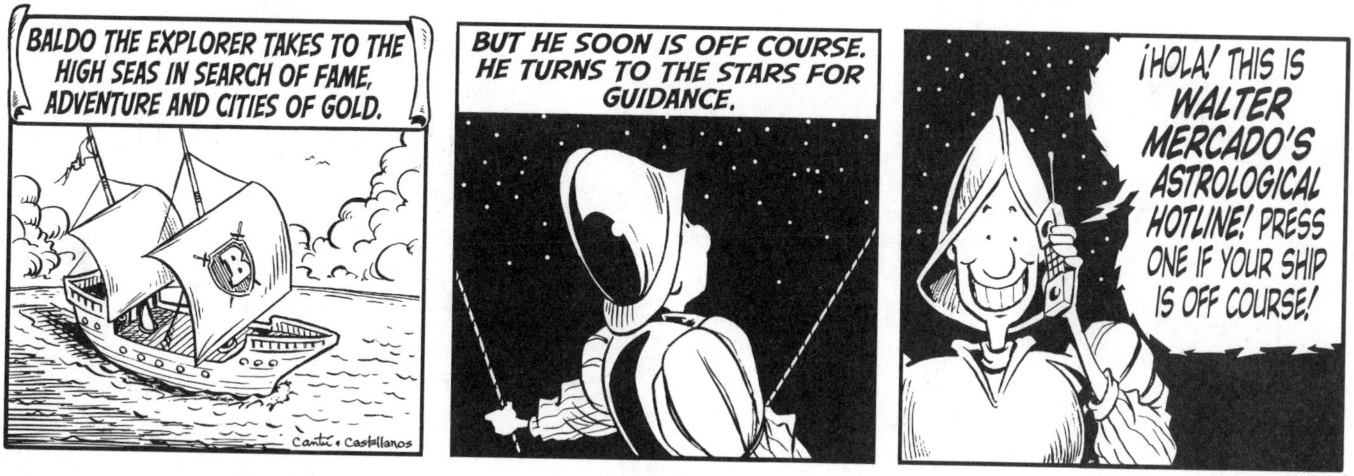
BALDO THE EXPLORER TAKES TO THE HIGH SEAS IN SEARCH OF FAME, ADVENTURE AND CITIES OF GOLD.
Cantú & Castellanos
BUT HE SOON IS OFF COURSE. HE TURNS TO THE STARS FOR GUIDANCE.
¡HOLA! THIS IS WALTER MERCADO'S ASTROLOGICAL HOTLINE! PRESS ONE IF YOUR SHIP IS OFF COURSE!

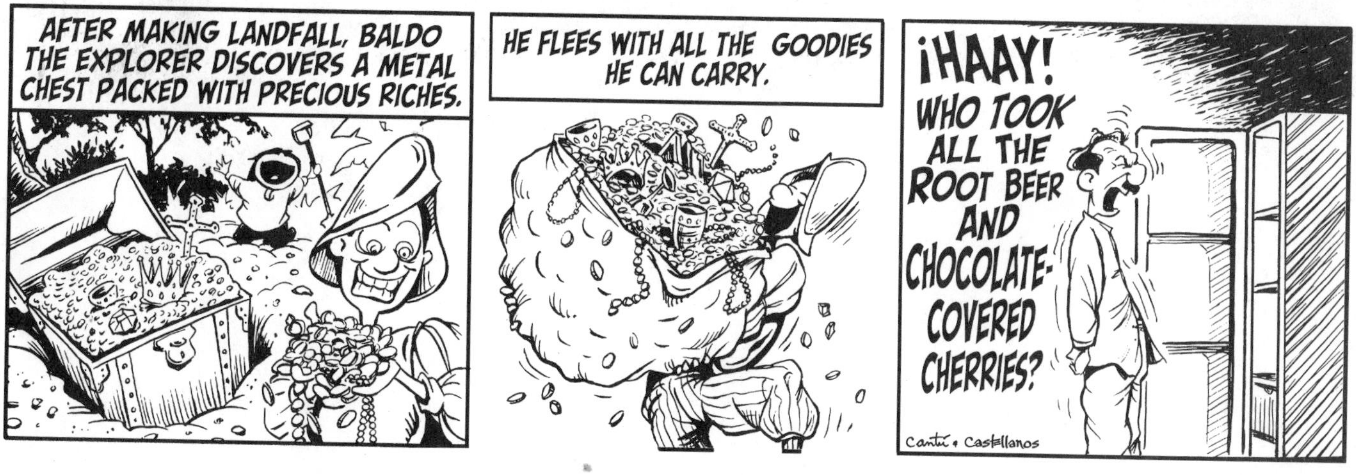
AFTER MAKING LANDFALL, BALDO THE EXPLORER DISCOVERS A METAL CHEST PACKED WITH PRECIOUS RICHES.
HE FLEES WITH ALL THE GOODIES HE CAN CARRY.
¡HAAY!
WHO TOOK ALL THE ROOT BEER AND CHOCOLATE-COVERED CHERRIES?
Cantú & Castellanos

BALDO, TIME FOR CHURCH!
YAWN!
STRETCH!
SWIP! SWIP!
I'M READY!
DAD **WAY OVER-REACTS** TO MY JOKES.

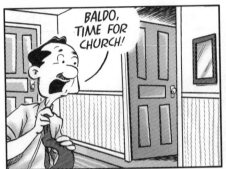

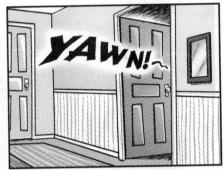

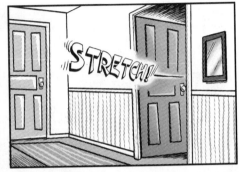

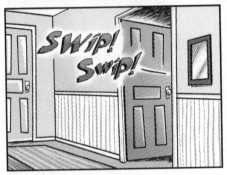

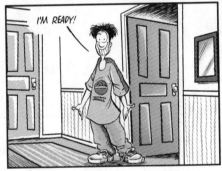

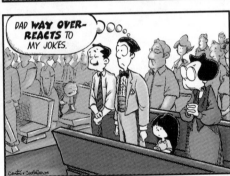

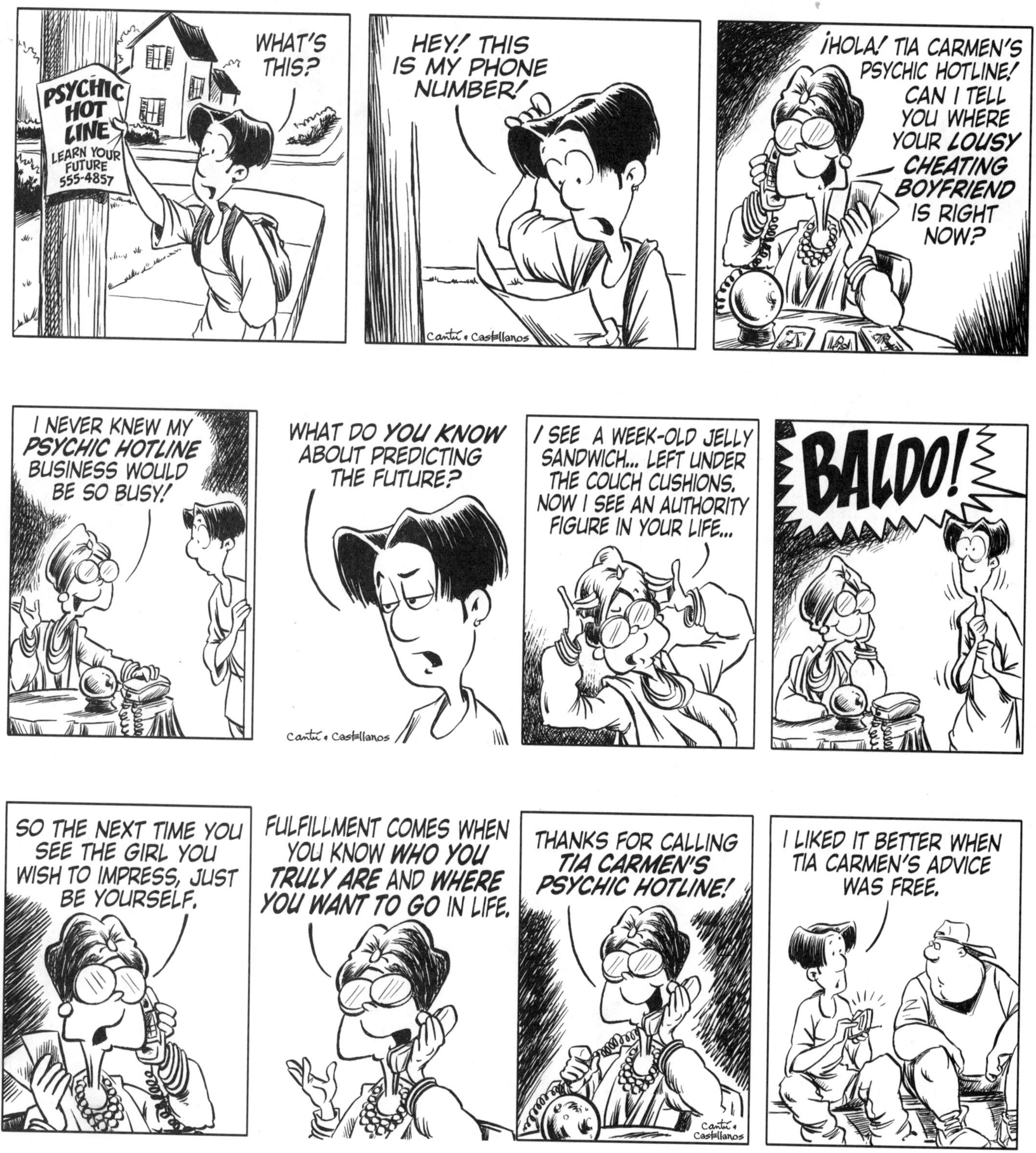
PSYCHIC HOT LINE
LEARN YOUR FUTURE 555-4857
WHAT'S THIS?
HEY! THIS IS MY PHONE NUMBER!
Cantú & Castellanos
¡HOLA! TIA CARMEN'S PSYCHIC HOTLINE! CAN I TELL YOU WHERE YOUR **LOUSY CHEATING BOYFRIEND** IS RIGHT NOW?
I NEVER KNEW MY **PSYCHIC HOTLINE** BUSINESS WOULD BE SO BUSY!
WHAT DO **YOU KNOW** ABOUT PREDICTING THE FUTURE?
Cantú & Castellanos
I SEE A WEEK-OLD JELLY SANDWICH... LEFT UNDER THE COUCH CUSHIONS. NOW I SEE AN AUTHORITY FIGURE IN YOUR LIFE...
BALDO!
SO THE NEXT TIME YOU SEE THE GIRL YOU WISH TO IMPRESS, JUST BE YOURSELF.
FULFILLMENT COMES WHEN YOU KNOW **WHO YOU TRULY ARE** AND **WHERE YOU WANT TO GO** IN LIFE.
THANKS FOR CALLING **TIA CARMEN'S PSYCHIC HOTLINE!**
Cantú & Castellanos
I LIKED IT BETTER WHEN TIA CARMEN'S ADVICE WAS FREE.

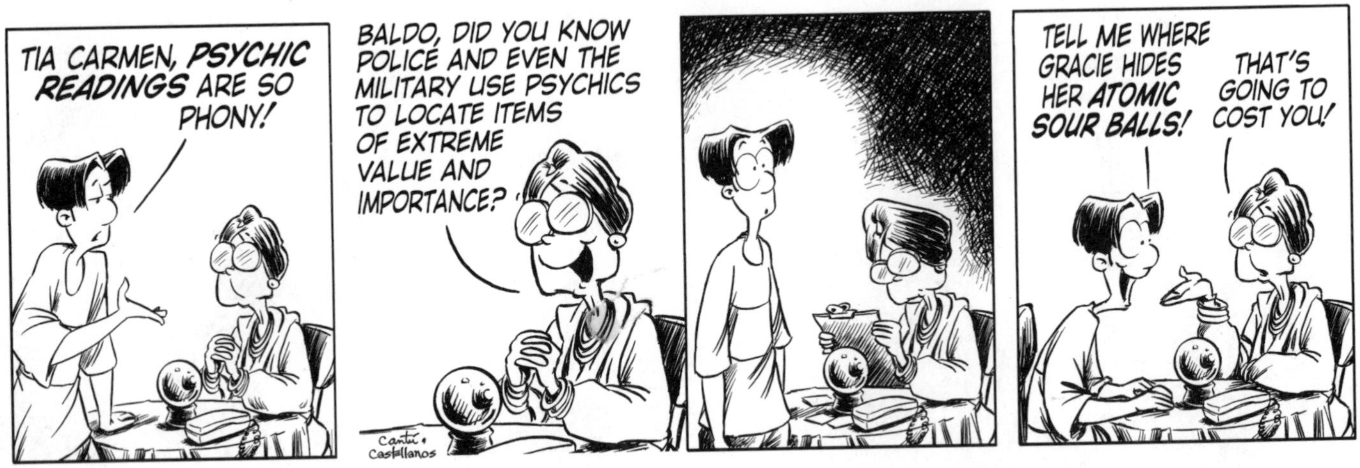
TIA CARMEN, PSYCHIC READINGS ARE SO PHONY!
BALDO, DID YOU KNOW POLICE AND EVEN THE MILITARY USE PSYCHICS TO LOCATE ITEMS OF EXTREME VALUE AND IMPORTANCE?
TELL ME WHERE GRACIE HIDES HER ATOMIC SOUR BALLS!
THAT'S GOING TO COST YOU!
Cantú & Castellanos

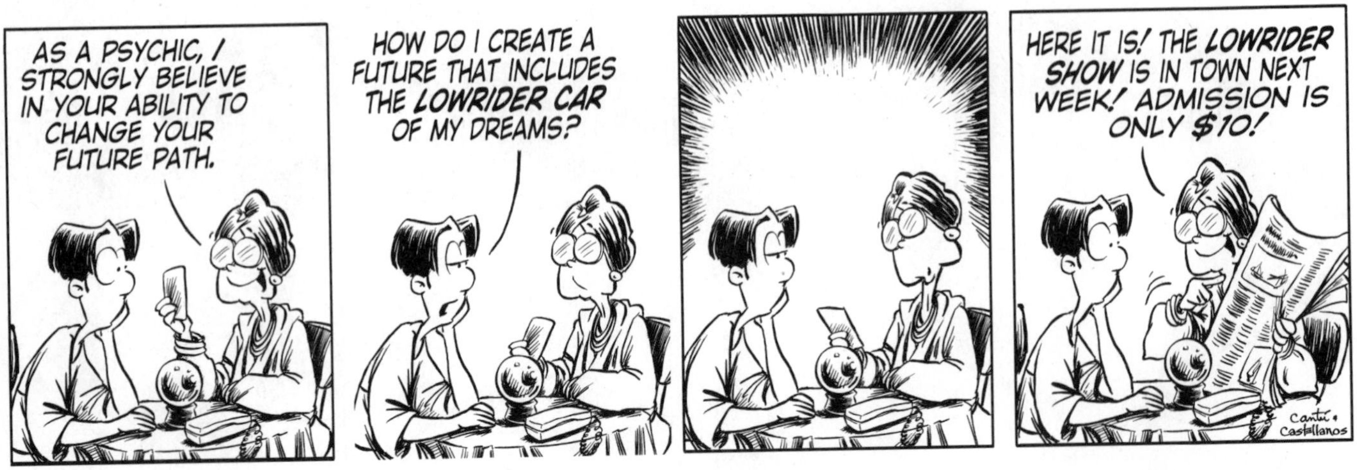
AS A PSYCHIC, I STRONGLY BELIEVE IN YOUR ABILITY TO CHANGE YOUR FUTURE PATH.
HOW DO I CREATE A FUTURE THAT INCLUDES THE LOWRIDER CAR OF MY DREAMS?
HERE IT IS! THE LOWRIDER SHOW IS IN TOWN NEXT WEEK! ADMISSION IS ONLY $10!
Cantú & Castellanos

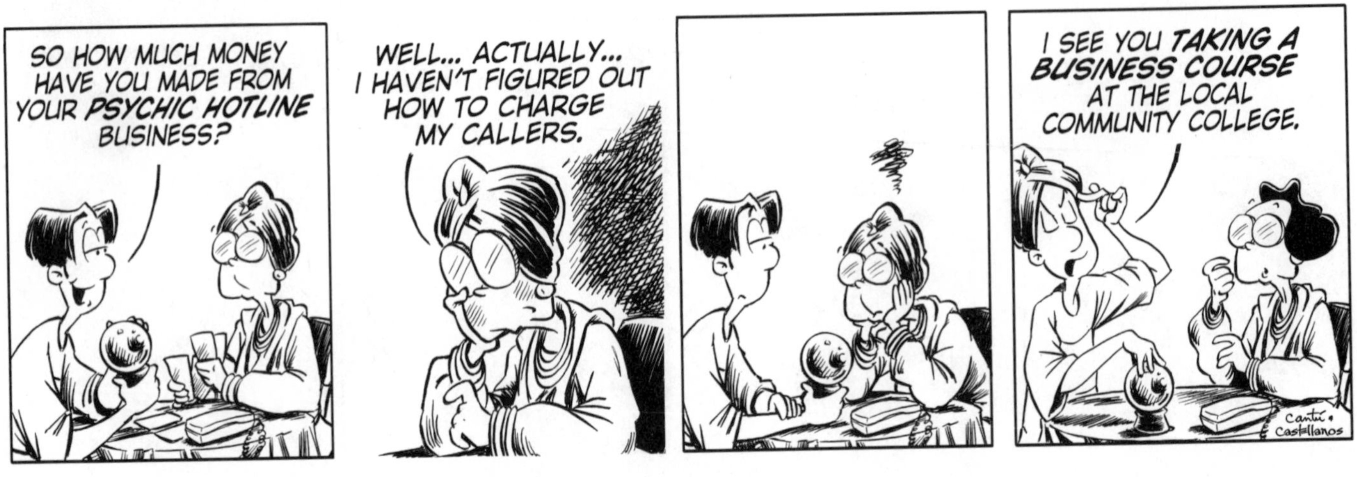
SO HOW MUCH MONEY HAVE YOU MADE FROM YOUR PSYCHIC HOTLINE BUSINESS?
WELL... ACTUALLY... I HAVEN'T FIGURED OUT HOW TO CHARGE MY CALLERS.
I SEE YOU TAKING A BUSINESS COURSE AT THE LOCAL COMMUNITY COLLEGE.
Cantú & Castellanos

THROUGH PAST LIFE REGRESSION, WE WILL DISCOVER YOUR PAST LIVES...
AND HOW TO INTEGRATE THEM WITH YOUR PRESENT LIFE'S PATH.
I SEE... THE WORD... KAN.
LADY KAN AL-IKAL WAS A HIGH RULER IN PRE-COLLUMBIAN AMERICA!
OFF MY THRONE, CHILD!
DAD! GRACIE'S BEING BOSSY AGAIN!

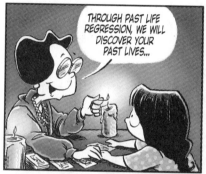

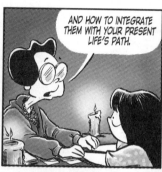

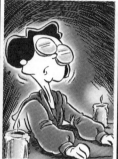

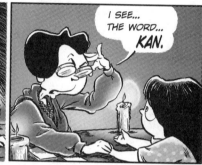

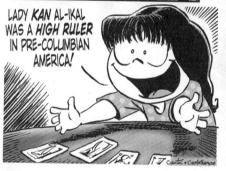

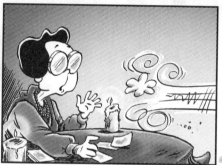

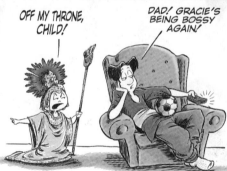

WE'LL RETURN TO OUR *"CHARLIE'S ANGELS"* MARATHON AFTER THESE MESSAGES.

LIVING ... IN ... THE ... 1970s ...

MUST ... HAVE ... BEEN ...

ZZZZZZZZZ

DYN-O-MITE!

Cantú • Castellanos

LOOK, BALDO! IT'S THE NEW *SANTANA* ALBUM.

C'MON, CRUZ, IT'S *1974!* SANTANA IS SO-O-O-O-O '60s!

ONLY PERFORMERS WHO *TOUCH THE SOUL* AND CONNECT ON A *MAGICAL LEVEL* BECOME LEGENDARY *POP ICONS* WHO *TRANSCEND TIME.*

Cantú • Castellanos

NOW LOOK AT *PAPER LACE.* I BET *THIS BAND* WILL BE CHURNING OUT HITS IN *25 YEARS!*

DAD! GRACIE BROKE MY *FLIP WILSON* LUNCH BOX!

HERE COMES THE JUDGE... HERE COMES THE JUDGE... HERE COMES THE JUDGE...

OK, WHAT SEEMS TO BE THE PROBLEM?

Cantú • Castellanos

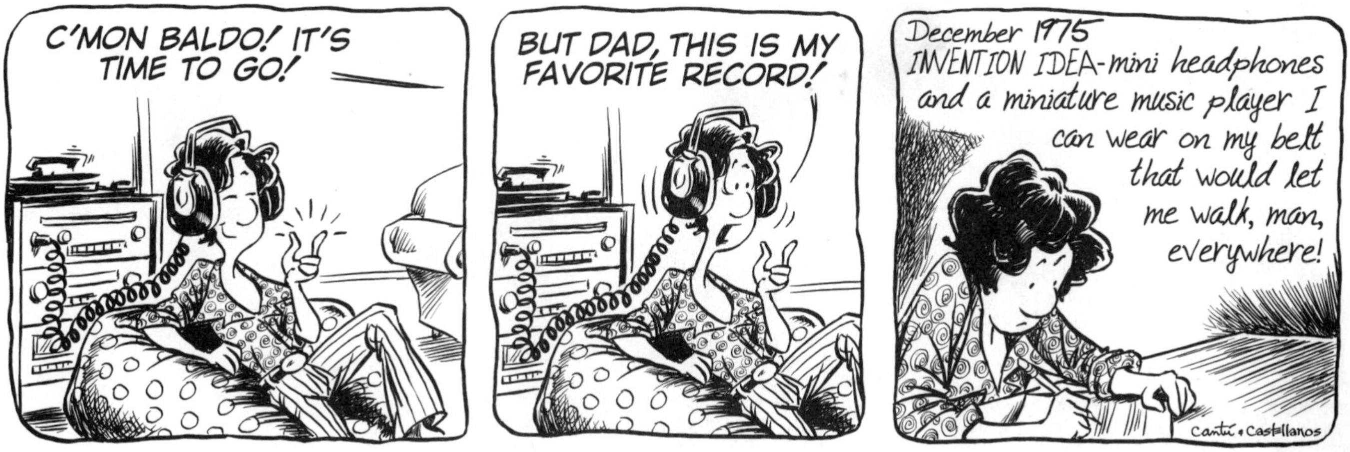
C'MON BALDO! IT'S TIME TO GO!
BUT DAD, THIS IS MY FAVORITE RECORD!
December 1975
INVENTION IDEA-mini headphones and a miniature music player I can wear on my belt that would let me walk, man, everywhere!
Cantú & Castellanos

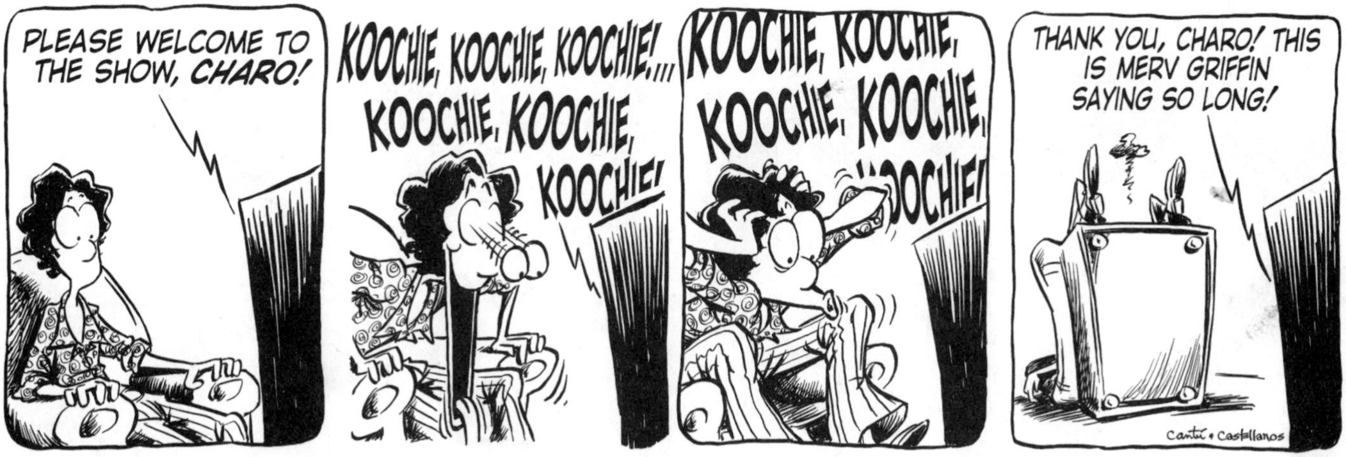
PLEASE WELCOME TO THE SHOW, CHARO!
KOOCHIE, KOOCHIE, KOOCHIE!,,,
KOOCHIE, KOOCHIE,
KOOCHIE!
KOOCHIE, KOOCHIE,
KOOCHIE, KOOCHIE,
THANK YOU, CHARO! THIS IS MERV GRIFFIN SAYING SO LONG!
Cantú & Castellanos

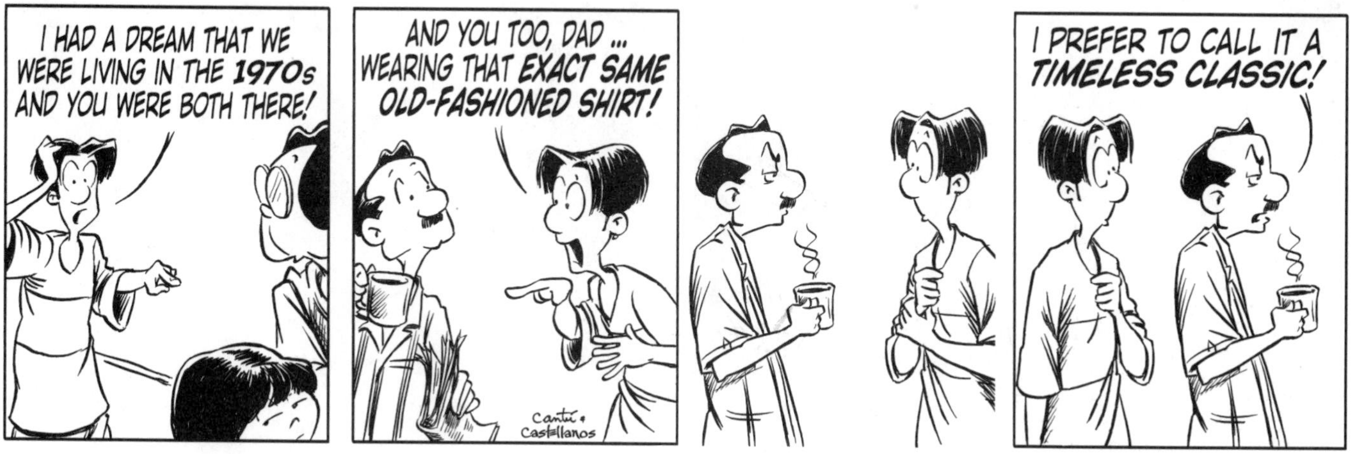
I HAD A DREAM THAT WE WERE LIVING IN THE 1970s AND YOU WERE BOTH THERE!
AND YOU TOO, DAD ... WEARING THAT EXACT SAME OLD-FASHIONED SHIRT!
Cantú & Castellanos
I PREFER TO CALL IT A TIMELESS CLASSIC!

TULI'S TATTOO UNIVERSE
OPEN
WHAT'S THAT ONE?
THAT'S A BOLTED SUN.
IS THAT A JAGUAR?
IT'S A BLACK TIGER.
THAT ONE LOOKS COOL!
THAT'S A FLAMING SKULL AND CROSSBONES.
OK. THANKS. BYE.
WHEN IT COMES TO LIVING WILD, YOU'RE ONLY A WINDOW SHOPPER.

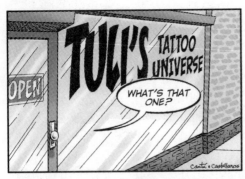

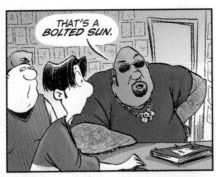

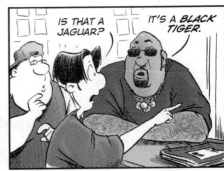

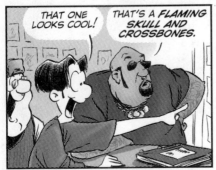

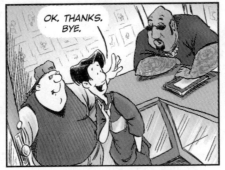

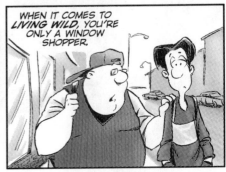

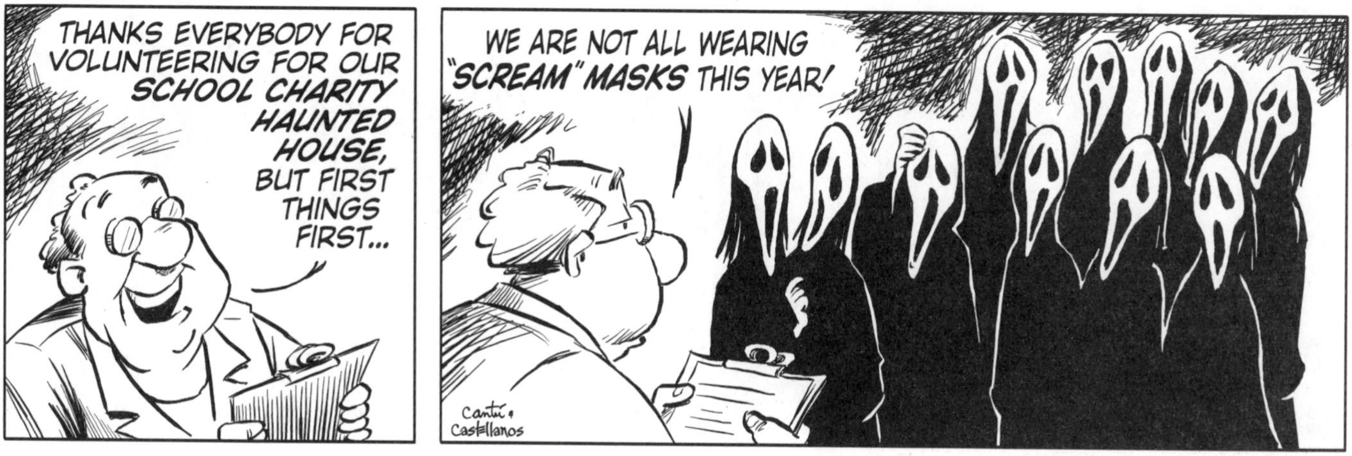
THANKS EVERYBODY FOR VOLUNTEERING FOR OUR SCHOOL CHARITY HAUNTED HOUSE, BUT FIRST THINGS FIRST...
WE ARE NOT ALL WEARING "SCREAM" MASKS THIS YEAR!
Cantú & Castellanos

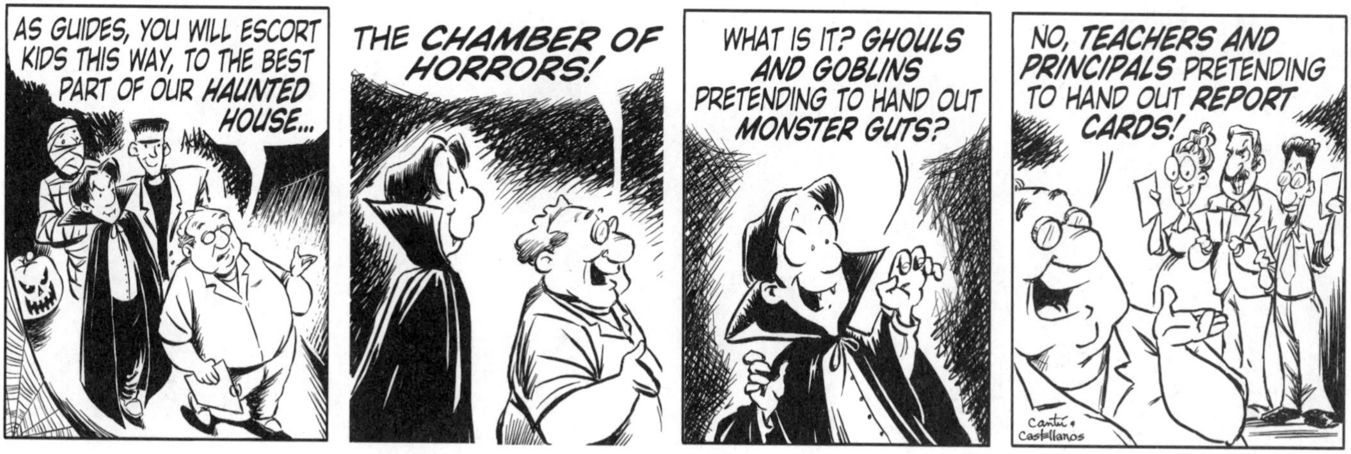
AS GUIDES, YOU WILL ESCORT KIDS THIS WAY, TO THE BEST PART OF OUR HAUNTED HOUSE...
THE CHAMBER OF HORRORS!
WHAT IS IT? GHOULS AND GOBLINS PRETENDING TO HAND OUT MONSTER GUTS?
NO, TEACHERS AND PRINCIPALS PRETENDING TO HAND OUT REPORT CARDS!
Cantú & Castellanos

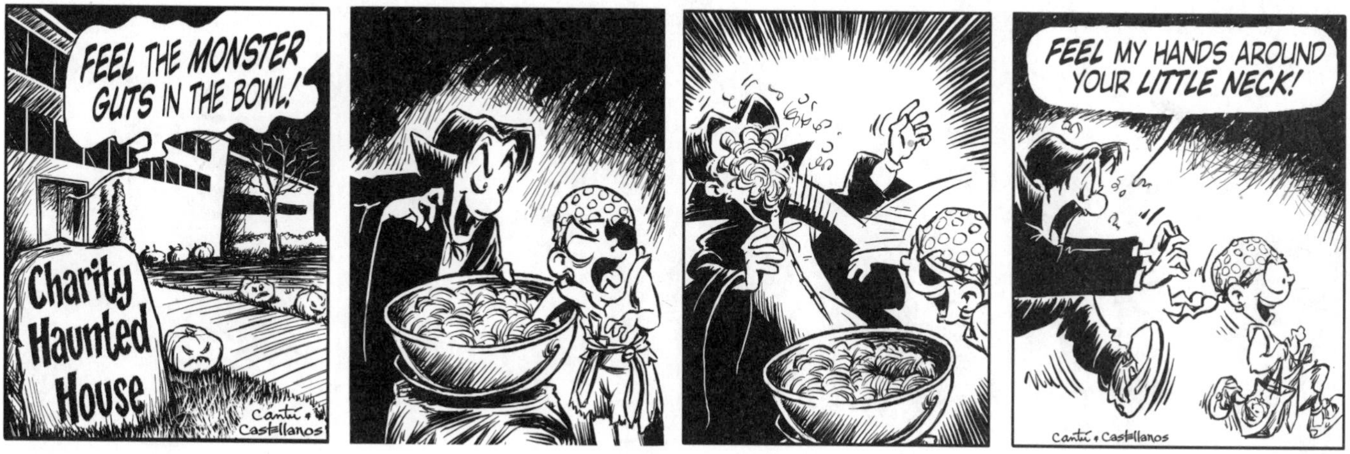
FEEL THE MONSTER GUTS IN THE BOWL!
Charity Haunted House
Cantú & Castellanos
FEEL MY HANDS AROUND YOUR LITTLE NECK!
Cantú & Castellanos

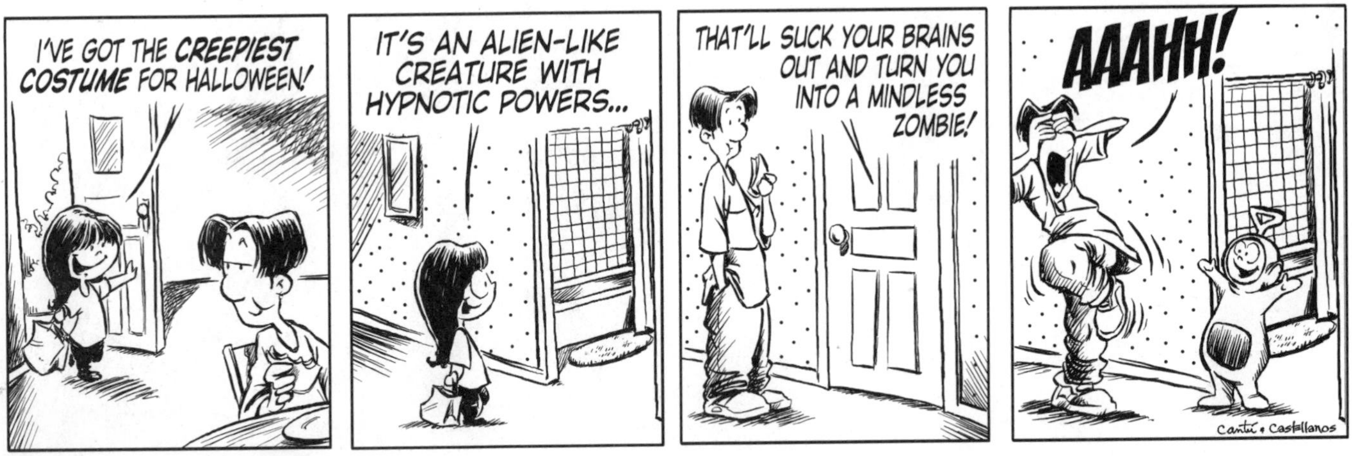
I'VE GOT THE **CREEPIEST COSTUME** FOR HALLOWEEN!
IT'S AN ALIEN-LIKE CREATURE WITH HYPNOTIC POWERS...
THAT'LL SUCK YOUR BRAINS OUT AND TURN YOU INTO A MINDLESS ZOMBIE!
AAAHH!
Cantú & Castellanos

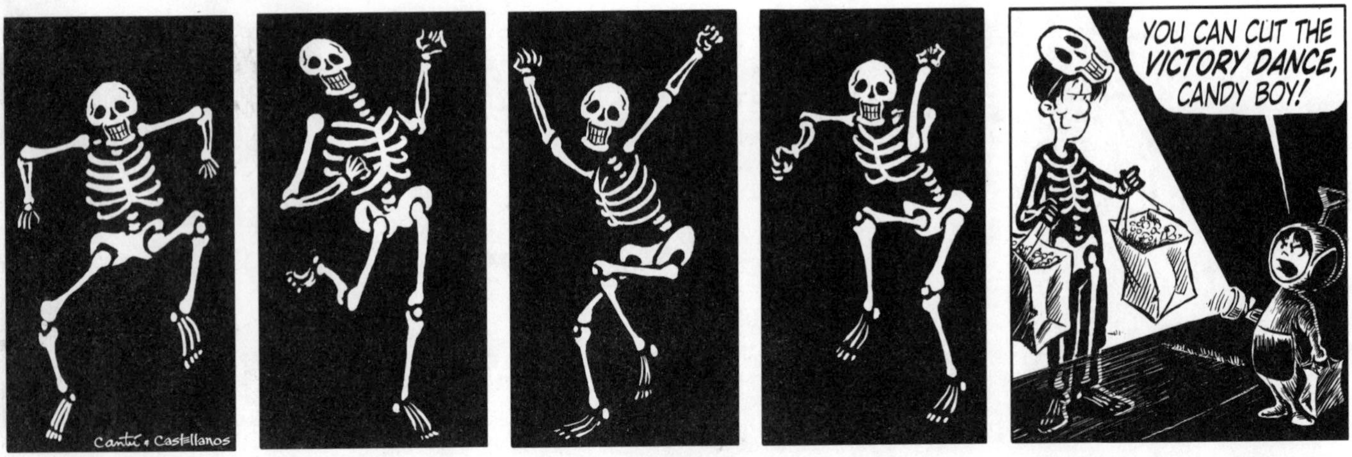
Cantú & Castellanos
YOU CAN CUT THE **VICTORY DANCE,** CANDY BOY!

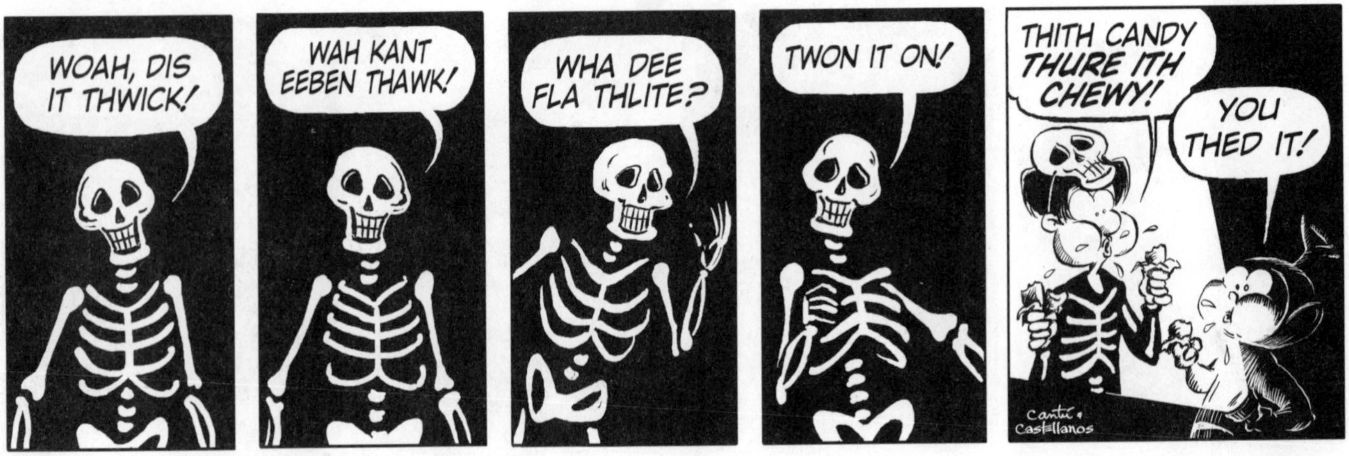
WOAH, DIS IT THWICK!
WAH KANT EEBEN THAWK!
WHA DEE FLA THLITE?
TWON IT ON!
THITH CANDY **THURE ITH CHEWY!**
YOU THED IT!
Cantú & Castellanos

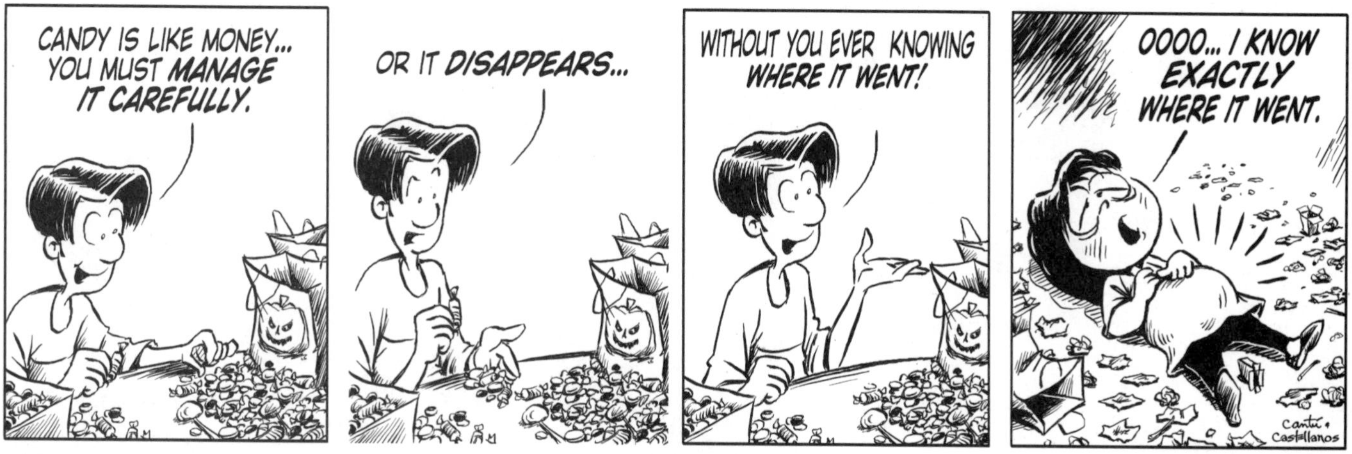
CANDY IS LIKE MONEY... YOU MUST MANAGE IT CAREFULLY.
OR IT DISAPPEARS...
WITHOUT YOU EVER KNOWING WHERE IT WENT!
OOOO... I KNOW EXACTLY WHERE IT WENT.
Cantú & Castellanos

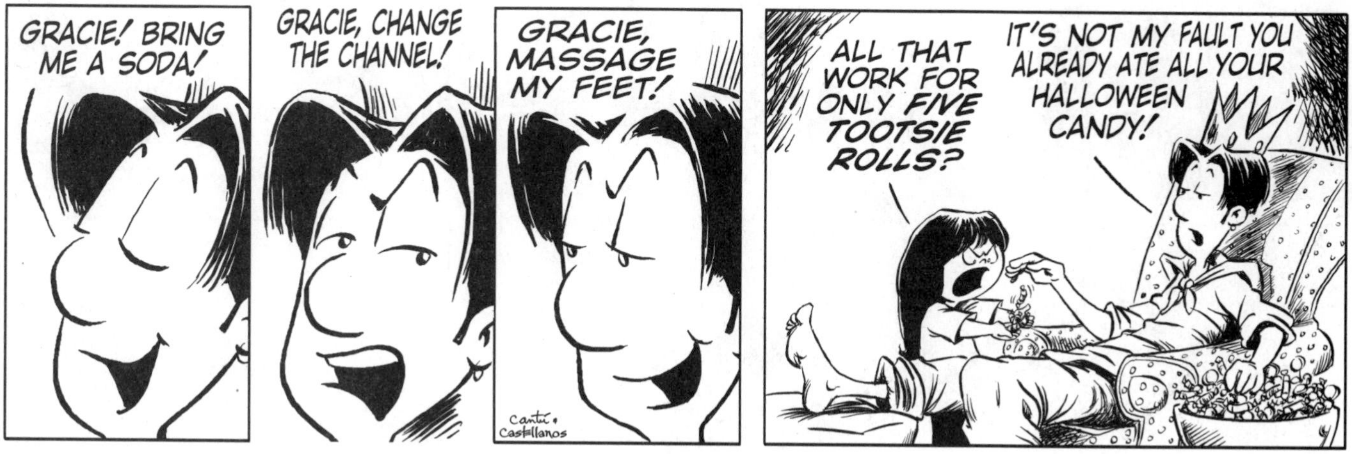
GRACIE! BRING ME A SODA!
GRACIE, CHANGE THE CHANNEL!
GRACIE, MASSAGE MY FEET!
Cantú & Castellanos
ALL THAT WORK FOR ONLY FIVE TOOTSIE ROLLS?
IT'S NOT MY FAULT YOU ALREADY ATE ALL YOUR HALLOWEEN CANDY!

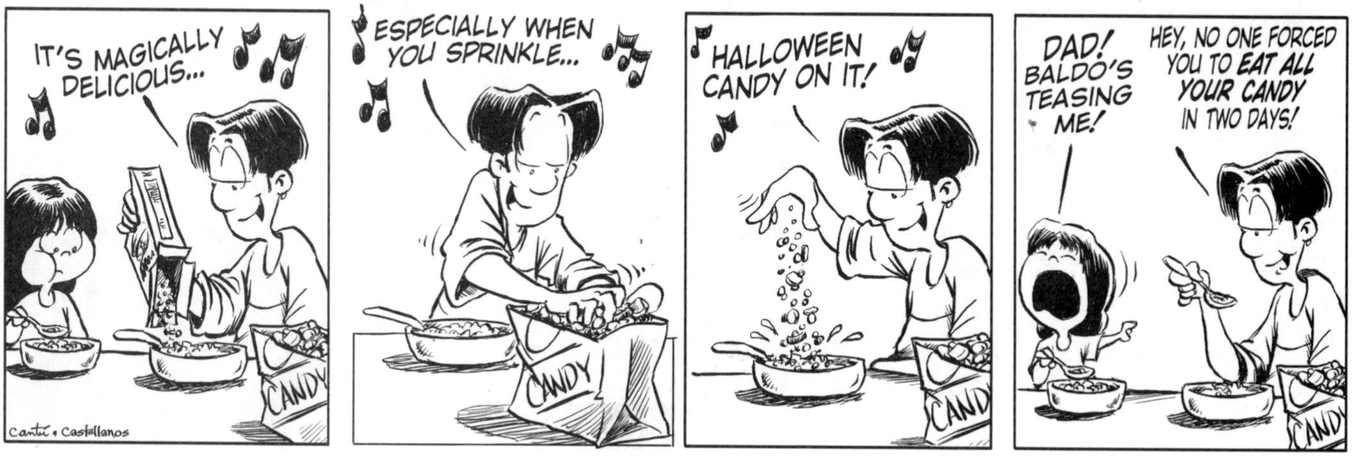
IT'S MAGICALLY DELICIOUS...
Cantú & Castellanos
ESPECIALLY WHEN YOU SPRINKLE...
CANDY
HALLOWEEN CANDY ON IT!
DAD! BALDO'S TEASING ME!
HEY, NO ONE FORCED YOU TO EAT ALL YOUR CANDY IN TWO DAYS!

YES, DOCTOR, BALDO IS REALLY NOT FEELING WELL.
HIS STOMACH HURTS AND HE'S COUGHING.
SOUNDS LIKE HE NEEDS A LITTLE CHAMOMILE TEA.
HE'S FUSSY AND RESTLESS...
CHAMOMILE IS A GOOD HARMONIZING HERB.
AND HE HAS A SLIGHT FEVER.
I'LL PREPARE A HOT, STRONG CUP OF CHAMOMILE TEA WITH A LITTLE LINDEN AND ELDER FLOWERS.
TIA CARMEN, PLEASE, I CAN'T HEAR THE DOCTOR!
Cantú & Castellanos
HAVE YOU HEARD OF CHAMOMILE?

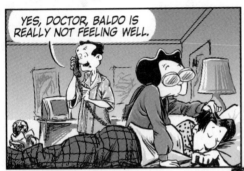

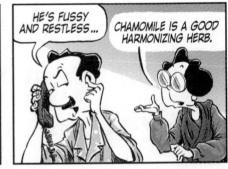

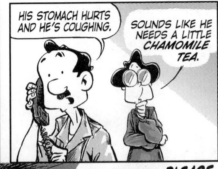

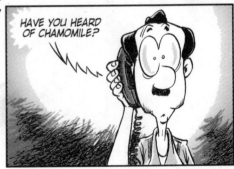

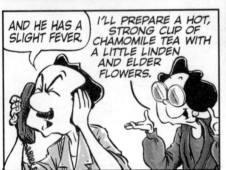

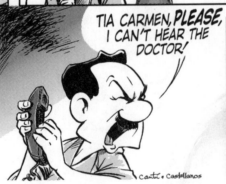

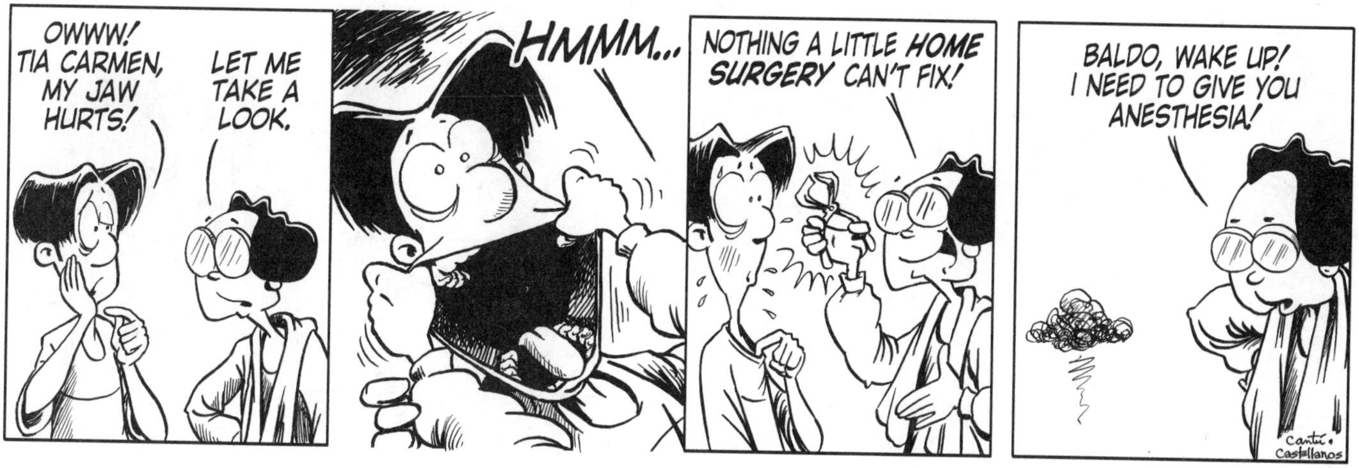
OWWW! TIA CARMEN, MY JAW HURTS!
LET ME TAKE A LOOK.
HMMM...
NOTHING A LITTLE **HOME SURGERY** CAN'T FIX!
BALDO, WAKE UP! I NEED TO GIVE YOU ANESTHESIA!

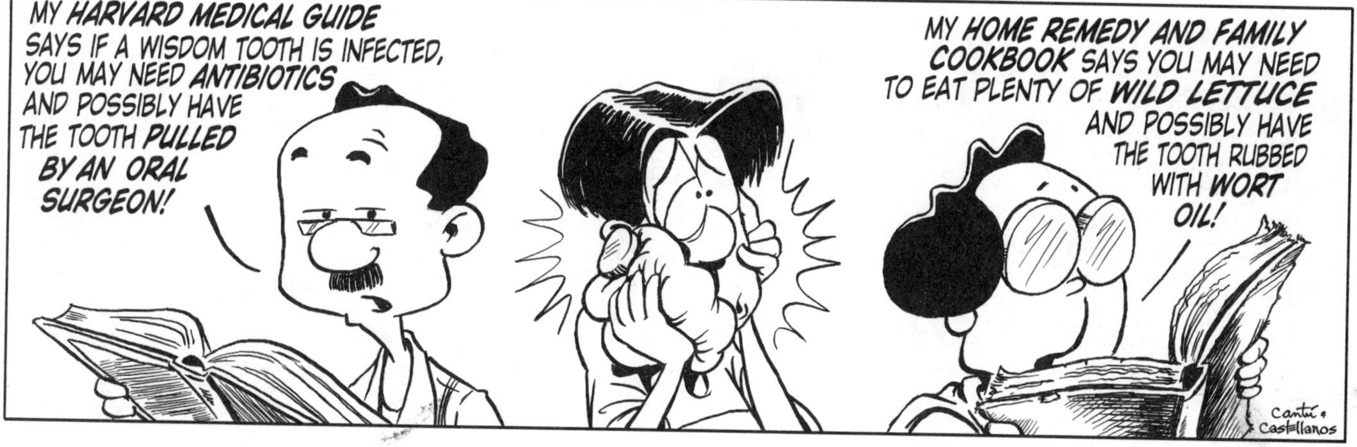
MY **HARVARD MEDICAL GUIDE** SAYS IF A WISDOM TOOTH IS INFECTED, YOU MAY NEED **ANTIBIOTICS** AND POSSIBLY HAVE THE TOOTH **PULLED BY AN ORAL SURGEON!**
MY **HOME REMEDY AND FAMILY COOKBOOK** SAYS YOU MAY NEED TO EAT PLENTY OF **WILD LETTUCE** AND POSSIBLY HAVE THE TOOTH RUBBED WITH **WORT OIL!**

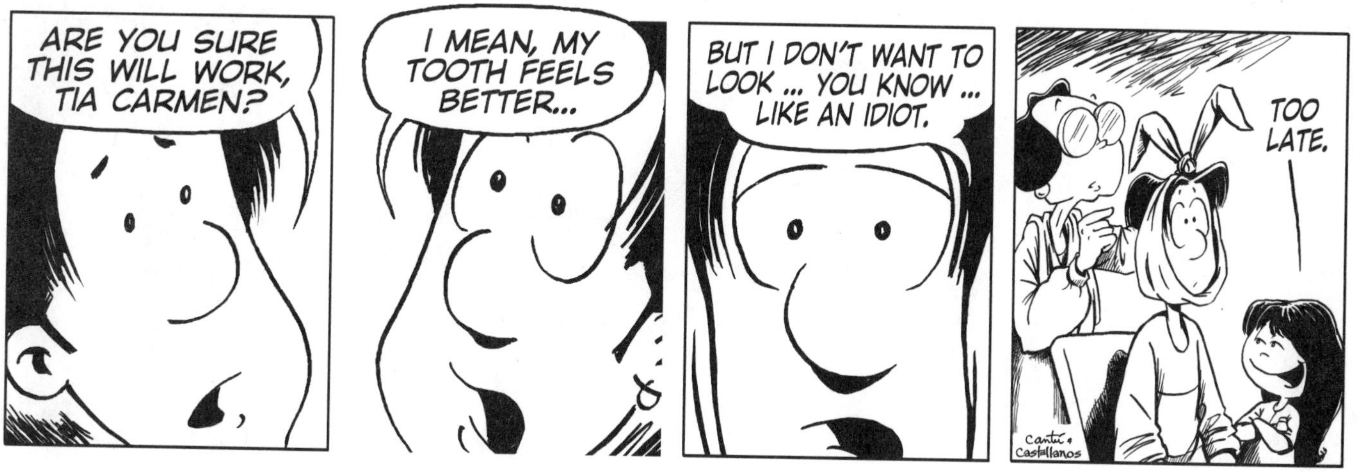
ARE YOU SURE THIS WILL WORK, TIA CARMEN?
I MEAN, MY TOOTH FEELS BETTER...
BUT I DON'T WANT TO LOOK ... YOU KNOW ... LIKE AN IDIOT.
TOO LATE.

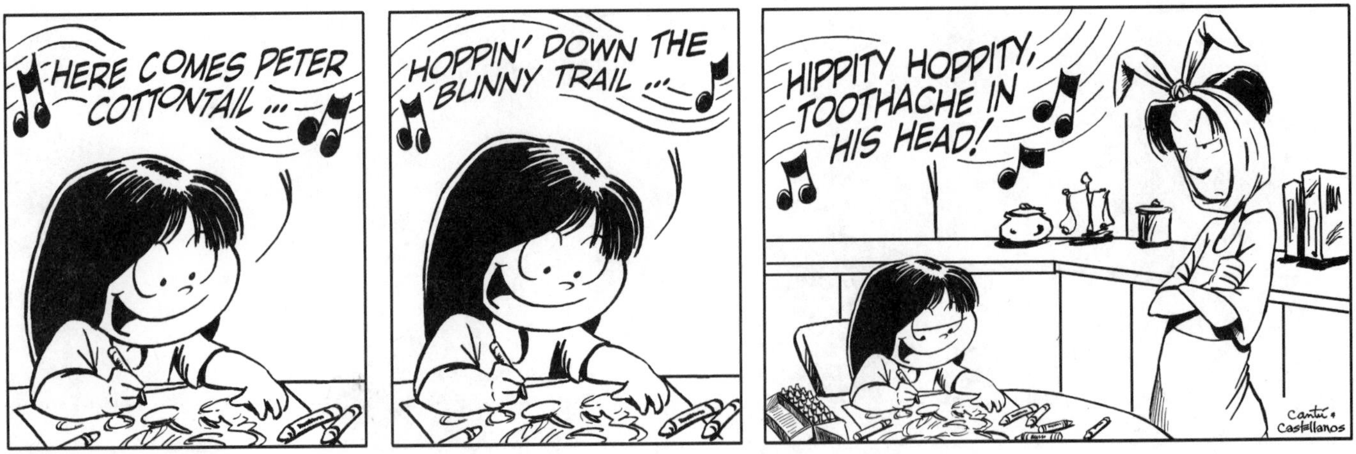
HERE COMES PETER COTTONTAIL ...
HOPPIN' DOWN THE BUNNY TRAIL ...
HIPPITY HOPPITY, TOOTHACHE IN HIS HEAD!

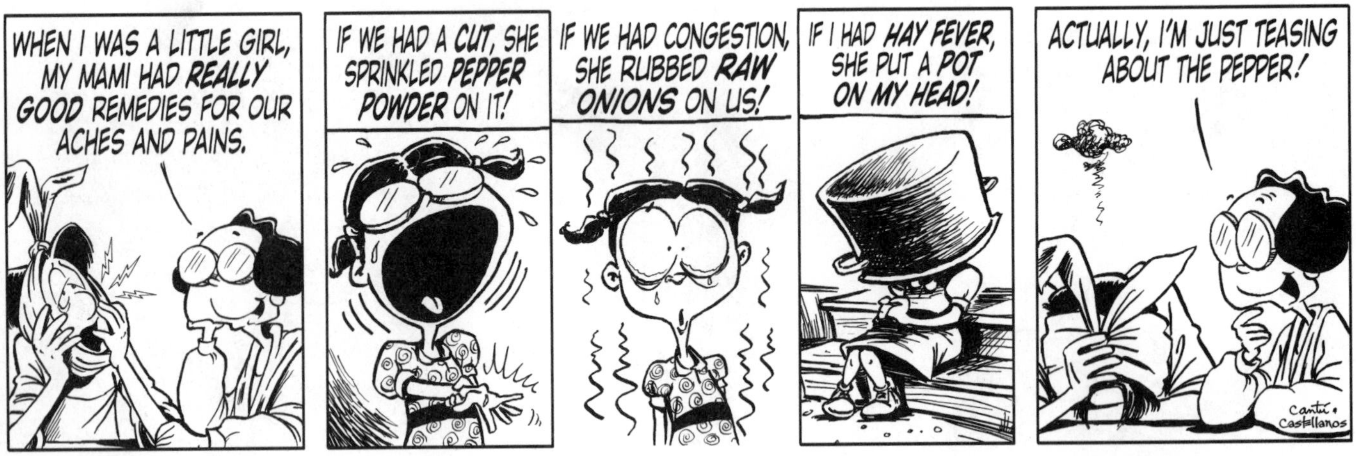
WHEN I WAS A LITTLE GIRL, MY MAMI HAD REALLY GOOD REMEDIES FOR OUR ACHES AND PAINS.
IF WE HAD A CUT, SHE SPRINKLED PEPPER POWDER ON IT!
IF WE HAD CONGESTION, SHE RUBBED RAW ONIONS ON US!
IF I HAD HAY FEVER, SHE PUT A POT ON MY HEAD!
ACTUALLY, I'M JUST TEASING ABOUT THE PEPPER!

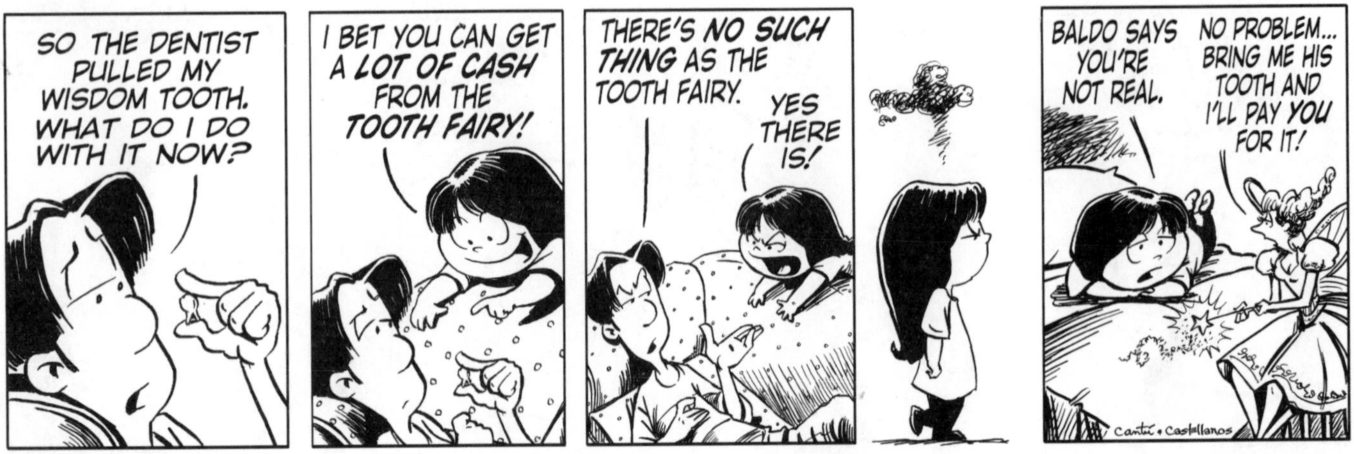
SO THE DENTIST PULLED MY WISDOM TOOTH. WHAT DO I DO WITH IT NOW?
I BET YOU CAN GET A LOT OF CASH FROM THE TOOTH FAIRY!
THERE'S NO SUCH THING AS THE TOOTH FAIRY.
YES THERE IS!
BALDO SAYS YOU'RE NOT REAL.
NO PROBLEM... BRING ME HIS TOOTH AND I'LL PAY YOU FOR IT!

CRUZ, LOOK! RALPHIE SOLD ME PART OF THE OLD HYDRAULIC SYSTEM OFF HIS LOWRIDER CAR!
YOU PUT IT ON YOUR BIKE?
YEAH! I JUST FLIP THE SWITCH...
RRMMMMBLL!!
FWIP
BOING!
I'VE NEVER SEEN A LOWRIDER BIKE FLY SO HIGH.

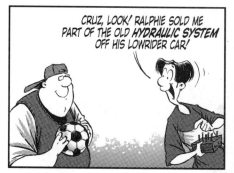

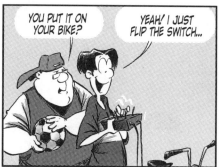

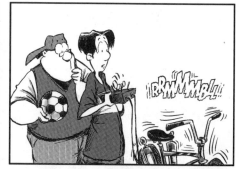

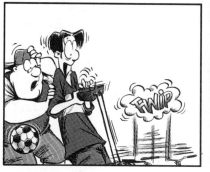

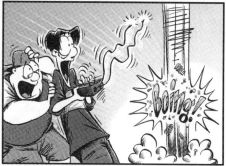

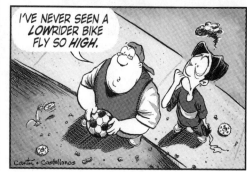

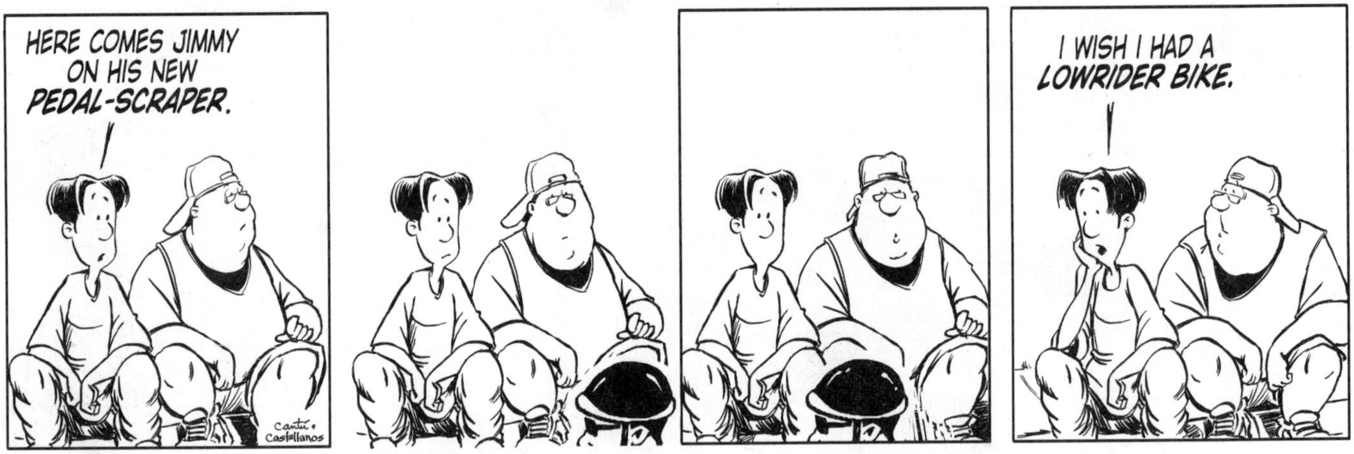
HERE COMES JIMMY ON HIS NEW PEDAL-SCRAPER.
I WISH I HAD A LOWRIDER BIKE.

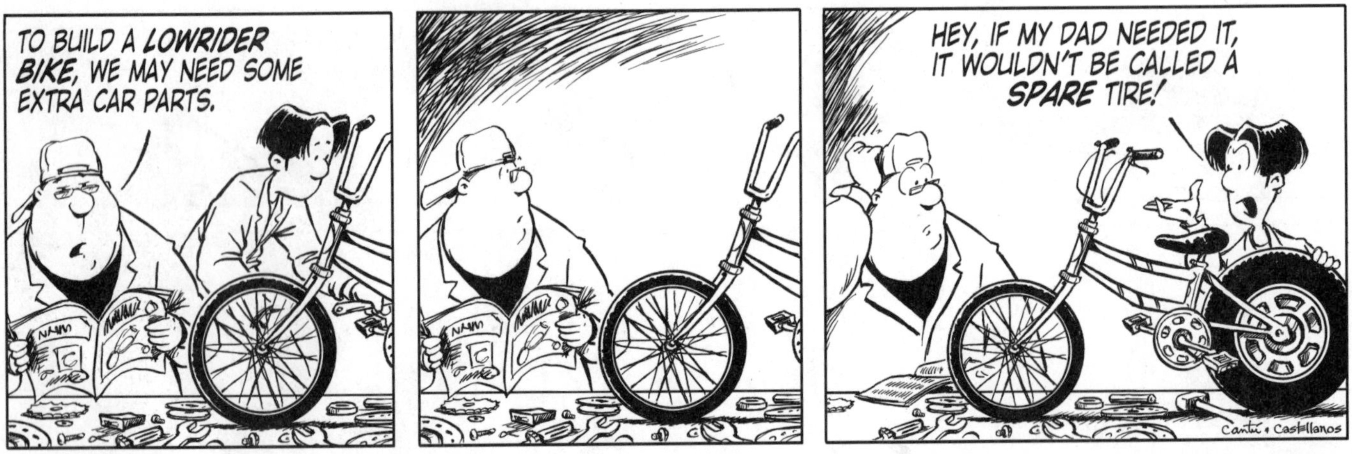
TO BUILD A LOWRIDER BIKE, WE MAY NEED SOME EXTRA CAR PARTS.
HEY, IF MY DAD NEEDED IT, IT WOULDN'T BE CALLED A SPARE TIRE!

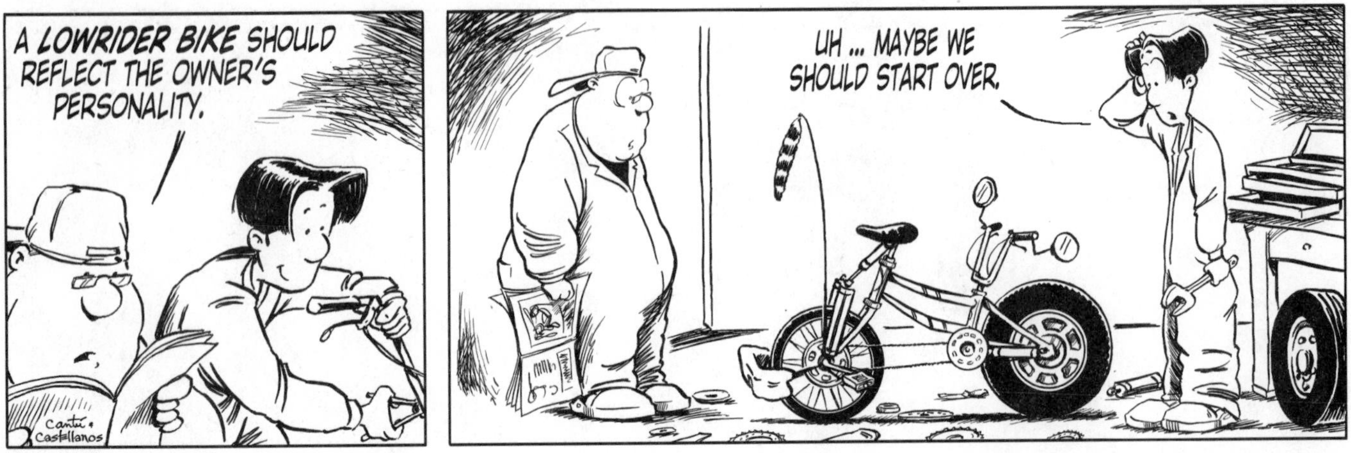
A LOWRIDER BIKE SHOULD REFLECT THE OWNER'S PERSONALITY.
UH ... MAYBE WE SHOULD START OVER.

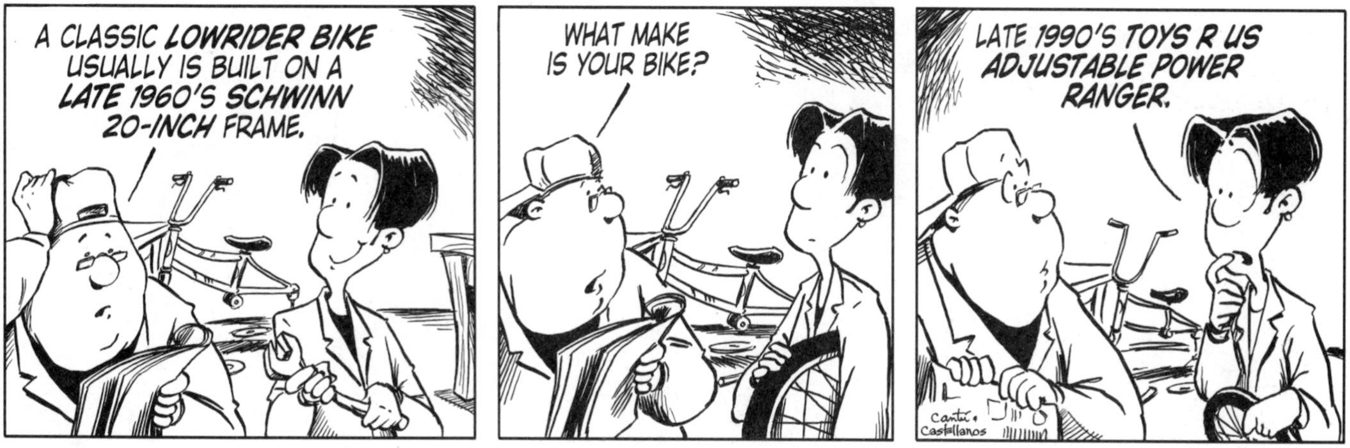
A CLASSIC LOWRIDER BIKE USUALLY IS BUILT ON A LATE 1960'S SCHWINN 20-INCH FRAME.
WHAT MAKE IS YOUR BIKE?
LATE 1990'S TOYS R US ADJUSTABLE POWER RANGER.
Cantú • Castellanos

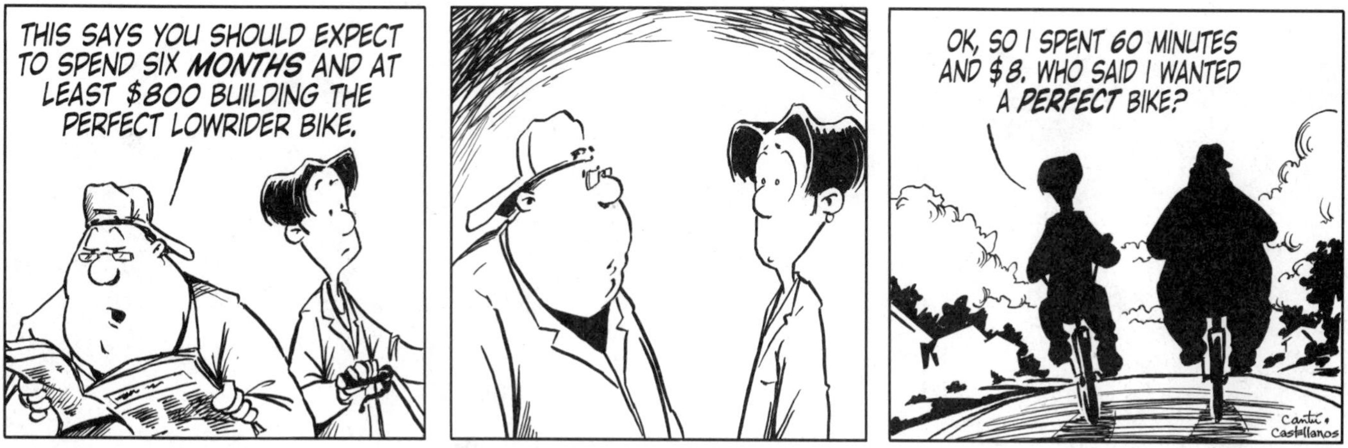
THIS SAYS YOU SHOULD EXPECT TO SPEND SIX MONTHS AND AT LEAST $800 BUILDING THE PERFECT LOWRIDER BIKE.
OK, SO I SPENT 60 MINUTES AND $8. WHO SAID I WANTED A PERFECT BIKE?
Cantú • Castellanos

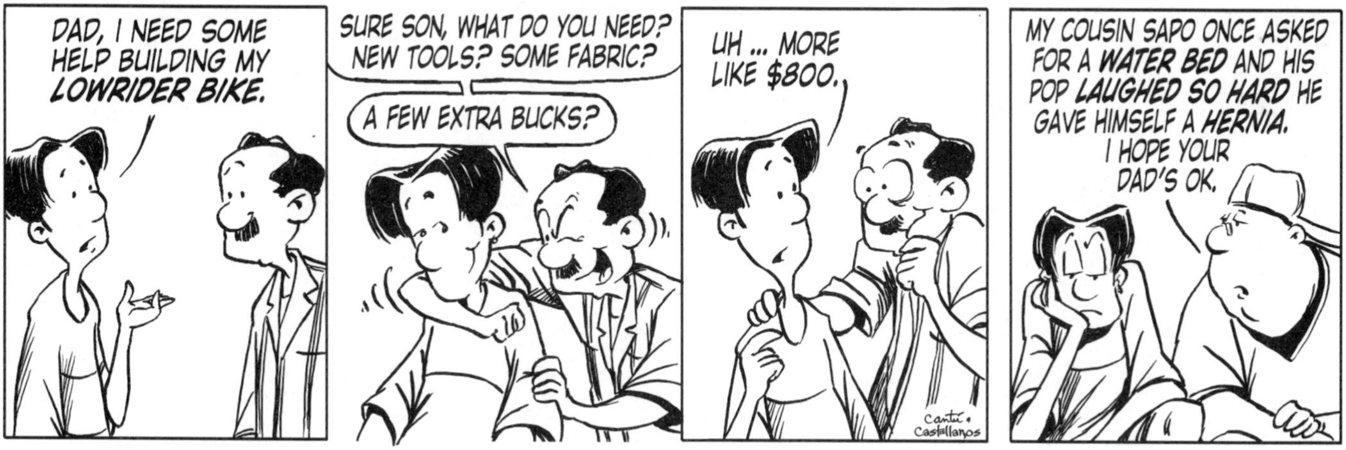
DAD, I NEED SOME HELP BUILDING MY LOWRIDER BIKE.
SURE SON, WHAT DO YOU NEED? NEW TOOLS? SOME FABRIC?
A FEW EXTRA BUCKS?
UH ... MORE LIKE $800.
Cantú • Castellanos
MY COUSIN SAPO ONCE ASKED FOR A WATER BED AND HIS POP LAUGHED SO HARD HE GAVE HIMSELF A HERNIA.
I HOPE YOUR DAD'S OK.

I NEED A BETTER SET OF WHEELS
I MEAN, I GUESS IT'S OK...
IT GETS ME WHERE I NEED TO GO...
AND IT'S LOW MAINTENANCE.
BUT MY BIKE JUST DOESN'T COMPARE TO A '64 IMPALA CONVERTIBLE!

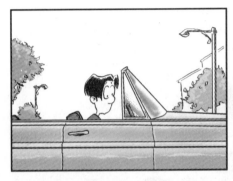

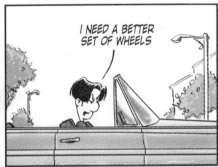

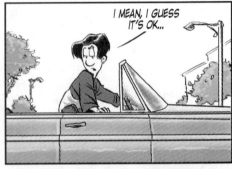

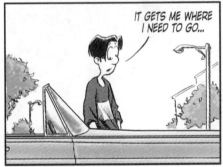

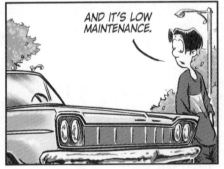

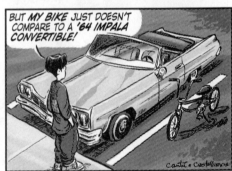

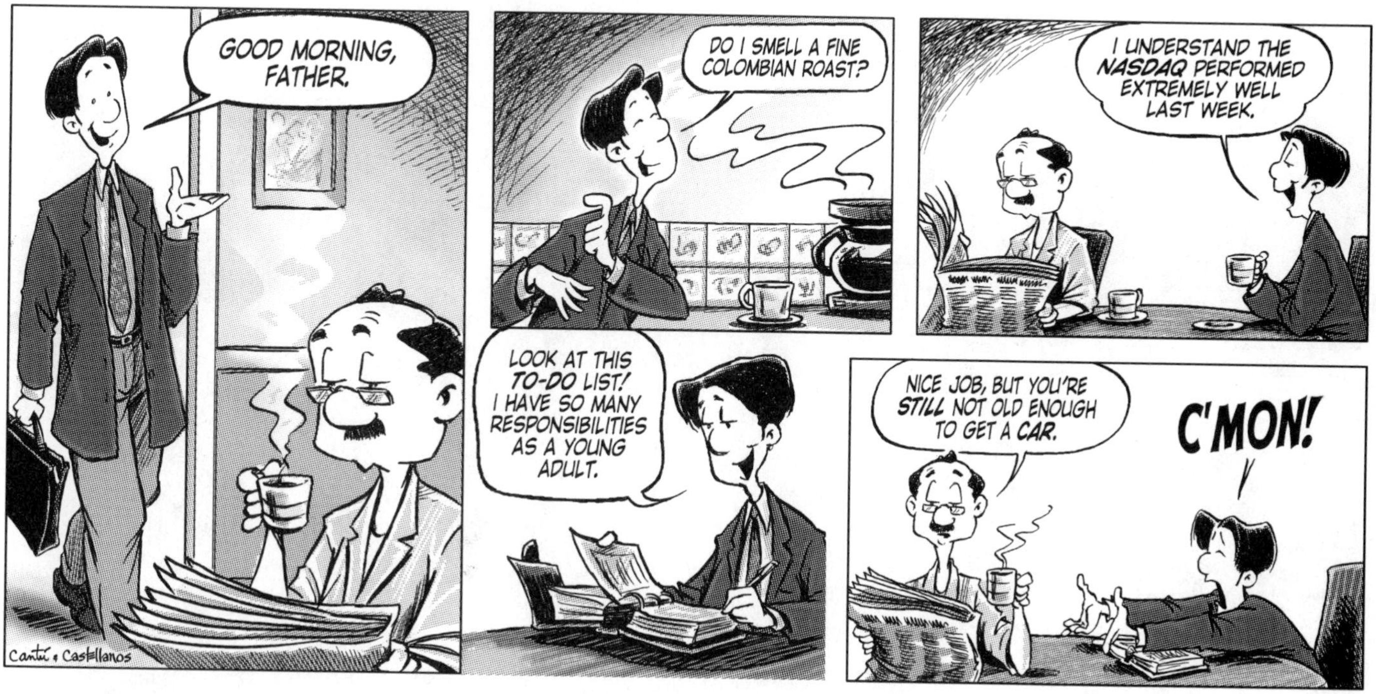
GOOD MORNING, FATHER.
DO I SMELL A FINE COLOMBIAN ROAST?
I UNDERSTAND THE NASDAQ PERFORMED EXTREMELY WELL LAST WEEK.
LOOK AT THIS TO-DO LIST! I HAVE SO MANY RESPONSIBILITIES AS A YOUNG ADULT.
NICE JOB, BUT YOU'RE STILL NOT OLD ENOUGH TO GET A CAR.
C'MON!
Cantú & Castellanos

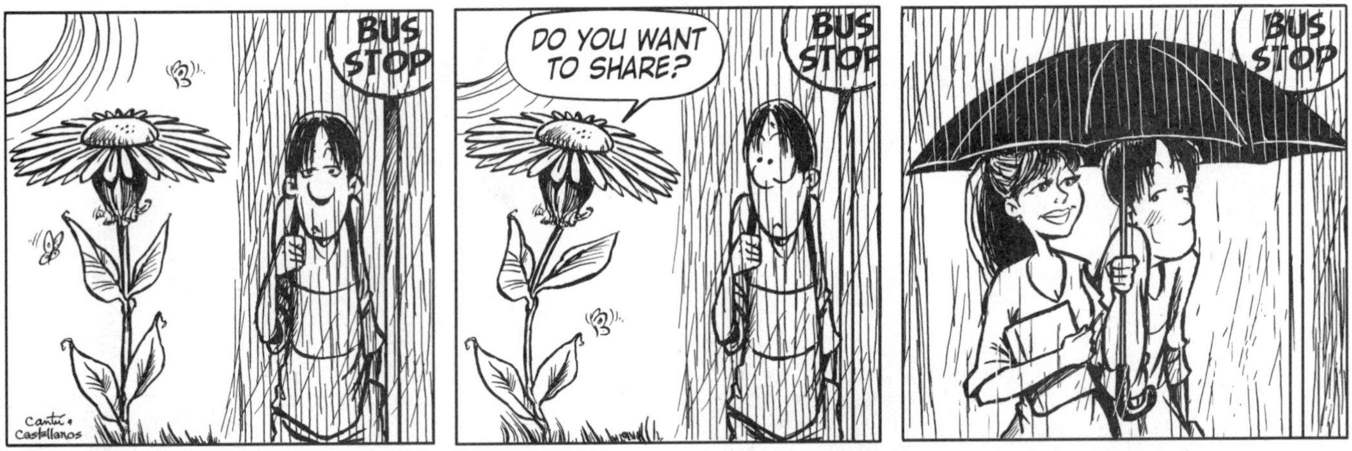
BUS STOP
DO YOU WANT TO SHARE?
BUS STOP
BUS STOP

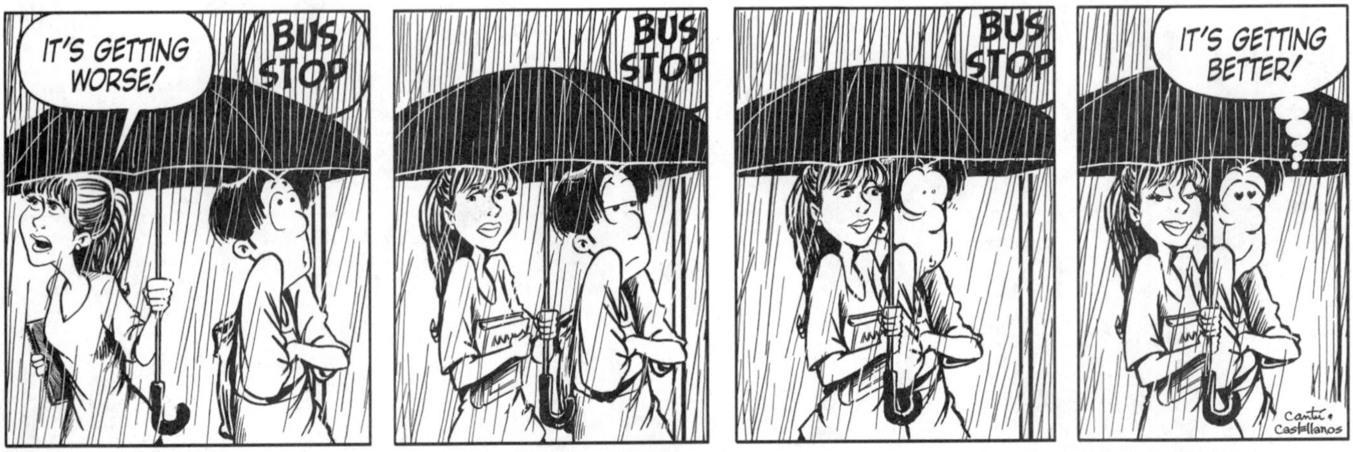
IT'S GETTING WORSE!
BUS STOP
BUS STOP
BUS STOP
IT'S GETTING BETTER!

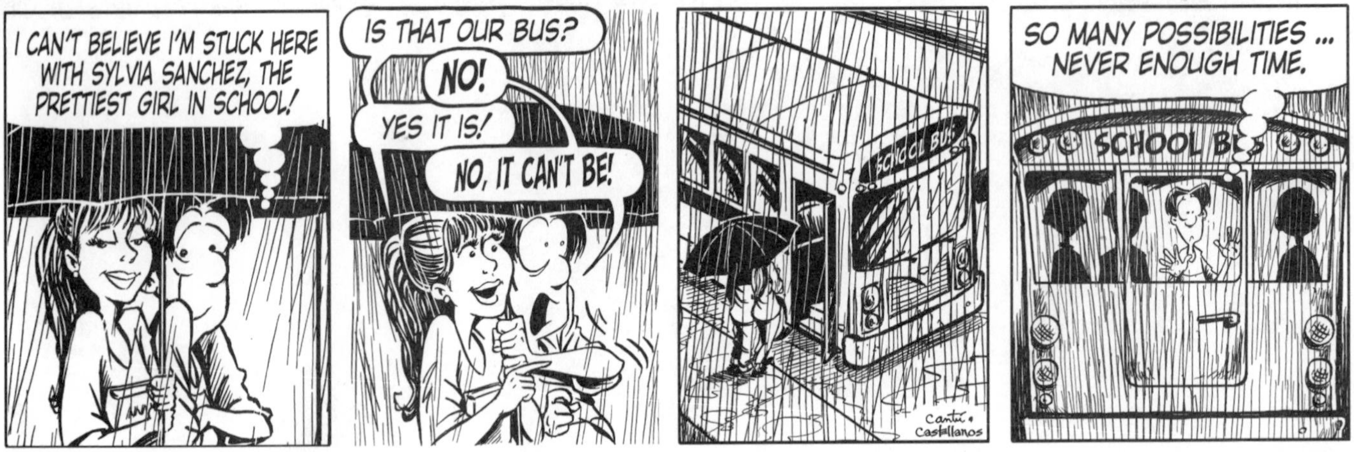
I CAN'T BELIEVE I'M STUCK HERE WITH SYLVIA SANCHEZ, THE PRETTIEST GIRL IN SCHOOL!
IS THAT OUR BUS?
NO!
YES IT IS!
NO, IT CAN'T BE!
SO MANY POSSIBILITIES ... NEVER ENOUGH TIME.
SCHOOL BUS

I HATE LIFE-CHANGING DECISIONS!
I MEAN, ONE CHOICE REPRESENTS FAMILIARITY, SOMETHING I'M COMFORTABLE WITH.
THE OTHER MEANS CHANGE. IT MAY TAKE A WHILE, BUT I'M SURE I'LL GET USED TO IT.
WHATEVER I DO, IT'S TIME TO MAKE A DECISION...
AND STICK WITH IT!
MEN'S DEPT.
SO IS IT BOXERS OR BRIEFS?
DON'T RUSH ME!

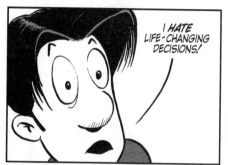

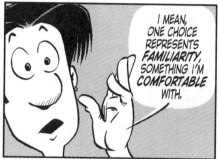

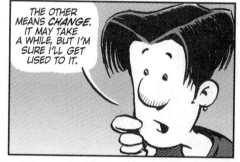

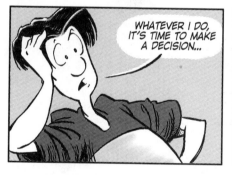

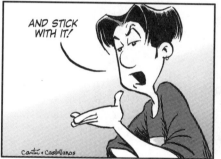

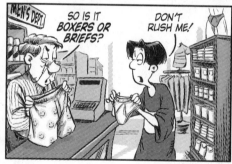

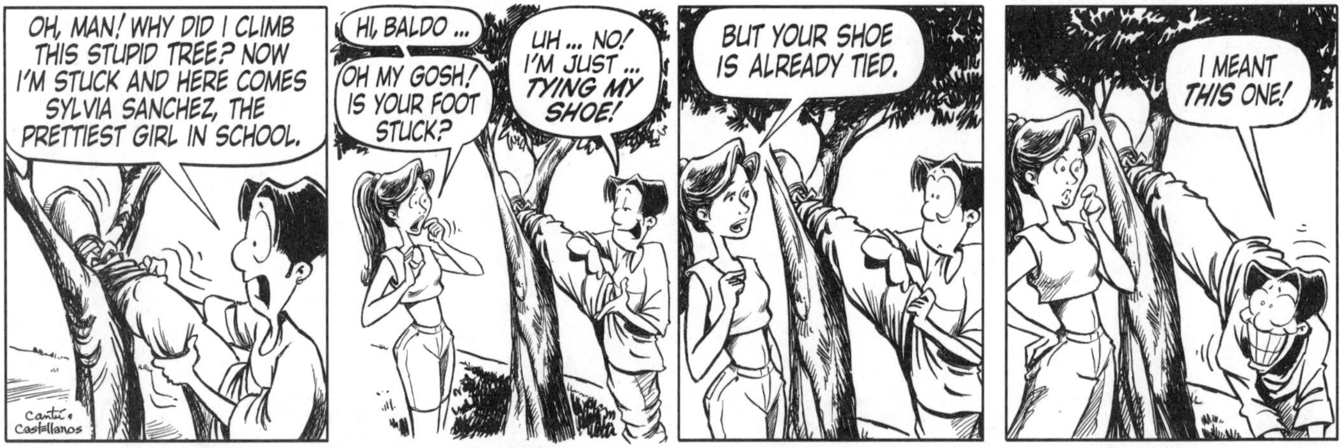
OH, MAN! WHY DID I CLIMB THIS STUPID TREE? NOW I'M STUCK AND HERE COMES SYLVIA SANCHEZ, THE PRETTIEST GIRL IN SCHOOL.
HI, BALDO ...
OH MY GOSH! IS YOUR FOOT STUCK?
UH ... NO! I'M JUST ... TYING MY SHOE!
BUT YOUR SHOE IS ALREADY TIED.
I MEANT THIS ONE!
Cantú & Castellanos

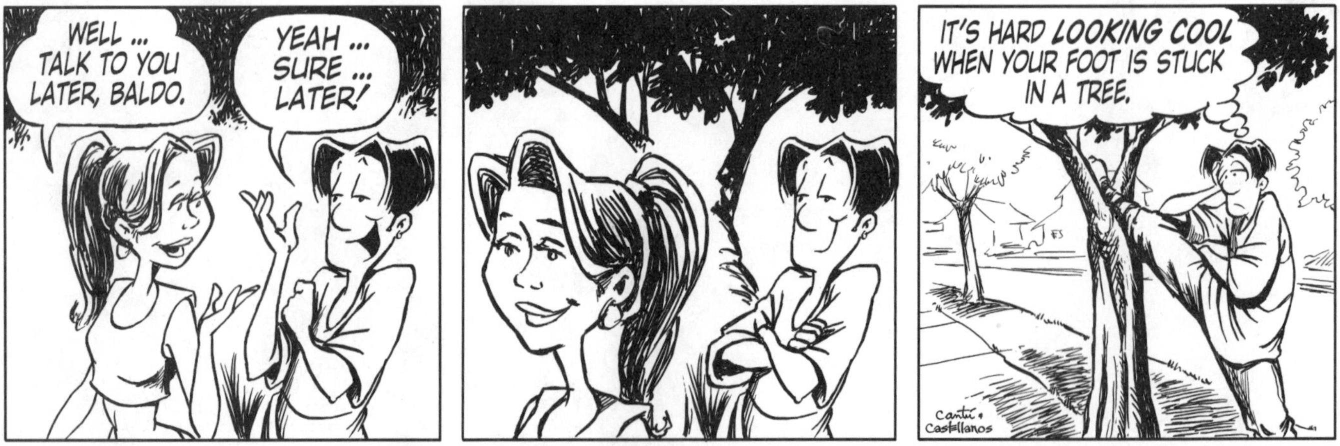
WELL ... TALK TO YOU LATER, BALDO.
YEAH ... SURE ... LATER!
IT'S HARD LOOKING COOL WHEN YOUR FOOT IS STUCK IN A TREE.
Cantú & Castellanos

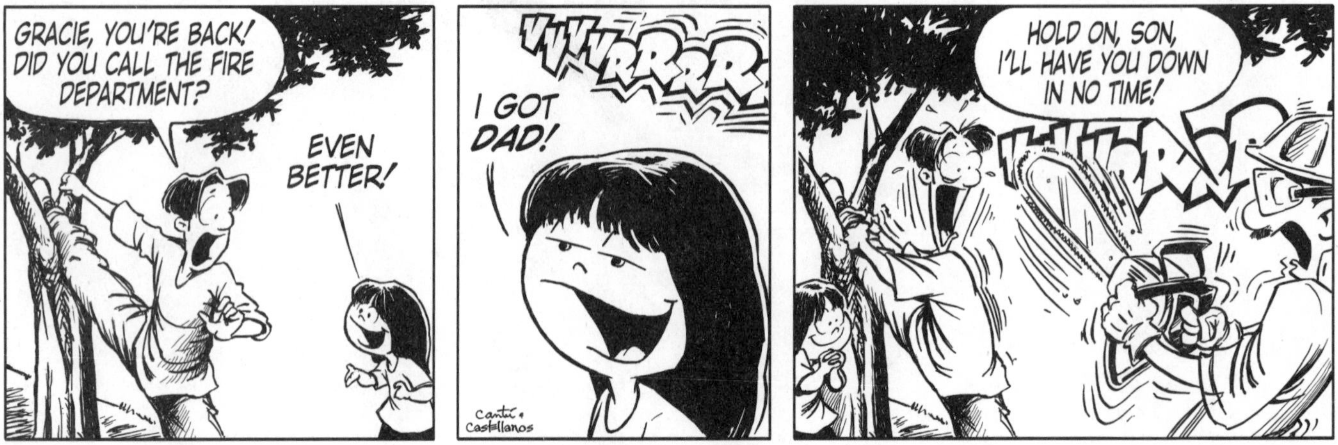
GRACIE, YOU'RE BACK! DID YOU CALL THE FIRE DEPARTMENT?
EVEN BETTER!
VVVVRRRR
I GOT DAD!
HOLD ON, SON, I'LL HAVE YOU DOWN IN NO TIME!
Cantú & Castellanos

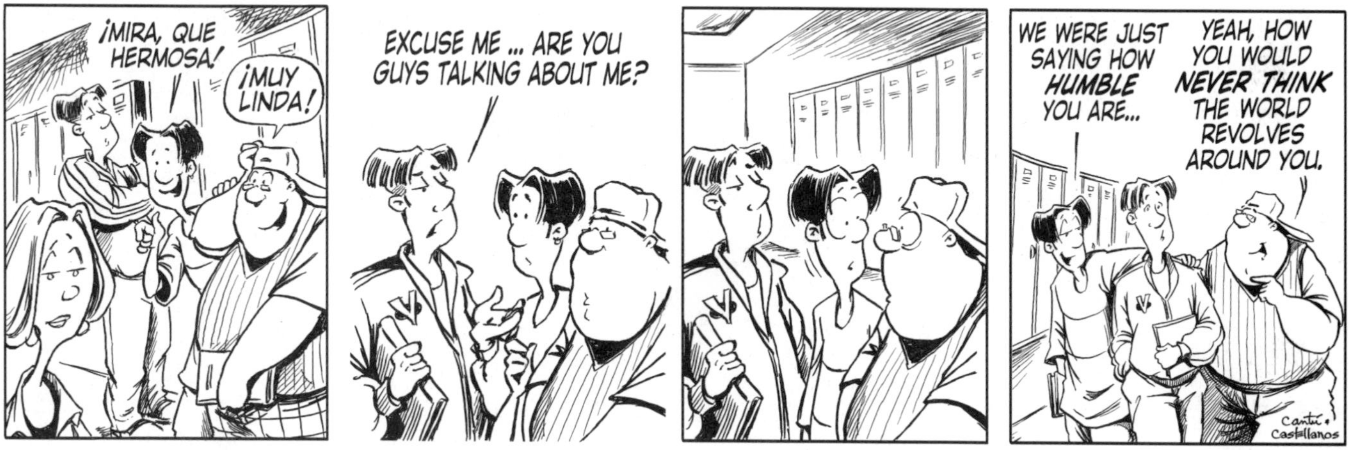
¡MIRA, QUE HERMOSA!
¡MUY LINDA!
EXCUSE ME ... ARE YOU GUYS TALKING ABOUT ME?
WE WERE JUST SAYING HOW **HUMBLE** YOU ARE...
YEAH, HOW YOU WOULD **NEVER THINK** THE WORLD REVOLVES AROUND YOU.
Cantú & Castellanos

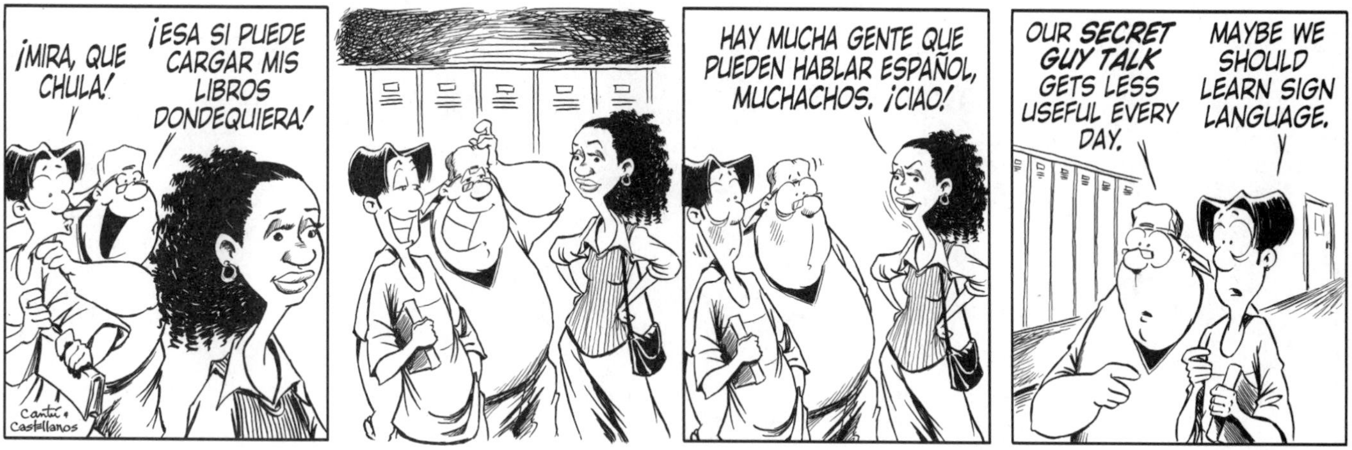
¡MIRA, QUE CHULA!
¡ESA SI PUEDE CARGAR MIS LIBROS DONDEQUIERA!
Cantú & Castellanos
HAY MUCHA GENTE QUE PUEDEN HABLAR ESPAÑOL, MUCHACHOS. ¡CIAO!
OUR **SECRET GUY TALK** GETS LESS USEFUL EVERY DAY.
MAYBE WE SHOULD LEARN SIGN LANGUAGE.

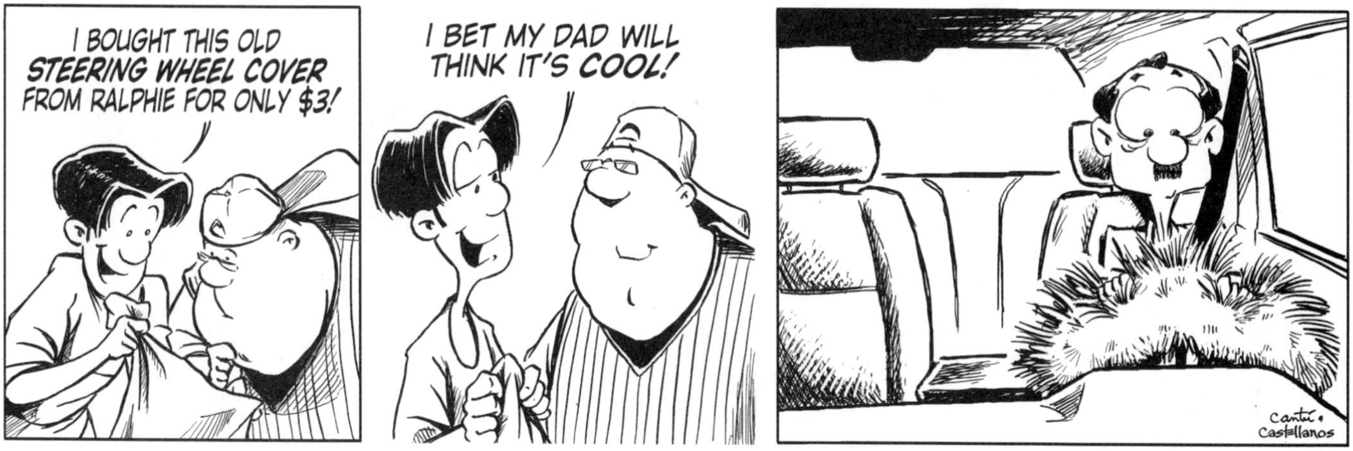
I BOUGHT THIS OLD **STEERING WHEEL COVER** FROM RALPHIE FOR ONLY $3!
I BET MY DAD WILL THINK IT'S **COOL**!
Cantú & Castellanos

IF MY EARS WERE SMALLER AND FACE ROUNDER ...
IF I HAD A STRONGER CHIN AND A PERFECT SMILE ...
IF MY HAIR, NOSE AND EYES WERE DIFFERENT ...
JUST CALL ME MR. STUDLY!
I'D BE SO NOT LIKE ME.
HEY! WHAT'S THE PROBLEMA, MAN?
Cantú • Castellanos

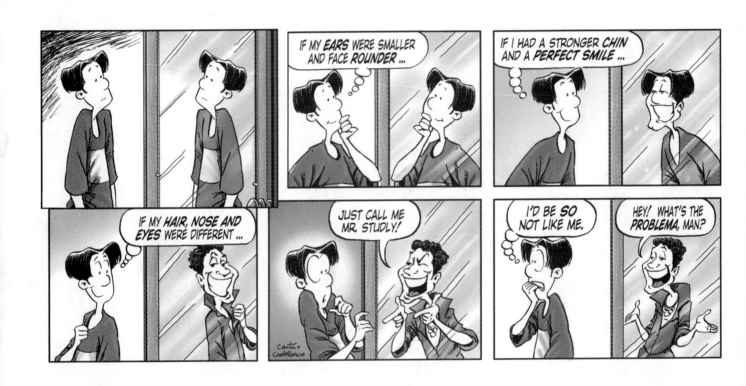

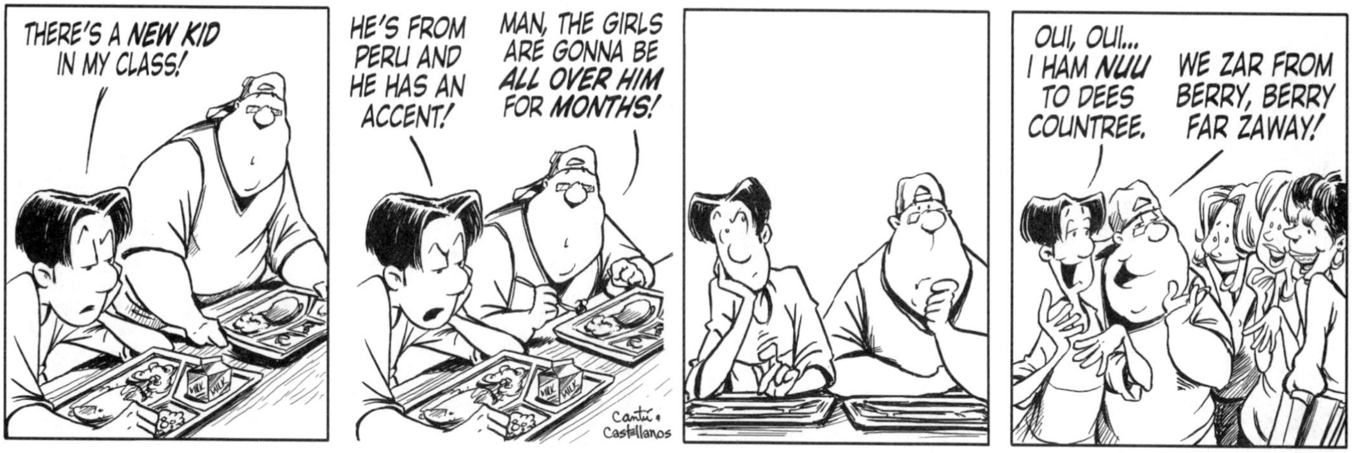
THERE'S A **NEW KID** IN MY CLASS!
HE'S FROM PERU AND HE HAS AN ACCENT!
MAN, THE GIRLS ARE GONNA BE **ALL OVER HIM** FOR **MONTHS!**
OUI, OUI... I HAM **NUU** TO DEES COUNTREE.
WE ZAR FROM BERRY, BERRY FAR ZAWAY!

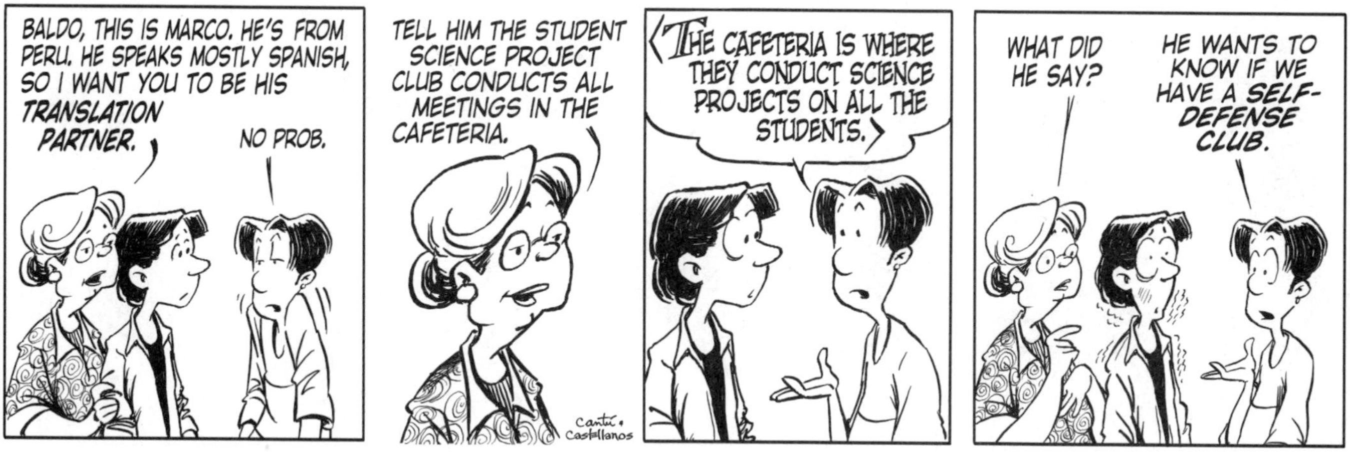
BALDO, THIS IS MARCO. HE'S FROM PERU. HE SPEAKS MOSTLY SPANISH, SO I WANT YOU TO BE HIS **TRANSLATION PARTNER.**
NO PROB.
TELL HIM THE STUDENT SCIENCE PROJECT CLUB CONDUCTS ALL MEETINGS IN THE CAFETERIA.
‹THE CAFETERIA IS WHERE THEY CONDUCT SCIENCE PROJECTS ON ALL THE STUDENTS.›
WHAT DID HE SAY?
HE WANTS TO KNOW IF WE HAVE A **SELF-DEFENSE CLUB.**

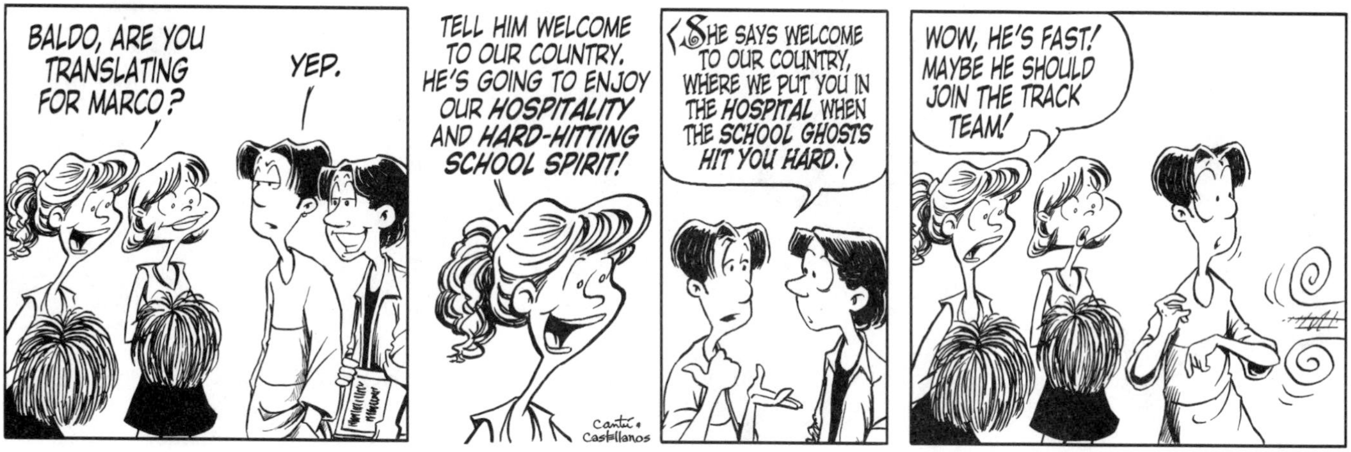
BALDO, ARE YOU TRANSLATING FOR MARCO?
YEP.
TELL HIM WELCOME TO OUR COUNTRY. HE'S GOING TO ENJOY OUR **HOSPITALITY** AND **HARD-HITTING SCHOOL SPIRIT!**
‹SHE SAYS WELCOME TO OUR COUNTRY, WHERE WE PUT YOU IN THE **HOSPITAL** WHEN THE **SCHOOL GHOSTS HIT YOU HARD.**›
WOW, HE'S FAST! MAYBE HE SHOULD JOIN THE TRACK TEAM!

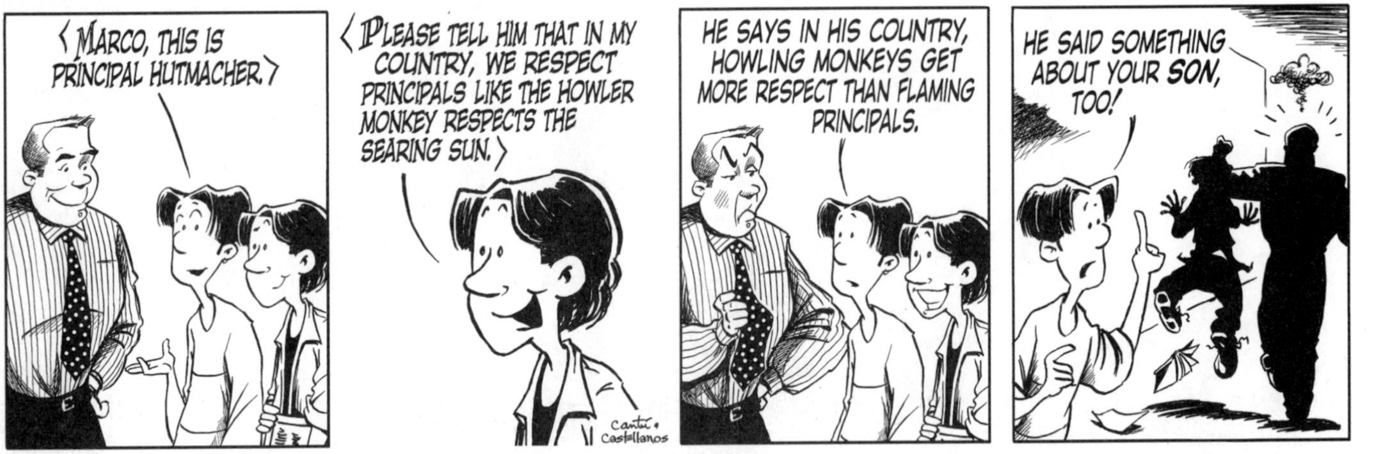
< MARCO, THIS IS PRINCIPAL HUTMACHER. >
< PLEASE TELL HIM THAT IN MY COUNTRY, WE RESPECT PRINCIPALS LIKE THE HOWLER MONKEY RESPECTS THE SEARING SUN. >
Cantú • Castellanos
HE SAYS IN HIS COUNTRY, HOWLING MONKEYS GET MORE RESPECT THAN FLAMING PRINCIPALS.
HE SAID SOMETHING ABOUT YOUR **SON**, TOO!

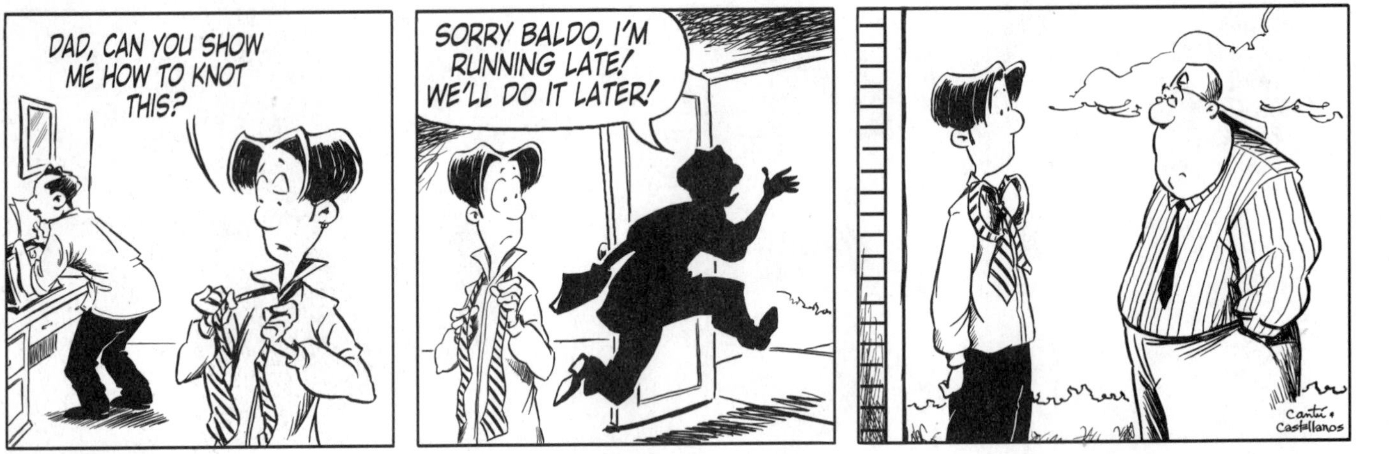
DAD, CAN YOU SHOW ME HOW TO KNOT THIS?
SORRY BALDO, I'M RUNNING LATE! WE'LL DO IT LATER!
Cantú • Castellanos

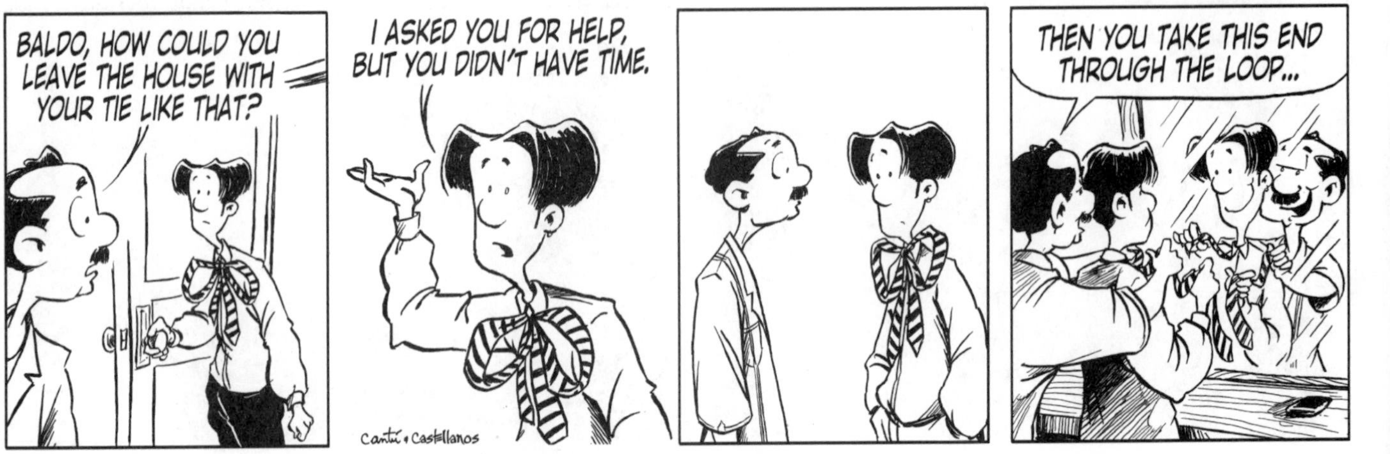
BALDO, HOW COULD YOU LEAVE THE HOUSE WITH YOUR TIE LIKE THAT?
I ASKED YOU FOR HELP, BUT YOU DIDN'T HAVE TIME.
Cantú • Castellanos
THEN YOU TAKE THIS END THROUGH THE LOOP...

Combat Zone
BLEEP!
ZAP!
BEEP!
Combat Zone
CLING!
THUMP!
BLIP!
ZZZZZ
WE CLOSE IN 5 MINUTES
mbat Zone
BLEEP!
ZAP!
BEEP!
Combat Zone
Zip!
Blip!
FwiP!
Yawn!
REALLY ... YOU HAVE TO LEAVE NOW.
Combat Z
C'MON BALDO!
BLAP!
PING!
GOODNIGHT!
Zone
LATER.

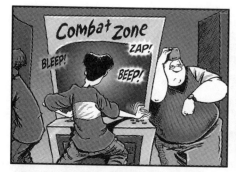

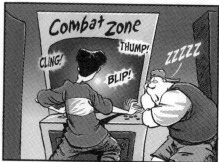

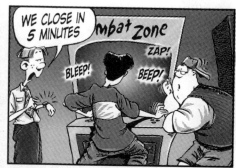

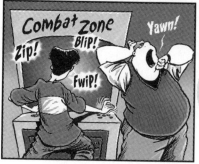

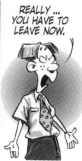

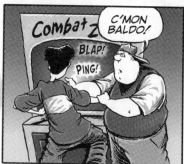

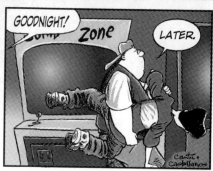

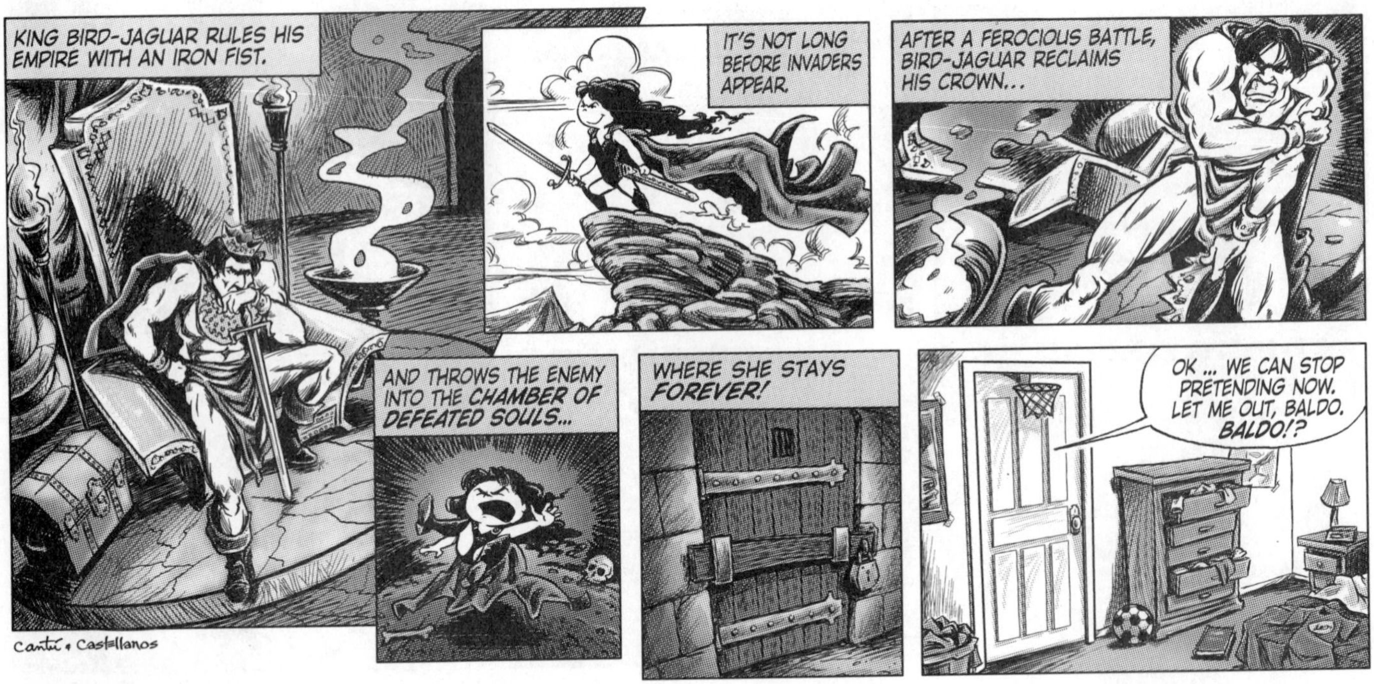
KING BIRD-JAGUAR RULES HIS EMPIRE WITH AN IRON FIST.
IT'S NOT LONG BEFORE INVADERS APPEAR.
AFTER A FEROCIOUS BATTLE, BIRD-JAGUAR RECLAIMS HIS CROWN...
AND THROWS THE ENEMY INTO THE CHAMBER OF DEFEATED SOULS...
WHERE SHE STAYS FOREVER!
OK ... WE CAN STOP PRETENDING NOW. LET ME OUT, BALDO. BALDO!?
Cantú & Castellanos

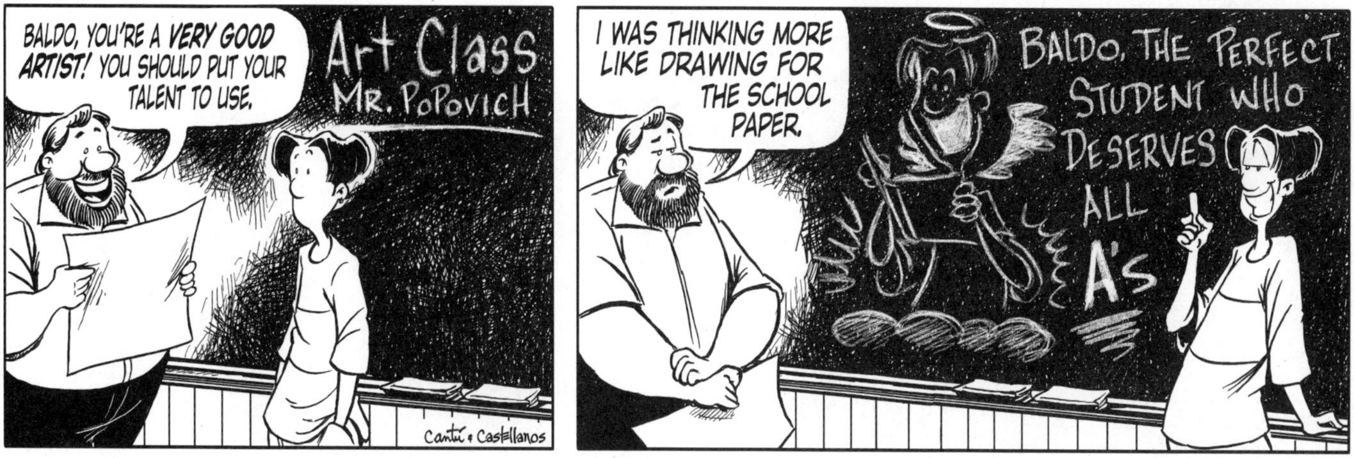
BALDO, YOU'RE A VERY GOOD ARTIST! YOU SHOULD PUT YOUR TALENT TO USE.
Art Class
MR. POPOVICH
Cantú & Castellanos
I WAS THINKING MORE LIKE DRAWING FOR THE SCHOOL PAPER.
BALDO, THE PERFECT STUDENT WHO DESERVES ALL A'S

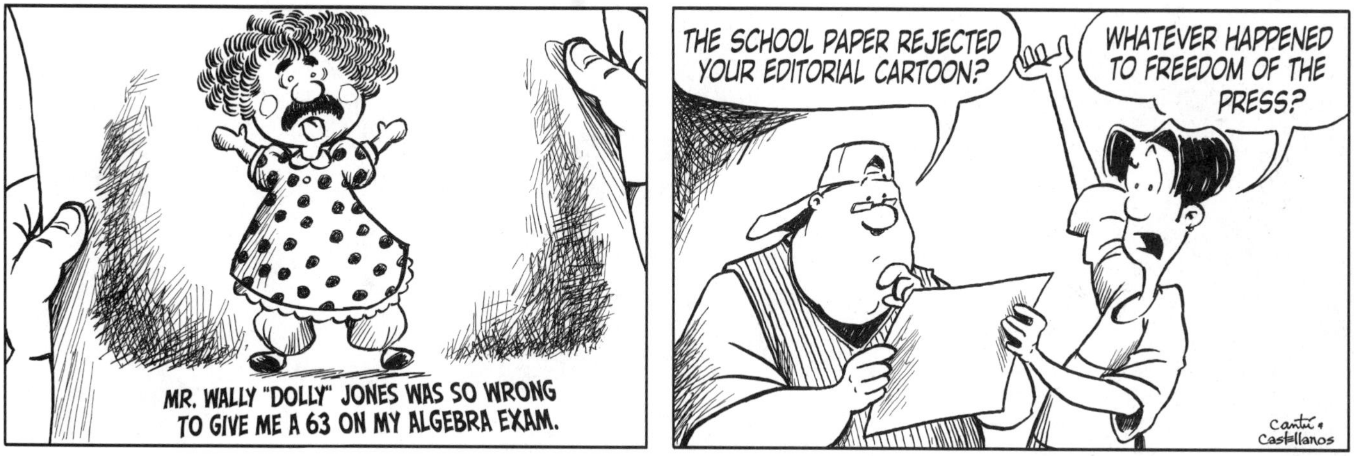
MR. WALLY "DOLLY" JONES WAS SO WRONG TO GIVE ME A 63 ON MY ALGEBRA EXAM.
THE SCHOOL PAPER REJECTED YOUR EDITORIAL CARTOON?
WHATEVER HAPPENED TO FREEDOM OF THE PRESS?
Cantú & Castellanos

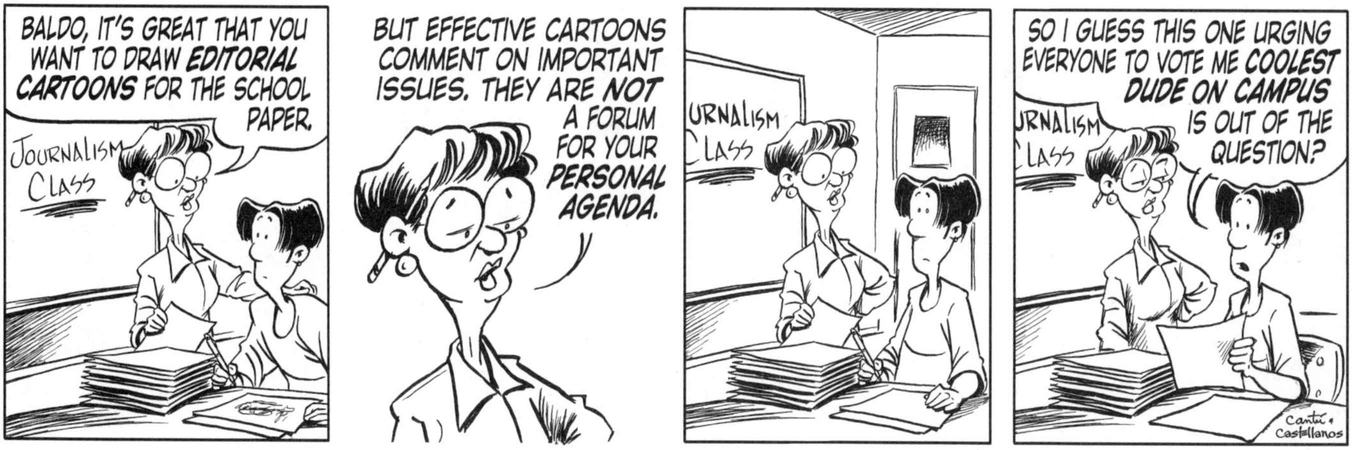
BALDO, IT'S GREAT THAT YOU WANT TO DRAW EDITORIAL CARTOONS FOR THE SCHOOL PAPER.
JOURNALISM CLASS
BUT EFFECTIVE CARTOONS COMMENT ON IMPORTANT ISSUES. THEY ARE NOT A FORUM FOR YOUR PERSONAL AGENDA.
SO I GUESS THIS ONE URGING EVERYONE TO VOTE ME COOLEST DUDE ON CAMPUS IS OUT OF THE QUESTION?
Cantú & Castellanos

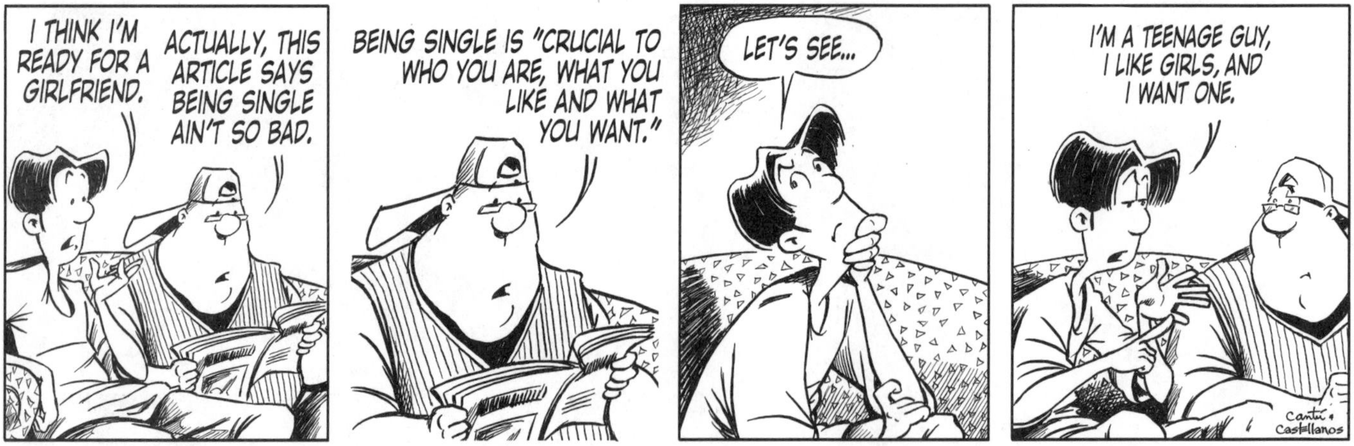
I THINK I'M READY FOR A GIRLFRIEND.
ACTUALLY, THIS ARTICLE SAYS BEING SINGLE AIN'T SO BAD.
BEING SINGLE IS "CRUCIAL TO WHO YOU ARE, WHAT YOU LIKE AND WHAT YOU WANT."
LET'S SEE...
I'M A TEENAGE GUY, I LIKE GIRLS, AND I WANT ONE.
Cantú & Castellanos

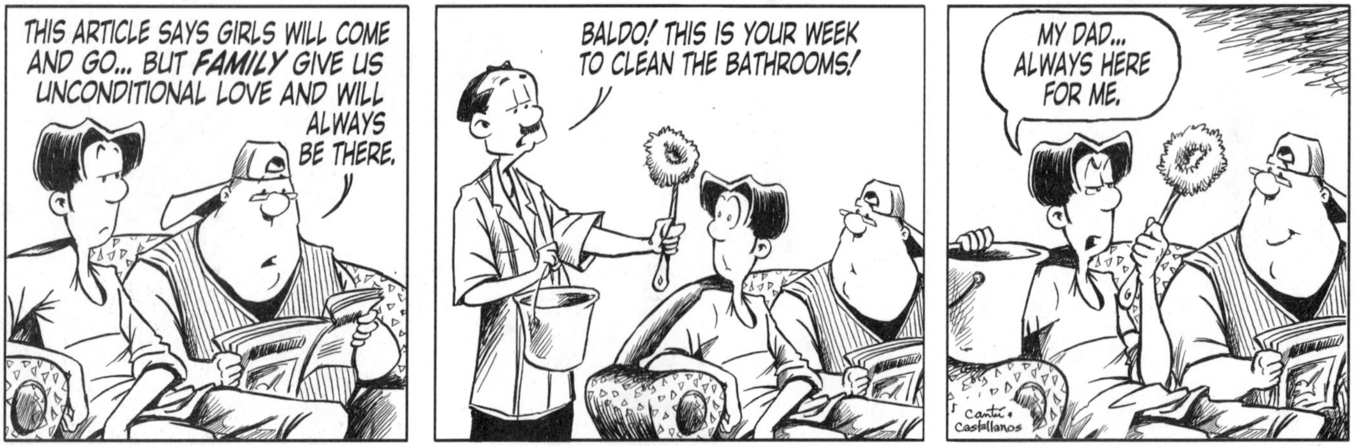
THIS ARTICLE SAYS GIRLS WILL COME AND GO... BUT **FAMILY** GIVE US UNCONDITIONAL LOVE AND WILL ALWAYS BE THERE.
BALDO! THIS IS YOUR WEEK TO CLEAN THE BATHROOMS!
MY DAD... ALWAYS HERE FOR ME.
Cantú & Castellanos

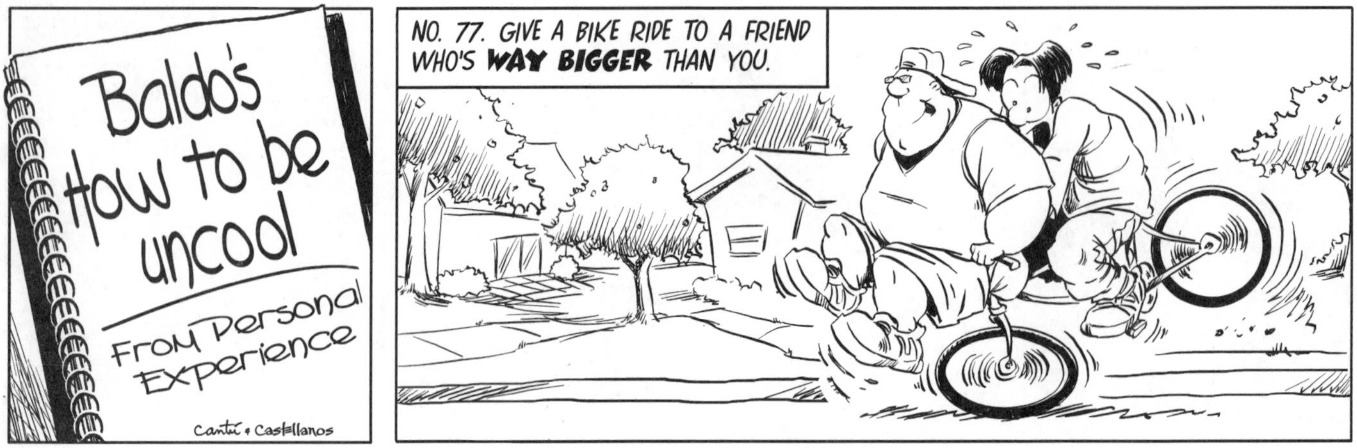
Baldo's How to be uncool
From Personal Experience
Cantú & Castellanos
NO. 77. GIVE A BIKE RIDE TO A FRIEND WHO'S **WAY BIGGER** THAN YOU.

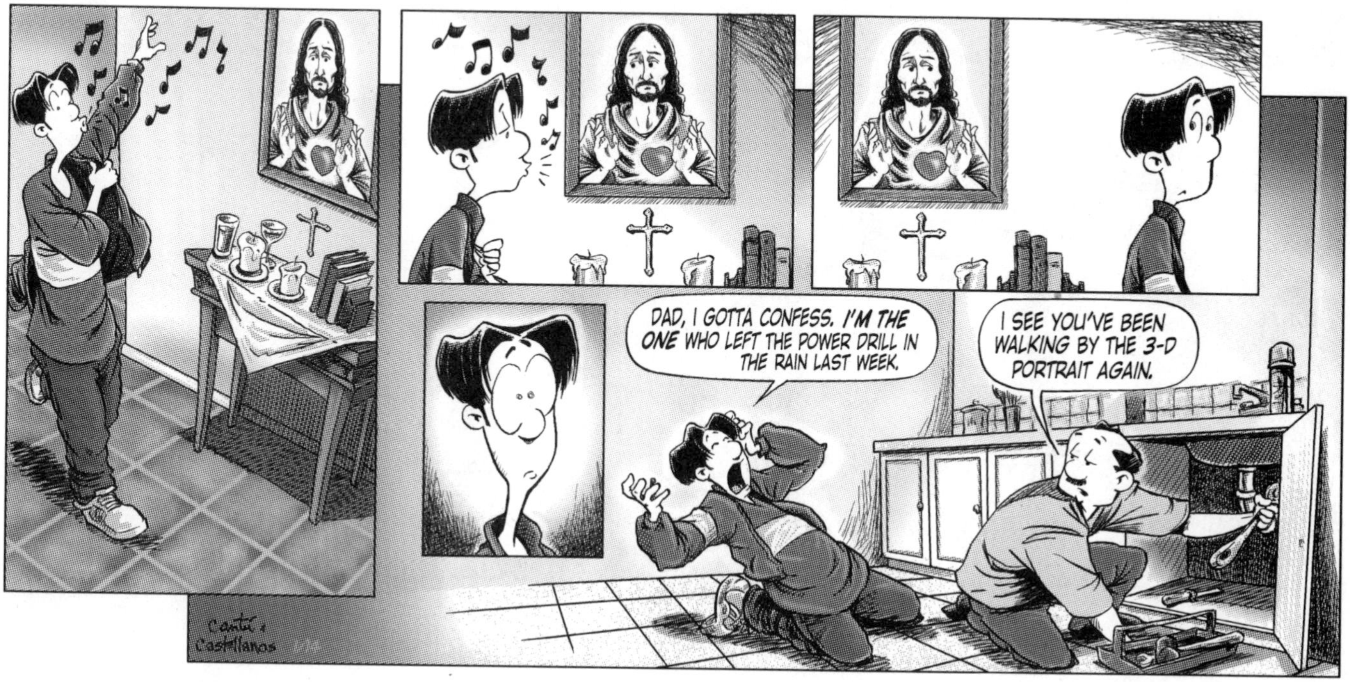
DAD, I GOTTA CONFESS. I'M THE ONE WHO LEFT THE POWER DRILL IN THE RAIN LAST WEEK.
I SEE YOU'VE BEEN WALKING BY THE 3-D PORTRAIT AGAIN.
Cantú & Castellanos

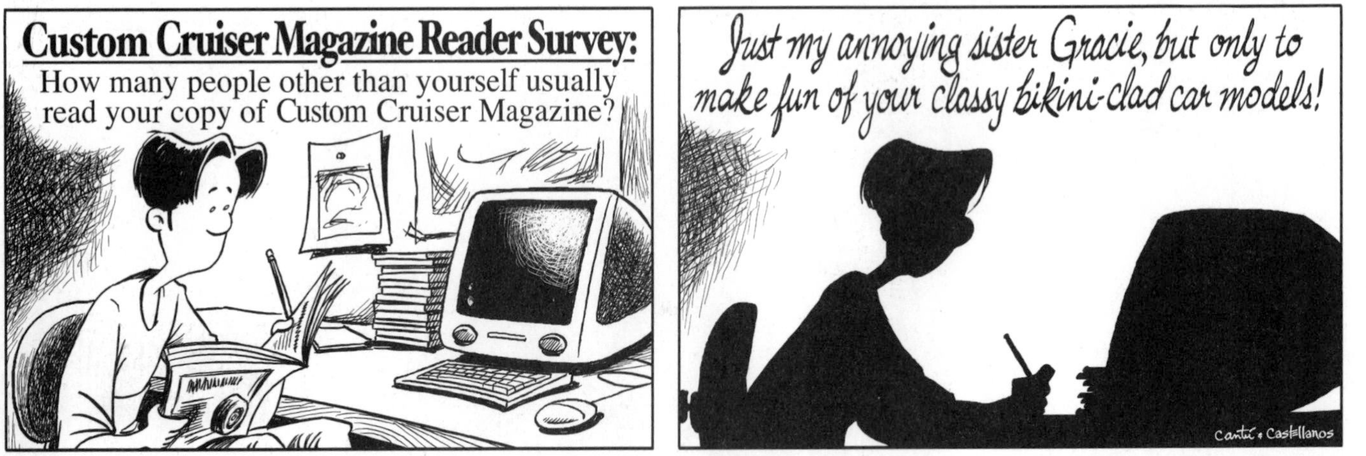
Custom Cruiser Magazine Reader Survey:
How many people other than yourself usually read your copy of Custom Cruiser Magazine?
Just my annoying sister Gracie, but only to make fun of your classy bikini-clad car models!
Cantú • Castellanos

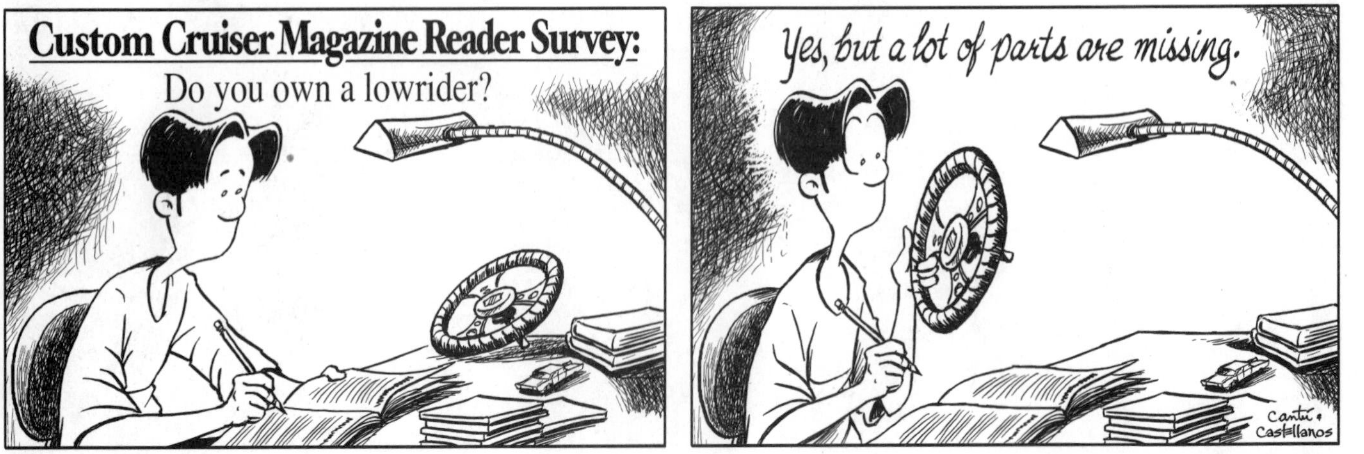
Custom Cruiser Magazine Reader Survey:
Do you own a lowrider?
Yes, but a lot of parts are missing.
Cantú • Castellanos

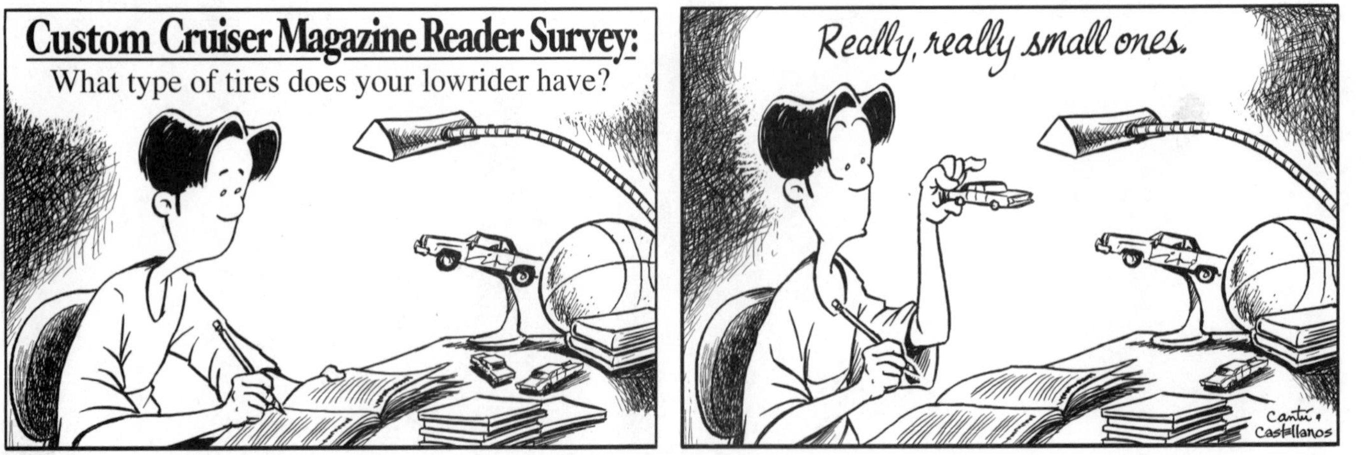
Custom Cruiser Magazine Reader Survey:
What type of tires does your lowrider have?
Really, really small ones.
Cantú • Castellanos

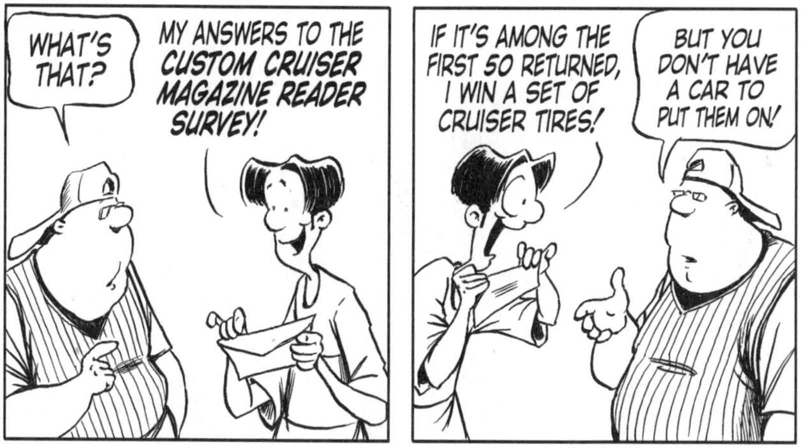
WHAT'S THAT?
MY ANSWERS TO THE *CUSTOM CRUISER MAGAZINE READER SURVEY!*
IF IT'S AMONG THE FIRST 50 RETURNED, I WIN A SET OF CRUISER TIRES!
BUT YOU DON'T HAVE A CAR TO PUT THEM ON!
THOUGH I GUESS THAT HASN'T STOPPED YOU BEFORE.
Cantú • Castellanos

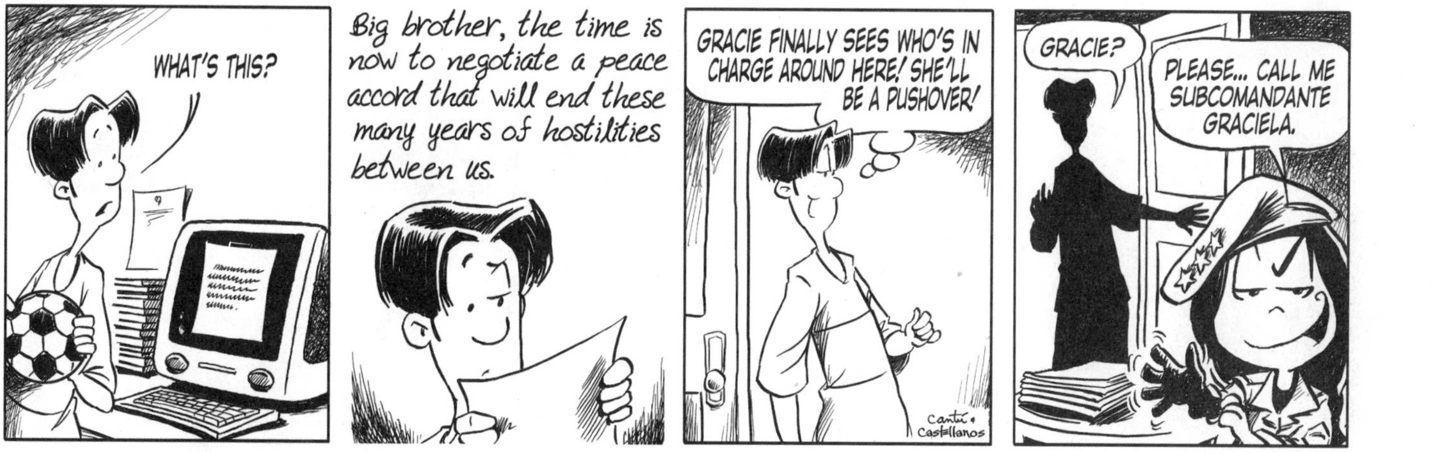
WHAT'S THIS?
Big brother, the time is now to negotiate a peace accord that will end these many years of hostilities between us.
GRACIE FINALLY SEES WHO'S IN CHARGE AROUND HERE! SHE'LL BE A PUSHOVER!
Cantú • Castellanos
GRACIE?
PLEASE... CALL ME SUBCOMANDANTE GRACIELA.

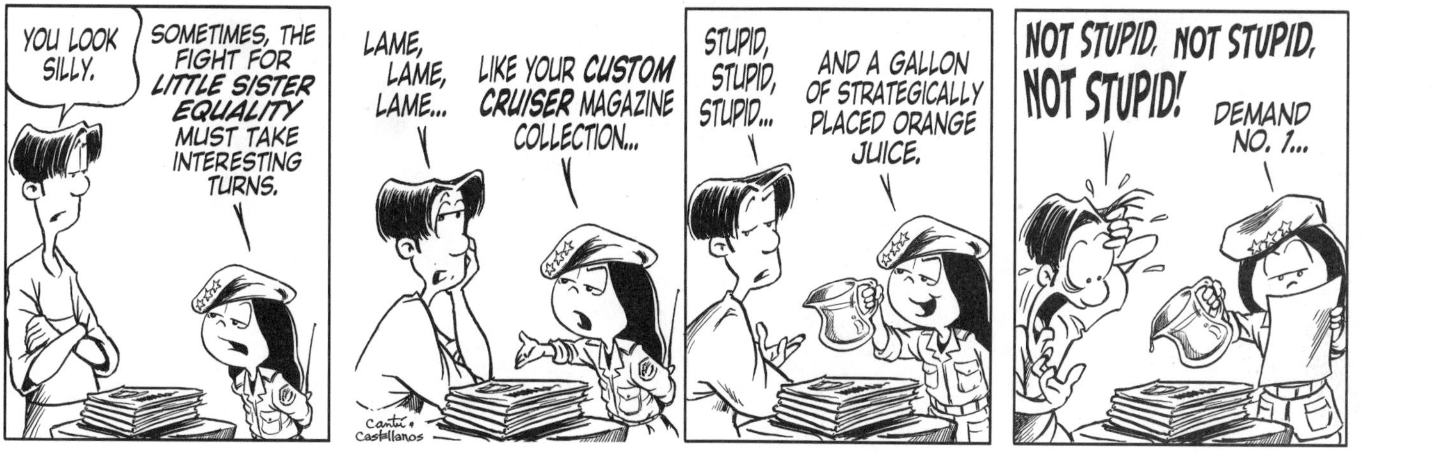
YOU LOOK SILLY.
SOMETIMES, THE FIGHT FOR *LITTLE SISTER EQUALITY* MUST TAKE INTERESTING TURNS.
LAME, LAME, LAME...
LIKE YOUR *CUSTOM CRUISER* MAGAZINE COLLECTION...
Cantú • Castellanos
STUPID, STUPID, STUPID...
AND A GALLON OF STRATEGICALLY PLACED ORANGE JUICE.
NOT STUPID, NOT STUPID, NOT STUPID!
DEMAND NO. 1...

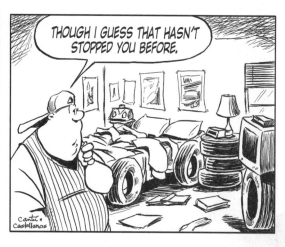

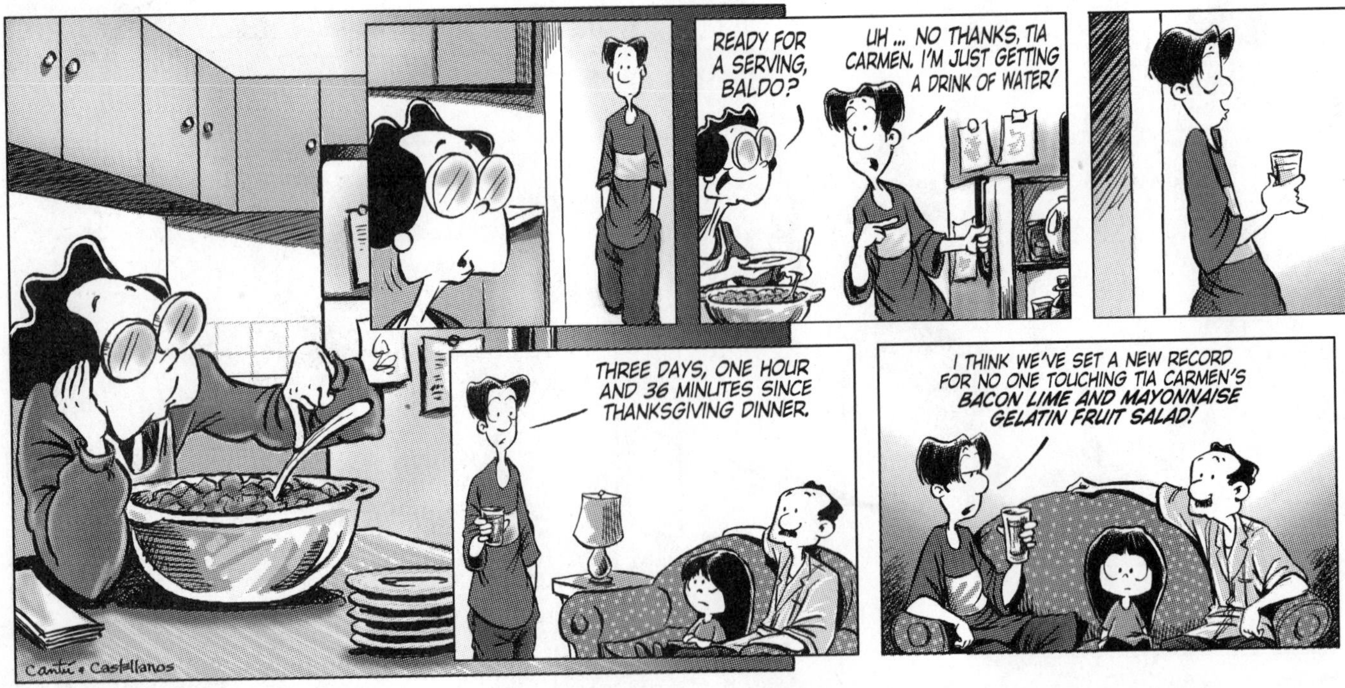
Cantú • Castellanos
READY FOR A SERVING, BALDO?
UH ... NO THANKS, TIA CARMEN. I'M JUST GETTING A DRINK OF WATER!
THREE DAYS, ONE HOUR AND 36 MINUTES SINCE THANKSGIVING DINNER.
I THINK WE'VE SET A NEW RECORD FOR NO ONE TOUCHING TIA CARMEN'S BACON LIME AND MAYONNAISE GELATIN FRUIT SALAD!

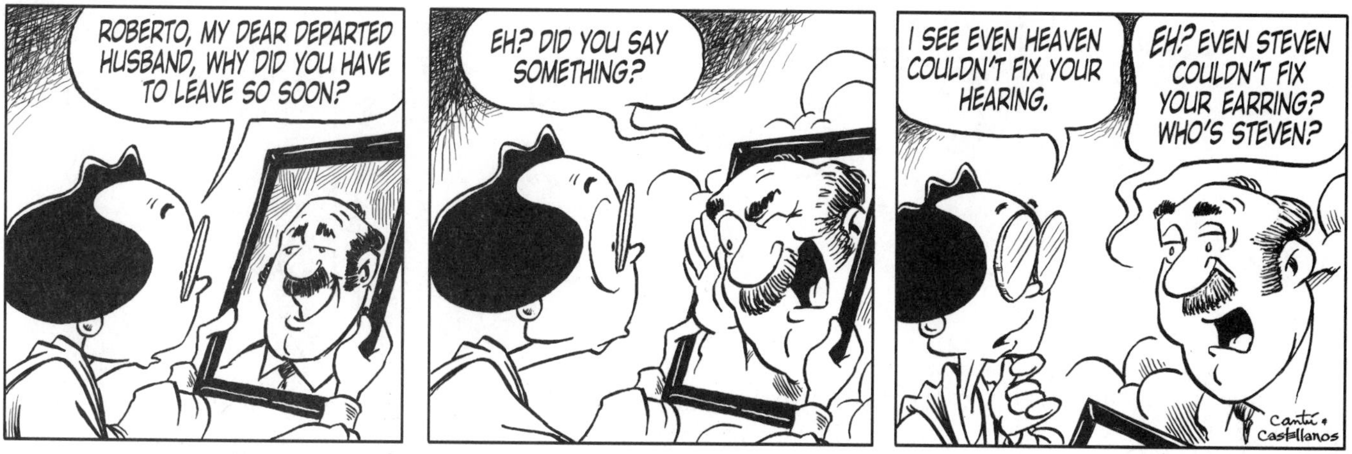
ROBERTO, MY DEAR DEPARTED HUSBAND, WHY DID YOU HAVE TO LEAVE SO SOON?
EH? DID YOU SAY SOMETHING?
I SEE EVEN HEAVEN COULDN'T FIX YOUR HEARING.
EH? EVEN STEVEN COULDN'T FIX YOUR EARRING? WHO'S STEVEN?
Cantú & Castellanos

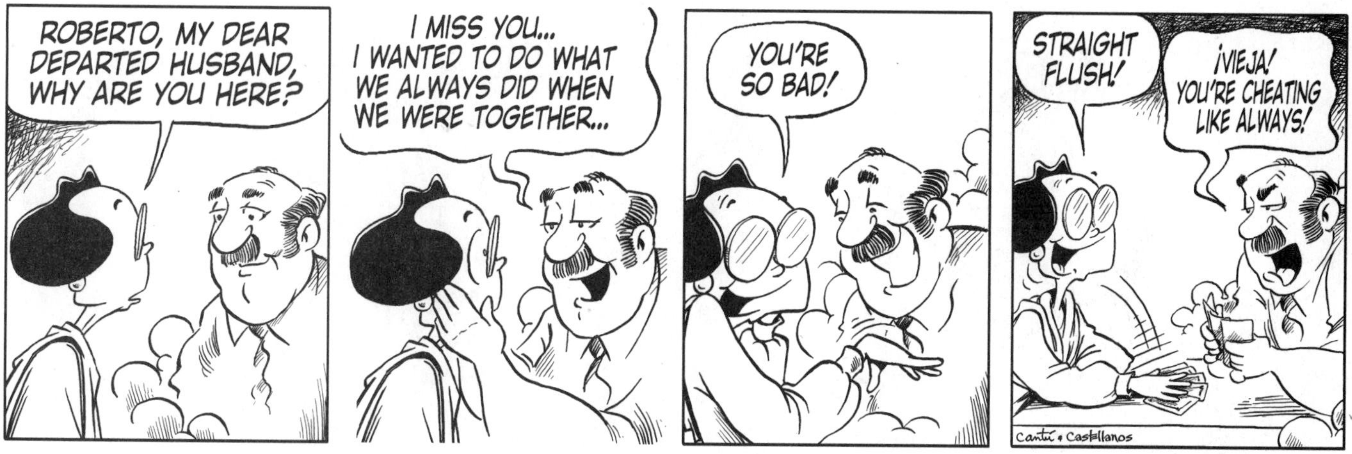
ROBERTO, MY DEAR DEPARTED HUSBAND, WHY ARE YOU HERE?
I MISS YOU... I WANTED TO DO WHAT WE ALWAYS DID WHEN WE WERE TOGETHER...
YOU'RE SO BAD!
STRAIGHT FLUSH!
¡VIEJA! YOU'RE CHEATING LIKE ALWAYS!
Cantú & Castellanos

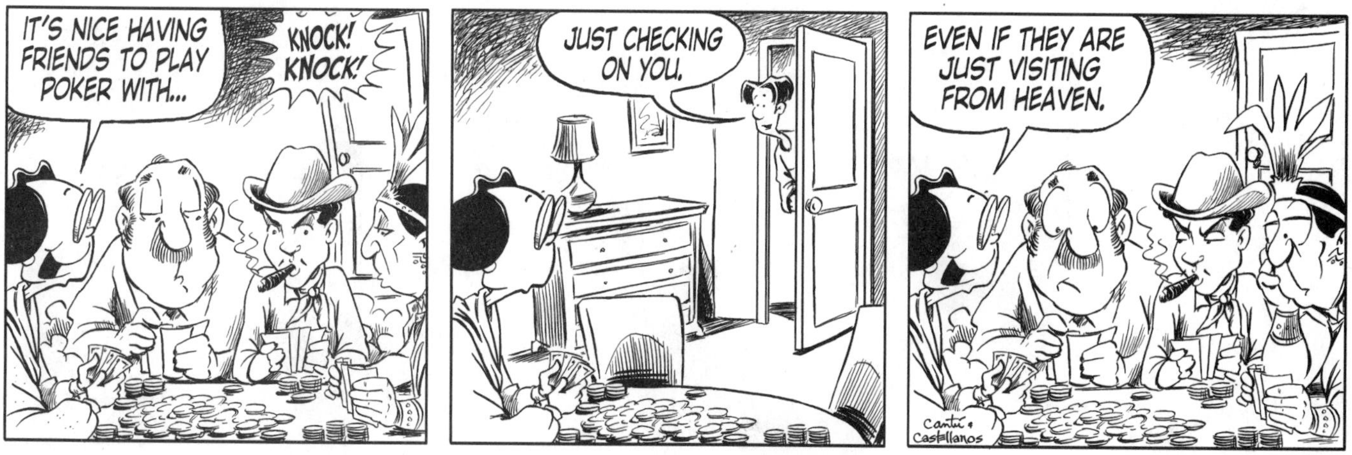
IT'S NICE HAVING FRIENDS TO PLAY POKER WITH...
KNOCK! KNOCK!
JUST CHECKING ON YOU.
EVEN IF THEY ARE JUST VISITING FROM HEAVEN.
Cantú & Castellanos

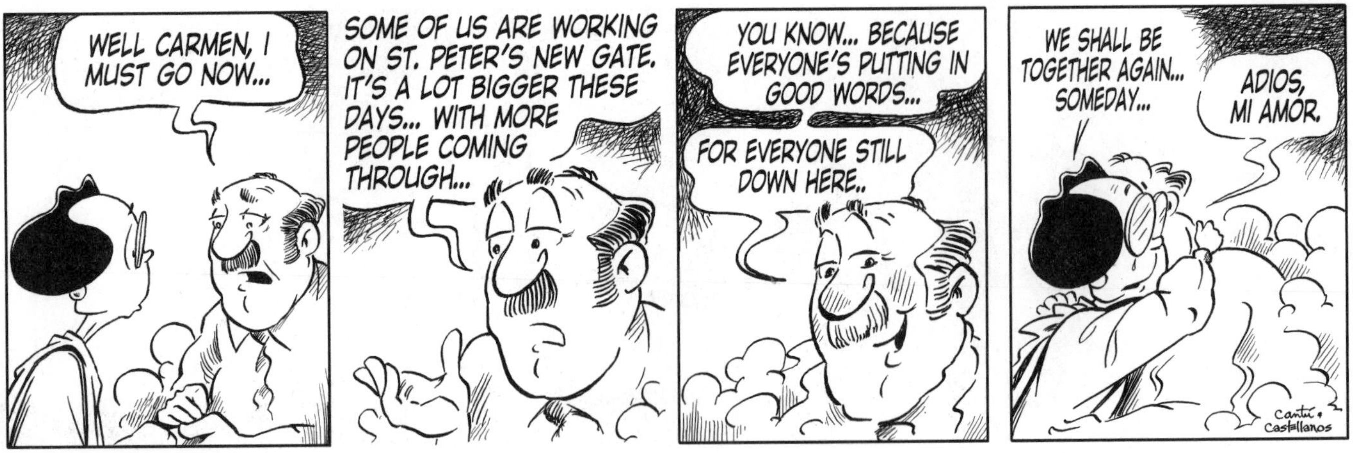
WELL CARMEN, I MUST GO NOW...
SOME OF US ARE WORKING ON ST. PETER'S NEW GATE. IT'S A LOT BIGGER THESE DAYS... WITH MORE PEOPLE COMING THROUGH...
YOU KNOW... BECAUSE EVERYONE'S PUTTING IN GOOD WORDS...
FOR EVERYONE STILL DOWN HERE..
WE SHALL BE TOGETHER AGAIN... SOMEDAY...
ADIOS, MI AMOR.
Cantú & Castellanos

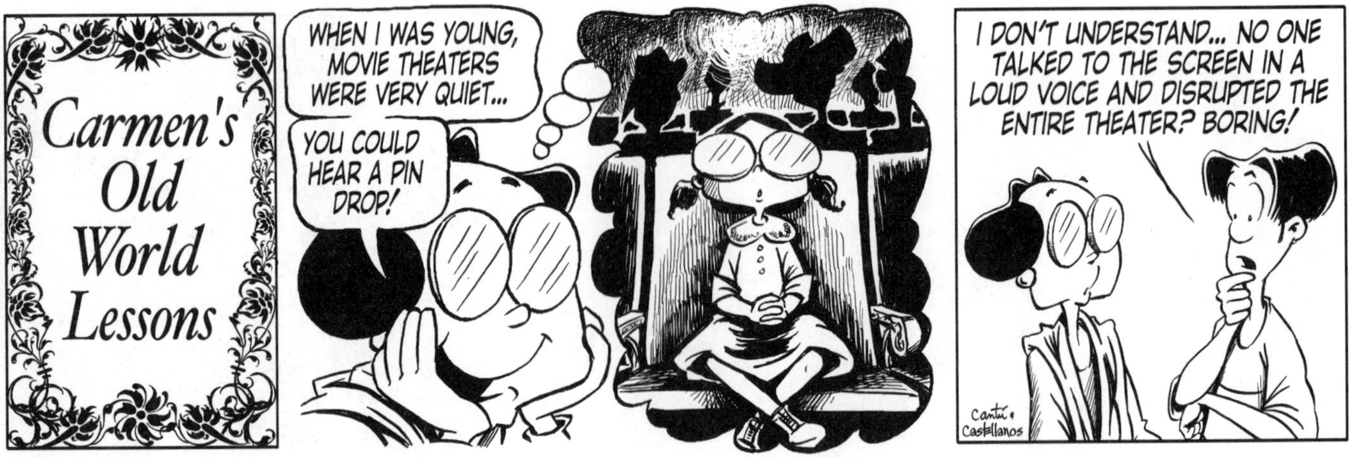
Carmen's Old World Lessons
WHEN I WAS YOUNG, MOVIE THEATERS WERE VERY QUIET...
YOU COULD HEAR A PIN DROP!
I DON'T UNDERSTAND... NO ONE TALKED TO THE SCREEN IN A LOUD VOICE AND DISRUPTED THE ENTIRE THEATER? BORING!
Cantú & Castellanos

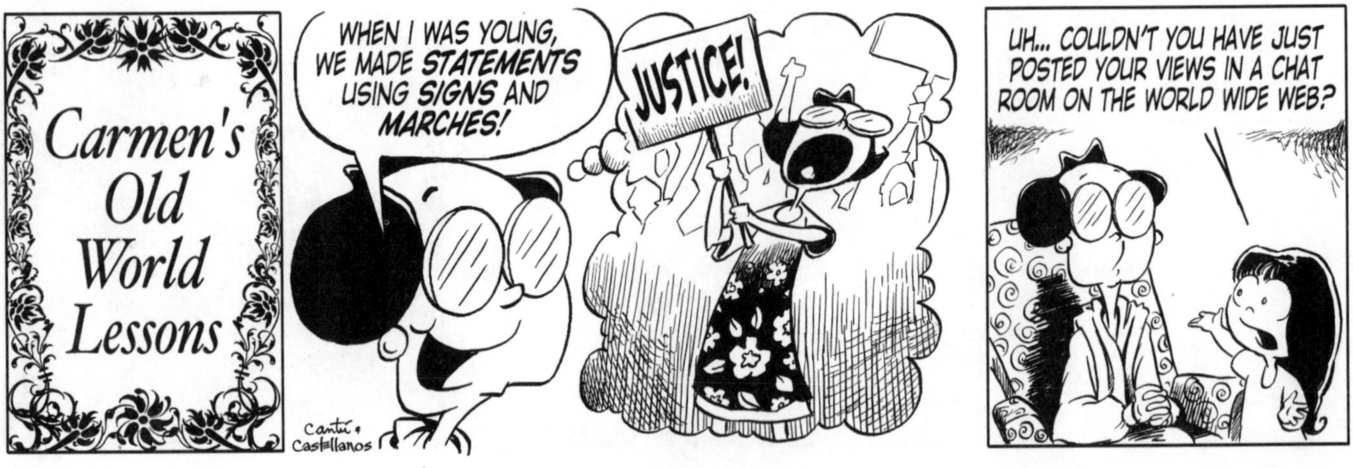
Carmen's Old World Lessons
WHEN I WAS YOUNG, WE MADE STATEMENTS USING SIGNS AND MARCHES!
JUSTICE!
UH... COULDN'T YOU HAVE JUST POSTED YOUR VIEWS IN A CHAT ROOM ON THE WORLD WIDE WEB?
Cantú & Castellanos

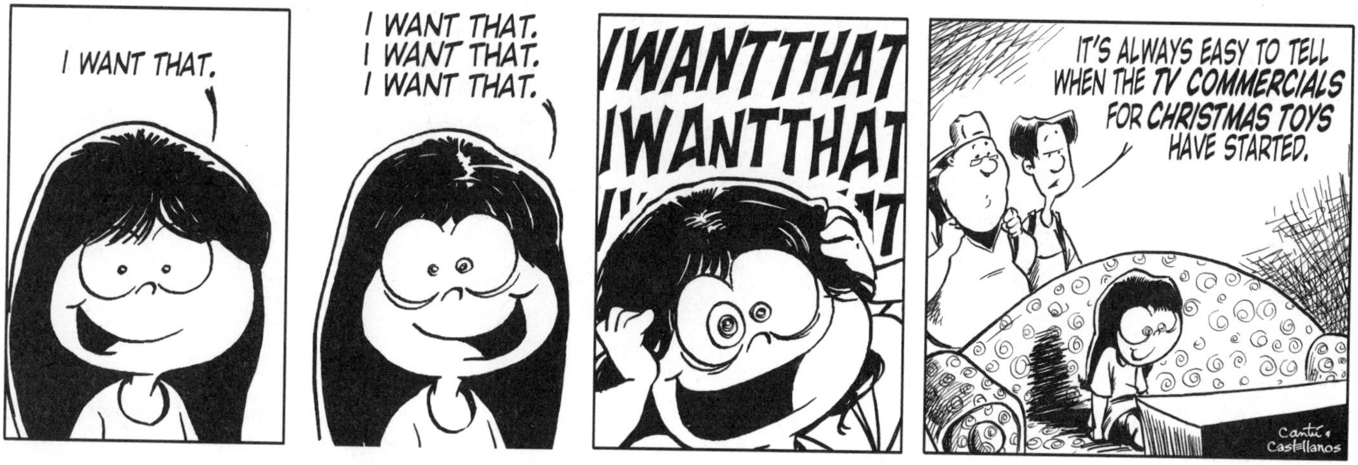
I WANT THAT.
I WANT THAT.
I WANT THAT.
I WANT THAT.
IWANTTHAT
IWANTTHAT
IT'S ALWAYS EASY TO TELL WHEN THE *TV COMMERCIALS* FOR *CHRISTMAS TOYS* HAVE STARTED.

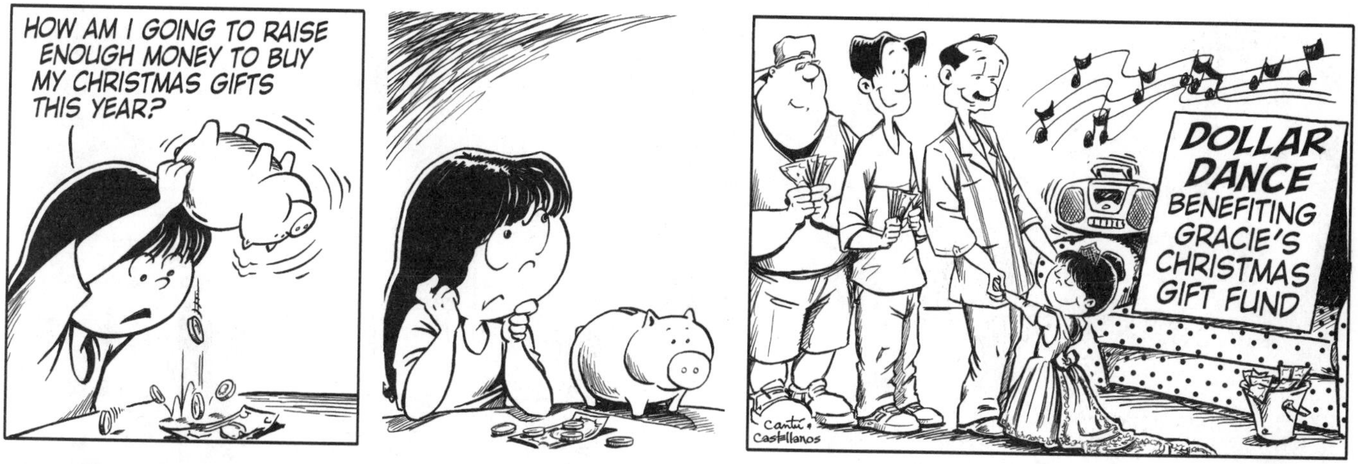
HOW AM I GOING TO RAISE ENOUGH MONEY TO BUY MY CHRISTMAS GIFTS THIS YEAR?
DOLLAR DANCE
BENEFITING GRACIE'S CHRISTMAS GIFT FUND

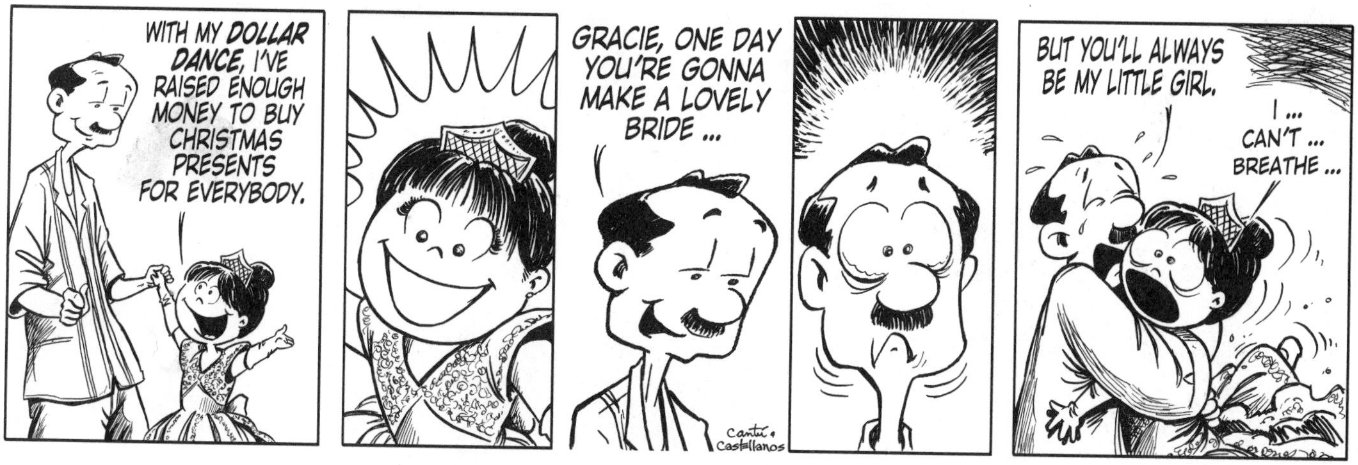
WITH MY *DOLLAR DANCE*, I'VE RAISED ENOUGH MONEY TO BUY CHRISTMAS PRESENTS FOR EVERYBODY.
GRACIE, ONE DAY YOU'RE GONNA MAKE A LOVELY BRIDE ...
BUT YOU'LL ALWAYS BE MY LITTLE GIRL.
I ... CAN'T ... BREATHE ...

THEN YOU LICK IT HERE...
Cantú & Castellanos
FOLD THE FLAP OVER LIKE THIS... AND SEAL IT!
THIS TELLS OUR MAILMAN THAT WE'VE PAID OUR MONEY TO HAVE IT DELIVERED TO COUSIN ALBERTO.
THEN WE JUST PUT IT OUT HERE.
SO WHEN DOES IT LEAVE? IS THERE A SEND BUTTON OR SOMETHING?

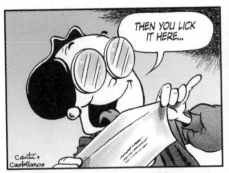

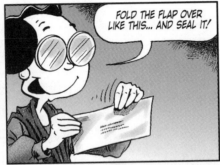

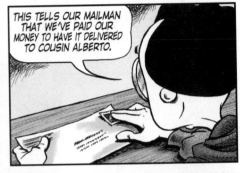

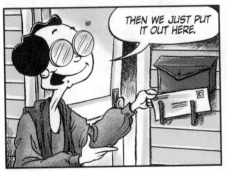

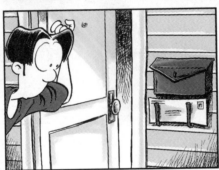

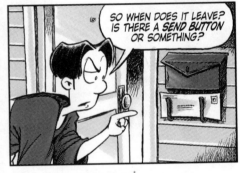

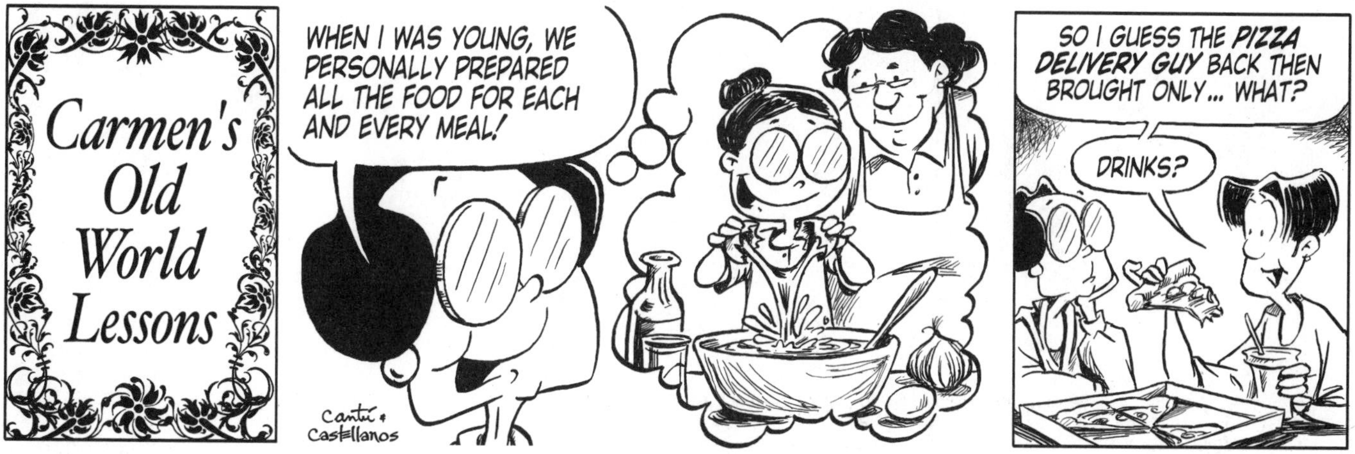
Carmen's Old World Lessons
WHEN I WAS YOUNG, WE PERSONALLY PREPARED ALL THE FOOD FOR EACH AND EVERY MEAL!
Cantú & Castellanos
SO I GUESS THE PIZZA DELIVERY GUY BACK THEN BROUGHT ONLY... WHAT?
DRINKS?

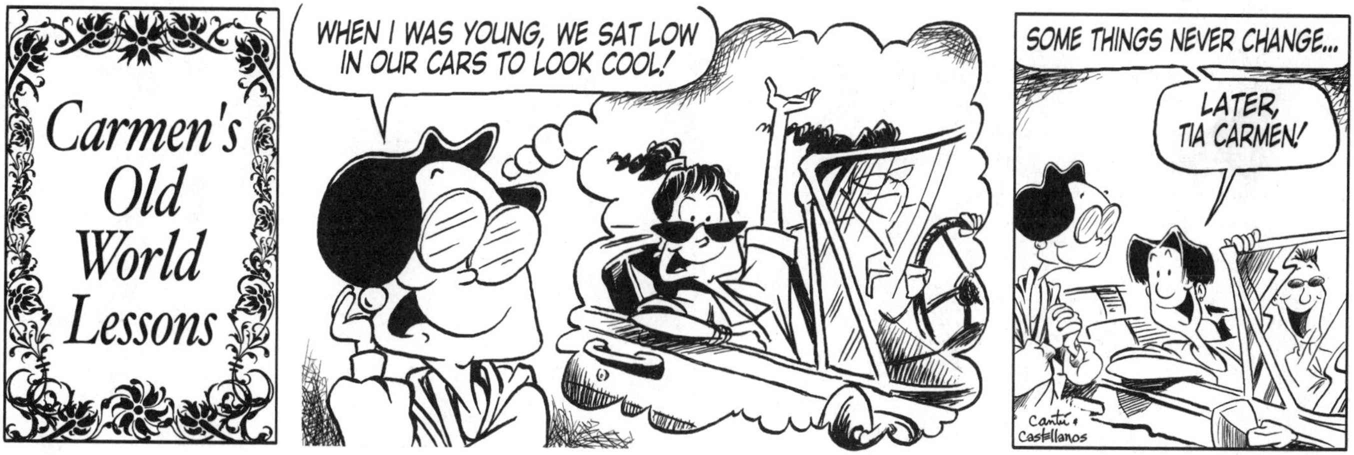
Carmen's Old World Lessons
WHEN I WAS YOUNG, WE SAT LOW IN OUR CARS TO LOOK COOL!
SOME THINGS NEVER CHANGE...
LATER, TIA CARMEN!
Cantú & Castellanos

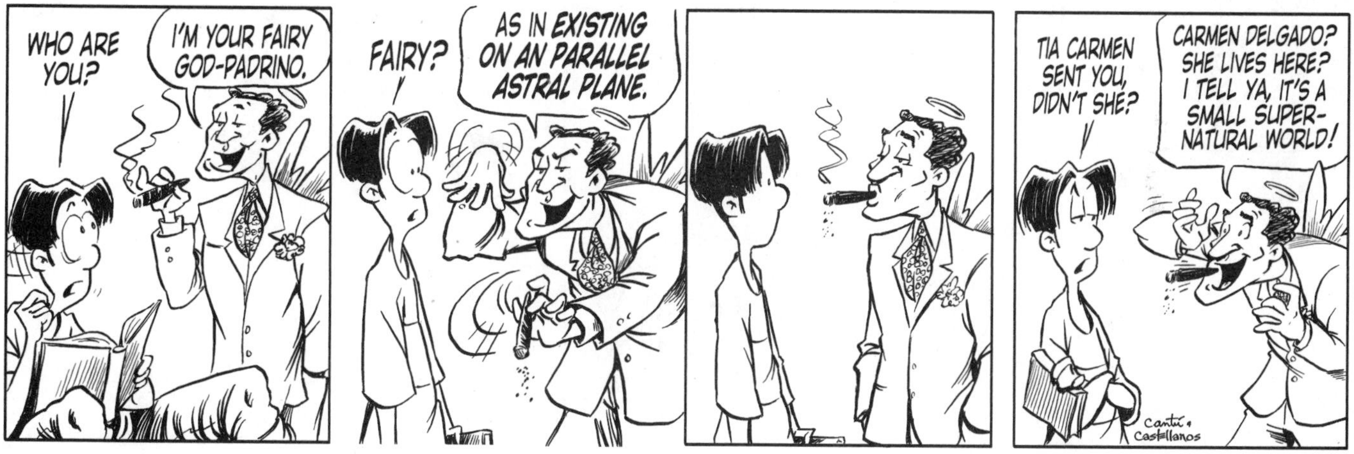
WHO ARE YOU?
I'M YOUR FAIRY GOD-PADRINO.
FAIRY?
AS IN EXISTING ON AN PARALLEL ASTRAL PLANE.
TIA CARMEN SENT YOU, DIDN'T SHE?
CARMEN DELGADO? SHE LIVES HERE? I TELL YA, IT'S A SMALL SUPER-NATURAL WORLD!
Cantú & Castellanos

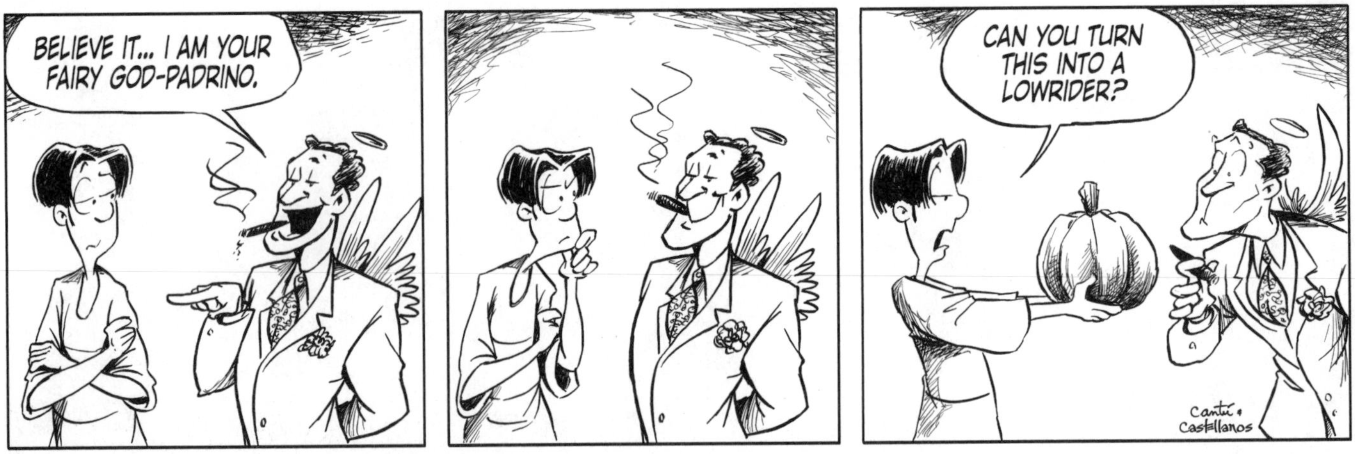
BELIEVE IT... I AM YOUR FAIRY GOD-PADRINO.
CAN YOU TURN THIS INTO A LOWRIDER?

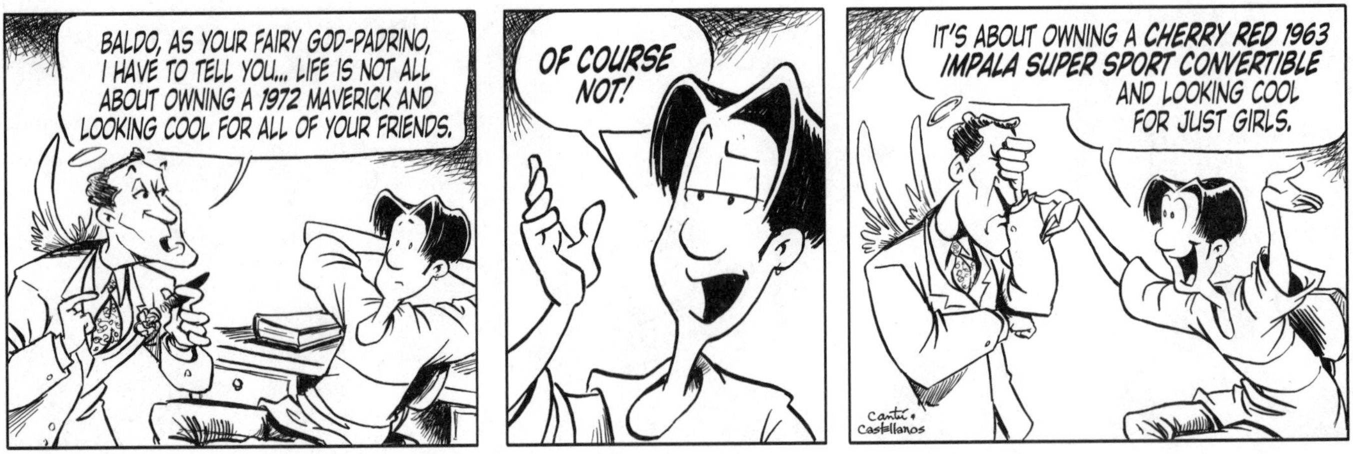
BALDO, AS YOUR FAIRY GOD-PADRINO, I HAVE TO TELL YOU... LIFE IS NOT ALL ABOUT OWNING A 1972 MAVERICK AND LOOKING COOL FOR ALL OF YOUR FRIENDS.
OF COURSE NOT!
IT'S ABOUT OWNING A CHERRY RED 1963 IMPALA SUPER SPORT CONVERTIBLE AND LOOKING COOL FOR JUST GIRLS.

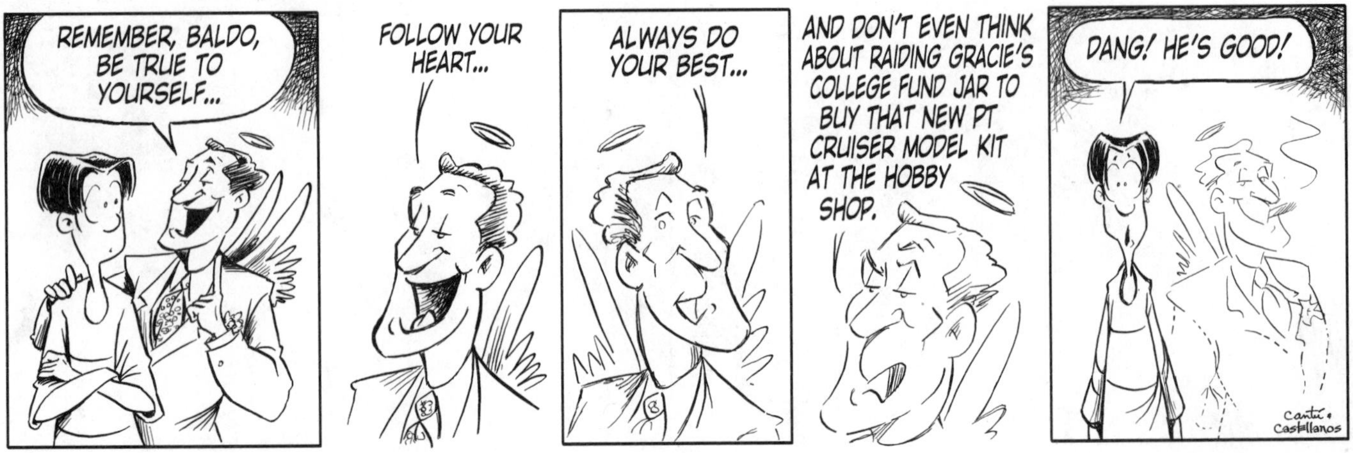
REMEMBER, BALDO, BE TRUE TO YOURSELF...
FOLLOW YOUR HEART...
ALWAYS DO YOUR BEST...
AND DON'T EVEN THINK ABOUT RAIDING GRACIE'S COLLEGE FUND JAR TO BUY THAT NEW PT CRUISER MODEL KIT AT THE HOBBY SHOP.
DANG! HE'S GOOD!

NACHO MUCHO GRANDE!
ENCHURITO!
Conte • Castellanos
NACHEESEBURGER! TAMACHILE!
GORDODITA!
DON'T!
CHALUPO SUPREMO!
FAJITACO!
BURITATOE!
STOP IT!
QUESATILLA!
CHIMICHANGO!
HAMBURRITO!
PLEASE!
MAN, I NEVER KNEW *BUTCHERED SPANISH WORDS* FROM FAST-FOOD MENUS DROVE MY DAD SO CRAZY!

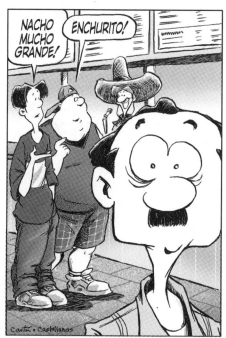

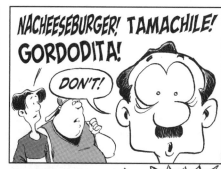

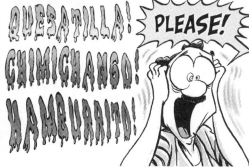

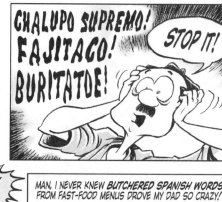

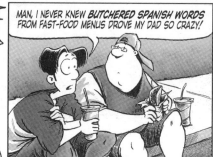

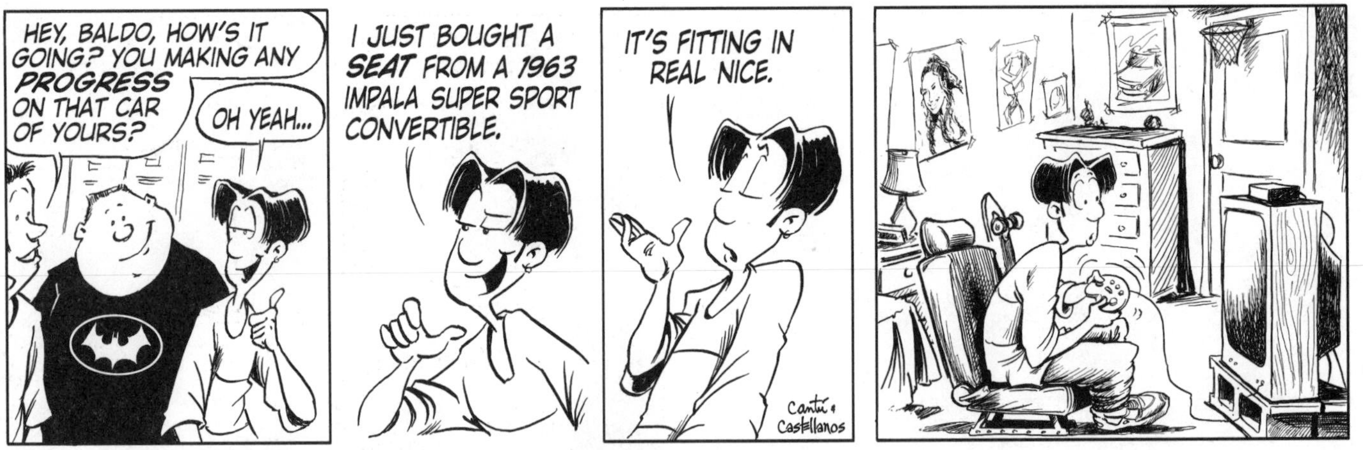
HEY, BALDO, HOW'S IT GOING? YOU MAKING ANY PROGRESS ON THAT CAR OF YOURS?
OH YEAH...
I JUST BOUGHT A SEAT FROM A 1963 IMPALA SUPER SPORT CONVERTIBLE.
IT'S FITTING IN REAL NICE.
Cantú & Castellanos

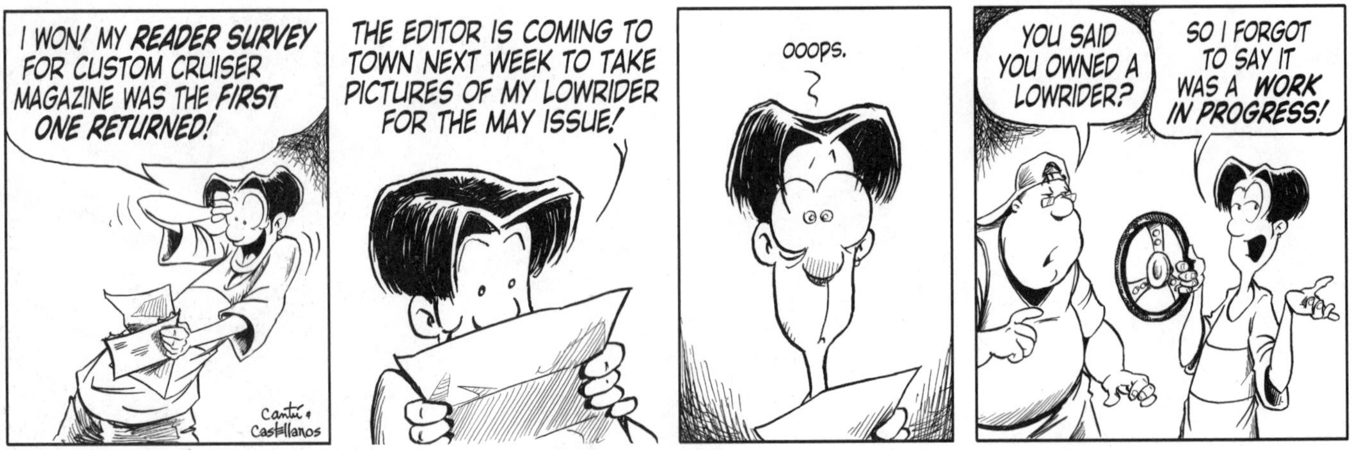
I WON! MY READER SURVEY FOR CUSTOM CRUISER MAGAZINE WAS THE FIRST ONE RETURNED!
Cantú & Castellanos
THE EDITOR IS COMING TO TOWN NEXT WEEK TO TAKE PICTURES OF MY LOWRIDER FOR THE MAY ISSUE!
OOOPS.
YOU SAID YOU OWNED A LOWRIDER?
SO I FORGOT TO SAY IT WAS A WORK IN PROGRESS!

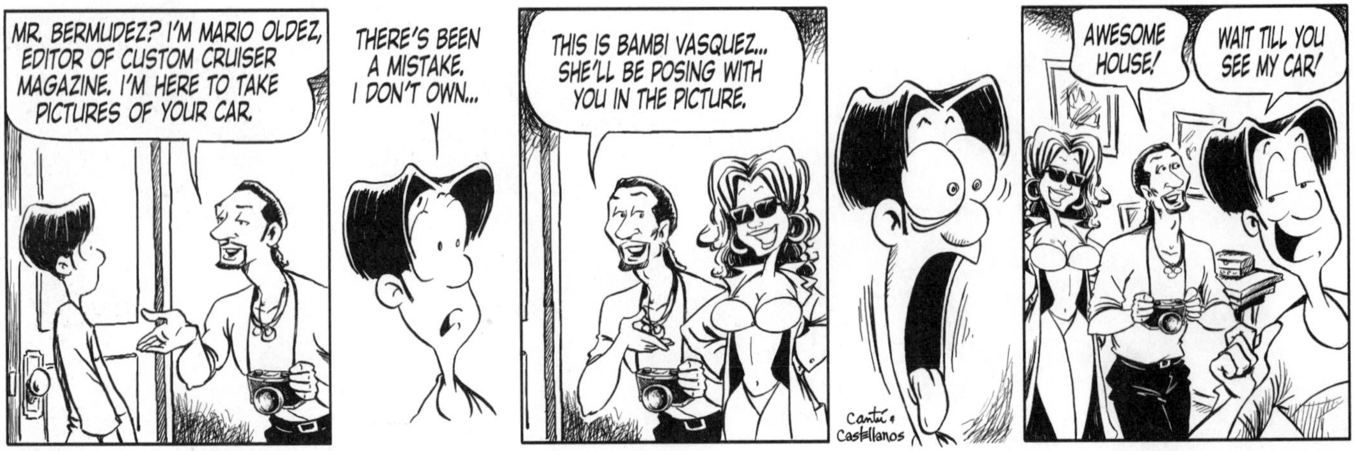
MR. BERMUDEZ? I'M MARIO OLDEZ, EDITOR OF CUSTOM CRUISER MAGAZINE. I'M HERE TO TAKE PICTURES OF YOUR CAR.
THERE'S BEEN A MISTAKE. I DON'T OWN...
THIS IS BAMBI VASQUEZ... SHE'LL BE POSING WITH YOU IN THE PICTURE.
Cantú & Castellanos
AWESOME HOUSE!
WAIT TILL YOU SEE MY CAR!

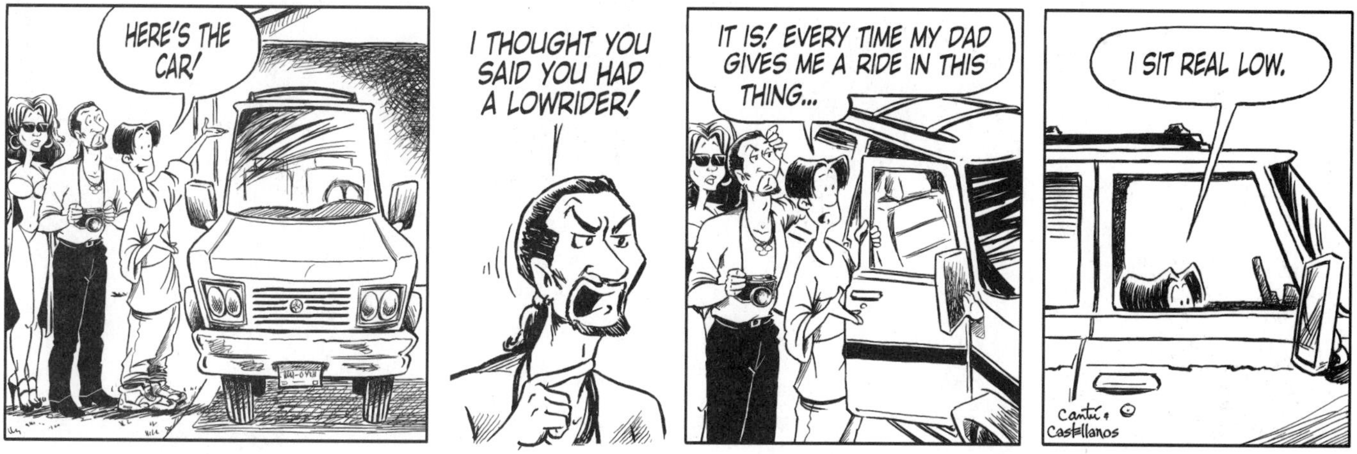
HERE'S THE CAR!
I THOUGHT YOU SAID YOU HAD A LOWRIDER!
IT IS! EVERY TIME MY DAD GIVES ME A RIDE IN THIS THING...
I SIT REAL LOW.
Cantú & Castellanos

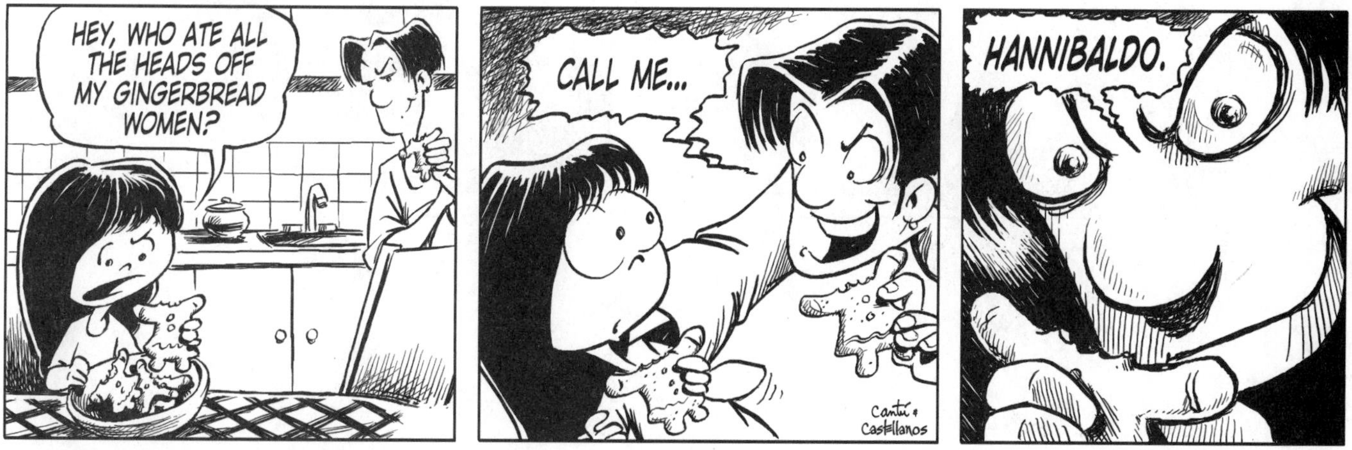
HEY, WHO ATE ALL THE HEADS OFF MY GINGERBREAD WOMEN?
CALL ME...
HANNIBALDO.
Cantú & Castellanos

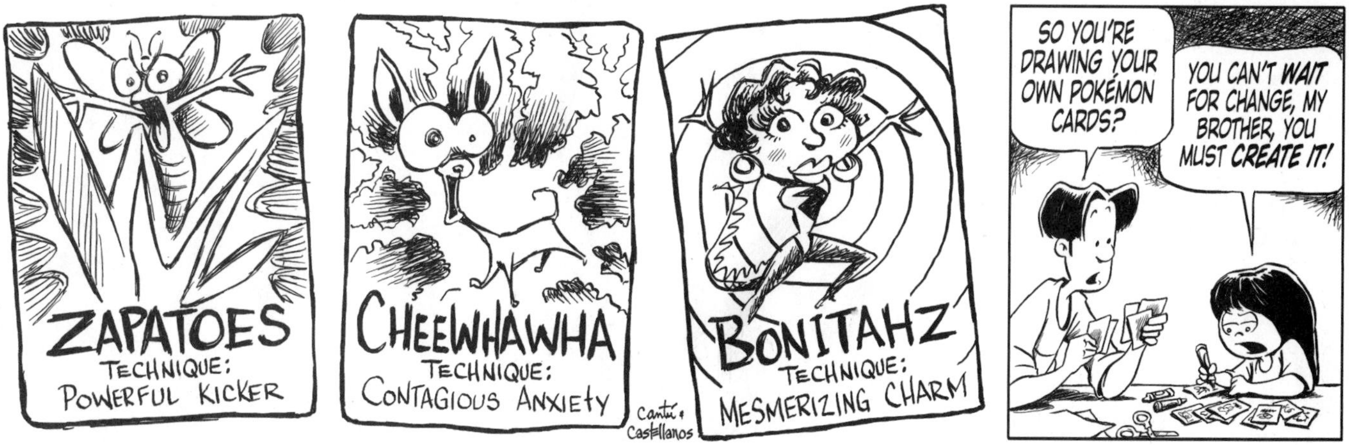
ZAPATOES
TECHNIQUE:
POWERFUL KICKER
CHEEWHAWHA
TECHNIQUE:
CONTAGIOUS ANXIETY
BONITAHZ
TECHNIQUE:
MESMERIZING CHARM
SO YOU'RE DRAWING YOUR OWN POKÉMON CARDS?
YOU CAN'T WAIT FOR CHANGE, MY BROTHER, YOU MUST CREATE IT!
Cantú & Castellanos

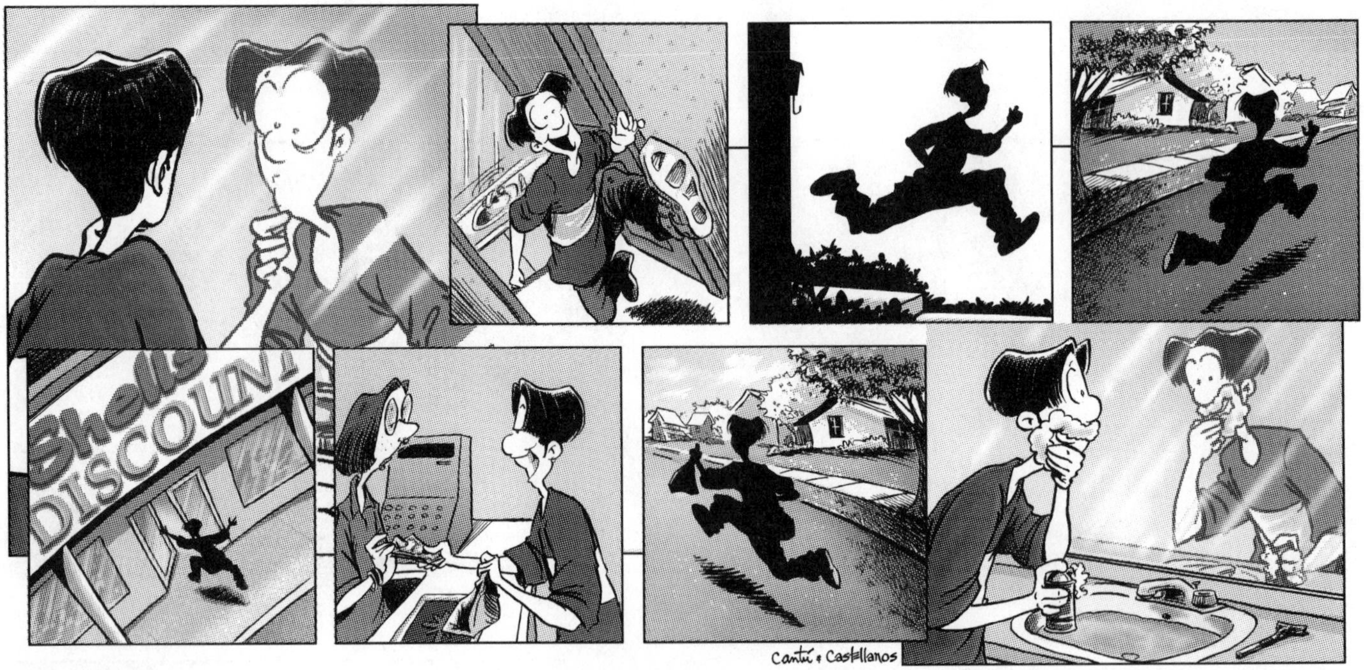
DISCOUN
Cantú & Castellanos

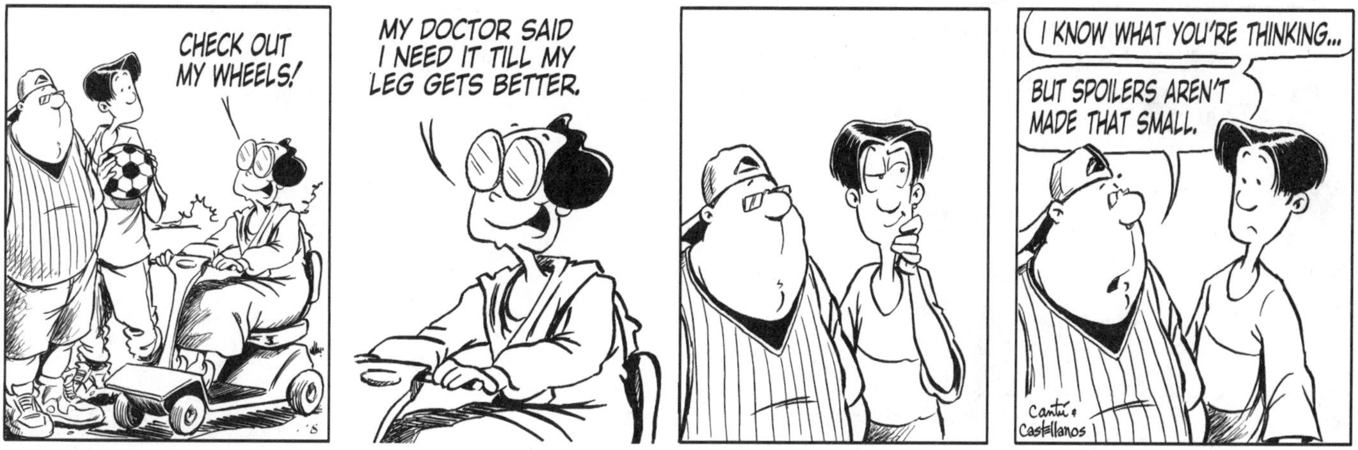
CHECK OUT MY WHEELS!
MY DOCTOR SAID I NEED IT TILL MY LEG GETS BETTER.
I KNOW WHAT YOU'RE THINKING...
BUT SPOILERS AREN'T MADE THAT SMALL.

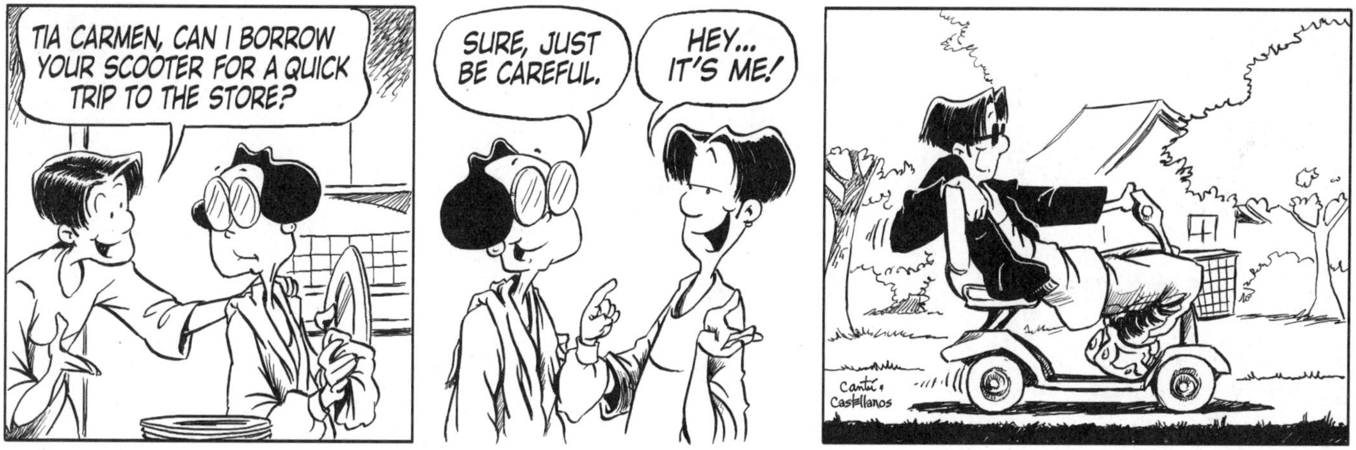
TIA CARMEN, CAN I BORROW YOUR SCOOTER FOR A QUICK TRIP TO THE STORE?
SURE, JUST BE CAREFUL.
HEY... IT'S ME!

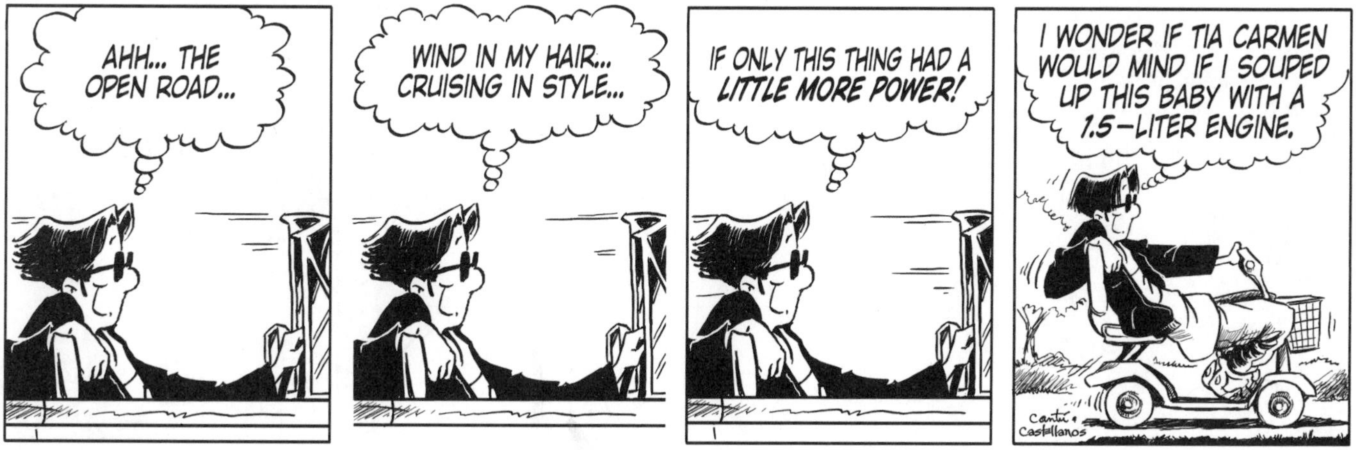
AHH... THE OPEN ROAD...
WIND IN MY HAIR... CRUISING IN STYLE...
IF ONLY THIS THING HAD A *LITTLE MORE POWER!*
I WONDER IF TIA CARMEN WOULD MIND IF I SOUPED UP THIS BABY WITH A *1.5*–LITER ENGINE.

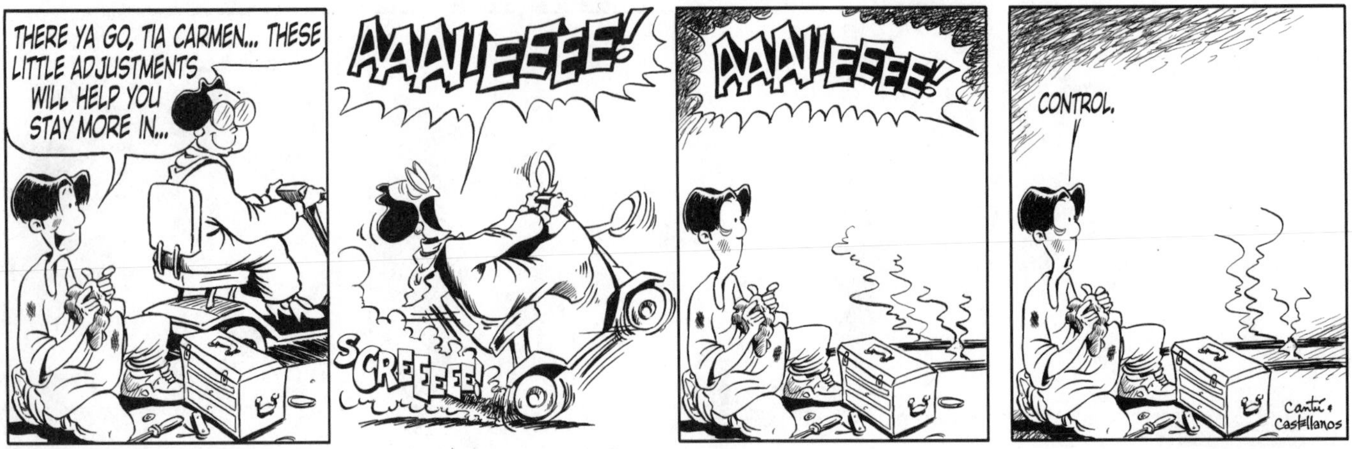
THERE YA GO, TIA CARMEN... THESE LITTLE ADJUSTMENTS WILL HELP YOU STAY MORE IN...
AAAIIEEEE!
SCREEEEEE!
AAAIIEEEE!
CONTROL.
Cantú & Castellanos

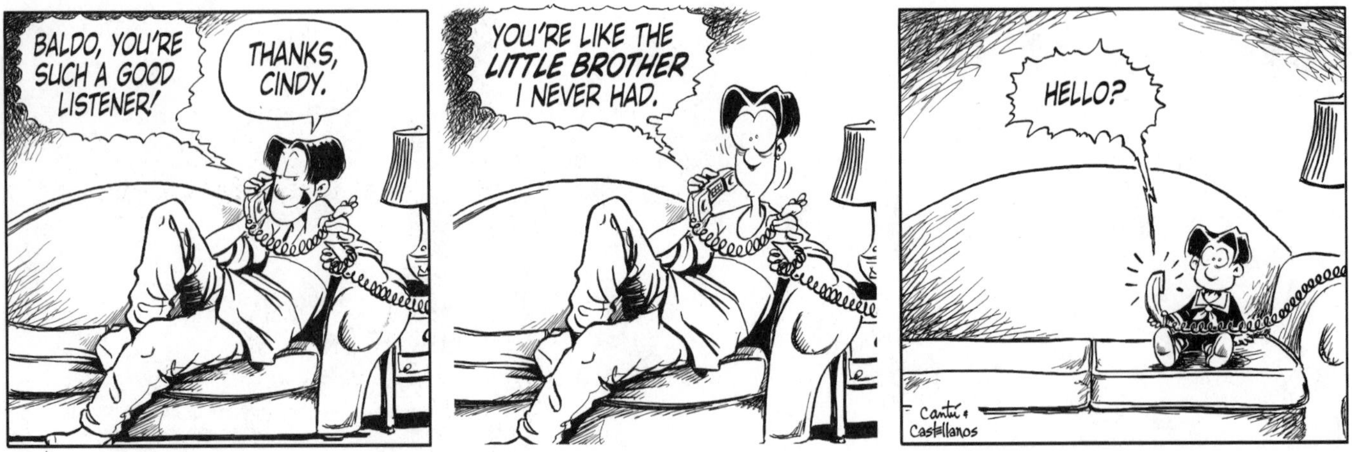
BALDO, YOU'RE SUCH A GOOD LISTENER!
THANKS, CINDY.
YOU'RE LIKE THE *LITTLE BROTHER* I NEVER HAD.
HELLO?
Cantú & Castellanos

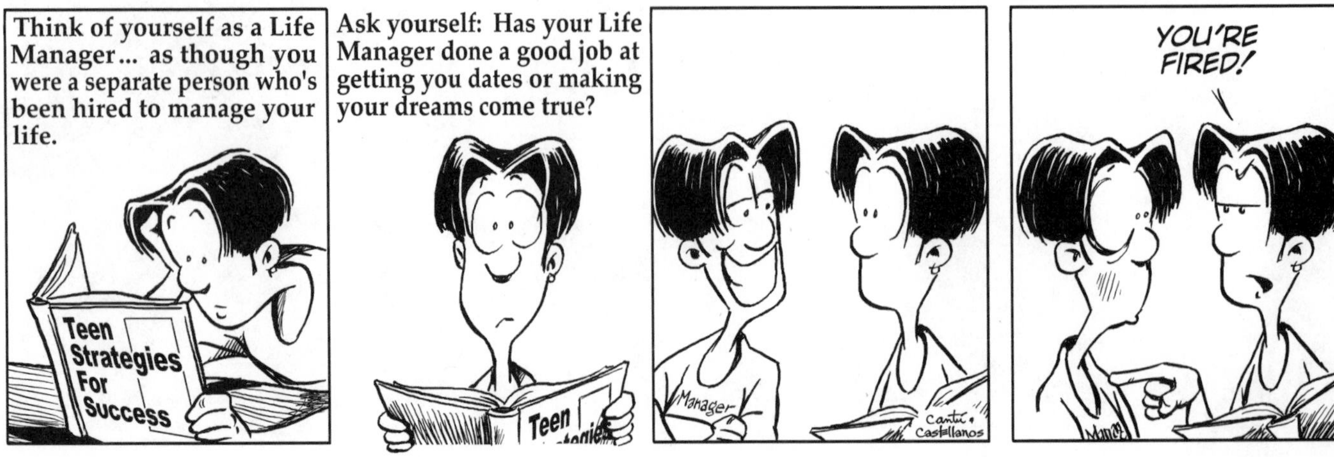
Think of yourself as a Life Manager... as though you were a separate person who's been hired to manage your life.
Teen Strategies For Success
Ask yourself: Has your Life Manager done a good job at getting you dates or making your dreams come true?
Manager
Cantú & Castellanos
YOU'RE FIRED!

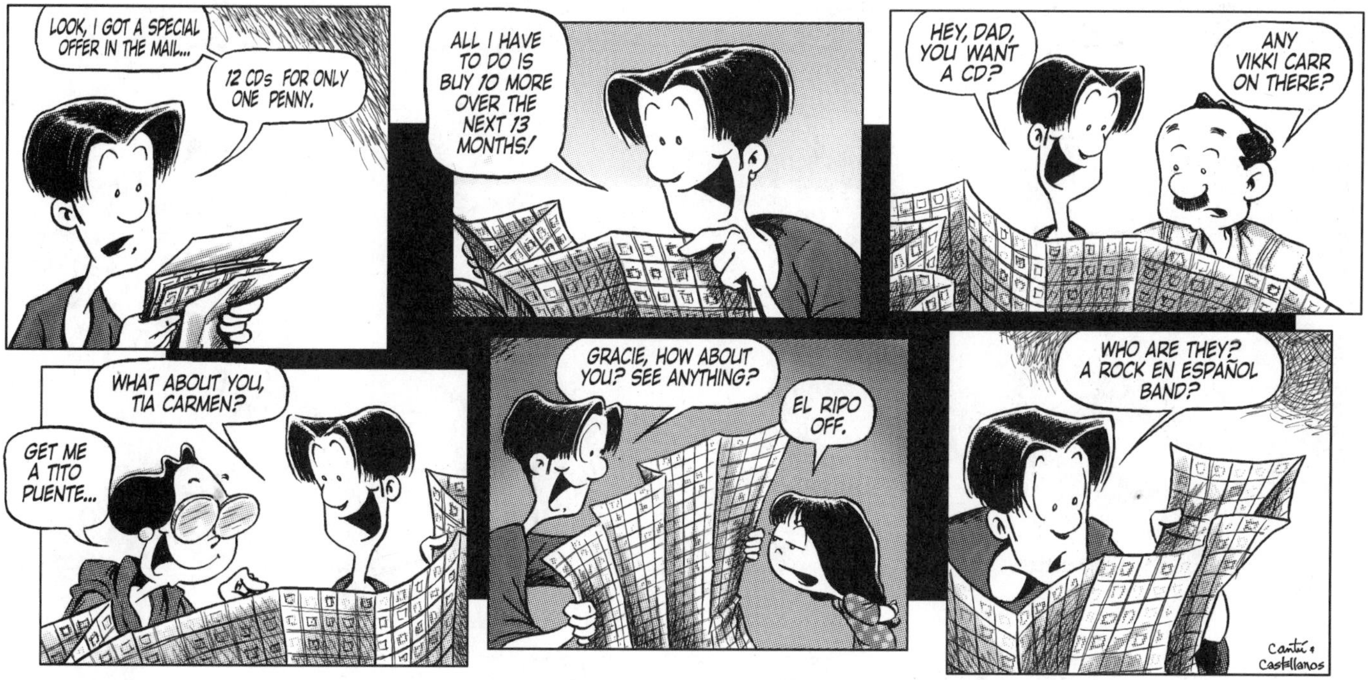
LOOK, I GOT A SPECIAL OFFER IN THE MAIL...
12 CDs FOR ONLY ONE PENNY.
ALL I HAVE TO DO IS BUY 10 MORE OVER THE NEXT 13 MONTHS!
HEY, DAD, YOU WANT A CD?
ANY VIKKI CARR ON THERE?
WHAT ABOUT YOU, TIA CARMEN?
GET ME A TITO PUENTE...
GRACIE, HOW ABOUT YOU? SEE ANYTHING?
EL RIPO OFF.
WHO ARE THEY? A ROCK EN ESPAÑOL BAND?
Cantú & Castellanos

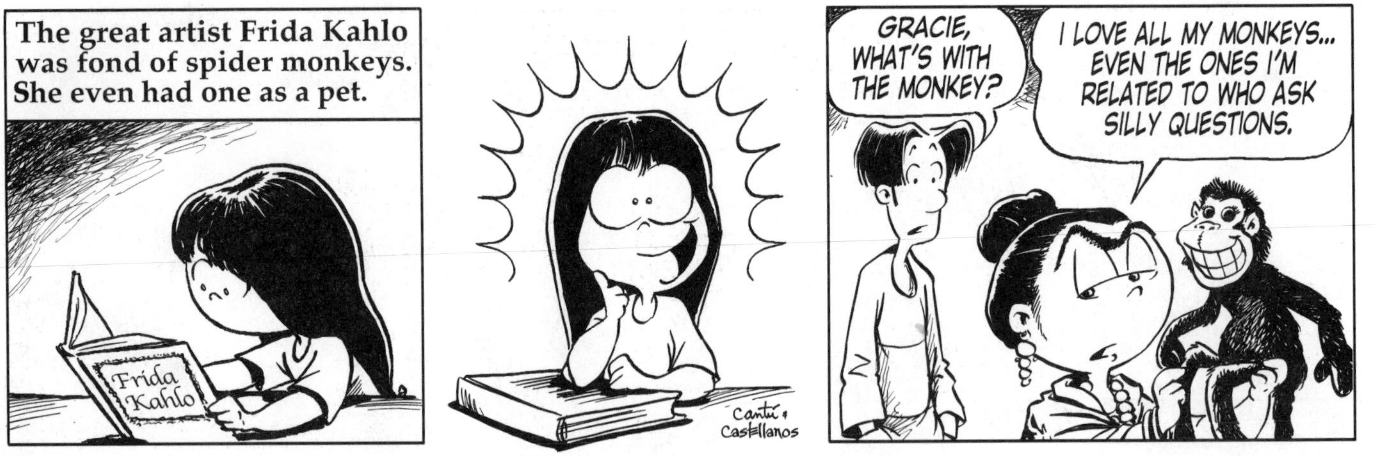
The great artist Frida Kahlo was fond of spider monkeys. She even had one as a pet.
Frida Kahlo
GRACIE, WHAT'S WITH THE MONKEY?
I LOVE ALL MY MONKEYS... EVEN THE ONES I'M RELATED TO WHO ASK SILLY QUESTIONS.

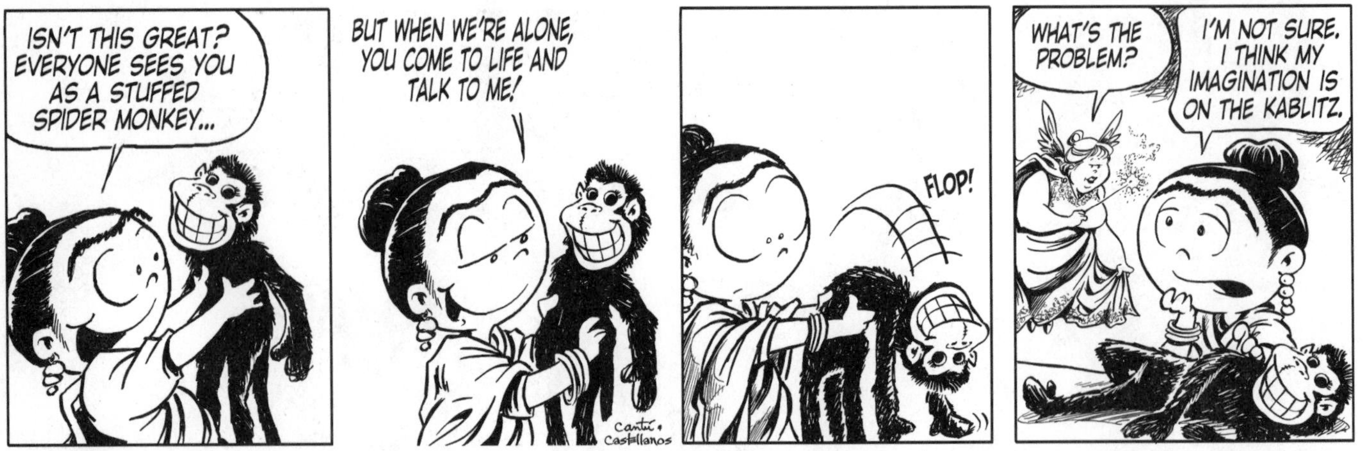
ISN'T THIS GREAT? EVERYONE SEES YOU AS A STUFFED SPIDER MONKEY...
BUT WHEN WE'RE ALONE, YOU COME TO LIFE AND TALK TO ME!
FLOP!
WHAT'S THE PROBLEM?
I'M NOT SURE. I THINK MY IMAGINATION IS ON THE KABLITZ.

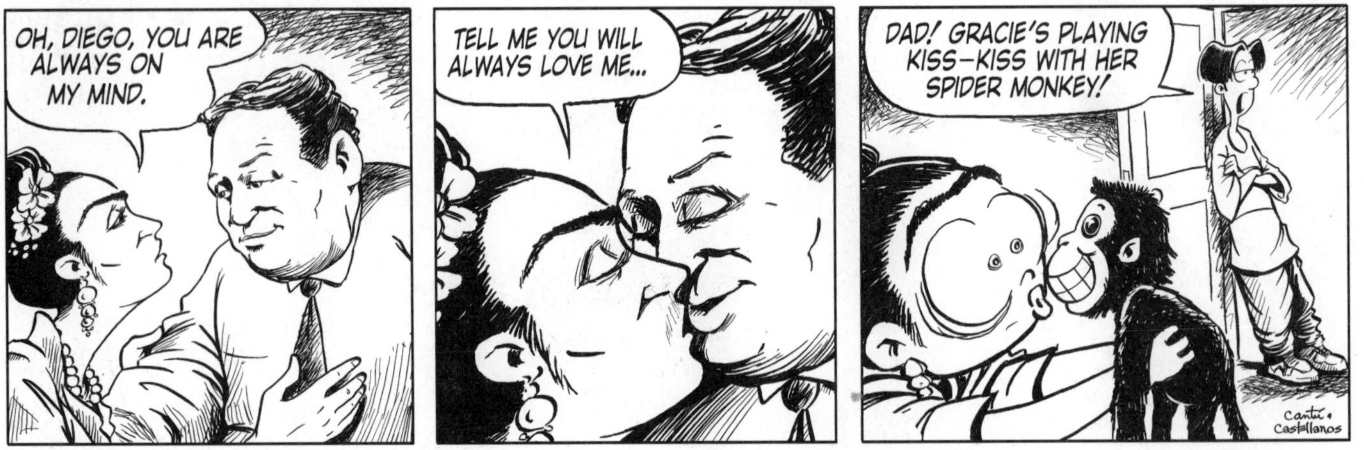
OH, DIEGO, YOU ARE ALWAYS ON MY MIND.
TELL ME YOU WILL ALWAYS LOVE ME...
DAD! GRACIE'S PLAYING KISS-KISS WITH HER SPIDER MONKEY!

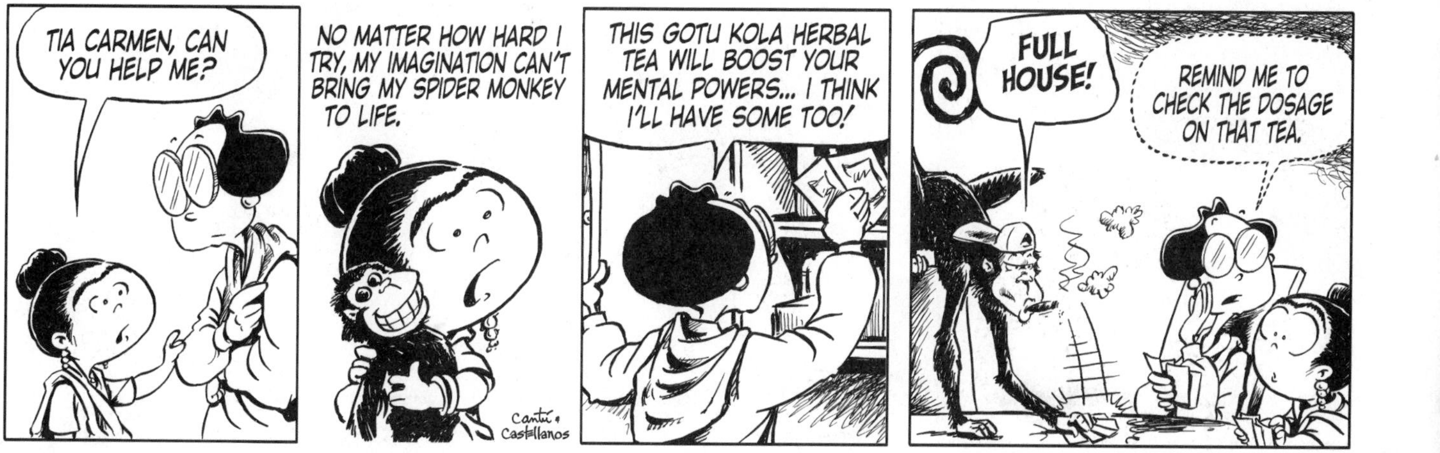
TIA CARMEN, CAN YOU HELP ME?
NO MATTER HOW HARD I TRY, MY IMAGINATION CAN'T BRING MY SPIDER MONKEY TO LIFE.
THIS GOTU KOLA HERBAL TEA WILL BOOST YOUR MENTAL POWERS... I THINK I'LL HAVE SOME TOO!
FULL HOUSE!
REMIND ME TO CHECK THE DOSAGE ON THAT TEA.

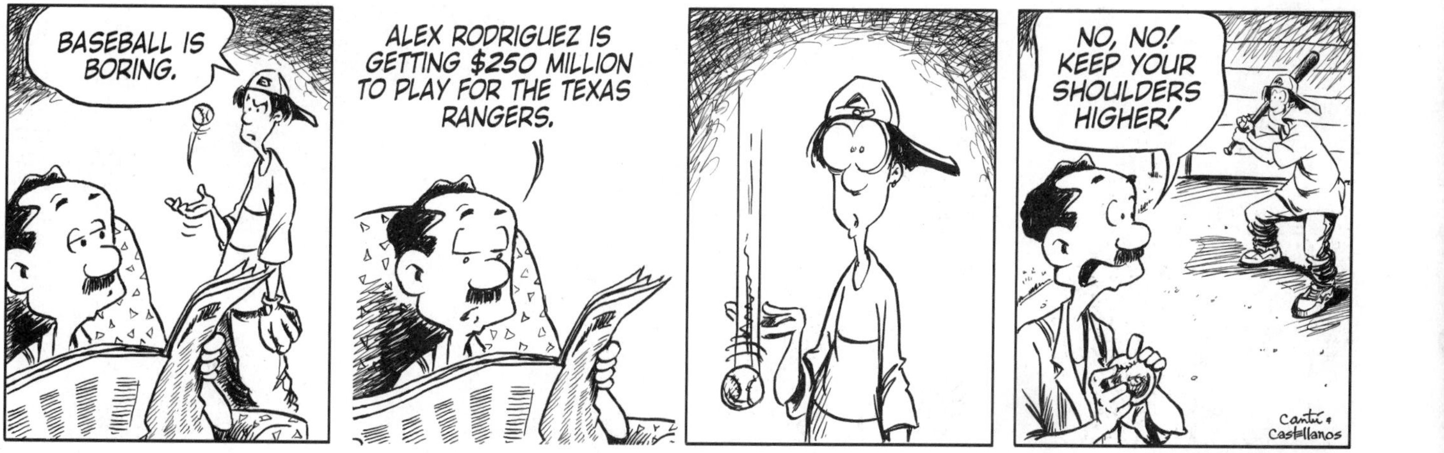
BASEBALL IS BORING.
ALEX RODRIGUEZ IS GETTING $250 MILLION TO PLAY FOR THE TEXAS RANGERS.
NO, NO! KEEP YOUR SHOULDERS HIGHER!

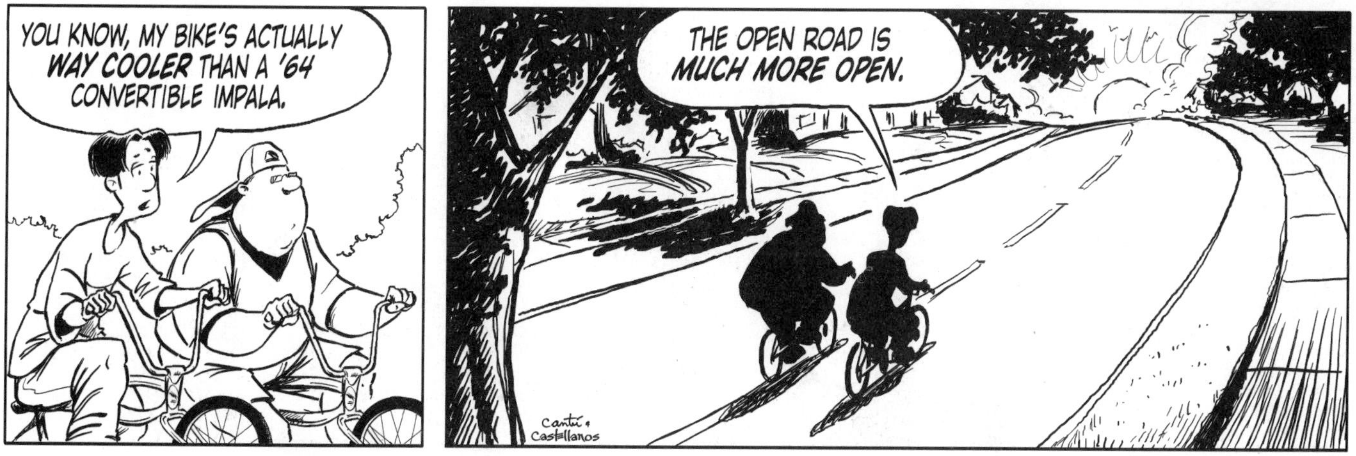
YOU KNOW, MY BIKE'S ACTUALLY WAY COOLER THAN A '64 CONVERTIBLE IMPALA.
THE OPEN ROAD IS MUCH MORE OPEN.

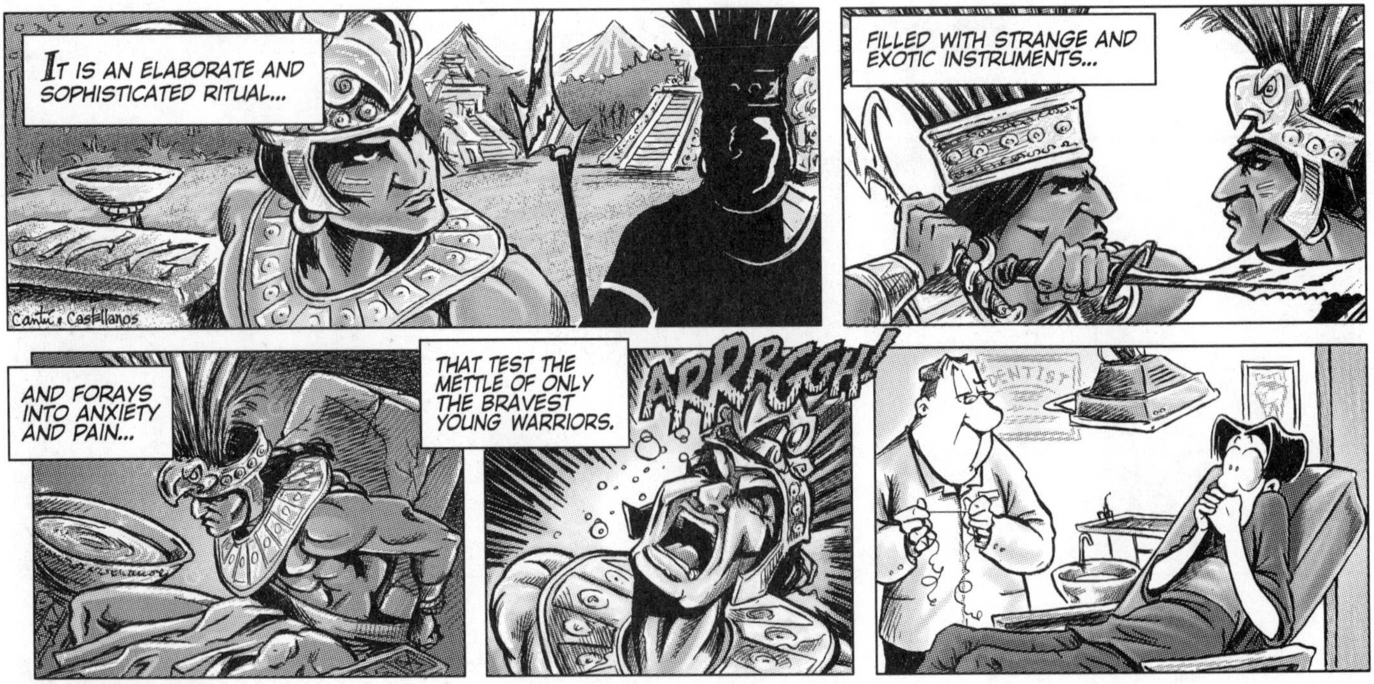
IT IS AN ELABORATE AND SOPHISTICATED RITUAL...
Cantú & Castellanos
FILLED WITH STRANGE AND EXOTIC INSTRUMENTS...
AND FORAYS INTO ANXIETY AND PAIN...
THAT TEST THE METTLE OF ONLY THE BRAVEST YOUNG WARRIORS.
ARRRGGH!
DENTIST

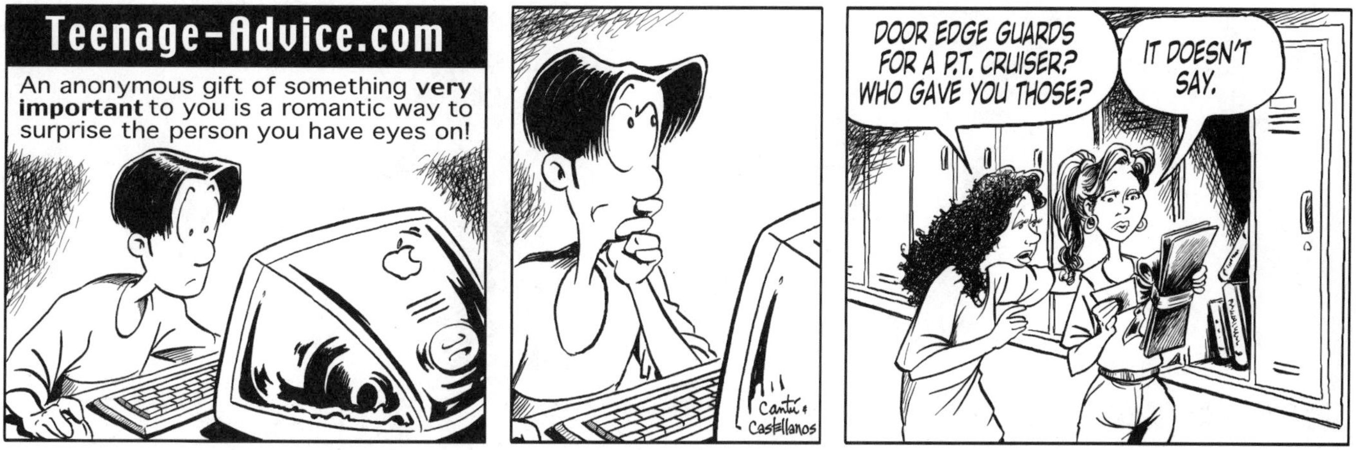
Teenage-Advice.com
An anonymous gift of something **very important** to you is a romantic way to surprise the person you have eyes on!
Cantú & Castellanos
DOOR EDGE GUARDS FOR A P.T. CRUISER? WHO GAVE YOU THOSE?
IT DOESN'T SAY.

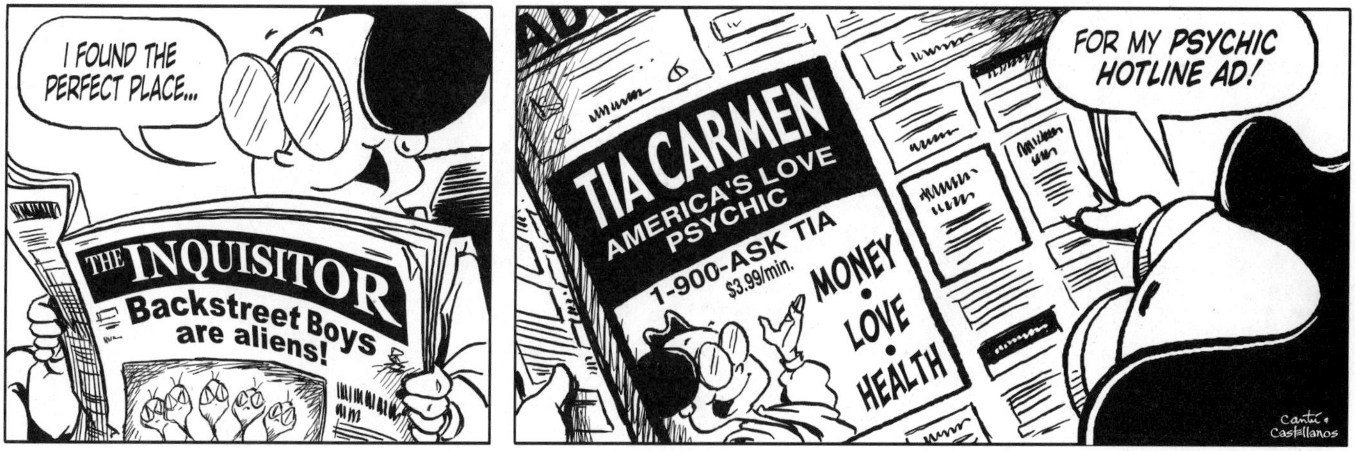
I FOUND THE PERFECT PLACE...
THE INQUISITOR
Backstreet Boys are aliens!
TIA CARMEN
AMERICA'S LOVE PSYCHIC
1-900-ASK TIA
$3.99/min.
MONEY • LOVE • HEALTH
FOR MY **PSYCHIC HOTLINE AD!**
Cantú & Castellanos

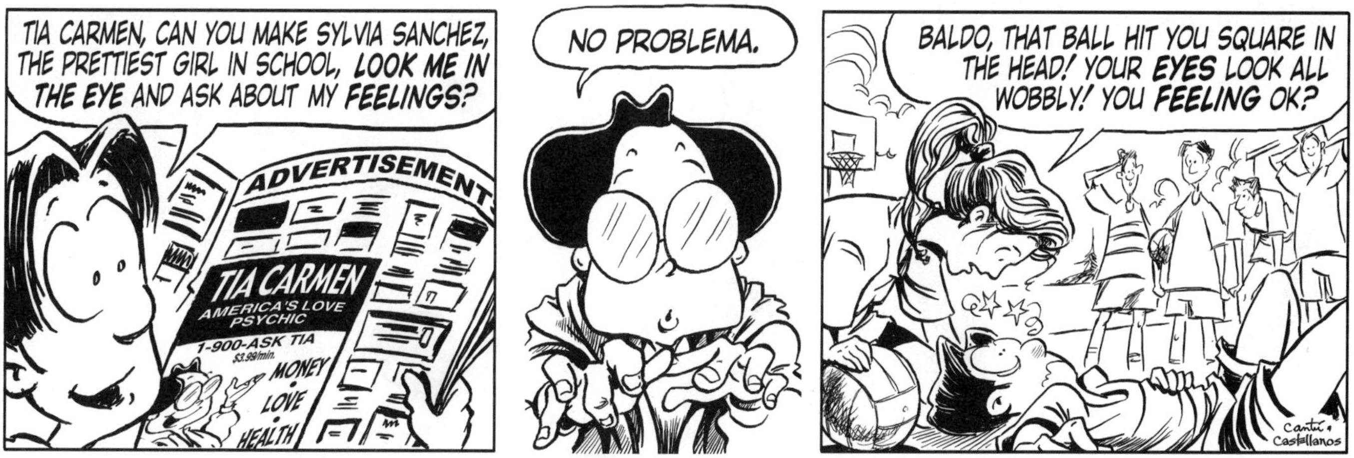
TIA CARMEN, CAN YOU MAKE SYLVIA SANCHEZ, THE PRETTIEST GIRL IN SCHOOL, **LOOK ME IN THE EYE** AND ASK ABOUT MY **FEELINGS?**
ADVERTISEMENT
TIA CARMEN
AMERICA'S LOVE PSYCHIC
1-900-ASK TIA
$3.99/min.
MONEY • LOVE • HEALTH
NO PROBLEMA.
BALDO, THAT BALL HIT YOU SQUARE IN THE HEAD! YOUR **EYES** LOOK ALL WOBBLY! YOU **FEELING** OK?
Cantú & Castellanos

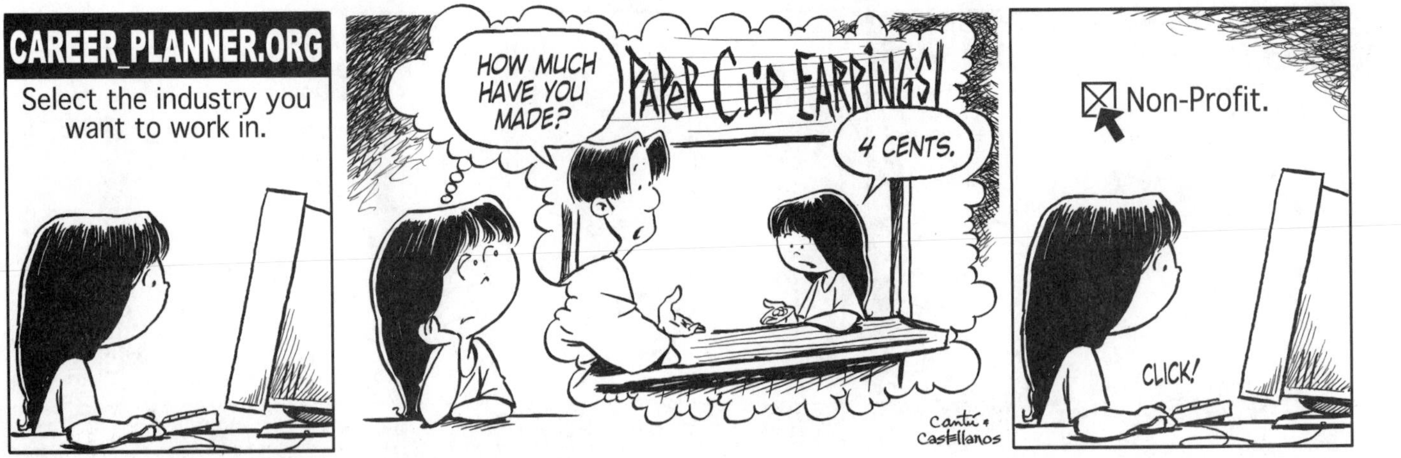
CAREER_PLANNER.ORG
Select the industry you want to work in.
HOW MUCH HAVE YOU MADE?
PAPER CLIP EARRINGS!
4 CENTS.
Cantú & Castellanos
Non-Profit.
CLICK!

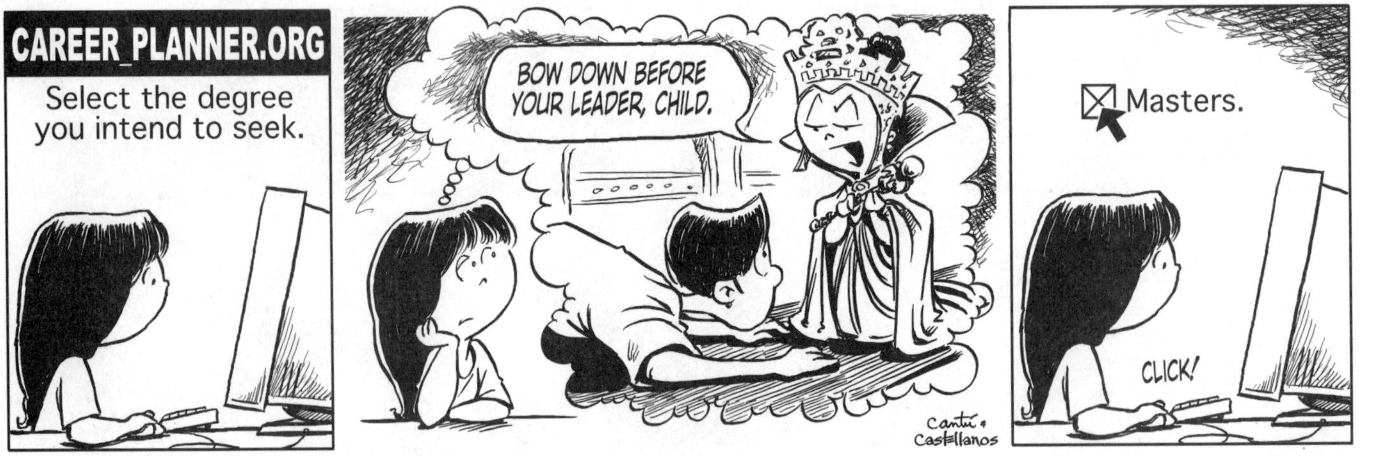
CAREER_PLANNER.ORG
Select the degree you intend to seek.
BOW DOWN BEFORE YOUR LEADER, CHILD.
Cantú & Castellanos
Masters.
CLICK!

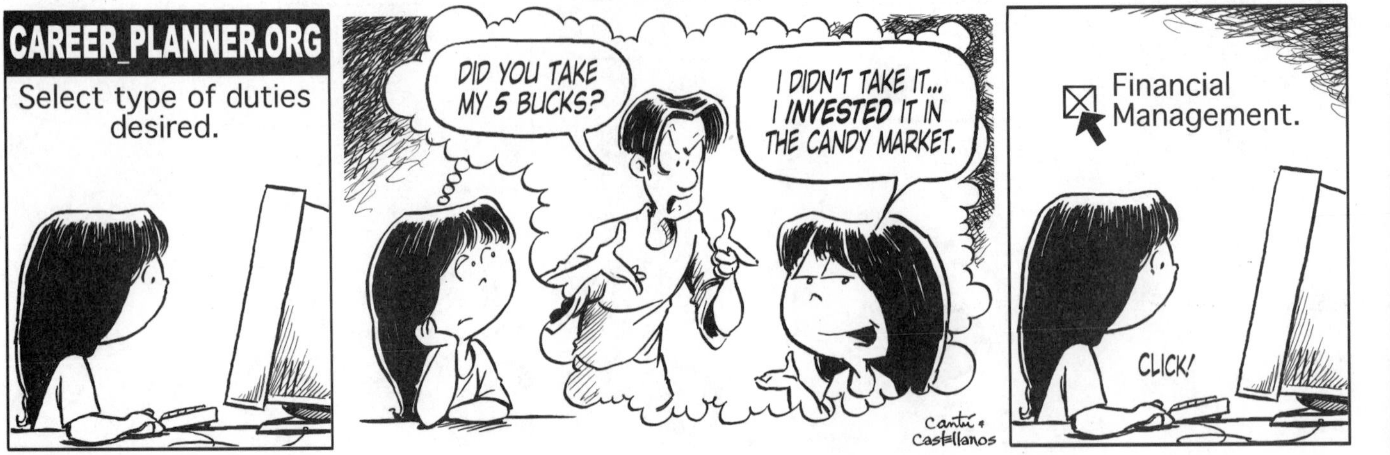
CAREER_PLANNER.ORG
Select type of duties desired.
DID YOU TAKE MY 5 BUCKS?
I DIDN'T TAKE IT... I INVESTED IT IN THE CANDY MARKET.
Cantú & Castellanos
Financial Management.
CLICK!

JENNIFER!
WHERE HAVE YOU BEEN?
YOU'RE LOOKING GOOD, MISS LOPEZ!
IT'S BEEN SO LONG SINCE WE TALKED...
LET'S JUST RUN AWAY... YOU AND ME...
Cantú & Castellanos
I WISH I HAD A BIG-SCREEN TV.
ME TOO.
LARGE SCREEN TV SALE!

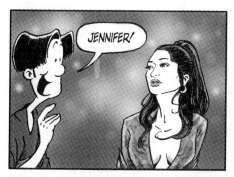

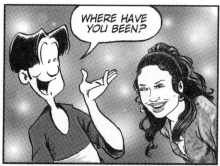

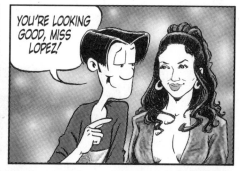

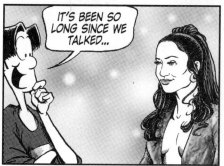

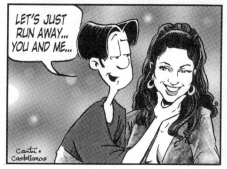

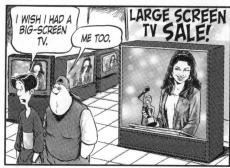

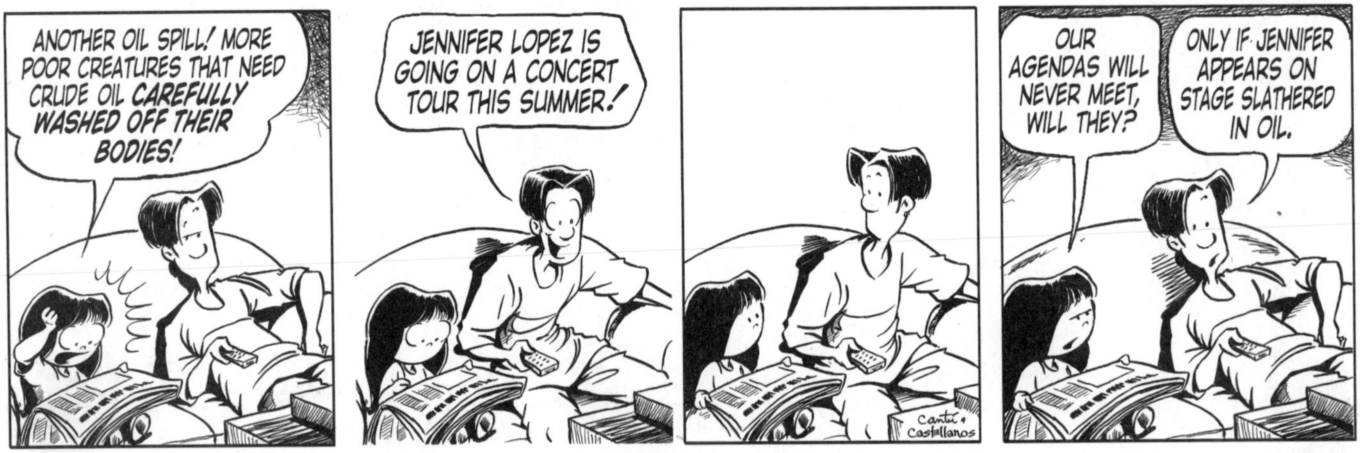
ANOTHER OIL SPILL! MORE POOR CREATURES THAT NEED CRUDE OIL CAREFULLY WASHED OFF THEIR BODIES!
JENNIFER LOPEZ IS GOING ON A CONCERT TOUR THIS SUMMER!
OUR AGENDAS WILL NEVER MEET, WILL THEY?
ONLY IF JENNIFER APPEARS ON STAGE SLATHERED IN OIL.
Cantú & Castellanos

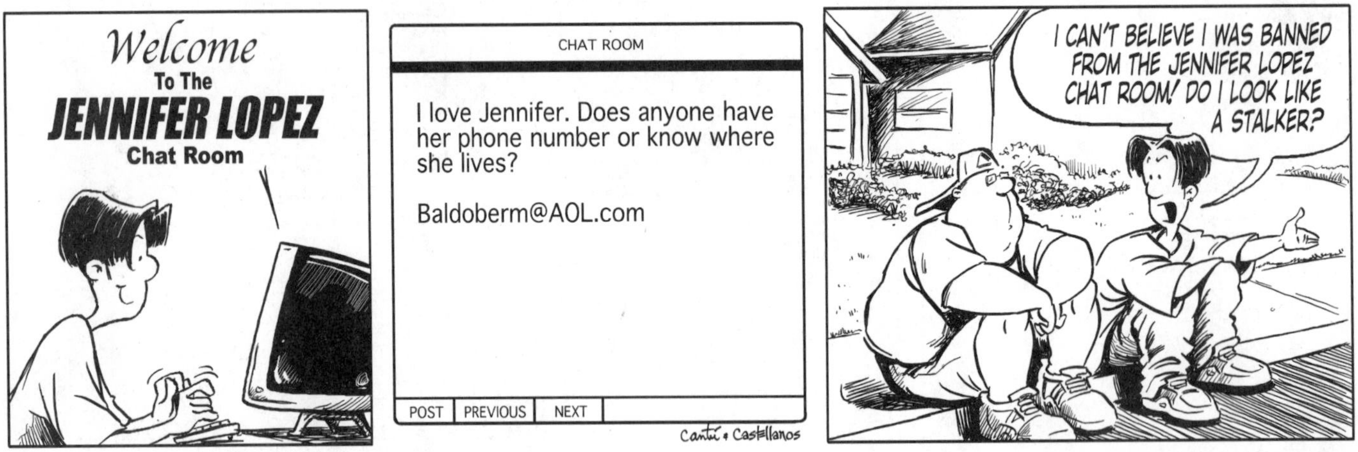
Welcome
To The
JENNIFER LOPEZ
Chat Room
CHAT ROOM
I love Jennifer. Does anyone have her phone number or know where she lives?
Baldoberm@AOL.com
POST
PREVIOUS
NEXT
Cantú & Castellanos
I CAN'T BELIEVE I WAS BANNED FROM THE JENNIFER LOPEZ CHAT ROOM! DO I LOOK LIKE A STALKER?

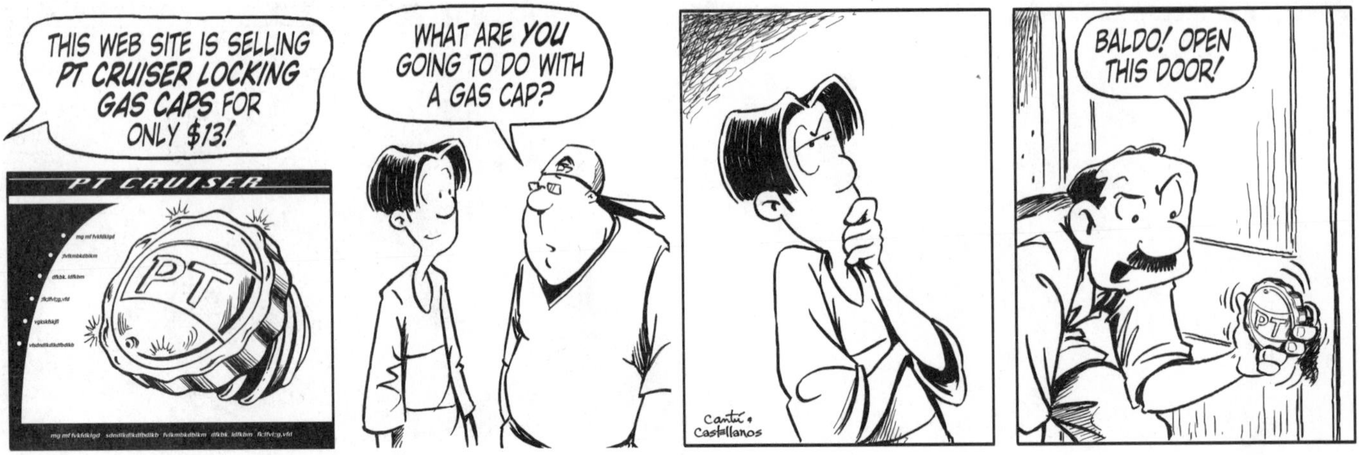
THIS WEB SITE IS SELLING PT CRUISER LOCKING GAS CAPS FOR ONLY $13!
PT CRUISER
PT
WHAT ARE YOU GOING TO DO WITH A GAS CAP?
Cantú & Castellanos
BALDO! OPEN THIS DOOR!
PT

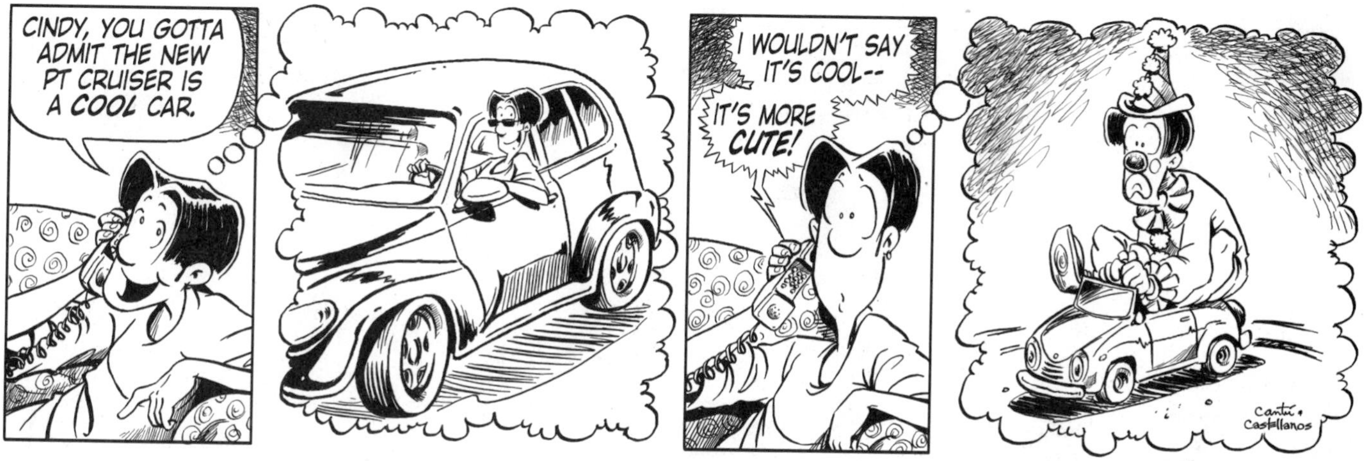
CINDY, YOU GOTTA ADMIT THE NEW PT CRUISER IS A **COOL** CAR.
I WOULDN'T SAY IT'S COOL--
IT'S MORE **CUTE!**
Cantú & Castellanos

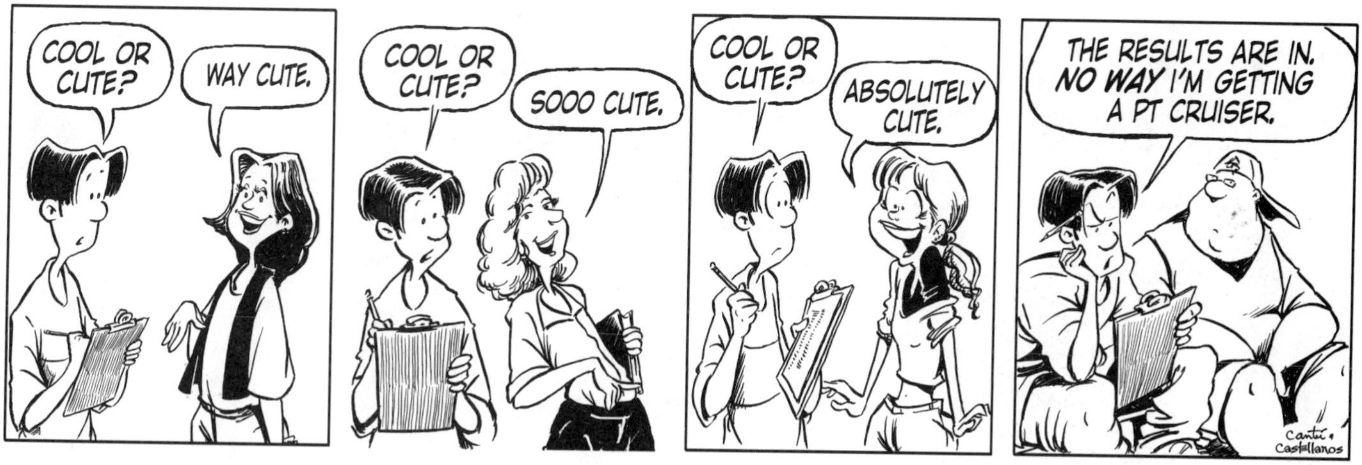
COOL OR CUTE?
WAY CUTE.
COOL OR CUTE?
SOOO CUTE.
COOL OR CUTE?
ABSOLUTELY CUTE.
THE RESULTS ARE IN. **NO WAY** I'M GETTING A PT CRUISER.
Cantú & Castellanos

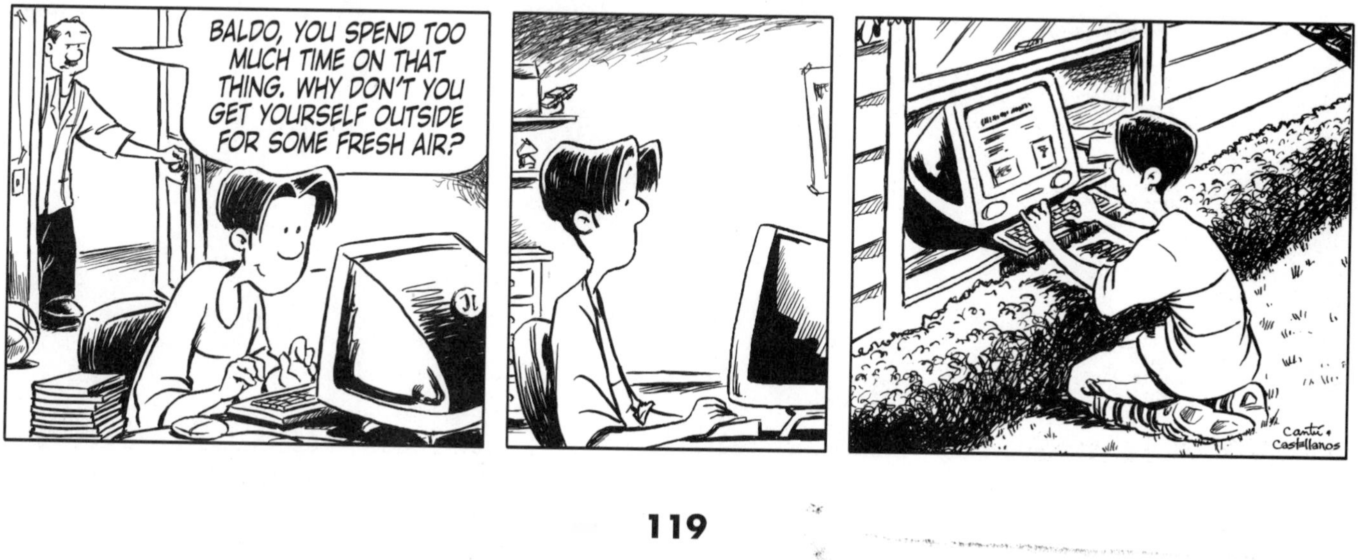
BALDO, YOU SPEND TOO MUCH TIME ON THAT THING. WHY DON'T YOU GET YOURSELF OUTSIDE FOR SOME FRESH AIR?
Cantú & Castellanos

WHO ARE YOU?
YO... I'M YOUR FAIRY GOD-PADRINO.
BUT THE LAST TIME YOU WERE HERE, YOU LOOKED DIFFERENT.
YEAH, BUT THIS LOOK DOES NADA FOR CLIENT RETENTION.
SnaP!
THIS IS COOLER... SO ALL MY HOMIES CAN CONNECT WITH WHAT I'M SAYING, KNOW WHAT I'M SAYING?
WORD!
HEY! WHERE YOU GOING? WHAT ABOUT A WRESTLER? WILL YOU LISTEN TO MY AGE-OLD WISDOM IF I'M A PROFESSIONAL WRESTLER?
Cantú & Castellanos

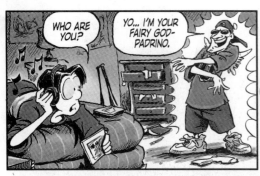

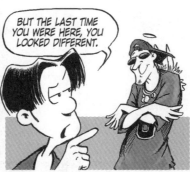

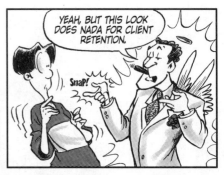

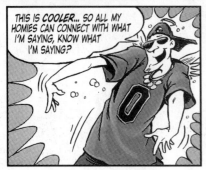

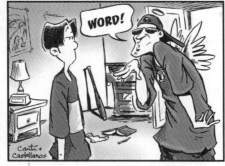

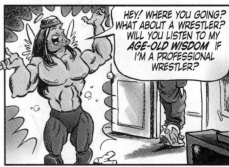

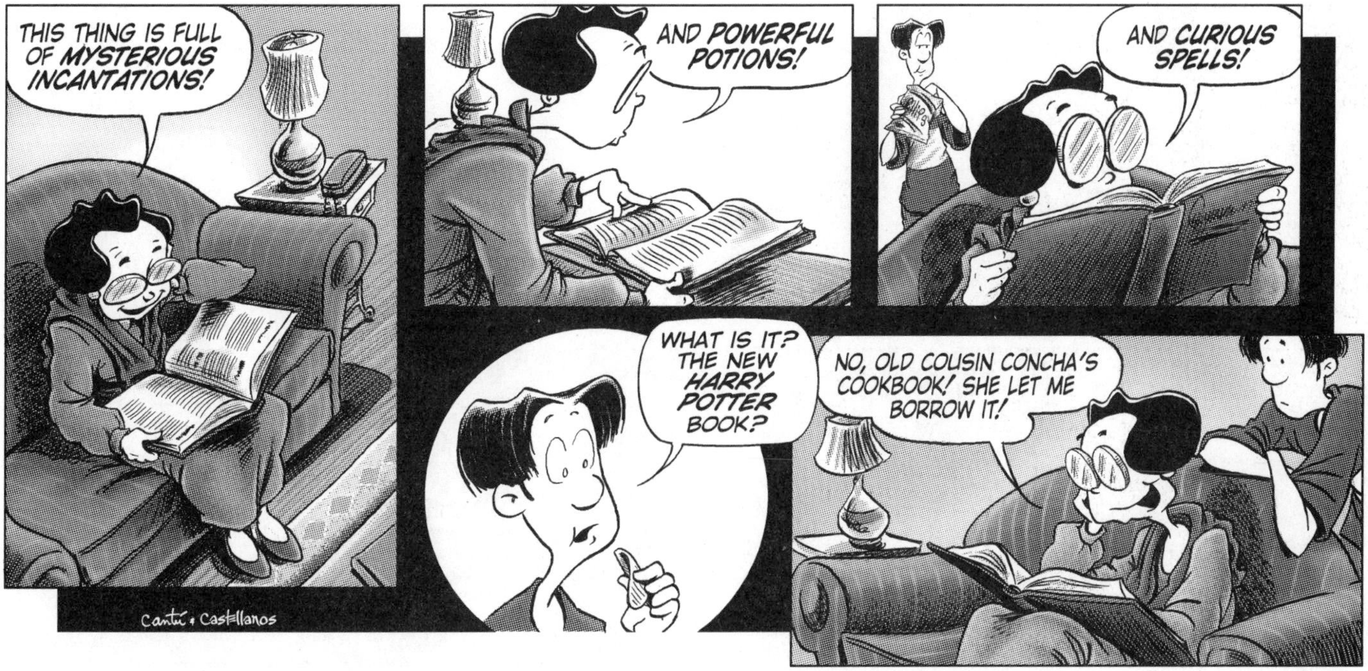
THIS THING IS FULL OF MYSTERIOUS INCANTATIONS!
AND POWERFUL POTIONS!
AND CURIOUS SPELLS!
WHAT IS IT? THE NEW HARRY POTTER BOOK?
NO, OLD COUSIN CONCHA'S COOKBOOK! SHE LET ME BORROW IT!
Cantú + Castellanos

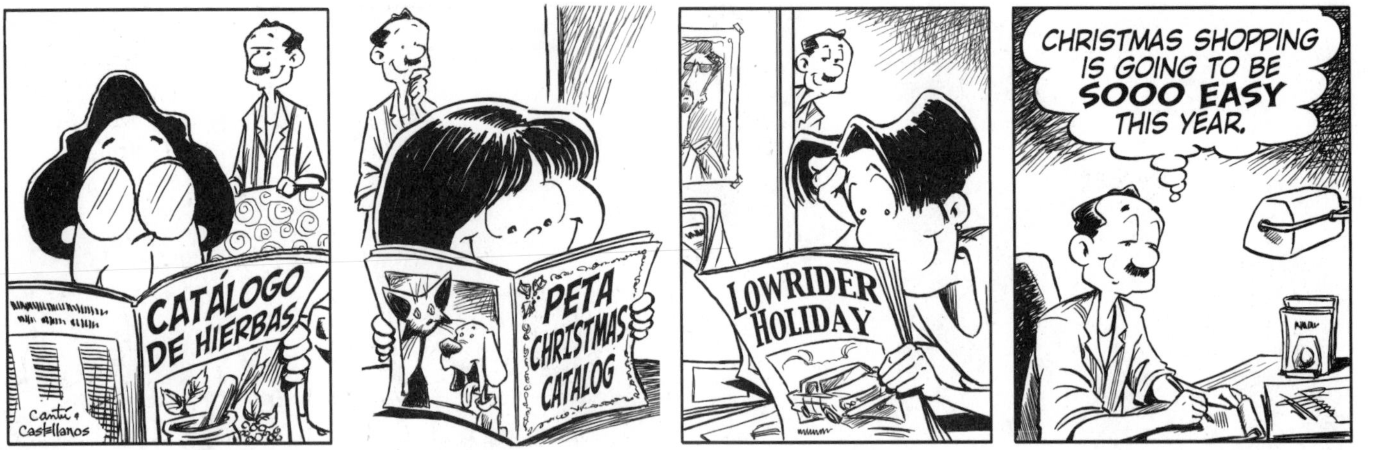
CATÁLOGO DE HIERBAS
Cantú & Castellanos
PETA CHRISTMAS CATALOG
LOWRIDER HOLIDAY
CHRISTMAS SHOPPING IS GOING TO BE **SOOO EASY** THIS YEAR.

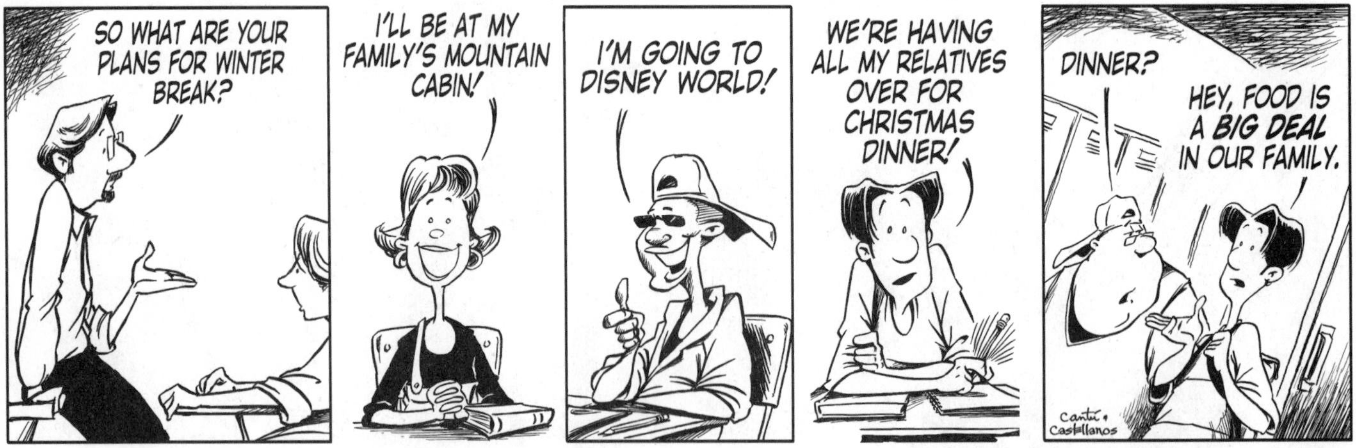
SO WHAT ARE YOUR PLANS FOR WINTER BREAK?
I'LL BE AT MY FAMILY'S MOUNTAIN CABIN!
I'M GOING TO DISNEY WORLD!
WE'RE HAVING ALL MY RELATIVES OVER FOR CHRISTMAS DINNER!
DINNER?
HEY, FOOD IS A ***BIG DEAL*** IN OUR FAMILY.
Cantú & Castellanos

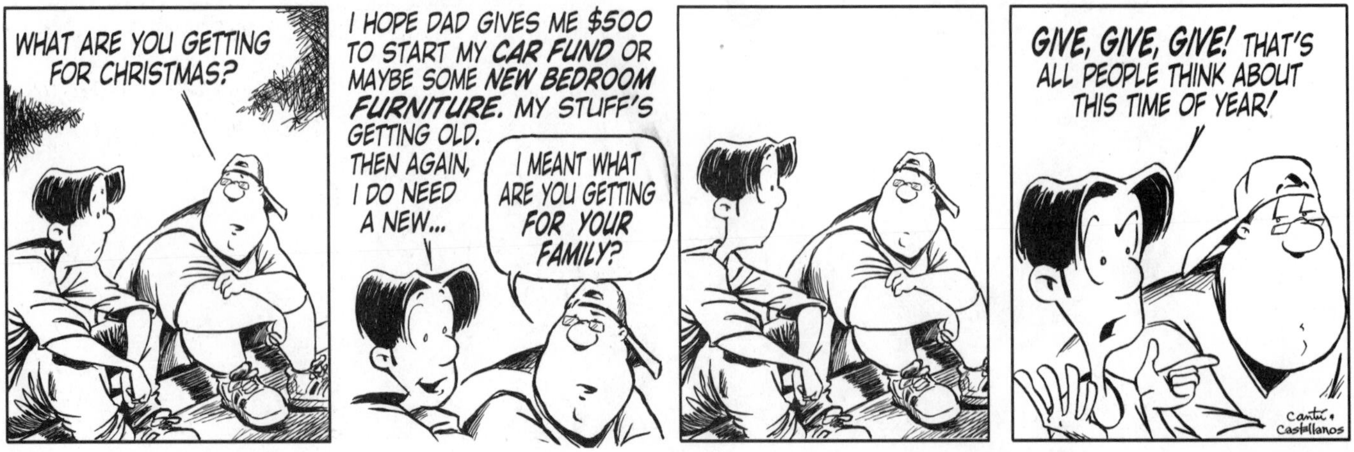
WHAT ARE YOU GETTING FOR CHRISTMAS?
I HOPE DAD GIVES ME $500 TO START MY ***CAR FUND*** OR MAYBE SOME ***NEW BEDROOM FURNITURE.*** MY STUFF'S GETTING OLD. THEN AGAIN, I DO NEED A NEW...
I MEANT WHAT ARE YOU GETTING ***FOR YOUR FAMILY?***
GIVE, GIVE, GIVE! THAT'S ALL PEOPLE THINK ABOUT THIS TIME OF YEAR!
Cantú & Castellanos

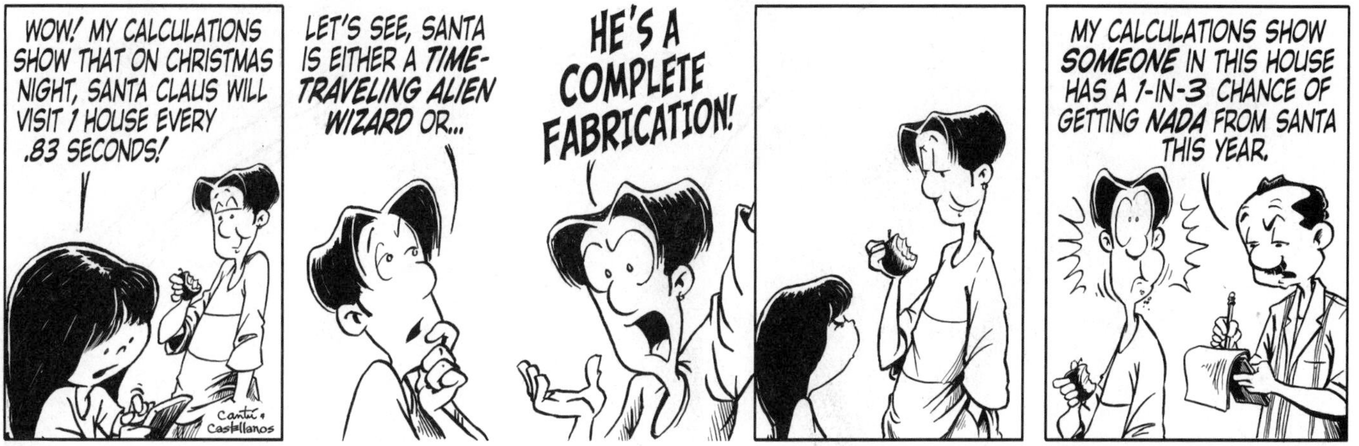
WOW! MY CALCULATIONS SHOW THAT ON CHRISTMAS NIGHT, SANTA CLAUS WILL VISIT 1 HOUSE EVERY .83 SECONDS!
LET'S SEE, SANTA IS EITHER A TIME-TRAVELING ALIEN WIZARD OR...
HE'S A COMPLETE FABRICATION!
MY CALCULATIONS SHOW SOMEONE IN THIS HOUSE HAS A 1-IN-3 CHANCE OF GETTING NADA FROM SANTA THIS YEAR.

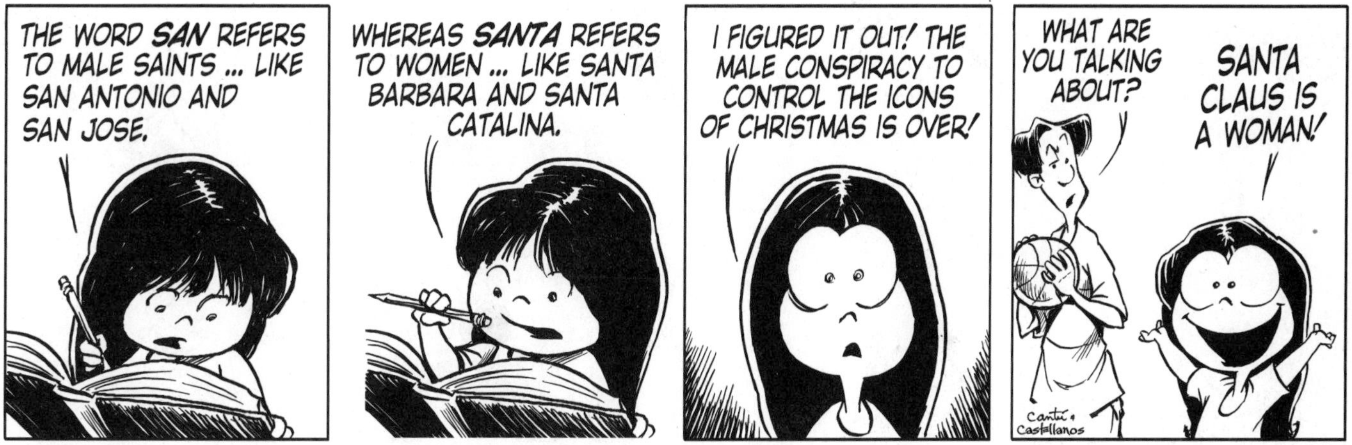
THE WORD SAN REFERS TO MALE SAINTS ... LIKE SAN ANTONIO AND SAN JOSE.
WHEREAS SANTA REFERS TO WOMEN ... LIKE SANTA BARBARA AND SANTA CATALINA.
I FIGURED IT OUT! THE MALE CONSPIRACY TO CONTROL THE ICONS OF CHRISTMAS IS OVER!
WHAT ARE YOU TALKING ABOUT?
SANTA CLAUS IS A WOMAN!

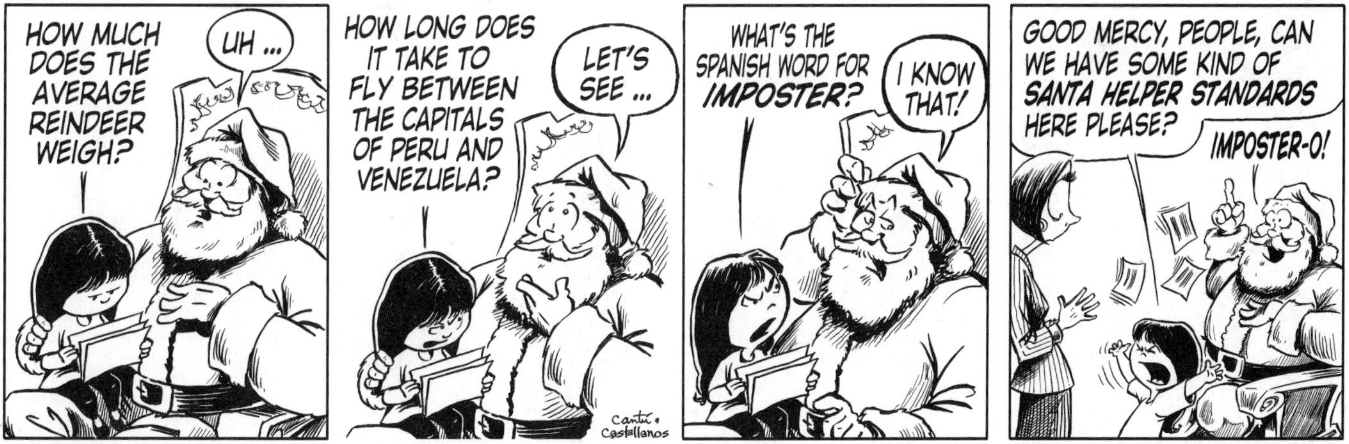
HOW MUCH DOES THE AVERAGE REINDEER WEIGH?
UH ...
HOW LONG DOES IT TAKE TO FLY BETWEEN THE CAPITALS OF PERU AND VENEZUELA?
LET'S SEE ...
WHAT'S THE SPANISH WORD FOR IMPOSTER?
I KNOW THAT!
GOOD MERCY, PEOPLE, CAN WE HAVE SOME KIND OF SANTA HELPER STANDARDS HERE PLEASE?
IMPOSTER-O!

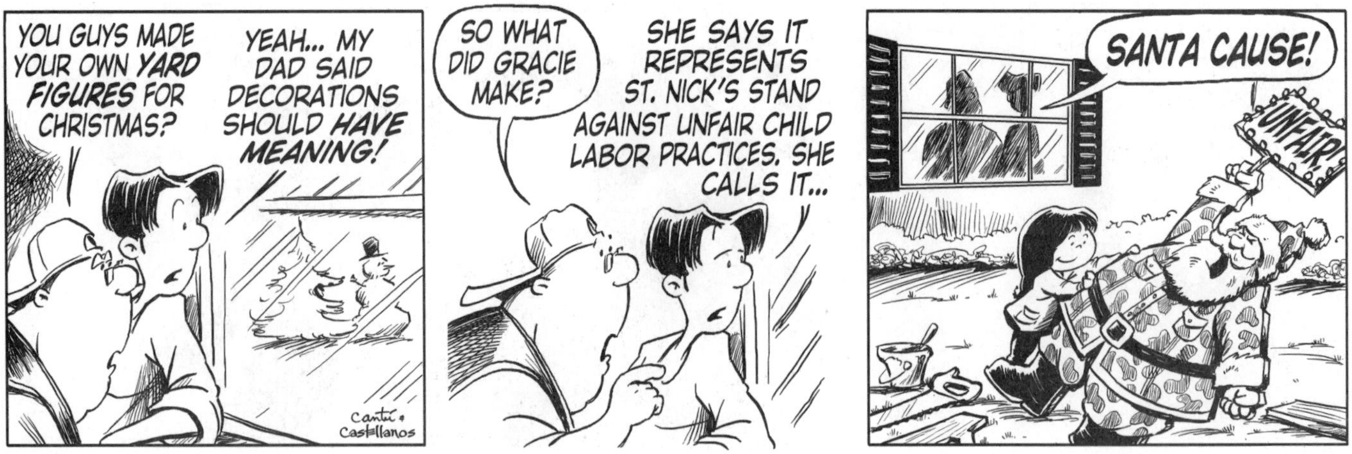
YOU GUYS MADE YOUR OWN *YARD FIGURES* FOR CHRISTMAS?
YEAH... MY DAD SAID DECORATIONS SHOULD *HAVE MEANING!*
Cantú & Castellanos
SO WHAT DID GRACIE MAKE?
SHE SAYS IT REPRESENTS ST. NICK'S STAND AGAINST UNFAIR CHILD LABOR PRACTICES. SHE CALLS IT...
SANTA CAUSE!
UNFAIR!

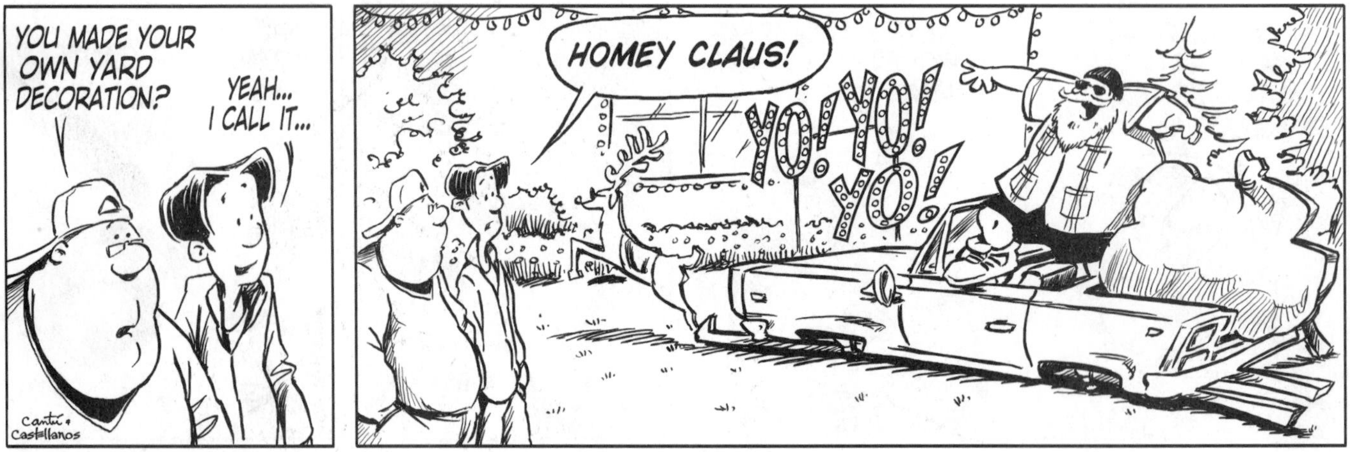
YOU MADE YOUR OWN YARD DECORATION?
YEAH... I CALL IT...
Cantú & Castellanos
HOMEY CLAUS!
YO! YO! YO!

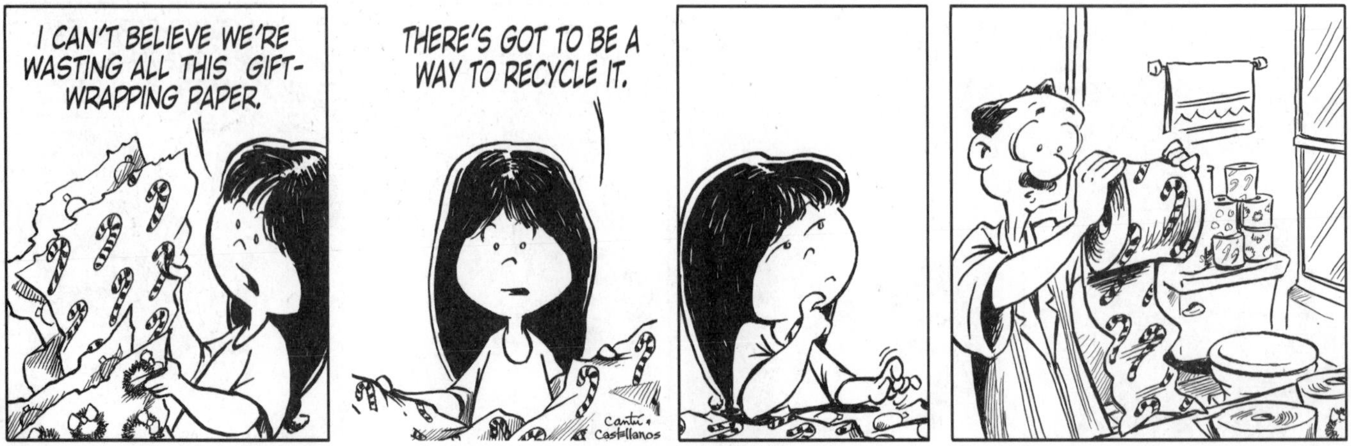
I CAN'T BELIEVE WE'RE WASTING ALL THIS GIFT-WRAPPING PAPER.
THERE'S GOT TO BE A WAY TO RECYCLE IT.
Cantú & Castellanos

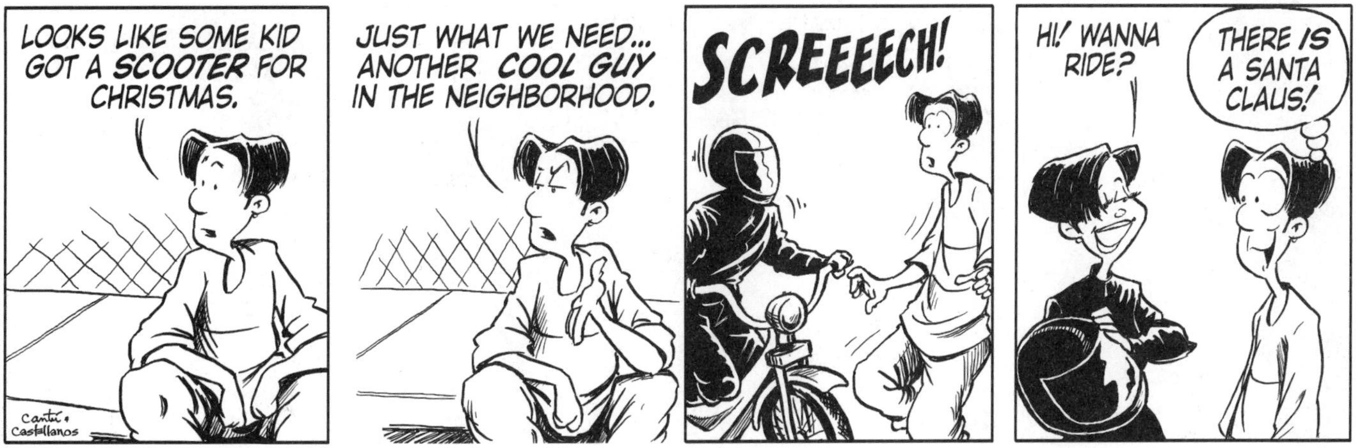
LOOKS LIKE SOME KID GOT A SCOOTER FOR CHRISTMAS.
Cantú & Castellanos
JUST WHAT WE NEED... ANOTHER COOL GUY IN THE NEIGHBORHOOD.
SCREEEEECH!
HI! WANNA RIDE?
THERE IS A SANTA CLAUS!

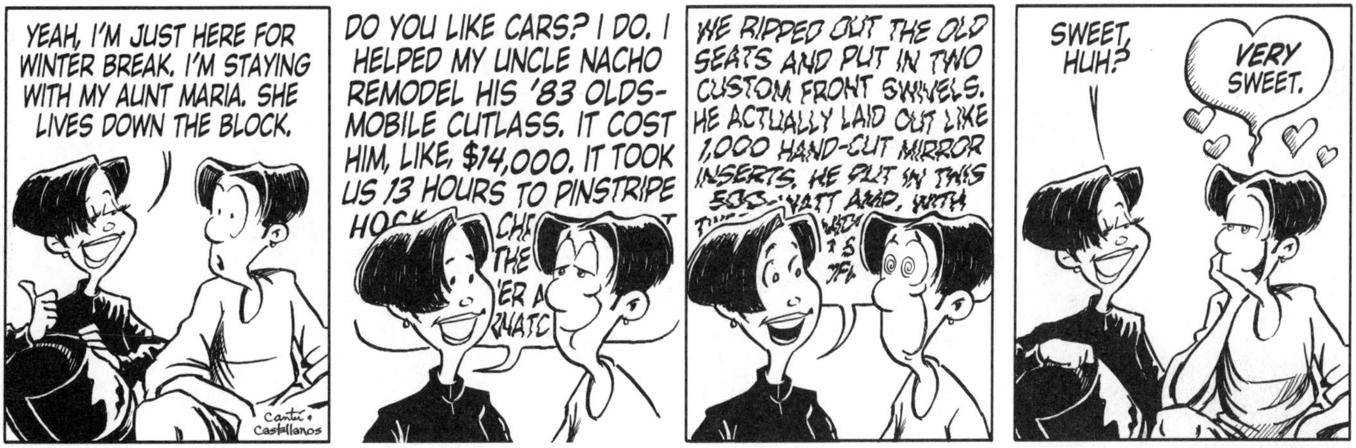
YEAH, I'M JUST HERE FOR WINTER BREAK. I'M STAYING WITH MY AUNT MARIA. SHE LIVES DOWN THE BLOCK.
Cantú & Castellanos
DO YOU LIKE CARS? I DO. I HELPED MY UNCLE NACHO REMODEL HIS '83 OLDS-MOBILE CUTLASS. IT COST HIM, LIKE, $14,000. IT TOOK US 13 HOURS TO PINSTRIPE
WE RIPPED OUT THE OLD SEATS AND PUT IN TWO CUSTOM FRONT SWIVELS. HE ACTUALLY LAID OUT LIKE 1,000 HAND-CUT MIRROR INSERTS. HE PUT IN THIS
SWEET, HUH?
VERY SWEET.

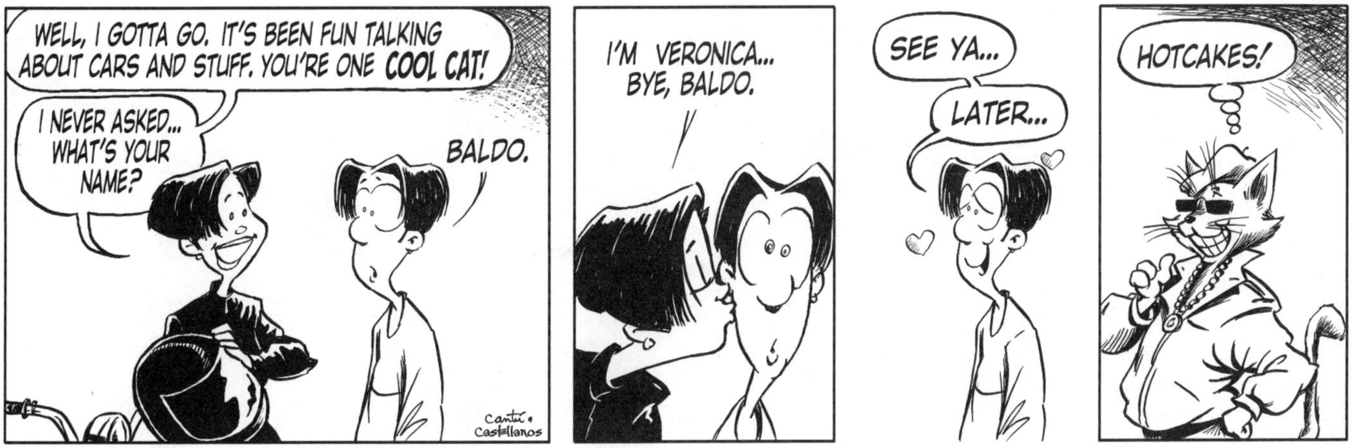
WELL, I GOTTA GO. IT'S BEEN FUN TALKING ABOUT CARS AND STUFF. YOU'RE ONE COOL CAT!
I NEVER ASKED... WHAT'S YOUR NAME?
BALDO.
Cantú & Castellanos
I'M VERONICA... BYE, BALDO.
SEE YA...
LATER...
HOTCAKES!

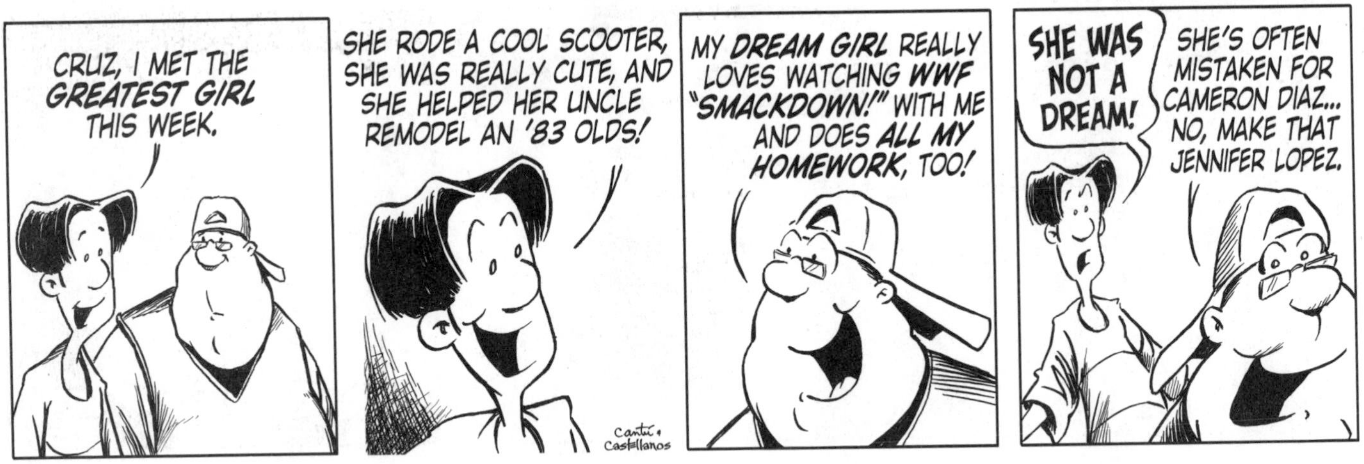
CRUZ, I MET THE GREATEST GIRL THIS WEEK.
SHE RODE A COOL SCOOTER, SHE WAS REALLY CUTE, AND SHE HELPED HER UNCLE REMODEL AN '83 OLDS!
MY DREAM GIRL REALLY LOVES WATCHING WWF "SMACKDOWN!" WITH ME AND DOES ALL MY HOMEWORK, TOO!
SHE WAS NOT A DREAM!
SHE'S OFTEN MISTAKEN FOR CAMERON DIAZ... NO, MAKE THAT JENNIFER LOPEZ.
Cantú & Castellanos

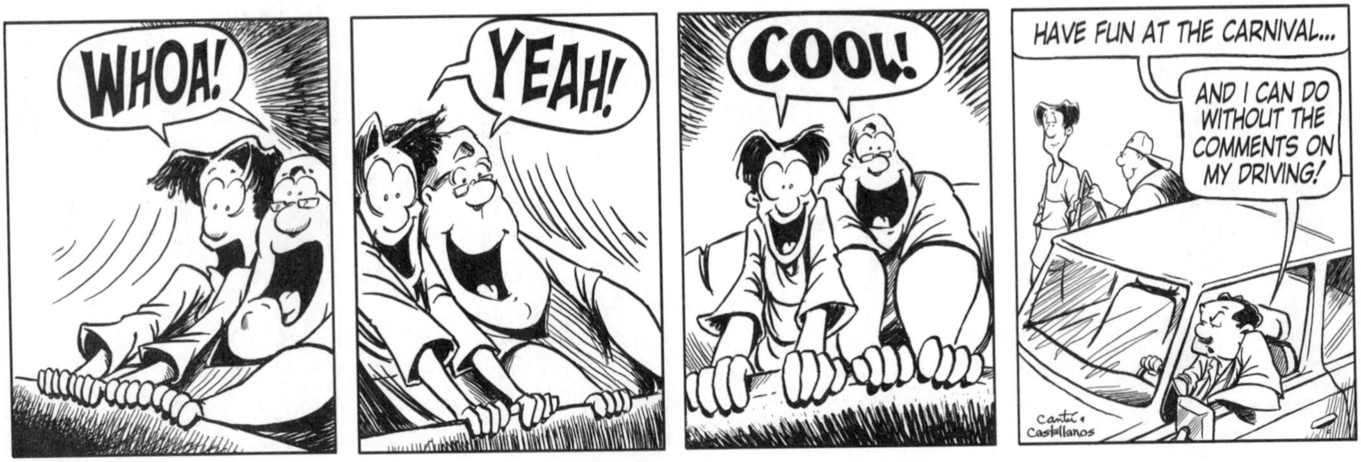
WHOA!
YEAH!
COOL!
HAVE FUN AT THE CARNIVAL...
AND I CAN DO WITHOUT THE COMMENTS ON MY DRIVING!
Cantú & Castellanos

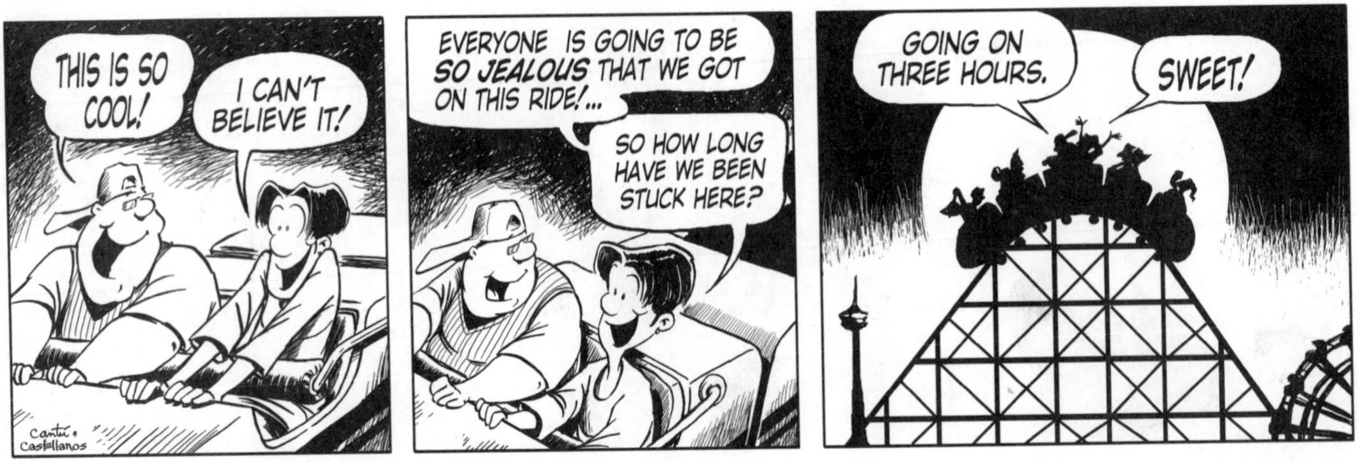
THIS IS SO COOL!
I CAN'T BELIEVE IT!
EVERYONE IS GOING TO BE SO JEALOUS THAT WE GOT ON THIS RIDE!...
SO HOW LONG HAVE WE BEEN STUCK HERE?
GOING ON THREE HOURS.
SWEET!
Cantú & Castellanos

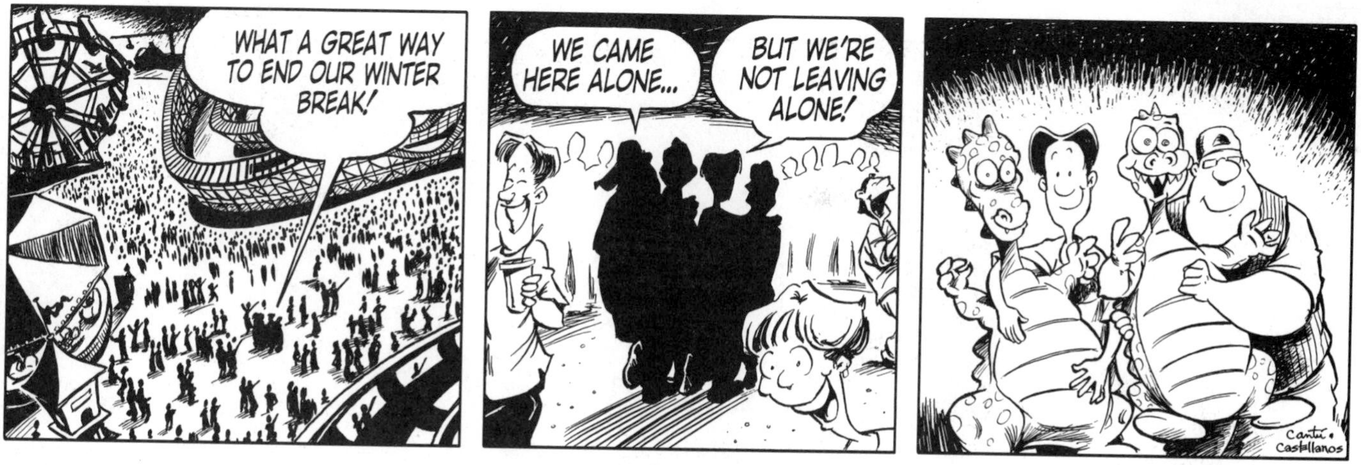
WHAT A GREAT WAY TO END OUR WINTER BREAK!
WE CAME HERE ALONE...
BUT WE'RE NOT LEAVING ALONE!
Cantú • Castellanos

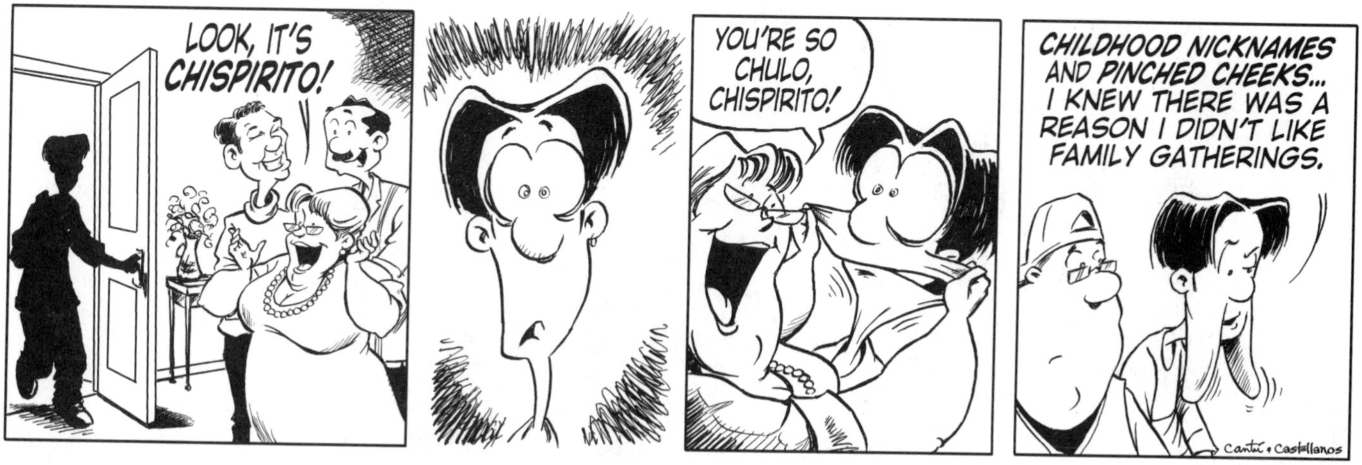
LOOK, IT'S CHISPIRITO!
YOU'RE SO CHULO, CHISPIRITO!
CHILDHOOD NICKNAMES AND PINCHED CHEEKS... I KNEW THERE WAS A REASON I DIDN'T LIKE FAMILY GATHERINGS.
Cantú • Castellanos

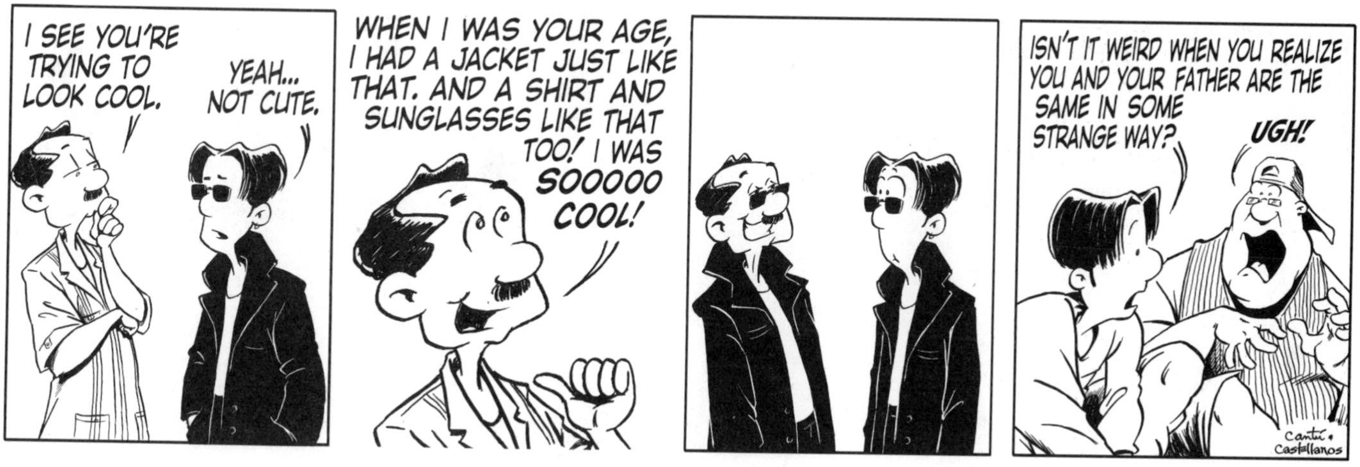
I SEE YOU'RE TRYING TO LOOK COOL.
YEAH... NOT CUTE.
WHEN I WAS YOUR AGE, I HAD A JACKET JUST LIKE THAT. AND A SHIRT AND SUNGLASSES LIKE THAT TOO! I WAS SOOOOO COOL!
ISN'T IT WEIRD WHEN YOU REALIZE YOU AND YOUR FATHER ARE THE SAME IN SOME STRANGE WAY?
UGH!
Cantú • Castellanos

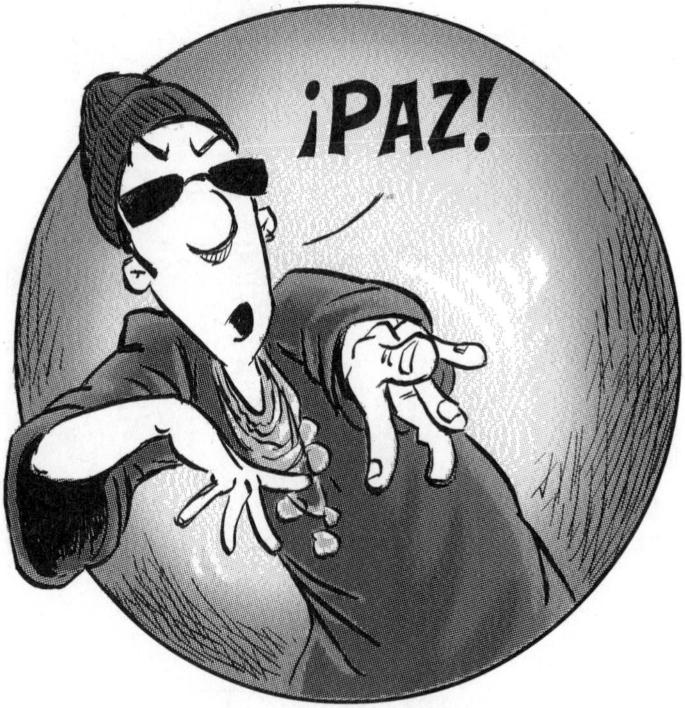
¡PAZ!

c/s